MW00816716

We Believe in Jesus Christ

Essays on Christology

Curtis A. Jahn
Compiling Editor

NORTHWESTERN PUBLISHING HOUSE
Milwaukee, Wisconsin

The cover illustration of Jesus reflects the contents of the essays in this book: ancient biblical teachings applied to contemporary church life. Jesus is portrayed as fully human and as using hand gestures that ancient Christian artists employed to symbolize the divine blessings Jesus gives us through his Word.

Cover illustration by Paul Burmeister.

All Scripture quotations, unless otherwise indicated, are taken from the HOLY BIBLE, NEW INTERNATIONAL VERSION®. NIV®. Copyright © 1973, 1978, 1984 by International Bible Society. Used by permission of Zondervan Publishing House. All rights reserved.

The "NIV" and "New International Version" trademarks are registered in the United States Patent and Trademark Office by International Bible Society. Use of either trademark requires the permission of International Bible Society.

All rights reserved. No part of this publication may be reproduced, stored in a retrieval system, or transmitted in any form or by any means—electronic, mechanical, photocopying, recording, or otherwise—except for brief quotations in reviews, without prior permission from the publisher.

Library of Congress Card 98-67601
Northwestern Publishing House
1250 N. 113th St., Milwaukee, WI 53226-3284
© 1999 by Northwestern Publishing House
Published 1999
Printed in the United States of America
ISBN 0-8100-0917-X

CONTENTS

THE CONTRIBUTORS

Richard D. Balge, professor, Wisconsin Lutheran Seminary,
Mequon, Wisconsin

Forrest L. Bivens, professor, Wisconsin Lutheran Seminary,
Mequon, Wisconsin

Leroy A. Dobberstein, professor, Wisconsin Lutheran Seminary,
Mequon, Wisconsin

David M. Gosdeck, professor, Martin Luther College,
New Ulm, Minnesota

Eric S. Hartzell, pastor, Cross and Crown Exploratory Mission,
Georgetown, Texas

James R. Janke, pastor, Bethel Ev. Lutheran Church,
Sioux Falls, South Dakota

Paul M. Janke, pastor, St. Peter Ev. Lutheran Church,
Modesto, California; president, Arizona-California District

John C. Jeske, professor emeritus, Wisconsin Lutheran Seminary,
Mequon, Wisconsin

Richard E. Lauersdorf, first vice president,
Wisconsin Evangelical Lutheran Synod,
Milwaukee, Wisconsin

Wayne D. Mueller, administrator for Parish Services,
Wisconsin Evangelical Lutheran Synod,
Milwaukee, Wisconsin

Ernst H. Wendland, professor emeritus, Wisconsin Lutheran Seminary,
Mequon, Wisconsin

Paul O. Wendland, professor, Martin Luther College,
New Ulm, Minnesota

We believe in Jesus Christ. This book's title is a fitting theme for any Epiphany, particularly as we approach a new millennium. And since *epiphany* means "unveiling, revelation," it seems fitting to turn to the book of Revelation for enlightenment. For, as John was inspired to write, it is "the revelation of Jesus Christ" (Rev 1:1).

Not surprisingly, in this last Epiphany before the year 2000, spiritual conditions are no different than they were at the end of the first Christian century. There were those then who were tempted to become utterly worldly, indulging all the ungodly impulses of the sinful nature. There were also some who were inclined to withdraw from this present evil world. Idly they waited for the Lord's return.

As a new millennium approaches, aren't the temptations still the same? Our flesh also is tempted to indulge in behavior characterized by the pagan Greek philosophy of "Let's eat, drink, and be merry for tomorrow we die." It's been reported that it may already be too late to acquire really good bottles of champagne for New Year's Eve 1999. Many of them have been bought and stored, anticipating a really big bash, a mindless, uninhibited bacchanalia when the clock strikes midnight on December 31, 1999.

For others, the approaching new millennium may signal the start of The Millennium, the mistaken notion of a one-thousand-year reign of Christ on earth. They eagerly and energetically are promoting an anticipated victory of Christ's heavenly forces on earth, the beginning of heaven on earth.

Under such conscience-numbing and faith-disturbing circumstances, it might be hard for Christians to maintain their religious sanity and moral sanctity. We're not immune to temptation. But a good antidote is what the book of Revelation reveals about why we believe in Jesus Christ.

Revelation affirms that the source of what we believe about Jesus Christ is heaven sent. It comes to us by way of revelation, divine revelation. The book begins, "The revelation of Jesus Christ" (1:1). And in this witness that Jesus gives, John is inspired to call him "the faithful witness" (1:5). And because this revelation of Jesus Christ about himself is God's faithful witness, the one who believes it is called blessed (22:7).

No revelation about Jesus Christ needs to be invented; it has been revealed, given by divine inspiration. All that remains to be done is for this

vii

revelation to be proclaimed. And then the same one who inspired it, the Holy Spirit, brings people to believe it.

The Holy Spirit did not inspire the faithless strategy of attempting to win more people for the gospel by proclaiming less of it. Such "gospel reductionism," inspired by the father of lies, the devil, continues as the eternally essential revelation about Jesus Christ in Holy Scripture is denied or hopelessly compromised.

Any such denial or compromise of the gospel flies in the face of the clear warning also revealed by God through John: "I warn everyone who hears the words of the prophecy of this book: If anyone adds anything to them, God will add to him the plagues described in this book. And if anyone takes words away from this book of prophecy, God will take away from him his share in the tree of life and in the holy city, which are described in this book" (22:18,19).

Jesus Christ is the epicenter of the gospel; there can be no other. No wonder, once, in John's vision, there was weeping in heaven when no one could be found to open the scroll and reveal what was inside—no one, that is, until the Lamb stepped forward. And then the song rang out: "You are worthy to take the scroll and to open its seals, because you were slain, and with your blood you purchased men for God from every tribe and language and people and nation. You have made them to be a kingdom and priests to serve our God, and they will reign on the earth" (5:9,10).

Here, in this song of praise to the Lamb, we see the mission thrust of our title, *We Believe in Jesus Christ*. John was privileged to see the fruits of the gospel's proclamation about Jesus Christ: "After this I looked and there before me was a great multitude that no one could count, from every nation, tribe, people and language, standing before the throne and in front of the Lamb" (7:9).

And the reason why such an assembly could be before the throne is clearly stated: "These are they who have come out of the great tribulation; they have washed their robes and made them white in the blood of the Lamb" (7:14).

And here are the eternal results of such belief in Jesus Christ: "Therefore, 'they are before the throne of God and serve him day and night in his temple; and he who sits on the throne will spread his tent over them. Never again will they hunger; never again will they thirst. The sun will not beat upon them, nor any scorching heat. For the Lamb at the center of the throne will be their shepherd; he will lead them to springs of living water. And God will wipe away every tear from their eyes' " (7:15-17).

We believe in Jesus Christ. He is the sum and substance of God's revelation. With this collection of essays, we privately affirm and publicly confess this saving truth. In faith we treasure all the precious details regarding him. With fidelity we proclaim them. We do so that even before one day gives way to a new millennium or the twinkling of an eye gives way to eternity, in faith we can eagerly anticipate the fulfillment of the Savior's words: "Yes, I am coming soon." (22:20). And so, with John, we pray, "Amen. Come, Lord Jesus" (22:20). This we confidently pray, for *we believe in Jesus Christ.*

"The grace of the Lord Jesus be with God's people. Amen" (22:21).

Karl R. Gurgel, president
Wisconsin Evangelical Lutheran Synod
Epiphany 1999

ABBREVIATIONS

References to the Book of Concord

AC	Augsburg Confession
Ap	Apology of the Augsburg Confession
SA	Smalcald Articles
Tr	Treatise on the Power and Primacy of the Pope
SC	Small Catechism
LC	Large Catechism
FC	Formula of Concord
FC RN	Rule and Norm of the Formula of Concord
FC Ep	Epitome of the Formula of Concord
FC SD	Solid (Thorough) Declaration of the Formula of Concord

References to Editions and Translations of the Book of Concord

Tappert *The Book of Concord: The Confessions of the Evangelical Lutheran Church*. Translated and edited by Theodore G. Tappert. Philadelphia: Fortress Press, 1959.

Triglot *Concordia Triglotta: The Symbolical Books of the Ev. Lutheran Church*. St. Louis: Concordia Publishing House, 1921.

References to Luther's Works

LW *Luther's Works*. Edited by Jaroslav Pelikan and Helmut T. Lehmann, American Edition, 55 vols. St. Louis: Concordia Publishing House; Philadelphia: Fortress Press, 1955–1986.

St. L. *Dr. Martin Luthers Sammtliche Schriften*. St. Louis: Concordia Publishing House, 1882.

WA *D. Martin Luthers Werke. Kritische Gesamtausgabe*. Weimar, 1883ff.

References to Church Fathers

ANF   *The Ante-Nicene Fathers of the Church*. A. Roberts, editor. 10 vols. Reprint. Grand Rapids: Eerdmans Publishing Company, 1987.

NPNF   *The Nicene and Post-Nicene Fathers of the Church*. First Series: 11 vols. Second Series: 14 vols. Philip Schaff, editor. Reprint. Grand Rapids: Eerdmans Publishing Company, 1988.

References to Hymns

CW   *Christian Worship: A Lutheran Hymnal*. Third printing. Milwaukee: Northwestern Publishing House, 1993.

TLH   *The Lutheran Hymnal*. St. Louis: Concordia Publishing House, 1941.

Richard E. Lauersdorf

South Atlantic District Convention
St. Petersburg, Florida
June 8–10, 1998

"Jesus!" Is there any greater name under heaven? For us as believers Jesus Christ is the most wonderful person—period! "The Word!" Is there any greater book under heaven? For us as believers the Holy Scripture is the most wonderful book—period! When we say "wonderful," we don't mean number one on some long list of personalities or books. We aren't identifying Jesus and the Word as the best liked or the best seller out of many. Both Jesus and the Word are in a class by themselves. The Bible is God's Word, and Jesus is God's Word. Both are God speaking to us in a most wonderful way about a subject that is more than wonderful—our salvation.

Nor can we ever separate Jesus and the Word. Without Holy Scripture we would know nothing about Jesus. He whose birth divides human history, whose teachings transform peoples' lives, whose work prepared pardon for sin, peace with God, and promise of eternal life, would be unknown to us without the Word. In history, as humans recorded it, we find only one early reference to Jesus. The Roman author Tacitus, writing about A.D. 112, makes passing reference to the crucifixion of Jesus under Pontius Pilate. There is nothing more without the Word; nothing more about him who is our Savior. Nor does Jesus walk among us visibly to speak to us as he did to the first disciples. There is no daily e-mail from him updating us on the latest kingdom news, no regular visits asking us how it's going. Just the Word, the Word that God has given us in written form, his Word, to tell us about Jesus Christ the Savior, who is God's Word in the flesh. And without the message of Jesus, the written Word would have nothing to say. Pull the scarlet thread of Christ Jesus

1

out of Scripture, and its fabric falls apart. Pluck out the central message of salvation through Christ, and the Bible's reason for existing vanishes.

Do you begin to see where our essay is heading? Your assignment to me was to lead you in a study of how Jesus is the final Word from God. You've asked me to show how in Jesus, God has revealed his saving will to us, how complete that revelation is in Jesus, and how we therefore have in Jesus what we have needed for the past 150 years of our synod and the past 25 years of your district and what we will need for the new millennium, both for our salvation and for our blessed work of spreading that salvation. And that cannot be done without talking about those two wonderful items—Jesus and the Word. So let's look at what the Word says about Jesus and what Jesus says about the Word.

The inspired Word

The God of the Bible is a God who speaks. From creation on he reveals himself by speaking. Unlike idols, he does not remain silent, but expresses his nature and thoughts, his will and plans, his work in the past, present, and future. In the Garden of Eden he spoke directly to Adam and Eve in a fellowship that one day will be fully ours again in heaven. When sin ruined that relationship, he spoke again, lovingly and graciously, the first promise of the Savior, who would come from the woman's seed to crush Satan's head. Note, he spoke to save! He came seeking sinners who scurried around in the garden, attempting in fright to hide from him. He came to reveal his loving plan of salvation to blind sinners who had not even the faintest inkling of it or the slightest ability to ferret it out.

Beginning with Moses he spoke through his written Word. Again the purpose was the same. He spoke through the written Word to save. That's why he guided those human authors in ways we do not fully understand, moving them to write, directing their thoughts, and recording their words in exactly the form he wanted. Of course, there were human elements involved. Luke did research (Lk 1:1-4); Ezra cited the records of the king of Persia (Ezr 6:3-12); but many things came by direct revelation, as Paul pointed out: "'No eye has seen, no ear has heard, no mind has conceived what God has prepared for those who love him'—but God has revealed it to us by his Spirit" (1 Co 2:9,10). The authors used their own language, vocabularies, and styles, but God provided the impulse to write, the message to be conveyed, and the words to do it. Through these human authors God was speaking to us just as if he were standing at our side, speaking his words in our ears, his exact words, which can only all be true.

We call this important teaching "verbal inspiration," using a word found only once in Scripture, in 2 Timothy 3:16, "All Scripture is *God-breathed*" (one word in Greek—*theopneustos*). But this is not the only passage nor the

We Believe in Jesus Christ

only word about this supremely important subject in the Bible. Every prophetic utterance that begins with "This is what the LORD says," every passage that tells us God spoke the message, emphasizes verbal inspiration. Again and again the Bible speaks on this subject, more times than, or at least as many times as, any other teaching. Moses and the prophets, the evangelists and the apostles, were men who "spoke from God as they were carried along by the Holy Spirit" (2 Pe 1:21). They wrote not according to their own will but the will of the Spirit. Some critics point out that Peter used the word *spoke* instead of *wrote*, in this passage. For Peter, as well as elsewhere in Scripture, these two words, *spoke* and *wrote* are interchangeable. In 2 Peter 1:19 Peter said, "We have the *word* of the prophets made more certain," and in 1:20 he refers to the "prophecy of *Scripture*." The prophets were long dead; Peter had their words not in oral but written form. But to him they were God's words, and God's words were true.

How reliable is the written Word? So reliable that Paul could take a single statement of the Old Testament (Ge 15:6) and use it to establish an important truth in Romans 4:3, "Abraham believed God, and it was credited to him as righteousness." So reliable that Paul could take a singular form in Genesis 12:7 and say of it in Galatians 3:16, "The promises were spoken to Abraham and to his seed. The Scripture does not say 'and to seeds,' meaning many people, but 'and to your seed,' meaning one person, who is Christ." So reliable that Jesus could take a single word in Psalm 82:6 and remind the Pharisees accusing him of blasphemy in John 10:34-36, "Is it not written in your Law, 'I have said you are gods'? If he called them 'gods,' to whom the word of God came—and the Scripture cannot be broken—what about the one whom the Father set apart as his very own and sent into the world?" Jesus was right, "the Scripture cannot be broken." It is God-breathed, his own Word for all the ages to come, absolutely reliable down to every word.

And the Scripture is God's living Word. Christ and the apostles regarded the Old Testament not as something just inspired in the past, but as God speaking today. Over 40 times Old Testament quotes are introduced not with "said," but "says" (Mt 22:43, Ro 10:11, Heb 3:7). The Word that goes forth from God's mouth (Isa 55:11) is "living and active. Sharper than any double-edged sword . . ." (Heb 4:12). No wonder the author of Hebrews urges, "See to it that you do not refuse him who *speaks*" (12:25). Here too in the power of God's living Word lies the answer for critics who accuse us of arguing in a circle when we use Scripture's own statements to prove its inspiration. The Pharisees hurled the same charge at Jesus. "Here you are, appearing as your own witness; your testimony is not valid," they snapped at him, only to have him answer, "Even if I testify on my own behalf, my testimony is valid, for I know where I came from and where I am going. But you have no idea where I came from or where I am going" (Jn 8:13,14). We know from where that Word has come and what it has done to our hearts. Just as we believe the sun shines because we see its light, we believe the Word is his because in it we have met the living God who saves us.

Some have argued that only when Scripture speaks about salvation is it God speaking. When it deals with history, science, geography, astronomy, they say it presents man's dated, fallible thinking. How presumptuous for man to strive to superimpose his puny mind on God's Word. Scripture is God's inerrant Word, no matter how far the subject matter seems removed from its central theme of salvation. How arrogant for man to judge what of Scripture directly or indirectly has a bearing on his salvation when God has told us plainly why he speaks to us. Though standing alone, the doctrine of verbal inspiration does not save us, yet it serves to enforce and validate all of Scripture's teachings, including its central theme of salvation. To attack verbal inspiration is to attack our salvation, for we correctly sing, "Jesus loves me, this I know, for the Bible tells me so." As someone pointed out, the doctrine of salvation through Christ runs like a scarlet thread through all of Holy Scripture, but the doctrine of verbal inspiration is the silken thread that gives strength to the Bible's fabric.

The incarnate Word

Not only did God speak to mankind by his inspired, written Word but also by his Son. In fact, God's greatest, clearest act of communication came in the ministry of his Son on earth. That's why the Bible calls Jesus-come-into-the-flesh *the Word.* Such an expression for us might seem like a strange way of speaking. We don't usually think of a word being a person, but a sound in audible form that we use to convey a concept. Yet the expression, though beyond our grasping, fits eminently. Jesus is the Word, God's personal message to us. An old Greek proverb states, "A word is the image of the soul." From a man's words we gain insight into his thoughts, feelings, and attitudes. Just as we use words to show others what's in our hearts, so God showed us his heart by sending his Son into this world. Jesus came to earth not to bring a new revelation, but to be the revelation of God. In Jesus, the incarnate Word, we sinful human beings can see and know the invisible, unapproachable God. To see Jesus is to see God. To hear Jesus is to hear God. To look at Jesus is to look into God's heart, overflowing with love and grace for lost sinners. In fact, all who would know God must come to know him through Jesus.

But let's allow Scripture to speak. Particularly does the apostle John, who walked and talked with Jesus, describe our Savior as the Word. John begins his gospel with sentences that soar off the page. "In the beginning was the Word," he writes (1:1), already telling us that Jesus is God because only God existed in the beginning. "And the Word was with God," he continues (1:1), using a preposition that meant face-to-face with God in the closest relationship possible. "And the Word was God," he concludes (1:1). From the beginning Jesus was together with God and was God, the second person of the Holy Trinity, one with the Father. What this means John then details in 1:18, "No one has ever seen God, but God the One and Only, who is at the Father's side, has made him known." In Jesus the eternal, invisible God has graciously stepped into our world to speak to us.

The apostle Paul picked up this same theme in Colossians 1:15, where he wrote of Christ, "He is the image of the invisible God." The word *image* means not just like God, but the perfect expression, the perfect revelation of God. That's what Jesus is, God revealed for our salvation.

John also began his first epistle with the thought of Jesus being the Word. "That which was from the beginning, which we have heard, which we have seen with our eyes, which we have looked at and our hands have touched—this we proclaim concerning the Word of life" (1:1). Notice John writes "that," not "who," referring not only to the person, but the message. And notice what he calls God's revelation in Christ come into the flesh; he calls it "the Word of life." In Jesus, God's message to the world was a message of life—glorious, eternal life in heaven.

In his last book, the book of Revelation, John came back to the same thought. Of that rider on the white horse, he wrote, "He is dressed in a robe dipped in blood, and his name is the Word of God" (19:13). "Word" . . . "Word of life". . . and now here, and only here in Scripture, "Word of God." Jesus is God's Word to us, showing us in person especially God's thoughts of salvation for us. He who once said, "Out of the overflow of the heart the mouth speaks" (Mt 12:34), was God's mouth, revealing clearly God's saving heart to us.

Hebrews 1 echoes the same thought. The unnamed author was writing to Christians tempted to turn away from Christ in order to avoid persecution. Trying to show them what a supreme treasure they had in Christ, one that they surely would not want to discard, he gets right to the point in the opening verses of the epistle. "In the past God spoke to our forefathers through the prophets at many times and in various ways," he begins (1:1). That was God speaking, he said, in various forms of law, history, poetry, prophecy, used by Moses through Malachi. But their message had been incomplete. More was to come, not to cancel what had been divinely recorded, but to finish it. "You must listen to him," the great Old Testament prophet Moses had said of the greater prophet yet to come (Dt 18:15).

And then it happened. "In these last days," in this New Testament period of time in which we live and after which comes only eternity, God "has spoken to us by his Son" (Heb 1:2). Through the prophets and now through his Son, God was speaking. The prophets spoke for God; the Son spoke as God. That Son, come into the flesh to be the Redeemer, is the one to whom the Old Testament pointed. Even more, he is the ultimate Word and the perfect revelation of God. To reinforce this glorious thought, the author of Hebrews describes Jesus as "the radiance of God's glory and the exact representation of his being" (1:3). "Radiance" is an inner brightness that shines out like the sun in the sky with its streaming light. All of God's attributes radiate forth in Jesus. To see Jesus is to see the God of glory just as to see the light is to see the sun. Jesus is the "exact representation of his being." An exact representation is some exact impression made by a tool, like a coin stamped by a die. So Jesus exactly represents the Father. To know Jesus is to know God's nature or glory. "God in focus," we might call Jesus. The Savior expressed it much better when he said in John 14:9, "Anyone who has seen me has seen the Father."

The point is clear. In and through the incarnate Christ, man has the most complete revelation of God. And what a revelation it is—one of grace and mercy and love. What a revelation it is—one of a divine heart that will do anything to save us. No wonder Paul wrote, "No matter how many promises God has made, they are 'Yes' in Christ" (2 Co 1:20). But note carefully where we find the incarnate Word. Not only is Christ Jesus God's Word in the flesh, the heart and fulfillment of Holy Scripture, but he also is found only there—in the written Word.

The inspired Word and the incarnate Word

When Jesus, God's incarnate Word, spoke, he spoke exactly what God spoke in the written Word. The written Word spoke of Jesus, and Jesus spoke in accord with the written Word. Christ and Scripture speak as God to man, and both say the same thing.

Let's examine briefly how Christ used the Scriptures. Again and again he turned to Holy Scripture, under differing circumstances but always as the final authority. Those who count and tally tell us 10% of Christ's daily conversation was words from Scripture. In Nazareth near the beginning of his ministry, he read and expounded Isaiah 61:1,2 to the people (Lk 4:16-21), the only time the Bible records Jesus as actually reading the Old Testament. Other times he quoted from memory or referred to something he or his hearers had read in it. His life, work, and speech were saturated with Holy Scripture, knowing it, using it, quoting it, so that many marveled, "How did this man get such learning without having studied?" (Jn 7:15). Interesting, isn't it, that he who spoke with divine authority as God's eternal Word used and bowed to Holy Scripture without reservation. Interesting also, isn't it, what this fact has to say about our attitude toward the written Word. After Jesus' resurrection it was still the written Word. On the way to Emmaus in that Bible class in which we wish we could have participated, Jesus didn't dazzle those two disciples with his risen person, but pointed them patiently and convincingly to the Word. "Were not our hearts burning within us while he talked with us on the road and opened the Scriptures to us?" those disciples marveled after Jesus broke the bread at their table (Lk 24:32). A bit later, in that locked room in Jerusalem with the others, Jesus still directed his disciples to the Scriptures. "This is what I told you while I was still with you: Everything must be fulfilled that is written about me in the Law of Moses, the Prophets and the Psalms," Jesus reminded those cautiously rejoicing disciples (24:44). "Then he opened their minds so they could understand the Scriptures" (24:45). The Incarnate Word used the Book for himself and for his disciples. He was not only the great message of that Book, but also its great teacher.

Always when Christ used Scripture, it was with dynamic testimony to its inspiration and authority. "The Scripture cannot be broken," he testified (Jn 10:35), stating an indisputable fact. Words that come from God, every one of them, must be true. "Until heaven and earth disappear, not the smallest letter, not the least stroke of a pen, will by any means disappear from the Law until everything is accomplished," he asserted (Mt 5:18). Words that come from God must be eternal, every one of them. For Jesus, accounts like the creation of the first couple (Mt 19:4,5), the murder of Abel (Lk 11:51), Noah and the flood (Mt 24:37), Sodom and Lot's wife (Lk 17:29,32), the manna in the wilderness (Jn 6:31,51), the bronze serpent (Jn 3:14), Elijah and the widow of Zarephath (Lk 4:26), Jonah and Nineveh (Mt 12:40,41) were not human myths, but historical facts. It almost seems that Jesus deliberately authenticated many of the passages of Scripture under attack today.

Especially did Jesus demonstrate how the Scriptures were written to testify of him. Referring to the Old Testament in his sparring with hostile Jews, he said, "You diligently study the Scriptures because you think that by them you possess eternal life. These are the Scriptures that testify about me" (Jn 5:39). They "testify about me," he claimed, using a strong word that originally came from the law courts and that implied truthfulness and honesty. To those same Jews he also said, "If you believed Moses, you would believe me, for he wrote about me" (Jn 5:46). On Easter eve, as we quoted earlier, in order to give his confused disciples the key to the Bible, Jesus said, "Everything must be fulfilled that is written about me in the Law of Moses, the Prophets and the Psalms" (Lk 24:44). The Old Testament, to which those terms referred, "were written about me," he said.

The Old Testament centered in Jesus. So does the New Testament. Luke wrote his gospel to set forth "all that Jesus began to do and to teach until the day he was taken up to heaven" (Ac 1:1,2). Paul refused to know anything "except Jesus Christ and him crucified" when working among the Corinthians (1 Co 2:2). Timothy learned from infancy in his mother's house "the Holy Scriptures, which [were] able to make [him] wise for salvation through faith in Christ Jesus" (2 Ti 3:15). And John had one purpose in mind when he penned his gospel, "That you may believe that Jesus is the Christ, the Son of God, and that by believing you may have life in his name" (Jn 20:31).

God's written Word is christocentric. At its center is the Savior. Everything it contains revolves around him. Though it cover other topics and convey other blessings, though it speak of sin and shame as well as of faith and faithfulness, yet in one way or another it connects everything with Christ, its center. Luther said it well, "God is concerned with the revelation and knowledge of his Son throughout the Scriptures of the Old and New Testaments; it all concerns his Son."[1]

Where else can mankind learn about God's Son, its only Savior? The written Word and the incarnate Word cannot be separated. Faith in Christ is also and always faith in the words and promises of God. To believe in Christ is to believe in the Bible, and to believe in the Bible is to believe in Christ. The incarnate Word taught this when in his high priestly prayer he asked his Father, "I pray also for those who will believe in me through their message," referring to the Word spoken by those who would go out in his name (Jn 17:20). With Peter, Christians turn to the Christ of Scriptures confessing, "Lord, to whom shall we go? You have the words of eternal life" (Jn 6:68).

Critics have attacked this inseparable relationship between Christ, the incarnate Word, and Scripture, God's written Word. The Word of God, they claim, is a person, not a book. For them the written Word is God's Word only when it speaks about Christ or at best when what it says has a direct bearing on Christ, whom they describe as God's real Word. "Our faith must be in a person, not a book," is their learned claim. *Christian Dogmatics,* the primary textbook used in all seminaries of the Evangelical Lutheran Church in America, contains such a statement. The author Carl Braaten writes:

> It is finally for the sake of Christ alone that the church continues to regard the Bible as a book without equal in the history of human literature. For this reason the churches that claim the heritage of Luther and of the Reformation still affirm the Bible as the Word of God. This is not meant in the fundamentalistic sense that everything in the Bible stands directly as the Word of God. . . . This evaluation of the Bible as the Word of God is asserted with greater difficulty today than in Luther's time and with greater awareness of the historical problems involved in Biblical interpretation. . . . The role of the Bible in constructive theology is radically qualified today by historical consciousness. Luther believed that the literal meaning of Scripture is identical with its historical content; things happened exactly as they were written down. Today it is impossible to assume the literal historicity of all

---

[1]WA 48:143. Quoted by Ludwig Wiesinger, "Is the Bible the Word of God?" *Wisconsin Lutheran Quarterly,* Vol. 69, No. 1 (January 1972), p. 14.

---

things recorded. What the biblical authors report is not accepted as literal transcript of the factual course of events. Therefore, critical scholars inquire behind the text and attempt to reconstruct the real history that took place.[2]

What a far cry from what the incarnate Word said. In John 17:17 he prayed to his Father for his followers, "Sanctify them by the truth; your word is truth." With this prayer he asked his Father to set his disciples apart in God's truth, which is God's Word. God's Word is God's truth, the source of power, saving faith, holiness. Jesus also is the Word and God's truth. Yes, Jesus as God's personal Word is distinguished from the Scriptures, God's prophetic Word, but we dare never disassociate him from that written Word, for he is its center and fulfillment. Only God's Word as we have it reveals and puts us in touch with the Savior. Use the sharp teeth of human reason on God's Word, and you're sawing away at the same time at the Savior it alone can bring.

Others, because of our insistence upon the Bible as God's inspired Word, accuse us of bibliolatry, that is, of worshiping the Bible. The Jews of Jesus' day were guilty of just that. They were proud possessors of God's Word, zealous defenders of its every letter, but failed to recognize him of whom the Old Testament spoke and who was its very substance. When the incarnate Word stood among them, they held the Bible in one hand while crucifying him with the other hand.

The warning is always in place: beware of believing that the Bible is true without really believing the truth it presents. We worship not the written Word but the incarnate Word it presents. The Scripture reveals our Savior and leads us to him, and therefore we hold it in high esteem. But Christ alone is our Savior, and him alone we adore.

In summary, we quote from "The Statement on Scripture," adopted by the WELS at its 1959 convention:

> God reveals Himself to men primarily through His incarnate Son, whom He attests and presents to His Church through Scripture. The purpose of Scripture is to proclaim Christ as the Savior of sinners (Jn 5:39; Ac 10:43). All Scripture is written because of Christ and has a connection with the revelation of God in Christ, some passages directly, some more remotely. Every word of Scripture is therefore an organic part of the Scripture's witness to Christ. And Scripture is the complete message of God to sinners. By it man is freed from carnal security and self-righteousness, is delivered from despair,

---

[2]Carl Braaten and Robert Jensen, editors, *Christian Dogmatics*, Vol. 1 (Philadelphia: Fortress Press, 1984), pp. 76,77.

---

and regains by faith the lost image of God. Gal 3:26; cf. 4:31; Jas 1:18; 1 Pe 1:23; Jn 8:31,32.[3]

The all-sufficient Word

"Scripture is the complete message of God to sinners," we have just heard. To put it another way, Scripture is sufficient. That's not to say that the inspired Word, like some encyclopedia, strives to tell man everything he can ever know. The Creator gave the creature a mind that can be used to learn about agriculture, architecture, astronomy, and the like. Need we add the thought that when the written Word does deal with such areas, it is always right and we subject our reason to what it has to say? Nor does the word *sufficient* imply that the Word reveals all the thoughts and counsels of God. "Now I know in part," Paul had to admit, even as he looked forward to heaven, where he said, "I shall know fully, even as I am fully known" (1 Co 13:12).

However, and mark this well, Scripture does teach whatever we need to know to be saved. Or to put it another way, Scripture is all-sufficient to accomplish the purpose for which God gave it. Isn't that what Paul tells us in Romans 15:4? "Everything that was written in the past was written to teach us, so that through endurance and the encouragement of the Scriptures *we might have hope.*" Isn't that what Paul told Timothy and us in 2 Timothy 3:15? "From infancy you have known the Holy Scriptures, which are able to make you wise *for salvation* through faith in Christ Jesus." With wonderful simplicity Jesus, the incarnate Word, emphasized the same important truth. In John 5:24 he told the hostile Jews, "Whoever hears my word and believes him who sent me has eternal life and will not be condemned; he has crossed over from death to life." "To my Word," Jesus was saying, to the Word which reveals the Father's saving will and already here and now brings the blessed crossing over from death to life. Later Jesus made the same point to his questioning disciples, "The words I have spoken to you are spirit and they are life" (Jn 6:63). What more do we need for our salvation? God's Word with its message of salvation in Christ says it all. No wonder Christ urges us to hold to his Word so that we may know the truth and be free (Jn 8:31,32). No wonder he also commands us to avoid those who teach otherwise (Ro 16:17), even if it were some angel from heaven preaching some other gospel (Gal 1:6-9).

Hebrews chapter 1 sounds a similar note of sufficiency. Verse 1 tells us, "In the past God spoke to our forefathers through the prophets at many times and in various ways." God's message through the Old Testament authors was

---

[3]*Doctrinal Statements of the WELS,* Prepared by the Commission on Inter-Church Relations of the Wisconsin Evangelical Lutheran Synod (Milwaukee: Northwestern Publishing House, 1997), pp. 7,8.

We Believe in Jesus Christ

partial and preparatory; it pointed to the fulfillment of his promise of salvation in Christ. Verse 2 continues, "But in these last days he has spoken to us by his Son."

God's message to us in "these last days," the time period that Jesus ushered in and that ends in eternity, is full and final. What more need our Father say than what he has said in Christ? Even the verb form the author used in Hebrews for "has spoken" points to finality, conveying the thought that God's revelation in Christ is not some continuous process, but one completed. Christ is the completed revelation of God. In him God has spoken to us fully about his love and life, his pardon and peace. In Christ we have God's final word to the world. And that final word is deposited only in Holy Scripture.

Moreover, Scripture has the power to work acceptance of salvation in the human heart. The gospel is "the power of God for the salvation of everyone who believes" (Ro 1:16). The Scriptures "are able to make you wise for salvation through faith in Christ Jesus (2 Ti 3:15). "The word of God . . . is at work in you who believe" (1 Th 2:13). "Through the living and enduring word of God" we are born again (1 Pe 1:23). "Through the word of truth" our loving God "chose to give us birth" (Jas 1:18). These and other references remind us how God has packed in his Word not only his message of salvation, but also his awesome power to split open human hearts to believe the message. What a sufficient Word we have—one that not only conveys Christ, but also creates and continues faith in him as our only Savior. God's Word with its message of salvation in Christ has it all.

Pointing to Scripture's purpose to prove its sufficiency, as we have just done, is not merely human argument. He who gave us Scripture used the same approach. To Martha, who questioned her sister's sitting at Jesus' feet, Jesus gave the reminder, "Only one thing is needed" (Lk 10:42). To the Jews who questioned him, Jesus responded, "You diligently study the Scriptures . . . [they] testify about me" (Jn 5:39). To the Jews who believed him, he replied, "If you hold to my teaching, you are really my disciples. Then you will know the truth, and the truth will set you free" (Jn 8:31,32). Through his Old Testament servant Moses, he issued the strong warning "Do not add to what I command you and do not subtract from it, but keep the commands of the LORD your God that I give you" (Dt 4:2). Through his New Testament servant John, he stated it even more strictly: "I warn everyone who hears the words of the prophecy of this book: If anyone adds anything to them, God will add to him the plagues described in this book. And if anyone takes words away from this book of prophecy, God will take away from him his share in the tree of life and in the holy city, which are described in this book" (Rev 22:18,19).

To those who argue that such prohibitions apply to us and not to God, we reply, "Of course. God is not bound by his own decrees, but we are. God can add to these books when he pleases, but we dare not." Nor should we expect the divine Author to do so either. He has given us his Word for the express purpose of making us wise for salvation through faith in Christ Jesus. What more need he tell us? Anything new would have to agree with what he has already said in his Word. He who builds his church on the "foundation of the apostles and prophets, with Christ Jesus himself as the chief cornerstone" binds us to the same sufficient Word (Eph 2:20).

Already in Paul's day it began, just a handful of years after the Master Teacher's ascension. The apostle felt constrained to warn Timothy: "The time will come when men will not put up with sound doctrine. Instead, to suit their own desires, they will gather around them a great number of teachers to say what their itching ears want to hear. They will turn their ears away from the truth and turn aside to myths" (2 Ti 4:3,4). How necessary Paul's warning is today. We need not look far to find those who want to mortar additional bricks into the foundation of the apostles and prophets or who want to smash bricks out of that foundation. Around us are those who say the church must determine what is truth or your heart and head must help you find the truth. *Schwaermer,* Luther called all those who forsake the all-sufficient Word. Like a swarm of bees such enthusiasts buzz around, but they have no solid foundation on which to land. Let's look at some of the errors, noticing as we do how they all point to man. Instead of letting the all-sufficient Scripture illumine man, these approaches make the colossal mistake of trying to illumine Scripture. Forgotten, unnoticed, ignored, rejected are the inspired words of the psalmist, "Your word is a lamp to my feet and a light for my path" (119:105).

Today we are living in what some call the post-modern age. The premodern age, when thinkers believed reason and revelation brought objective truth, has been pushed into the closet. The modern age, which followed with its stress upon reason as the only source and sifter of truth, has been swept under the carpet. Today they profoundly tell us we are in the post-modern age, when more and more people believe there is no such thing as absolute truth. Truth is what becomes true for you. Truth is what you feel. As a result, there are no moral absolutes, and what you feel as religious truth is just as valid as what others feel. How sad. Those who step off the solid ground of God's Word into the subjective swamp of the human heart can only be sucked down, down, down.

Not all have abandoned reason as the umpire of religious truth. The followers of Zwingli and Calvin live on in the Reformed churches, still measuring Scripture by their minds. Ulrich Zwingli was a contemporary of Martin Luther, but differed mightily in his approach to Scripture. While Luther was first a theologian and then a thinker, Zwingli was first a thinker and then a theologian. For Luther the Scriptures were the final authority. Reason was a servant to be used in studying it. For Zwingli reason was the master and was to be used to judge the Scriptures. See the difference? Luther accepted what Scripture said even when what it said appeared illogical. Zwingli accepted

We Believe in Jesus Christ

what Scripture said only when it agreed with human logic. For him and his followers what could not be understood was then no object of faith. For them infant Baptism is not essential, the real presence of Christ's body and blood in the Sacrament not possible, divine election to salvation without also then divine election to damnation unthinkable. His followers claim to have extricated themselves from the straitjacket of Scripture only to handcuff themselves to their own minds. Which approach would we prefer? Scripture, which is God's solid, sufficient Word, or human reason, which is flawed and fallible? Those who look into their heads for answers will find what they deserve, answers that can hardly be called God's truth or hardly serve as solid footing for eternity.

The reliance on human reason is also the driving force behind the historical-critical approach to Scripture. At the risk of oversimplifying, let me try to explain. This approach postulates that nothing the Bible says is to be accepted as true. Instead, the biblical text must prove its truthfulness to the mind of the scholar. The scholar approaches the text in light of the comparable literature of its day and seeks to judge its reasonable truthfulness from the harmony the text shows with such literature. For example, did Paul really speak about the headship of man as divine, eternal principle, or was he stating the passing practice of his day? Do you begin to see what such a historical-critical approach does to Scripture? It reduces it from a book that is God's truth in all it says to one filled only with likelihoods and possibilities to be decided by the scholar's mind. Does this appeal to reason sound new and mysterious? Hardly! The approach is as old as the Garden of Eden, and note who used it there: "He [the devil] said to the woman, 'Did God really say, "You must not eat from any tree in the garden"?'" (Ge 3:1).

Still others abandon the sufficient Word or strive to augment it with new revelations. The 17th-century Society of Friends was the first of many in this approach. Its leader, George Fox, taught members to look for "inner light" rather than into Scripture for guidance. Because the receiving of such direct revelation from God was usually accompanied by shaking and physical agitation, these people were labeled "Quakers." The Pentecostals and charismatics of today are of similar stripe. Their preoccupation with special gifts and prophecies elevates current communication with God ahead of a Book from the past. Others like Mary Baker Eddy, who claimed her writings as the key to Scripture, and Joseph Smith Sr., who penned the *Book of Mormon* as a more valuable edition than Scripture, belong to the same camp. Note again where all these approaches center—in the subjective heart of man, a place more filled with darkness than light and where the prince of darkness finds it easy to masquerade as an angel of light.

The Roman Church has attacked Scripture's sufficiency from yet another direction. The fourth Session of the Council of Trent in 1546 described the Roman Church as the official interpreter and custodian of Scripture. Not the

Word but the church sets doctrine. Not what God has said but what the church has said, is saying, or will say is to be believed. Lest someone protest that the Roman Church has changed, we quote from its *Catechism of the Catholic Church*, published in 1994 and described by Pope John Paul II as "a sure norm for teaching the faith."[4] Paragraph 82 of that catechism states: "The Church, to whom the transmission and interpretation of Revelation is entrusted, does not derive her certainty about all revealed truths from the Holy Scriptures alone. Both Scripture and Tradition must be accepted and honored with equal sentiment of devotion and reverence." Paragraph 85 further claims: "The task of giving an authentic interpretation of the Word of God, whether in its written form or in the form of Tradition, has been entrusted to the living, teaching office of the Church alone. Its authority in this matter is exercised in the name of Jesus Christ. This means that the task of interpretation has been entrusted to the bishops in communion with the successor of Peter, the Bishop of Rome." "Thus says the Lord" has been turned into "thus says Rome."

Thank God for using his servant Luther to restore the teaching of Scripture's sufficiency. The great Reformer wrote, "Everything that is to be held, all and sufficient, is in Scripture. If it is not there, you should say, 'When did God ever say this?'"[5] "Be it ever so good, outside of the Book of the Holy Ghost, namely Holy Scripture, one does not find Christ."[6] "Our doctrine is in the Scriptures, therefore we should not look anywhere else, but all Christians should keep this book in daily use."[7] By God's grace Luther's slogan *sola Scriptura* is ours. Now let those who preach and teach follow Paul's example and proclaim "the whole will of God" (Ac 20:27), and let those who listen search for nothing more and be satisfied with nothing less than the all-sufficient Word.

Our work with the all-sufficient Word

"God's Word is our great heritage and shall be ours forever," we love to sing and then add the prayer, "Lord, grant, while worlds endure, we keep its teachings pure throughout all generations" (CW 293). Thank God we can sing such words and know them still to be true for us and for our synod, now approaching 150 years of existence. God in his grace has more than smiled on us. While other church bodies, including some Lutherans, are working overtime squandering their inheritance and scratching around trying to justify their existence, we know what we have. But do we always *treasure* that pure Word? And do we always treasure it for the right reason? Remember it is not the Book

---

[4]John Paul II, "Apostolic Constitution *Fidei Depositum*," *Catechism of the Catholic Church* (United States Catholic Conference, Inc., Libreria Editrice Vaticana, 1994), p. 5.
[5]St. L. XII:169.
[6]St. L. IX:1775.
[7]St. L. XII:32.

We Believe in Jesus Christ

we worship, but the Savior it brings us. Viewing the Scriptures as the inerrant, inspired Word is extremely important for us, not because that teaching saves us, but because it guarantees God's salvation to us. Teaching all its words correctly is our ongoing concern, but again remember the reason why. Every teaching of Scripture revolves around its central message of God's salvation in Christ. When we deflect, dent, or disfigure any teaching of the Bible, we at the same time, or eventually, detract from Scripture's central teaching. In Scripture God has revealed his saving face to us with all its priceless love. Anything that clouds the mirror of his Word helps to hide the Savior's face. "Let me see my Savior's face, let me all his beauties trace; show those glorious truths to me which are only known to Thee" (TLH 234:2), the hymn writer taught us to pray to the Holy Spirit. And that face is seen most clearly on the pages of his pure Word. Our first response to God's sufficient Word is treasuring it as a precious gift that God by his grace alone has kept on deposit among us.

Treasuring God's Word involves ongoing efforts to preserve that Word among us. As a sausage lover I was thrilled to find near our new home a meat market that had won several blue ribbons for its product. Imagine my consternation when I read in a newspaper article one day that the meat market had been fined for adulterating its product. That impure stick of sausage didn't kill me, but impure teaching can. When man's teaching is mixed in with the Word, the result is always danger for the soul. How careful we who preach and teach must be about the purity of what we present. How careful those who listen and read must be to examine the Scriptures, as the Bereans did, to see if what our modern Pauls are presenting is the truth (Ac 17:11). How careful those who train our young men and women must be so that those future workers grow in knowledge of the truth and in the conviction that nothing but the truth be proclaimed to God's people. How blessed we have been in this regard. The South Atlantic District has many of the more recent products of our ministerial education system and can vouch for their concern for the Word. To treasure God's all sufficient Word means to work as hard as we know how to preserve it—under God's grace and for the right reason—that our Savior's face be seen most clearly.

Our working with God's Word involves, second, *turning* to it. Psalm 1, in describing the truly happy man says, "His delight is in the law of the LORD and on his law he meditates day and night" (1:2). Here, as in many passages, "law" refers to the whole Word of God. Notice the believer's reaction to God's instruction in the Word. He finds his delight in it. Notice his second reaction to God's Word. "He meditates day and night" in it. The word *meditate* pictures the low hum as the believer half-aloud reads and rereads to himself the precious words of his God. It's a healthy interest in and regular turning to that precious Word which the psalmist ascribes to the happy man.

How big is our Bible? We can only live by the part of the Bible we know. Martin Luther put it this way: "In truth, you cannot read too much in

Scripture; and what you read you cannot read too carefully; and what you read carefully you cannot understand too well; and what you understand well you cannot teach too well; and what you teach well you cannot live too well."[8] Turn to the Scripture. Live in the Scripture. Study the Scripture. Listen to the Scripture. Benefits will follow. Again, chief among those benefits will be seeing the Savior's face, knowing and appreciating, reveling in and responding to, our salvation in him. "They testify about me," Jesus said (Jn 5:39). That's reason enough to turn to the sufficient Word.

The past years in the WELS have seen increased emphasis placed on Bible class attendance. For good reason. Spiritual growth comes only through the Word. "Crave pure spiritual milk," Peter urged, "so that by it you may grow up in your salvation" (1 Pe 2:2). The more people drink the Word, the more growth there will be in salvation and Christian living. With growing optimism we note that in the WELS, Bible class attendance has gone up 30% in the past ten years or, should we say, has inched up to 14% of our communicants. But that still leaves 86% not regularly in the Word, at least in that forum. Checking the statistics for the South Atlantic District, we find an average of almost 30% of communicants in regular attendance at Bible class. Even as we thank God for turning this percentage to his Word, we increase our prayers and our efforts for the 70% still not there.

The past years have seen a flattening in worship attendance in the WELS, plateauing at 44.7% the past two years. Again, statistics aren't everything, but they do show us something. "If you hold to my teaching," Jesus said, using a word that meant to "live in his Word," ". . . you will know the truth, and the truth will set you free" (Jn 8:31,32). Home is where we live, where we "hang our hat." God's Word with its message of freedom from sin's clanking chains and hell's consuming fires should be home for us, a place where we dwell. Thank God that 60% of the South Atlantic District members find that home each week in public worship. But what about the 40% who do not? Even as we pray and direct our efforts to them, let's also remember this. Every sermon deserves maximum effort by the one who preaches as well as the one who listens. Every worship service demands the best music and direction by those who lead as well as the best efforts by those who participate. Our Savior speaks to us in our worship services, our Savior who wants us to see his face.

Turning to God's sufficient Word involves also our personal devotions. "No time," we say as we speed down life's freeway? It depends on our priorities. If I'm a diabetic, I take time for my insulin. If I'm a sports fan, I take time to watch ESPN. If I have a job, I show up at work, at least if I want a regular paycheck. If God's Word is "my joy and my heart's delight," I find

---

[8]*What Luther Says*, complied by Ewald M. Plass (St. Louis: Concordia Publishing House, 1959), no. 3547, p. 1110.

We Believe in Jesus Christ

time to "eat" it (Jer 15:16). And it does take time. Serious Bible study requires a time exposure, not a snapshot approach. Like piano playing, it takes time and practice. What benefits have we derived from our personal use of Scripture? What kind of methods or materials have we used? What have been some of the hindrances to our reading? How might our congregations help us with them? What kind of materials might aid us? How much personal use have we made of The People's Bible series or other WELS Bible study materials?

"Let the word of Christ dwell in you richly," Paul urges (Col 3:16). Turning to God's Word is to be no "hit or miss" affair, no "now you do it, now you don't" kind of activity. That Word is to "dwell" in us, to live in us, to make its home in us. And this it is to do "richly." Our hearts and lives are to be wide open with room for that blessed Word and its empowering message of salvation.

What God urges Christians to do, he repeats even more specifically to those he calls into public, or representative, ministry. Writing to his student and coworker, Paul stressed the need for Timothy to be "brought up in the truths of the faith and of the good teaching that you have followed" (1 Ti 4:6). Timothy needed to be "brought up," constantly nourished in God's Word if he was going to serve others well. "To the Word," Paul was telling him. "Keep on being fed by it. Don't ever stop. You need that Word if you are going to serve." In 2 Timothy 2:6 Paul stressed the same truth, though more graphically, "The hardworking farmer should be the first to receive a share of the crops." First the farmer needs to be nourished, or else he will produce less and less for anyone else. Paul was writing to Timothy, who was a pastor, about concerns much deeper than farming. How basic is the called servant's need for his own personal use of the Word!

Because called servants use God's Word in their daily work to meet the needs of others, they may forget about their own needs for it. Hurrying about their duties feverishly, caught up in the flurry of daily activities, they may forget something as basic as what it is they hold in their hands and how much they need it first for themselves before they offer it to others. One author put it this way:

> The great peril of the minister is that of deadening familiarity with the sublime. You will not have been long in the ministry before you discover that it is possible to be fussily busy about the Holy Place and yet to lose the wondering sense of the holy Lord. We may have much to do with religion and yet not be religious. We may indicate the way and yet not be found in it. We may be professors, but not pilgrims. Our studies may be workshops instead of upper rooms. Our share in the table provisions may be as servers instead of

guests. We may become so absorbed in words that we forget to heed the Word.[9]

"Let me see my Savior's face" needs to be the daily prayer and practice of every called worker.

When servants turn to the Word, they will be the first to benefit. Through the Word, the Spirit will renew them in the faith "that God was reconciling the world to himself in Christ, not counting men's sins against them. And he has committed to us the message of reconciliation" (2 Co 5:19). Through the Word the Spirit will convince them of the glorious truth "that one died for all, and therefore all died" (2 Co 5:14) and then commit them to the glorious task that "those who live should no longer live for themselves but for him who died for them and was raised again" (5:15). Or as Paul put it even more personally in Galatians 2:20, "I have been crucified with Christ and I no longer live, but Christ lives in me. The life I live in the body, I live by faith in the Son of God, who loved me and gave himself for me." Such truths each servant needs desperately for himself before taking them to others. And these are the truths that will aid him in serving others. When spirits sag and energy vanishes, God's servants turn to the Word. There in the message of God's grace in Christ they find both reason and strength for ministry. When problems persist and people perplex, God's servants turn to the Word. There in the message of God's grace in Christ they find new vitality and renewed zeal. When work becomes stale and ministry bland, God's servants turn to the Word. There in the message of God's grace in Christ they find again privilege in serving where he has placed them as bearers of his sufficient Word.

Our work with God's sufficient Word involves, third, *trusting* its power. That truth is so basic and yet so often smudged over or even forgotten. The words Jesus has spoken are spirit and life (Jn 6:63). God's Word is "fire" and "a hammer that breaks a rock in pieces" (Jer 23:29). His Word is "living and active. Sharper than any double-edged sword, it penetrates even to dividing soul and spirit, joints and marrow" (Heb 4:12). His gospel is "the power of God for the salvation of everyone who believes" (Ro 1:16). In his Word is power, the only power of which he promises, "It will not return to me empty, but will accomplish what I desire and achieve the purpose for which I sent it" (Isa 55:11). If God's people are to grow and then go, it can only happen through the power of the Word.

Problems arise when we try to tell the Word where to go and how it should cause people to grow. We forget that God, whose seed the Word is, is also the only One who makes it grow. Because we forget this basic truth, when the seed

---

[9]Paul Lindemann, *Ambassadors for Christ* (St. Louis: Concordia Publishing House, 1935), p. 32.

We Believe in Jesus Christ

doesn't seem to take root or bear the kind of fruit we expect, we are disappointed. Or even worse, we begin to distrust the seed and seek to supplement its strength. That's the fatal flaw of the Church Growth Movement. It distrusts the divine seed and shifts some of the trust to the efforts of the sower. Of course, we can keep our church grounds attractive and our buildings in good repair. We can meet people in the parking lot and greet them warmly at the door. We can follow up on our visitors right away on Monday and seek to form friendships with our neighbors. We can analyze communities before we plant and do ethnographic interviews with those of another culture. Such efforts are the prelude to sowing the Word, not attempts to power it. Watch out, though, when human efforts and gimmicks get in the way or seek to replace the Word. Only God's Word, as powered by the Spirit, works in the human heart. And it will work where and when God, whose Word it is, wants it to. "I planted the seed, Apollos watered it, but God made it grow," Paul said in 1 Corinthians 3:6. So must we. Our job is to sow and sow as best we know how. Our job is to trust the Word to work as God promises it will. How discouraging sowing the seed of God's Word would be if it fell only on stony, shallow, or weed-infested soils. What keeps us going is Jesus' promise that some seed will fall on soil that will produce a crop. No, not all the crops will have the same-size yield, but a crop will be produced nonetheless.

Don't we have a good example of this in your South Atlantic District? The seed has worked. Those people, and there are a few, who have been here the full 25 years might have wondered more than once. Those who are newer and striving to sow with might and main might still wonder. But growth has come. Like children whose steady growth we don't always notice because we see them day after day, until some visiting relative remarks, "My, how you've grown," or like some classmate whose waistline has expanded almost unnoticed till some smart-aleck remark by someone at a class reunion, so the South Atlantic District has grown. In 1973 there were 21 congregations, today 55. In 1973 there were three schools, today nine. In 1973 there were 2,257 baptized members, today 8,924. In 1973 there were 62 children baptized, last year 283. In 1973 there were 54 adults confirmed, last year 285. In 1973 there were 383 in Bible class, last year 1,986. And yes, we'll add it because we believe the Lord causes this also: in 1973 average offerings per communicant were $237.30, last year $903.17. Only the Lord can see the hearts involved in the statistics just quoted. Even more so, only the Lord can see the inner growth involved, that invisible growth in faith and knowledge, in comfort and confidence, in enthusiasm and energy for service that his all-sufficient Word brings. Today we thank him for that growth even as we ask for increased zeal to sow his Word and renewed trust in its divine power.

Lastly, our work with God's sufficient Word involves *taking* it to others. Mission work is not just something our 150-year-old synod does. It's not just something our mission congregations do. It's not just something our missionaries do in Tallahassee and Miami, Sharpsburg and Antigua, Cameroon and Canada, South East Asia and South America. It's something every believer does. With David who said it first and Paul who repeated it, for us too it's "I believed; therefore I have spoken" (2 Co 4:13). The children in our own family and in our church families are not just children. They are souls. Those who live next door to us are not just our neighbors. They are souls. Those five billion plus in the world's booming population are not just so many ciphers. They are souls. Those increasing numbers of citizens in our land of other cultures and from other countries are not just different. They are souls. The questions still rings out, "Can we whose souls are lighted with wisdom from on high, can we to those benighted the lamp of life deny?" Let our answer ring out even more loudly, "Salvation! Oh, salvation! The joyful sound proclaim till each remotest nation has learned Messiah's name" (CW 571:3). While our Lord leaves us here, let one eye be on his heaven and the other on the work he has given us, privileged work that he has entrusted to our hands along with his all-sufficient Word with which to do it.

Today, just as 150 years ago when the WELS began and centuries before that when the first sin brought those horrible shadows into Eden, dying sinners need to live, despairing sinners need to be comforted, doomed sinners need to learn of forgiveness. Today, just as 150 years ago when the WELS began and centuries before that when a loving God spoke to our sin-ravaged ancestors, only one word is sufficient for the task, JESUS—THE FINAL WORD FROM GOD.

WHAT DO WE MEAN, JESUS IS LORD OF THE CHURCH?

Wayne D. Mueller

Northern Wisconsin District Convention
Manitowoc, Wisconsin
June 15–17, 1998

Satan's current successes seem to belie Jesus' lordship of the church.

Apathy among many American Christians today makes the "lukewarm" Laodiceans look like zealots (Rev 3:16). The more they pursue wealth and personal freedom, the colder their hearts grow toward God. To attract ad revenue, Hollywood parades its self-serving immorality. The media continue to measure morality by public opinion. Thirty-five million infants have lost their lives on the altar of personal choice. Economic pragmatism and hedonism are prematurely putting the elderly to death. In fact, materialism threatens the life of anyone whose dollar value to society is questioned.

Most mainline denominations in our country long ago sold out their doctrinal birthright for politically correct "pottage." Once large and influential, church bodies now struggle to hold on to their dwindling membership with an impotent social gospel. They have forsaken the Word's power to wound the spiritually smug and bind up bleeding consciences. America's spiritual shepherds have lost the courage to call their people to choose between Baal and the Lord. The age of science has always caricatured Christians as hopelessly naive. But attacks on the Bible are no longer confined to public university classrooms. So-called Christian scholars challenge basic articles of faith more often and more boldly than secular skeptics.

The gospel is departing our country today as surely as God has in the past withdrawn it from other nations that grew indifferent to its lifesaving power. No one will deny that Christianity's once-strong influence on the

21

morals and manners of our society has eroded. Reluctantly, even we Christians must acknowledge that we are living in the post-Christian era of Western civilization.

All over the world, the gospel is under attack. Satan quickly closes many of the doors God opens to mission work. Overseas gospel outposts struggle with civil turmoil, political corruption, and religious competition. Physical persecution of Christians is increasing too. News reports of death and violence to Christians leak through from the former Soviet Union, China, and a host of Muslim countries. Even here at home, the pious Amish suffer increasingly brutal attacks in Wisconsin and Pennsylvania.

The concurrence of the impending new millennium and the 150th anniversary of our Wisconsin Synod provides us an obvious time to reflect on all this. Some retrospect is in place, but most of our thoughts will contemplate the present and anticipate the future. What comfort and hope does the Lord of the church offer us as we approach the third millennium since his first coming? What courage and impetus does the Lord of the church give us as we carry his message into the next millennium? As Satan attacks our confidence in these last and perilous days, what exactly does it mean, "Jesus is Lord of the church"?

Long ago St. Paul wrote, "No one can say, 'Jesus is Lord,' except by the Holy Spirit" (1 Co 12:3). Still today we depend on the Spirit, who first created our faith in Jesus to refresh our confidence that Jesus is still Lord of his church. Since faith itself derives from hearing the message of Christ, new strength of faith and new direction for these last days will also come from the Spirit's inspired Scripture.

The Lord Jesus is God

To understand Jesus' lordship of the church, we look first at how the Holy Spirit used the word for *lord* in reference to Jesus. The word he used in the New Testament is the Greek word for *lord, kurios. Kurios* occurs more than seven hundred times in the New Testament. Most of the time it refers to Jesus.

Two things, however, complicate an easy understanding of *kurios.* First, the word *lord* has many different shade of meanings. *Lord* is not properly a name but a title. This title applied to slave owners, kings, even husbands (1 Pe 3:7). In everyday use the word was simply a term of respect, like "sir," or "m'lord." "*In the ordinary, profane language* of the Greeks, the term *Kurios* meant 'master' or 'owner' and generally designated the subject of legitimate authority."[1]

In the four gospels, people often addressed Jesus as Lord in this common sense of the term. "Nor shall we feel surprise to learn that the simplest honorific titles are represented as those most frequently employed in addressing

---

[1] Lepold Sabourin, *The Names and Titles of Jesus* (New York: The Macmillan Company, 1967), pp. 253,254.

We Believe in Jesus Christ

Him—'Rabbi,' with its Greek renderings, 'Teacher' and 'Master,' and its Greek representative 'Lord'."[2] Many people called Jesus Lord merely to show respect for him as a spiritual master, that is, a teacher, or rabbi.

On the other hand, in the religious setting of the New Testament, *kurios* was often and obviously much more than a title of respect. This is clear when both God and Jesus are called Lord. This exalted understanding of *kurios* was passed down through the Septuagint. The Septuagint (LXX) is a Greek translation of the Old Testament Hebrew Scriptures, completed in the second century B.C. Greek was the language of commerce at that time.[3] Jews dispersed throughout Asia Minor and northern Egypt used the Septuagint to follow their Scriptures in the common language of the day and to win over for Judaism the people among whom they lived. The way the Septuagint used *kurios* profoundly affected the understanding of this word in Palestine during Jesus' ministry and at the time the New Testament was written. Most of the time, when Jesus was called Lord, the Septuagint flavor of *kurios* carried through and applied to him.

So the Greek *kurios* uniquely joins the Hebrew Old Testament witness to Jesus with the Greek New Testament. The Septuagint used *kurios* to translate the high and holy name God gave himself: Jehovah, or Jahweh. "The word *kurios,* "lord," as a name for God in the LXX is a strict translation only in cases where it is used for *Adoon* or *Adonai* (in the *ketib* [the traditional text]). As a rule, however, it is used as an expository equivalent for the divine name *Yaweh*."[4]

As you would expect, the Septuagint used the Greek *kurios* to translate some Hebrew words with the common meaning of "ruler" or "slave owner." Most often, however, the Septuagint used *kurios* to translate the Tetragrammaton (the four letter Hebrew word for *Jehovah,* or *Yahweh*), YHWH. Speaking of the Septuagint translation, one Greek scholar comments:

> In the religious sphere, then, *kurios* is reserved for the true God, and, apart from unimportant periphrases of the name in figurative speech, it is used regularly, i.e., some 6156 times, for the proper name Jehovah in all its pointings and in the combination *Yahweh Sebaoth* or in the short form *Yah.* Only by way of exception is *ho kurios* used for the other terms for God: 60 times for *El,* 23 for *Elohai,* 193 for *Elhohim,* and 3 for *Elohei Sebaoth.*[5]

---

[2]Benjamin B. Warfield, *The Lord of Glory* (Grand Rapids: Baker Book House, 1974), p. 3.
[3]A fairly detailed history of the formation of the Septuagint is found in Edersheim's, *The Life and Times of Jesus the Messiah,* Vol. 1 (Grand Rapids: William B. Eerdmans Publishing Company, 1953), pp. 17ff.
[4]Gerhard Kittel, ed., *Theological Dictionary of the New Testament* [TDNT], Vol. 3 (Grand Rapids: William B. Eerdmans Publishing Company, 1965), p. 1058.
[5]Ibid., p. 1059.

What Do We Mean, Jesus Is Lord of the Church?   23

Yet not only the Septuagint influenced how Jesus' immediate audience and later New Testament readers understood *kurios*. The secular world also used this word to denote an authority much higher than an earthly lord.

> *Kurios* was a synonym for "god" in the eastern Hellenistic religions of the Roman Empire. . . . By virtue of his political power the Roman emperor had himself called *Kurios*, a title that took on a religious character, when the Caesars received the honors of a cult. To adore Christ as the only *Kurios* was, then, to reject two false cults: the one of the Hellenistic deities and the other of the emperor.[6]

In this light, we can see why Jesus himself called his heavenly Father Lord. He authenticated his own ministry by quoting Isaiah's prophecy: "The Spirit of the Lord is on me, because he has anointed me to preach good news to the poor. . . . Today this Scripture is fulfilled in your hearing" (Lk 4:18,21). Jesus twice called God Lord when he answered Satan's temptations with Old Testament Bible passages: "Do not put the Lord your God to the test" and "Worship the Lord your God, and serve him only" (Mt 4:7,10).

Lord is the title Jesus invited his disciples to use when addressing the Father in prayer: "Ask the Lord of the harvest, therefore, to send out workers into his harvest field" (Mt 9:38). Jesus reminded the expert in the law that loving God as Lord is the first and greatest commandment: "Love the Lord your God with all your heart and with all your soul and with all your mind" (Mt 22:37).

We may be sure, then, that when the holy writers of the New Testament called Jesus *kurios*, they were stating that he is the Jehovah God. The Evangelical scholar Erickson explains:

> While the term can most certainly be used without any high christological connotations, there are several considerations which argue that the term signified divinity when it is applied to Jesus. First, in the Septuagint *kurios* is the usual translation of the name *Jehovah* and of the reverential *Adonai* which was ordinarily substituted for it. Further, several New Testament references to Jesus as "Lord" are quotations of Old Testament texts employing one of the Hebrew names for God (e.g., Ac 20:20-21 and Ro 10:13 [cf. Jl 2:31-32]; 1 Pe 3:15 [cf. Is 8:13]). These references make it clear that the apostles meant to give Jesus the title Lord in its highest sense. Finally, *kurios* is used in the New Testament to designate both God

---

[6]Sabourin, *The Names and Titles of Jesus*, pp. 253,254.

---

the Father, the sovereign God (e.g., Mt 1:20; 9:38; 11:25; Ac 17:24; Rev 4:11), and Jesus (e.g., Lk 2:11; Jn 20:28; Ac 10:36; 1 Co 2:8; Php 2:11; Jm 2:1; Rev 19:16). William Childs Robinson comments that when Jesus is addressed as the exalted God, he is so identified with God that there is ambiguity in some passages as to whether the Father or the Son is meant (e.g., Ac 1:24; 2:47; 8:39; 9:31; 11:21; 13:1-12; 16:14; 20:19; 21:14; cf. 18:26; Ro 14:11). For the Jews particularly, the term *kurios* suggested that Christ was equal with the Father.[7]

What does it mean, "Jesus is Lord of the church"? It means that the one who came to redeem his people is the very God who created all things. "In the beginning was the Word, and the Word was with God, and the Word was God. He was with God in the beginning. Through him all things were made; without him nothing was made that has been made. The Word became flesh and made his dwelling among us" (Jn 1:1-3,14). "He is the image of the invisible God, the firstborn over all creation. For by him all things were created: things in heaven and on earth . . . For God was pleased to have all his fullness dwell in him, and through him to reconcile to himself all things, whether things on earth or things in heaven, by making peace through his blood, shed on the cross" (Col 1:15,16,19,20).

When Scripture identifies Jesus as God, it fortifies our trust in the divine nature in the person of the Lord Jesus for these last and difficult days. John rightly warns us: "Watch out that you do not lose what you have worked for, but that you may be rewarded fully. Anyone who runs ahead and does not continue in the teaching of Christ does not have God; whoever continues in the teaching has both the Father and the Son" (2 Jn 8,9).

"Jesus is Lord of the church" means that he who guided his church through the christological controversies (arguments about whether Jesus is true God) of the early centuries is still God of his people. He is who he said he is, and he will continue to defend us against those who want to strip him of his divinity. He will guard his church against modernists who try to damn him with faint praise as a great teacher, martyr, or role model. Against the attacks of sects like the Mormons and the Jehovah's Witnesses, our Lord still insists, "I and the Father are one" (Jn 10:30). Jesus is God, and God is Jesus. Our Lord is of one essence with the Father. Thus Paul can say that God bought the church with his own blood (Ac 20:28). Daily the Lord of the church upholds our faith and establishes our ministry with the same assurance he gave Philip: "Anyone who has seen me has seen the Father" (Jn 14:9).

---

[7]Millard J. Erickson, *Christian Theology* (Grand Rapids: Baker Book House, 1985), pp. 690,691.

The Lord Jesus is the promised Messiah

By calling him Lord, the inspired authors of the New Testament identify Jesus as God. Yet by the use of the same word, the holy writers separate Jesus from the person of God the Father. While *kurios* identifies Jesus as Jehovah, it also distinguishes him from the Father. Although both Jesus and the Father are called Lord, *kurios* also designates Jesus as the Christ, the Messiah. As Lord, Jesus is at the same time true God and God's agent of salvation.

Jesus once posed this seeming conundrum to the teachers of the law: "David himself, speaking by the Holy Spirit, declared: 'The Lord said to my Lord: "Sit at my right hand until I put your enemies under your feet."' David himself calls him 'Lord.' How then can he be his son?" (Mk 12:36,37). A Lutheran scholar explains the significance of Jesus' challenge:

> The answer to this question should have been easy enough for scribes acquainted with O. T. doctrine. That Jesus is true God begotten of the Father from eternity, and also true man born of the virgin Mary, is not a doctrine first revealed in the N. T. The O. T. also has it. Compare Ps 2:7; Is 9:6; Mi 5:2; Ml 3:1; Ps 45:7; not to mention Ps 110 itself. Jesus knew only too well that the leaders, those who should have known better, had discarded this doctrine of the deity of the Messiah long ago and replaced it with the familiar belief in a temporal Messiah who was to lead his people to earthly glory."[8]

This distinction between the two Lords is found throughout the New Testament. In the same breath, Elizabeth called both the baby Jesus and the God who sent him Lord: "Why am I so favored, that the mother of my *Lord* should come to me? As soon as the sound of your greeting reached my ears, the baby in my womb leaped for joy. Blessed is she who has believed that what the *Lord* has said to her will be accomplished!" (Lk 1:43-45). Later, an angel Luke describes as "an angel of the Lord" (Lk 2:9), announced Jesus' birth by calling him Christ (Messiah) and Lord: "Today in the town of David a Savior has been born to you; he is Christ the Lord" (Lk 2:11).

When John the Baptist pointed to the coming of Jesus, he proclaimed that Jesus' ministry was in fulfillment of Isaiah's prophecy: "A voice of one calling in the desert, 'Prepare the way for the Lord, make straight paths for him'" (Mt 3:3). In the original prophecy, Isaiah spoke of preparing the way for *Jehovah,* which the Septuagint translated "Lord." Now John asserts that Jesus is the Lord for whom he is preparing the way.

---

[8]F. W. Wenzel, *The Wenzel Commentary* (Bemidji, Minnesota: Arrow printing, 1986) p. 594.

We Believe in Jesus Christ

St. Paul also set the two Lords side by side when he wrote, "Even if there are so-called gods, whether in heaven or on earth (as indeed there are many 'gods' and many 'lords'), yet for us there is but one God, the Father, from whom all things came and for whom we live; and there is but one Lord, Jesus Christ, through whom all things came and though whom we live" (1 Co 8:5,6). *The Expositor's Bible Commentary* explains:

> So Paul is teaching that the "so-called gods" of the pagans are unreal and that the real "gods" and "lords," whatever they may be, are all subordinate to the only one supreme God whom alone we recognize. Actually, Paul declares the Christian's "one God, the Father . . . one Lord, Jesus Christ, to be the source of all things and the One for whom all Christians live" (v 6). Concerning the world, the Father is the source of all creation, and Jesus Christ is the dynamic One through whom creation came into existence.[9]

While Paul's letters place Jesus and God side by side as Lord, they also carefully distinguish between the two persons. Warfield substantiates this distinction:

> Obviously the significance of the title "Lord" as applied to Jesus by Paul is not uninfluenced by its constant employment of God in the Greek Old Testament, and especially in those Old Testament passages which Paul applies to Jesus, in which "Lord" is the divine name (e.g., 2 Th 1:9; 1 Co 1:31; 10:9,26; 2 Co 3:16; 10:17; Ro 10:13; Eph 6:4; 2 Ti 2:19; 4:14. Is 45:23 is cited with reference to God in Rom 14:11, and with reference to Jesus in Php 2:10). Under the influence of these passages the title "Lord" becomes in Paul's hands almost a proper name, the specific designation for Jesus conceived as a divine person in distinction from God the Father. It is therefore employed of Jesus not merely constantly but almost exclusively. It is doubtful whether it is ever once employed of God the Father, outside of a few citations from the Old Testament: and in any case such employment of it is very exceptional. It is accordingly in point of fact the determinate title for Jesus as distinguished from God the Father. As such "the Lord Jesus Christ" is coupled with "God our Father" (or "the Father") as the co-source of that grace and peace which Paul is accustomed to invoke on his readers in

---

[9]Frank E. Gaebelein, ed., *The Expositor's Bible Commentary*, Vol. 10 (Grand Rapids: Zondervan Publishing House, 1976ff.), p. 239.

---

the addresses to his Epistles (1 Th 1:2; 2 Th 1:1,2; 1 Co 1:3; 2 Co 1:2; Gal 1:3; Ro 1:17; Eph 1:2; Php 1:2; 1 Ti 1:2; 2 Tm 1:2; Tit 1:4; cf. Eph 6:23; 1 Th 3:11; 2 Th 1:12). And throughout the Epistles Jesus as "the Lord" and the Father as "God" are set over against each other as distinct yet conjoined objects of the reverence of Christians, and distinct and yet conjoined sources of the blessings of which Christians are the recipients.[10]

As Peter, James, and John do in their epistles, Paul connects both Jesus and God with the title Lord in order to speak of Jesus' divinity but distinguishes between the persons in order to denote Jesus as the Messiah, or Christ, God's agent of salvation.[11] Paul demonstrates Jesus' saving messianic work by compounding his names and titles with Lord. Paul, James, Peter, and John all use compounds like Lord Jesus, Christ our Lord, Jesus Christ our Lord, our Lord Jesus Christ. The hundreds of occurrences of such compounds, the seemingly random interchangeability of them, and their use in scores of passages that speak of Jesus' saving work—all these serve to identify *Lord* with Christ's messianic office.

What does it mean, "Jesus is Lord of the church"? It means that Jesus is the focal point of all Scripture. All of the Bible points us to Jesus: the Old Testament by prophecy, the New by fulfillment. It means that all of God's promises can be trusted, that as surely as Jesus came by the prophets' testimony, so he will certainly come again by the word of the apostles. As Messiah, Jesus came in fulfillment of God's promise and will return in the same promise of God. As we seek mooring for our church in the uncertain days that lie ahead, we can be certain that if we set our anchor in the written Word, we will be tied to him for whom the Christian church is named.

In the certainty of Bible promises, the Holy Spirit restores to me the joy of my personal salvation. This is the joy the Spirit gave Andrew when he followed Jesus: " 'We have found the Messiah' (that is the Christ)" (Jn 1:41). Our elation is borne of the renewed trust that God keeps all his promises, not only to the church as a whole, but also to me personally. My growing faith breeds patient confidence. As Israel waited centuries for God to come and save, so we need divine patience to await God's salvation in the post-Christian era. God's Messiah, his Coming One, is coming again. "The Lord is not slow in keeping his promise, as some understand slowness. He is patient with you, not wanting anyone to perish, but everyone to come to repentance" (2 Pe 3:9).

---

[10]Warfield, *The Lord of Glory*, pp. 226,227.
[11]A list of Old Testament passages messianically applied in ancient rabbinic writings is in Edersheim's, *The Life and Times of Jesus the Messiah*, Vol. 2, Appendix IX, pp. 710ff.

We Believe in Jesus Christ

The Lord Jesus is the exalted God-man

The New Testament gives Jesus the title *Lord* to show him to be both God and Messiah. But following his resurrection and ascension, the title of Lord takes on a new, exalted significance. The divine Messiah who came to be the Savior of the church is now also Lord of the church in a special sense.

Before he was born and became the God-man, Jesus, the Son of God, possessed all the glory of the Godhead. In this sense, the Son of God was always Lord. Yet he veiled his glory as the only-begotten Son of God in the humility he took on at his conception. He kept this servant's form until his resurrection from the dead.

Throughout all the time of his humility, Jesus was truly and fully God. The many passages above that call him Lord prior to his resurrection attest to this. In addition, the inspired writers who wrote after his exaltation make it clear that Jesus was Lord of all even during the deepest moments of his humiliation. "The Bible says that the Jews crucified the Lord of Glory (1 Co 2:8). Peter told the Jews that they killed the Prince of life (Ac 3:15)."[12]

Yet Jesus declared himself Lord in a special way at his ascension. "All authority in heaven and on earth has been given to me" (Mt 28:18), he said. He was God and Lord from all eternity, but he did not receive the title of Lord according to his human nature until he completed his work as the Messiah. The glory accorded his human nature invoked the praises of the heavenly choir in St. John's vision of heaven: "Worthy is the Lamb, who was slain, to receive power and wealth and wisdom and strength and honor and glory and praise! . . . To him who sits on the throne and to the Lamb be praise and honor and glory and power, for ever and ever!" (Rev 5:12,13).

The Lutheran orthodox theologian Martin Chemnitz explains:

> Not only the saints in heaven but all creatures everywhere understand and recognize all this power which is given to Christ in time, in heaven, and on earth. Note this well, for it is the best and surest interpretation of all, and it is seen in the fact itself. Thus in Acts 2:36 we read: "God has made this Jesus, whom you crucified, both Lord and Christ," that is, King; and in John 13:13: "You call me Lord, and so I am." And in the preceding verses He has shown the reason that he is Lord, namely, that the Father has given all things into His hand. The context of these Scripture passages shows that all these things have been predicated of Christ with respect to his human nature,

---

[12]Siegbert Becker, "God Manifest in Flesh—The Mystery of the Personal Union," undated essay, Wisconsin Lutheran Seminary Library, essay file, p. 8.

---

according to which as a lamb He has been humiliated, put to death, and raised again.[13]

Jesus received the title Lord according to his human nature when his physical body rose from the grave. Easter thus marks the high point and divine proof of the believer's trust in his salvation. "As soon as the exinanition [humiliation] of Christ had accomplished its purpose, he was *exalted*, in that his human nature entered upon the *full and uninterrupted use* of the divine majesty communicated to it by virtue of the personal union. Beginning at the moment when his body was quickened in the tomb, it continues forever. Thus he was made Lord of all."[14]

What does it mean, "Jesus is Lord of the church"? It means that the "Lord, Jesus Christ, the only Son of God, eternally begotten of the Father, God from God . . . of one being with the Father . . . for us and for our salvation . . . became fully human."[15] That Jesus is Lord of the church means he was fully qualified to be my Savior. The Messiah whom God promised and sent was God and man in one person.

The Messiah had to be true God to save us because no mere man could rescue us from sin and death. "No man can redeem the life of another or give to God a ransom for him—the ransom for a life is costly, no payment is ever enough—that he should live on forever and not see decay" (Ps 49:7-9). "But"—since he is God—"now he has appeared once for all at the end of the ages to do away with sin by the sacrifice of himself" (Heb 9:26). God accepted the Lord's righteousness for all humans because the man Jesus was also true God. God accepted the Lord's death for all humans because the man Jesus died also as true God.

Our Messiah also had to be fully human in order to save us from our sins. "Since the children have flesh and blood, he too shared in their humanity so that by his death he might destroy him who holds the power of death—that is, the devil—and free those who all their lives were held in slavery by their fear of death" (Heb 2:14,15). God's justice demanded human perfection and human suffering as punishment for human imperfection. "For this reason he had to be made like his brothers in every way, in order that he might become a merciful and faithful high priest in service to God, and that he might make atonement for the sins of the people" (Heb 2:17).

"Jesus is Lord" comforts me for the trials that surely lie ahead in the end times. When Jesus was exalted, "his human nature entered upon the full and uninterrupted use of the divine majesty communicated to it by virtue of the per-

---

[13]Martin Chemnitz, *The Two Natures in Christ* (St. Louis: Concordia Publishing House, 1971), p. 320.
[14]John Schaller, *Biblical Christology* (Milwaukee: Northwestern Publishing House, 1981), p. 95.
[15]The Nicene Creed, *Christian Worship: A Lutheran Hymnal* (Milwaukee: Northwestern Publishing House, 1993), p. 18.

We Believe in Jesus Christ

sonal union."[16] For this reason I can be sure Jesus is physically present with me according to his promise, "Surely I am with you always, to the very end of the age" (Mt 28:20). I'm confident that the Jesus who fully understands my problems is fully capably of resolving them. "Because he himself suffered when he was tempted, he is able to help those who are being tempted" (Heb 2:18).

One of the most important ways in which the God-man upholds and strengthens his people for the last days is his Holy Supper. Because I understand how his human nature participates in the divine attributes, I come to the Lord's Supper with confidence. I know that with the bread and wine, I am receiving his true body and blood, not a mere representation or reminder of it. My Lord is not, as many still believe, physically confined to a chair next to God in heaven. Martin Luther reminds us of the connection between Jesus' lordship and the blessing of Holy Communion. We participate in his body and blood, unfettered by Reformed doubts about his real presence in the Supper. Reflecting Luther's thoughts, Chemnitz states:

> We content ourselves with the words of Christ by which in the institution of the Supper He affirms that that which is present in the Lord's Supper and shown and received with the mouth is His very body. But if someone asks how this is possible, and if he raised the objection that it conflicts with the true nature of the human body for it to be in many different places at the same time, then Luther advises this reply for the unlearned: Christ is not a mere man but also true, substantial, and perfect God and man in one inseparable person. And because the right hand of God where Christ's body is placed is everywhere and is not in one circumscribed, enclosed, and fenced-in place, and because He Himself has said of the bread of the Lord's Supper, "This is my body," it is a fact that without doubt and in keeping with his wisdom and omnipotence, which have neither mode nor boundary, that He can easily find a way, even though we may not understand it, whereby His body at the same time can be in heaven and in all places on earth where the Lord's Supper is observed according to His institution.[17]

The Lord Jesus is my Savior

Jesus completed in full the saving work God sent him to do. "God has raised this Jesus to life, and we are all witnesses of the fact. Exalted to the

---

[16]Schaller, *Biblical Christology*, p. 95.
[17]Chemnitz, *The Two Natures in Christ*, p. 464.

---

right hand of God, he has received from the Father the promised Holy Spirit. . . . Therefore let all Israel be assured of this: God has made this Jesus, whom you crucified, both Lord and Christ" (Ac 2:32,33,36). The one who served as my Prophet and Priest is now—also according to his human nature—my King. His saving work is done. Jesus, as God and man, is now the object of the church's faith and adoration.

St. Paul invited personal faith in this Lord: "I tell you that no one who is speaking by the Spirit of God says, 'Jesus be cursed,' and no one can say, 'Jesus is Lord,' except by the Holy Spirit" (1 Co 12:3). The Corinthians understood that confessing Jesus to be Lord was more than recognizing him as being equal with God. "Jesus is Lord" is the Spirit-created testimony to the work Jesus completed as the Messiah. Earlier, Paul said that this is a Spirit-created faith: "I resolved to know nothing while I was with you except Jesus Christ and him crucified. My message and my preaching were not with wise and persuasive words, but with a demonstration of the Spirit's power, so that your faith might not rest on men's wisdom, but on God's power" (1 Co 2:2,4,5).

To the first believers in the early church, Jesus was Lord in the sense of Messiah and Savior, the one who completed their redemption. When they proclaimed Jesus to be Lord, the secular sense of a bossy taskmaster was gone. To them, Lord was a title that expressed the comfort of the completed work of the crucified Christ.

That's why "Jesus is Lord" became the earliest creed by which the fledgling church proclaimed Jesus to be her Savior. This outward declaration expressed an inner trust: "'The word is near you; it is in your mouth and in your heart,' that is, the word of faith we are proclaiming: That if you confess with your mouth, 'Jesus is Lord,' and believe in your heart that God raised him from the dead, you will be saved. For it is with your heart that you believe and are justified, and it is with your mouth that you confess and are saved" (Ro 10:8-10).

Philippians 2 provides more evidence that the early church proclaimed "Jesus is Lord" as a confession of trust in Jesus as Savior. With these three simple words, they publicly accepted the exalted Jesus as Messiah. Because Jesus carried out his messianic work, even to the extreme point of a shameful death on a cross, and because God accepted his messianic work by exalting him, "every tongue [should] confess that Jesus Christ is Lord" (Php 2:11).

After Jesus rose from the dead, but before Paul wrote his Philippian letter, the whole Christian community had declared Jesus to be Lord in the sense of the divine Messiah. "The postpaschal formulation (cf. Lk 24:34; Mk 16:19ff.) is even more evident in the Fourth Gospel, where *kurios* is always used to designate the risen Jesus."[18] "The narrative in Acts revolves

---

[18]Sabourin, *The Names and Titles of Jesus*, p. 257.

We Believe in Jesus Christ

around the Jesus exalted to the right hand of God, whom God has made Lord and Christ (2:36). It is He who leads to eternal life; He is the Lord of life (3:15). He is the Savior, and there is salvation in no other (4:12). He deals out His blessings (3:16) and pours out the Holy Spirit on believers (2:33)."[19]

While the gospels call Jesus Lord to verify his divine credentials for his messianic work, the book of Acts and other New Testament writings call Jesus Lord to affirm that his work is completed. As a unit, the New Testament proclaims Jesus competent and his work completed. The title *Lord* invites us to see Jesus as the object of our faith, not as a taskmaster who now demands our obedience. When the church proclaims Jesus Christ as Lord, it is praise, not duty.

How we understand Jesus' lordship is evident in the church's life of sanctification. Jesus is the church's loving spiritual master. As such, he is the power and the motivator behind all Christian living. *Kurios* retains the basic sense of a slave owner, but brings with it a whole new spiritual dimension in connection with Christ. The service of the Christian is entirely willing. "It is for freedom that Christ has set us free. Stand firm, then, and do not let yourselves be burdened again by a yoke of slavery. . . . You who are trying to be justified by law have been alienated from Christ; you have fallen from grace. But by faith we eagerly await through the Spirit the righteousness for which we hope" (Gal 5:1,4,5).

Paul said, "I served the Lord with great humility and with tears, although I was severely tested by the plots of the Jews" (Ac 20:19). Paul reflected this same attitude in his inspired advice to the Roman Christians: "Never be lacking in zeal, but keep your spiritual fervor, serving the Lord. Be joyful in hope, patient in affliction, faithful in prayer" (Ro 12:11,12).

The church gives willing and thankful obedience to her Lord, not as to a demanding taskmaster but as to a loving Redeemer. This attitude of heart is also reflected in matters of Christian liberty. Paul writes: "Each [man] should be fully convinced in his own mind. He who regards one day as special, does so to the Lord. He who eats meat, eats to the Lord, for he gives thanks to God; and he who abstains, does so to the Lord and gives thanks to God. For none of us lives to himself alone and none of us dies to himself alone. If we live, we live to the Lord; and if we die, we die to the Lord. So, whether we live or die, we belong to the Lord" (Ro 14:5-8).

Sadly, what the Bible says about the meaning of *Lord* is not shared by all who proclaim Jesus as Lord today. Catholic and Reformed teachers still hold Jesus to be Lord more in the secular sense of a spiritual boss. This is also true of the Arminian branch of the Reformed church, which denies original sin and emphasizes personal choice in matters of faith. Many professing Christians

---

[19]Warfield, *The Lord of Glory*, p. 210.

---

still regard Jesus primarily as a master to whom we owe a legal debt. The theologies of these churches portray Jesus as a new Lawgiver.

> The Reformed Christian likes to view the worship service above all as a work of the believer which he owes to God, as a *duty to God*, a proof of his gratitude, so that he even comes very close to applying the idea of sacrifice to the service. For the Lutheran, on the other hand, the worship service is primarily *a service which God renders to us*, a way by which he bestows his grace on us, the high point of which is the sacrament, which, viewed as our activity is a seeking for grace, an enjoyment of God."[20]

What is true in many Protestant camps in regard to receiving salvation also influences the way many Reformed Christians live out their salvation. Lutheran theologian August Pieper writes: "According to the Reformed view, prayer is placed under the duties prescribed by the law for the believer. For that reason the *Heidelberg Catechism* treats it only *after* the Commandments, almost as the highest exercise, as a rendering of gratitude to God. For Lutherans it is just the opposite. There it is found under the means for the subjective appropriation of salvation."[21] For us Lutherans, Pieper says, prayer is a privilege granted by God, the response of a Spirit-wrought faith.

The same wrong-headed concept of *Lord* pervades Catholicism. After the Lutheran Reformation, Rome made it clear that obedience to Christ as a master was still necessary. Obedience to the Lord was a condition for receiving continued forgiveness and growth in justification. At the Council of Trent, Rome condemned anyone who taught otherwise: "If anyone says that the justice received is not preserved and is also not increased before God through good works, but that the works are only the fruit and the signs of the justification received, let him be anathema."[22]

Those who view the Lord of the church as a taskmaster invariably end up confusing law and gospel. Obedience to the law becomes a part of attaining salvation instead of thanksgiving for receiving it. Again Pieper comments:

> [For the Reformed] the law has a *positive* significance for the regenerate person *as such*, not just a negative one, in so far as he still has a side that has not yet been renewed. It must tell him what he as a believer and regenerate person must do. It

---

[20]August Pieper, "The Difference Between the Reformed and the Lutheran Interpretation of the So-Called Third Use of the Law," *The Wauwatosa Theology*, Vol. 2, Curtis A. Jahn, ed., (Milwaukee: Northwestern Publishing House, 1997), p. 107.
[21]Pieper, "The Difference," pp. 107,108.
[22]Canon XXIV, Council of Trent, quoted in Martin Chemnitz, *Examination of the Council of Trent*, Part 1 (St. Louis: Concordia Publishing House, 1971), p. 538.

must *prescribe* God's will to him and encourage him to carry it out. Accordingly, *the justified and regenerated person as such* needs the law, and for this reason, that as we have seen before, he has to do good works and in doing the same has to work out his salvation.[23]

For the Lutheran Christian, the Bible-based definition of *Lord* is gospel, not law. The Lord Jesus moves me to happy and willing service. He is not a spiritual whip or overseer. Greek scholar Werner Foerster notes, "In the designation of God as Lord is expressed the submission of man not so much to a power which he cannot resist as to a greatness in the face of which only humble reverence is befitting."[24] Professor John Schaller explains how Jesus displayed this kind of lordship toward his subjects: "Christ's Kingdom of Grace is the exercise of the power of his grace, when he creates, orders, and controls, by the force, not of an arbitrary sovereign will, but of a will acting according to his own redeeming grace, to bestow upon sinners the salvation he earned for them."[25]

So for Lutherans, the law continues to serve its purposes for our old Adam but does not impinge on our spiritual relationship with Christ as Lord. Lutheran theologian Gerhard wrote: "The regenerate Christian, in so far as he is a Christian and regenerated, needs no law, namely that drives and compels him, because he does good works on his own initiative. Since, however, he is not yet completely regenerated but is still partly under the old domination of the flesh, his stubborn flesh must be compelled by commands and threats and subjected to the rule of the spirit."[26]

What does it mean, "Jesus is Lord of the church"? It means that we celebrate the anniversary of the Wisconsin Synod as a gift of the Lord's saving grace to our church. Our milestone praise will not be self-congratulations for our faithful adherence to doctrine, our hard work, or our careful preservation of our fathers' heritage. Instead, our motto and motive is, *Soli deo gloria!* To our Lord alone be glory for all the blessings of personal life and for all the bounties of Wisconsin Synod ministry.

"Jesus is Lord of the church" means I will continue to seek his saving grace in the last and terrible days before his return. I will be wary of insidious incursions into his grace by those who want to turn my Savior into a moral supervisor. I see them not only in the traditional Reformed and Roman theologies, but also in the popular movements of the day: Promise Keepers, New Age, scouting, lodges, and social gospel. As I search the Scriptures, I plead with the Lord to immerse me in his amazing grace. I ask him to help me

---

[23]Pieper, "The Difference," p 105.
[24]TDNT, Vol. 3, p. 1053.
[25]Schaller, *Biblical Christology*, p. 158.
[26]Pieper, "The Difference," p. 104.

---

always to see the predominant New Testament meaning of *Lord* as "source of love and spiritual life for the church." I seek for myself and my church the closing blessing Paul offered the Romans: "The grace of our Lord Jesus be with you" (Ro 16:20).

The Lord is head of the church

Many New Testament passages stress the exalted, divine power of the resurrected Jesus. Jesus spoke of this power first at his trial (Jn 19:11), then again at his ascension: "All authority in heaven and on earth has been given to me" (Mt 28:18). Already now this power is absolute: "You have been given fullness in Christ, who is the head over every power and authority" (Col 2:10). At his return his sovereignty will have to be acknowledged by all, "even those who pierced him" (Rev 1:7).

Such passages clearly emphasize our Lord's ability to control all things. But it's equally important to note how our Lord exercises this absolute control. He exercises his lordship not over his church, but on behalf of his church. The Lord's might defends his people. His power does not coerce obedience; it protects those who have already come to faith.

When the New Testament was written, *kurios,* even in a secular sense, could have the meaning "a benevolent, protecting master." "The linking of a personal suffix with the designation 'lord' is an impressive reminder that 'already in primitive conditions the relation of the slave to his master as the latter's property was a guarantee of protection against danger from others.'"[27] When the Bible talks about Jesus' benevolent use of power, it is not out of touch with generally accepted uses of the word *lord.* Foerster notes that at times even pagan cultures would speak of their gods in this way:

> If all Semitic personal names which contain the name of a god, and which are formed with some other word than servant, speak of something which the god either has done or will do to save his worshipers, or mention a quality which is the basis for the certainty or hope that the god will intervene on their behalf, this implies that the god has the power to act for his servant in this way.[28]

The combination of our Lord's omnipotence and grace is beautifully joined in Paul's picture of him as head of his church. The apostle writes, "God placed all things under his feet and appointed him to be head over everything for the church, which is his body, the fullness of him who fills everything in every way" (Eph 1:22,23). Paul defines marital roles with the same picture:

[27]TDNT, Vol. 3, p. 1053.
[28]Ibid.

"Wives, submit to your husbands as to the Lord. For the husband is the head of the wife as Christ is the head of the church, his body, of which he is the Savior. Husbands, love your wives, just as Christ loved the church and gave himself up for her" (Eph 5:22,23,25). The Lord has a symbiotic relationship to his church, as a head has to its body. In this passage "Savior" serves as appositive and synonym for "head." It defines how the church understands Christ's headship. So we may understand Paul's words to the Colossians in the same sense: "He is the head of the body, the church" (Col 1:18).

Similarly, both the Old and New Testaments portray the Lord as bridegroom of the church. The bridegroom uses his authority to win the willing love of the bride and to control what might threaten her welfare. Isaiah writes: "I delight greatly in the Lord; my soul rejoices in my God. For he has clothed me with garments of salvation and arrayed me in a robe of righteousness, as a bridegroom adorns his head like a priest, and as a bride adorns herself with her jewels. . . . As a bridegroom rejoices over his bride, so will your God rejoice over you" (Isa 61:10; 62:5).

The persistent weakness of sinful man is to glory in power rather than in grace. Human perversion of God's spiritual lordship was deep rooted already when Jesus walked the earth. "Jesus knew only too well that the leaders, those who should have known better, had discarded this doctrine of the deity of the Messiah long ago and replaced it with the familiar belief in a temporal Messiah who was to lead his people to earthly glory."[29]

Even after his resurrection, Jesus had to shake this earthly view of his kingdom from the minds of his disciples. At his ascension the disciples asked him, "Lord, are you at this time going to restore the kingdom to Israel?" (Ac 1:6). They had visions of marching into Jerusalem, parading the risen and exalted Lord in front of the Sanhedrin that condemned him, forming an army to drive out the hated Romans, and reestablishing the earthly kingdom of David.

Jesus dislodged the disciples' misdirected lust for earthly power. He reminded them that just as he exercised his lordship to win souls and protect the church, the power he was bequeathing them was a gracious, spiritual power: "You will receive power when the Holy Spirit comes on you; and you will be my witnesses (Ac 1:8). The power the Lord left the church is not a worldly power, but a power to convert the world.

The power of the Holy Spirit that Jesus left his disciples then and now is the power to forgive and retain sins in the name of the Lord Jesus. "Jesus said, '. . . As the Father has sent me, I am sending you. . . . Receive the Holy Spirit. If you forgive anyone his sins, they are forgiven; if you do not forgive them, they are not forgiven'" (Jn 20:21-23). This is the power Paul told the

---

[29]Wenzel, *The Wenzel Commentary*, p. 594.

Corinthians to exercise in the name of the Lord: "When you are assembled in the name of our Lord Jesus and I am with you in spirit, and the power of our Lord Jesus is present, hand this man over to Satan, so that the sinful nature may be destroyed and his spirit saved on the day of the Lord" (1 Co 5:4,5).

Many who profess Christian faith nevertheless speak and act against Jesus' loving, spiritual lordship. Professor Schaller defines these weaknesses:

> As contradicting this scriptural view of the Kingdom of Grace we note both the Romanizing and the Millenarian errors. In the former, the church as an outward organization is held to be the visible Kingdom of Christ; in the latter, the expectation of a universal extension of the visible Kingdom of Christ on earth at some future date is a characteristic feature. These errors are not antagonistic, but rather complementary to one another. As they have developed side by side from the patristic age of the church, so they may now be found combined in the theologies of most sects.[30]

Kurt Marquart goes into more detail:

> Traditional Roman Catholicism errs here not by identifying the kingdom of grace with the church, but by equating this church with the papal dominion. The modern Calvinist dogmatician Berkhof . . . sees "Christian labor unions, and Christian political organizations" also as "manifestations of the Kingdom of God, in which groups of Christians seek to apply the principles of the Kingdom to every domain of life.[31]

Millennialists set aside Jesus' spiritual lordship for a thousand years of rule by force at the end of the world. Marquart speculates that millennialists substitute their anticipation of a rule of power for their lack of meaningful sacraments.

> Quite exotic is the "dispensationalist" scheme proposed by what is sometimes regarded as the most influential religious book in the United States, the Scofield Reference Bible. Biblical terms are gerrymandered there on a grand scale in the interest of an imaginary "kingdom, political, spiritual, Israelitish, universal, over which God's Son, David's heir, shall be King, and which shall be for one thousand years, the manifestation of righteousness of God in human affairs."

---

[30]Schaller, *Biblical Christology*, p. 202.
[31]Kurt Marquart, *The Church, and Her Fellowship, Ministry, and Governance* (Fort Wayne: International Foundation for Lutheran Confessional Research, 1990), p. 177.

We Believe in Jesus Christ

The church is demoted thereby to a sort of interim consolation prize, until the interrupted fulfillment of Lk 1:32 can be taken up again in the "political, spiritual, Israelitish" thousand years! Such surrogate "sacraments" are the fate of a moralistic pietism too lofty and "spiritual" to acknowledge the real sacraments.[32]

Our Lord operates with grace toward his church. His spiritual kingdom is "peace and joy in the Holy Spirit" (Ro 14:17). The Lord never exercises his omnipotent, physical power toward his church. By grace he wins people to faith and preserves them in faith.

But there is a kingdom of power in which Jesus operates for the protection of his church so that it may safely distribute his grace through the Word. History is his story. By his power, our Lord weaves enough peace into his story to allow us to dispense his grace. The Lord will protect his two witnesses, the law and the gospel, with whatever omnipotent means they need for their defense: "These [two witnesses] are the two olive trees and the two lampstands that stand before the Lord of the earth. If anyone tries to harm them, fire comes from their mouths and devours their enemies. This is how anyone who wants to harm them must die. These men have power to shut up the sky so that it will not rain during the time they are prophesying; and they have power to turn the waters into blood and to strike the earth with every kind of plague as often as they want" (Rev 11:4-6).

St. Paul exhorts Christians to pray for a peaceful context in which to preach the gospel: "I urge, then, first of all, that requests, prayers, intercession and thanksgiving be made for everyone—for kings and all those in authority, that we may live peaceful and quiet lives in all godliness and holiness. This is good, and pleases God our Savior, who wants all men to be saved and to come to a knowledge of the truth" (1 Ti 2:1-4).

So the vehemence of the Lord's almighty hand is felt by those who oppose his church. The prophetic psalms remind us that the Lord is in control: "Why do the nations conspire and the peoples plot in vain? The kings of the earth take their stand and the rulers gather together against the Lord and against his Anointed One. The One enthroned in heaven laughs; the Lord scoffs at them. Then he rebukes them in his anger and terrifies them in his wrath, saying, 'I have installed my King on Zion, my holy hill'" (Ps 2:1,2,4-6). Luther based "A Mighty Fortress," the battle hymn of the Reformation, on God's promises of protection to his church:

> There is a river whose streams make glad the city of God,
> the holy place where the Most High dwells.

---

[32]Ibid., p. 179.

> God is within her, she will not fall;
>> God will help her at break of day.
> Nations are in uproar, kingdoms fall;
>> he lifts his voice, the earth melts.
> The LORD Almighty is with us;
>> the God of Jacob is our fortress. (Ps 46:4-7)

Thus believers do not look to the Lord's creative might to force conversions, win political victories over their enemies, or control their flocks. But we do seek refuge in the Lord's power for the safety we need to proclaim his grace to the world. When Jesus sent his disciples out to witness, he urged them to confide in this safety: "Do not be afraid of them. . . . Do not be afraid of those who kill the body but cannot kill the soul. . . . So don't be afraid; you are worth more than many sparrows" (Mt 10:26,28,31). Likewise, St. Peter urges us to witness to the gospel without fear of physical consequences: "Even if you should suffer for what is right, you are blessed. 'Do not fear what they fear; do not be frightened.' But in your hearts set apart Christ as Lord. Always be prepared to give an answer to everyone who asks you to give the reason for the hope that you have" (1 Pe 3:14,15).

What does it mean, "Jesus is Lord of the church"? As we look back, we can see the Lord's gentle rule on behalf of the church. We praise him for holding our little synod in the palm of his Shepherd's hand for 150 years. We rejoice that he has used his power to defend us against and defeat every one of our spiritual enemies. We exult in retrospect that the power he granted to the Wisconsin Synod was not that of impressive numbers, political sway, secular honor, or institutional grandeur. But we humbly rejoice that we are privileged to wield the sword of the Word and exercise the Lord's great life-changing power by forgiving and retaining sins.

For the future, the confidence that Jesus is Lord of the church engenders an optimism that no human power or influence can. Our confidence that Jesus is in control even in the "post-Christian" era, moves us to renewed efforts at carrying out his Great Commission. Personal witness and congregational outreach mark the members of the Lord's church as his disciples. Like Gideon's army, we are confident of victory in the might of the Lord. When God grants success, we will tell those we have conquered with the means of grace, "I will not rule over you, nor will my son rule over you. The LORD will rule over you" (Jdg 8:23). We will wield the sword of the Spirit, knowing that as kings we will soon reign with the King of kings.

A spiritual understanding of Jesus' lordship of the church also impacts the practical way we church leaders administer the keys in our parishes until the Lord returns. Recently I wrote that the two different approaches to parish leadership devolve from the two different understandings of "Jesus is Lord":

There are two different views of Jesus as Lord of the church. One sees Jesus as sovereign controller of the Christian's life. Would-be disciples must choose Jesus as their master and then prove their choice by keeping their promises to obey. Jesus is the moral ruler of their lives. We see this picture of Jesus in action throughout history, from the Holy Roman Empire and John Calvin's Geneva to today's Christian Coalition and Church Growth.

Radically opposed to this view of the Lord is one that sees Jesus as the King of grace. In the eyes of his disciples, the authority of Jesus is based on his service to sinners as the Messiah, not his *modus operandi* for maintaining his kingdom. His kingdom is not of this world, so it is not run like worldly kingdoms.

In this radical scriptural view, the Lord is still head of his church, but head in the sense of the Savior of the body. This Sovereign does not compel faith or obedience. Rather, he loves the church, gives himself up for her, cleanses her, and presents his bride to himself spotless and holy (Eph 5:25-27).

This king of love is the same supreme ruler who holds sway over all creation. But he uses his sovereign power not to control his church, but to hold the church's enemies in check and finally defeat them.

As you might expect, the Lord's undershepherds usually tend toward one of these two views as they administer their parishes. Some equate a well-controlled parish with a well-administered one. Others see good order merely as an instrument to distribute mercy.

The difference between these two approaches is not subtle. One is secular; the other spiritual. One is legal; the other evangelical. One is mind control; the other is soul care. One aims at moral and organizational compliance; the other at salvation.

Distinctive Lutheran leadership is more than theological commitment to general gospel predominance. Leaders' attitudes and actions will demonstrate the gospel meaning of "Jesus is Lord."

That doesn't mean that loving church leadership lacks order. "For God is not a God of disorder but of peace" (1 Co 14:33).

Staying in control, however, is a lesser leadership challenge than displaying the Lord's love from the top down."[33]

The Lord Jesus is the Lord of glory

Even as we celebrate the Lord's wise and loving shepherding of our church for the past 150 years, our sinful flesh trembles at the prospect of what the future may bring. Although the Lord Jesus is already in full control of all things, his full power and glory are veiled until his final return. Until then, the Lord allows sin and evil to continue, in order that all the elect might be converted and gathered into his church. "The Lord is not slow in keeping his promise, as some understand slowness. He is patient with you, not wanting anyone to perish, but everyone to come to repentance" (2 Pe 3:9).

The ultimate demonstration of Jesus' lordship will come on the day named for him, "the day of the Lord" (1 Co 1:8; 5:5; 2 Co 1:14; 1 Th 5:2; 2 Th 2:2; 2 Pe 3:10). The lordly power believers accepted by faith will become forcefully evident to all by sight. The church waits in patient anticipation for the Lord's "appearing" (1 Ti 6:14). "The Lord is near" (Php 4:5). He is coming (1 Th 3:13; 4:15; 2 Th 2:1; 2 Pe 1:16; Jude 14). He will be revealed (2 Th 1:7), and then the church, the Lord's bride, will enter "into the eternal kingdom of our Lord" (2 Pe 1:11).

We hope for that full and final glory of Jesus' lordship, but while on earth, we accept the burden of suffering in his kingdom of grace. Scripture reverberates with optimistic statements of sharing his final victory. "In this world you will have trouble. But take heart! I have overcome the world" (Jn 16:33), Jesus assured his fearful disciples. Paul expresses this confidence to the Corinthians: "He has delivered us from such a deadly peril, and he will deliver us. On him we have set our hope that he will continue to deliver us" (2 Co 1:10). To Timothy, the apostle expresses similar hope: "The Lord will rescue me from every evil attack and will bring me safely to his heavenly kingdom. To him be glory for ever and ever" (2 Ti 4:18).

The day of the Lord will be a fateful day for every enemy of the church. "At that time the sign of the Son of Man will appear in the sky, and all the nations of the earth will mourn. They will see the Son of Man coming on the clouds of the sky, with power and great glory" (Mt 24:30). The church patiently suffers the trials of the last days without thoughts of physical revenge, knowing that final justice waits in the wings for its enemies:

> God is just: He will pay back trouble to those who trouble you and give relief to you who are troubled, and to us as well.

---

[33]Wayne Mueller, "Leadership: Top-Down Love," *Lutheran Leader*, Vol. 6, No. 4 (Summer 1998).

We Believe in Jesus Christ

This will happen when the Lord Jesus is revealed from heaven in blazing fire with his powerful angels. He will punish those who do not know God and do not obey the gospel of our Lord Jesus. They will be punished with everlasting destruction and shut out from the presence of the Lord and from the majesty of his power on the day he comes to be glorified in his holy people and to be marveled at among all those who have believed. (2 Th 1:6-10)

The shame and defeat of the Lord's enemies only begins when he returns. The Lord's "day" is actually an eternity. First Satan and his minions who plagued the church will meet their never-ending doom. "They marched across the breadth of the earth and surrounded the camp of God's people, the city he loves. But fire came down from heaven and devoured them. And the devil, who deceived them, was thrown into the lake of burning sulfur, where the beast and the false prophet had been thrown. They will be tormented day and night for ever and ever" (Rev 20:9,10).

Following Satan into hell are all those who followed his lead on earth: "Outside are the dogs, those who practice magic arts, the sexually immoral, the murderers, the idolaters and everyone who loves and practices falsehood" (Rev 22:15). St. John's vision of judgment day pictures the way in which the Lord's justice disposes of his enemies:

I saw the dead, great and small, standing before the throne, and books were opened. Another book was opened, which is the book of life. The dead were judged according to what they had done as recorded in the books. The sea gave up the dead that were in it, and death and Hades gave up the dead that were in them, and each person was judged according to what he had done. Then death and Hades were thrown into the lake of fire. The lake of fire is the second death. If anyone's name was not found written in the book of life, he was thrown into the lake of fire. (Rev 20:12-15)

Contrasted with the agony of those who opposed the Lord is the eternal bliss of those who anticipated their Lord's return. For the saints, the last day is a day of joy: "The Lord himself will come down from heaven, with a loud command, with the voice of the archangel and with the trumpet call of God, and the dead in Christ will rise first. After that, we who are still alive and are left will be caught up together with them in the clouds to meet the Lord in the air. And so we will be with the Lord forever" (1 Th 4:16,17). Since we have this knowledge in advance, our Lord urged us to look for that time with hope, not fear: "When these things begin to take place, stand up and lift up your heads, because your redemption is drawing near" (Lk 21:28).

As the terror of the Last Day is an eternal terror for the Lord's enemies, so the joy of his redeemed is an eternal day of bliss. Jesus gave John this vision of eternal bliss:

> I saw the Holy City, the new Jerusalem, coming down out of heaven from God, prepared as a bride beautifully dressed for her husband. And I heard a loud voice from the throne saying, "Now the dwelling of God is with men, and he will live with them. They will be his people, and God himself will be with them and be their God. He will wipe every tear from their eyes. There will be no more death or mourning or crying or pain, for the old order of things has passed away." (Rev 21:2-4)

Heaven is the highest meaning of "Lord of the church." There the full splendor of the Lord's grace and power will be enjoyed by his people. "No longer will there be any curse. The throne of God and of the Lamb will be in the city, and his servants will serve him. They will see his face, and his name will be on their foreheads. There will be no more night. They will not need the light of a lamp or the light of the sun, for the Lord God will give them light. And they will reign for ever and ever" (Rev 22:3-5).

What do we mean, Jesus is Lord of the church? As we look back for reasons to give thanks, we do not focus on the institutional, corporate, organizational, or visible blessings the Lord gave our synod. "We fix our eyes not on what is seen, but on what is unseen. For what is seen is temporary, but what is unseen is eternal" (2 Co 4:18). The Lord of the church's greatest blessings are the eternities of bliss he granted by grace to those who have gone before us. We praise the Lord for the forgiveness he distributed to them and us, for answered prayers, for the gifts and graces to serve, and for perseverance in the good fight of faith.

As we look forward, our greatest temptation is not to look far enough forward. Our sin is to look only at the immediate future, the stack of bills we have to pay, the apathy created by materialism, our failed attempts at outreach, the disaffection of our youth, and the shortage of workers for the harvest. Those who serve the Lord of the church always have as their goal the joy of heaven. Only that promised joy can propel us past the seemingly impossible predicaments that lie immediately in front of us. The Lord's resurrection leads us to work toward our own. Such long-range motivation is not pious, pie-in-the-sky rhetoric. It is spiritually pragmatic, godly practical, and all and only what we need to keep at the work of the kingdom. When St. Paul urged such dedication based on Christ's resurrection, he pointed to the Lord:

"Therefore, my dear brothers, stand firm. Let nothing move you. Always give yourselves fully to the work of the Lord, because you know that your labor in the Lord is not in vain" (1 Co 15:58).

We Believe in Jesus Christ

David M. Gosdeck

Michigan District Convention
Saginaw, Michigan
June 9–11, 1998

Wonder of wonders

The pitch lowers; the music softens; the soloist almost whispers. The words are barely audible. "He became incarnate." In the musical setting of the Mass, at these words of the Nicene Creed, the music invites the hearer to stand quietly before the great miracle and ponder the mystery. Each time the music bids us to feel anew the awe of the shepherds who first went to marvel at the great thing God had done. For "beyond all question, the mystery of godliness is great: He appeared in a body, was vindicated by the Spirit, was seen by angels, was preached among the nations, was believed on in the world, was taken up into glory" (1 Ti 3:16).

No Christian dare ever let the miracle of the incarnation become commonplace. Nor must we let the awe of it be lost in the Christmas season, the season in which our focus fixes most narrowly on "God become fully human." Indeed, the danger is great, for ". . . the mystery of Christ runs the risk of being disbelieved precisely because it is so incredibly wonderful. For God was in humanity. He who was above all creation was in our human condition; the invisible one was made visible in the flesh; he who is from the heavens and from on high was in the likeness of earthly things; the immaterial one who could be touched; he who was free in his own nature came in the form of a slave. . . ."[1]

---

[1]Cyril of Alexandria, *On the Unity of Christ* (Crestwood, New York: St. Vladimir's Seminary Press, 1995), p. 61.

The best way to approach this subject is with a sense of awe, for we can never understand nor comprehend the miracle. Nor should we attempt to. The truth is simple and clear. "The miracles recorded permit us not to entertain a doubt that God was born in the nature of man. But how—this, as being a subject unapproachable by the processes of reasoning, we decline to investigate."[2] "The manner of this union is entirely beyond conception."[3] The incarnation is the very heart of our message and the center of the gospel. "We cannot treat of and teach diligently enough that great compassion and the honor the Heavenly Father paid us by deigning to send His Son into the flesh."[4] With the angels we bow and worship. In the end we can exclaim with Gregory, "I cannot restrain my pleasure; I am rapt into God."[5]

Fully human

The testimony of Scripture to the full and real humanity of our Savior is overwhelming. But as we fix our attention on his humanity, we want always to remember that he is true God. In all that we say, we cannot lose sight of this truth. Scripture teaches with equal force that our Savior is one person who is both God and man.

From the beginning God had revealed that the coming Savior would be a real human being. In the first promise he said, "I will put enmity between you and the woman, and between your offspring and hers; he will crush your head, and you will strike his heel" (Ge 3:15). When he called Abram, he promised him, "All peoples on earth will be blessed through you" (Ge 12:3). He repeated that promise in Genesis chapter 15, and again, after Abraham's willingness to sacrifice Isaac, God swore by the most solemn oath, "Through your offspring all nations on earth will be blessed" (Ge 22:18). He sealed that same promise both to Isaac and Jacob (Ge 26:4; 28:14). Finally, out of their descendants, the people of Israel, he chose one family through which he would fulfill that promise. He chose David: "When your days are over and you rest with your fathers, I will raise up your offspring to succeed you, who will come from your own body, and I will establish his kingdom" (2 Sa 7:12). No one convinces us of the Savior's humanity more than Isaiah, as he pictures the Suffering Servant for us in chapter 53.

The New Testament confirms the promises of the Old. Matthew traces the genealogy of the Savior from Abraham to Joseph and Mary (Mt 1:1-16). Luke goes even further; he traces the Lord's genealogy from Joseph to Adam (Lk 3:23-37). Throughout the gospels, Christ calls himself "the Son of Man." In Romans Paul speaks of Christ, "who as to his human nature was a

---

[2]Gregory of Nyssa, *The Great Catechism*, NPNF 2:V:487.
[3]Cyril of Alexandria, *On the Unity of Christ*, p. 77.
[4]LW 5:224.
[5]Gregory of Nazianzen, *Oration on the Holy Lights*, NPNF 2:VII:357.

descendant of David" (1:3). Paul and the other apostles also use this description in other books of the New Testament. Paul attests to the real humanity of Christ in Galatians: "When the time had fully come, God sent his Son, born of a woman, born under law" (4:4).

For John no word more vividly describes the humanity of Christ than the Greek word *psalphizo,* "to touch with the hand." As he faced those who denied that Jesus was fully human, John wrote, "That which was from the beginning, which we have heard, which we have seen with our eyes, which we have looked at and *our hands have touched*—this we proclaim concerning the Word of life" (1 Jn 1:1). Even after many decades John remembered the night of the resurrection. Jesus appeared among them, but "they were startled and frightened, thinking they saw a ghost" (Lk 24:37; not for the first time— Mk 6:49). Jesus reassured them and commanded them, *"Touch me and see; a ghost does not have flesh and bones, as you see I have"* (Lk 24:39). It is as if John were saying to his readers, "Have no doubt in your minds; we touched him before and after his resurrection. Know without any doubt. Jesus was just as human as you and I are."

Jesus was a real human being. He was born (Lk 2:7). He was circumcised (Lk 2:21). He grew up (Lk 2:52). He was tempted (Lk 4:2). He hungered (Jn 4:8). He thirsted (Jn 4:7; 19:28). He was tired (Jn 4:6). He slept (Mk 4:38). He wept (Jn 11:35). He anguished (Mt 26:38). He suffered (Jn 19:5). He died (Lk 23:46). In every sense of the word, Jesus was fully human, except in one—he was without sin (Heb 4:15).

Throughout the history of the discussion of the humanity of Christ, the church fathers looked especially to three portions of Scripture. The first is John 1:14, "The Word became flesh." These words are a bare, stark statement of the reality of the incarnation, simply saying that it is so. In these four words we have the sum of the whole Scripture and the gospel itself. The Word, the second person of the Holy Trinity, the Son himself, became flesh. We notice immediately who initiates the action. The initiative lies with God. He takes the action. Our salvation begins and ends with the action of God. Salvation is wholly in God's hands. We are saved purely by grace. Irenaeus writes, "On this account, therefore, the Lord Himself, who is Emmanuel from the Virgin, is the sign of our salvation, since it was the Lord Himself who saved them, because they could not be saved by their own instrumentality; and therefore, when Paul sets forth human infirmity, he says, 'For I know that there dwelleth in my flesh no good thing,' showing that the 'good thing' of our salvation is not from us but from God."[6] Again he writes, ". . . according to the tender mercy of God the Father, who had compassion on his own handiwork, and gave to it salvation, restoring it by means of the Word—that is, by Christ—in

---

[6]Irenaeus, *Against the Heresies,* ANF I:451.

---

order that men might learn by actual proof that he receives incorruptibility not of himself, but by the free gift of God."[7] Defending Christianity against the charge that it has no trustworthy foundation, Origen writes, "Our agreement is based on such an important foundation, or rather not on a foundation but on a divine action, its origin was God."[8] Our salvation, our hope, and our future are secure because they rest wholly on God.

"The Word became flesh." He became as we are, human in every sense of the word. The apostle uses the term *flesh* in a figure of speech as a part for the whole to describe the whole human being. The word *flesh* is often used this way in Scripture (Lk 3:6[Greek]; Ac 2:17,26[Greek]; Jn 3:6). The word *flesh* also teaches us that Christ came in all weakness.

The second passage, and certainly a favorite, is Philippians 2:5-8: "Your attitude should be the same as that of Christ Jesus: Who, being in very nature God, did not consider equality with God something to be grasped, but made himself nothing [emptied], taking the very nature of a servant, being made in human likeness. And being found in appearance as a man, he humbled himself and became obedient to death—even death on a cross!" These words say far more than the bare truth that the Word became flesh. These words show us to what degree he became flesh and to what lengths he was willing to go for us. In short, he held nothing back.

Paul emphasizes that Christ was God in very nature. Unlike Adam and Eve and all sinners since, he did not need to strive to be as God or fall prey to the devil's temptation, "You will be like God" (Ge 3:5). For him it was no big deal; he was already by nature God. Yet in love he emptied himself, or made himself nothing. So he conformed himself to the limits of the creature he himself had made. He hid his divinity. But he went even further. He took the form, the very nature, of a slave. He was truly one of us in every way but one. The apostle carefully adds "in human likeness" for he was without sin. He was found in appearance as a man—he looked just like any other human being of his time. To the eye he looked no different; to the ear he sounded no different. He experienced and endured everything human, even death, and not just any death, but the most disgraceful death of that time, death on a cross. "All that is human has become his own. And so to say that he assumed the form of a slave expresses the whole mystery of the economy in the flesh."[9]

Christ did it all for us. "For there was no other way to honor the slave except by making the characteristics of the slave his very own so that they could be illumined from his own glory."[10] "He therefore yielded his neck to the law in company with us, because the plan of salvation so required it; for

---

[7]Ibid., p. 550.
[8]Origen, *Contra Celsus* (New York: Cambridge University Press, 1980), pp. 136,137.
[9]Cyril of Alexandria, *On the Unity of Christ*, p. 76.
[10]Ibid., p. 75.

---

it became him to fulfill all righteousness. For having assumed the form of a slave, as being now enrolled by reason of his human nature among those subject to the yoke, he once even paid the half shekel to the collectors of the tribute, although by nature free, and as the Son not liable to pay the tax. When therefore, thou seest him keeping the law, be not offended, . . . but rather reflect on the profoundness of the plan of salvation."[11] Because he took the form of a slave, we ought to expect that in his humanness he would be as we are. He endured everything we endure. He became as weak and poor as we are. He entered into the full measure of human littleness.

The third portion of Scripture to which the church fathers often referred is Hebrews 2:11,14-17: "Both the one who makes men holy and those who are made holy are of the same family. So Jesus is not ashamed to call them brothers. Since the children have flesh and blood, he too shared in their humanity so that by his death he might destroy him who holds the power of death—that is, the devil—and free those who all their lives were held in slavery by their fear of death. For surely it is not angels he helps, but Abraham's descendants. For this reason he had to be made like his brothers." This passage emphasizes God's great compassion for us. He is not ashamed to call us his own family. We sense the warmth and love in this word, *family*. To save us, he had to become one of us in every way. So he shared our flesh and blood. Thus he could die and by his dying end death. Our brother stood in our place, taking the death Adam brought into the world upon himself and thereby freeing us from it forever.

Even though the church fathers often had good reason to shrink away from Christ's humanity, nevertheless, they taught and confessed it with all its reality. Tertullian writes against those who denied the reality of Christ's suffering in the flesh:

> The Son of God was crucified; I am not ashamed because men must needs be ashamed of it. And the Son of God died; it is by all means to be believed, because it is absurd. And he was buried, and rose again; the fact is certain, because it is impossible. But how will all this be true in him, if he was not himself true—if he really had not in himself that which might be crucified, might die, might be buried, and might rise again? I mean this flesh suffused with blood, built up with bones, interwoven with nerves, entwined with veins, a flesh which knew how to be born, and how to die, human without doubt, as born of a human being.[12]

---

[11]Cyril of Alexandria, *A Commentary upon the Gospel according to St. Luke,* translated by Robert Payne Smith (Oxford University Press, 1859).
[12]Tertullian, *On the Flesh of Christ,* ANF III:525.

They took on the toughest issues and accepted the consequences of Christ's humanity. Did he grow as a normal, natural human being? Scripture says so. Do we accept the limits implied by such growth? Of course. Cyril of Alexandria writes:

> When the wise evangelist introduces the Word as having been made flesh, he shows him economically, allowing his flesh to obey the laws of its own nature. It belongs to manhood to advance in stature and wisdom, and one might say in grace also, for understanding unfolds in a certain fashion in each person according to the limits of the body. It would not have been impossible, or impractical, for God the Word who issued from the Father to have made that body which he united to himself rise up even from its swaddling bands, and bring it straight to the stature of perfect maturity. One might even say that it would have been plain sailing, quite easy for him to have displayed a prodigal wisdom in his infancy; but such a thing would have smacked of wonder-working, and would have been out of key with the plan of the economy. No, the mystery was accomplished quietly and for this reason he allowed the limitations of the manhood to have dominion over him.[13]

Describing the profound human feeling and the great anguish Christ clearly displayed during the last days of his life, Ambrose writes:

> As being man, he doubts; as man he is amazed. Neither his power nor his Godhead is amazed, but his soul; he is amazed by consequence of having taken human infirmity upon him. Finally he cried : 'My God, my God, why hast thou forsaken me?' As being man; he speaks, bearing with him my terrors, for when we are in the midst of danger we think ourself abandoned by God. As man, therefore, he is distressed, as man he weeps, as man he is crucified.[14]

We ought not be surprised at anything in which Jesus shows us that he is truly and fully human, but rather rejoice that in all things he was like me. For "it is profitable to me to know that for my sake Christ bore my infirmities, submitted to the affections of my body, that for me, that is to say for every man, he was made sin, and a curse, that for me and in me was he humbled and made subject, that for me he is the Lamb, the Vine, the Rock, the Servant, the Son of

---

[13]Cyril of Alexandria, *On the Unity of Christ*, pp. 109,110.
[14]Ambrose, *Of the Christian Faith*, NPNF 2:X:230.

We Believe in Jesus Christ

an handmaid, knowing not the day of judgment, for my sake ignorant of the day and hour"[15] We cannot fathom this miracle. We cannot understand it, but God does not ask us to. He bids only believe that for all humanity his Son became fully human so that in every way, in all stages and life experiences, he might walk in our steps and by this walking redeem and restore all of human life to God. Christ's psychology is beyond our analysis. That he should pray in anguish, struggling and wrestling to do his Father's will, is beyond us. We, in whose life sin and all that is natural to us without sin are totally intermingled so that we cannot separate what is normal from what is sinful, cannot but marvel at one who lived liked us, but never sinned. That was God's rescue: "What the law was powerless to do in that it was weakened by the sinful nature, God did by sending his own Son in the likeness of sinful man" (Ro 8:3).

Attacked on every side

In view of all the testimony of Scripture, one would think that no one could possibly deny that Christ was fully human. But many did, some crassly and crudely, others more subtly. Even today we still face the temptation not so much to deny, but at least to diminish Christ's humanity.

In general, three reasons lie behind the denial of Christ's humanity. Many felt that it was not worthy of God to become human, that somehow by becoming human God would lessen himself or pollute himself. This idea springs from a low view of creation and the material world. It also comes from a flawed view of God. It ignores the very reason for his becoming human, that is, his great love for man. Others felt that it was impossible for God to become human. The very act would endanger or threaten the deity of God because it would subject God to change and even possibly sin. All Greek philosophy taught that God was impassible and not subject to change. In the Bible itself God says, "I the LORD do not change" (Mal 3:6). Finally, the incarnation clearly challenges the freedom of man. It attacks his unlimited potential and his power to deliver and save himself. The desire to be godlike in thought and action lies coiled in the center of the human heart. It was, after all, the basis for the first temptation in Genesis 3:5 ("you will be like God"). To accept the incarnation is to admit one's sinfulness and the need for help and a savior. This is something man cannot and will not do for himself. This is how Jesus described man's natural way of thinking: "This is the verdict: Light has come into the world, but men loved darkness instead of light because their deeds were evil" (Jn 3:19).

Very early in the history of Christianity, Christ's humanity became an issue. The apostle John in his writings opposed teachers who denied the full

---

[15]Ibid., p. 236.

---

humanity of Christ. These teachers were probably influenced by a religious movement known as Gnosticism. Gnosticism's origins are obscure. It began outside of Christianity as a religious movement and drew from a wide range of thought in the ancient world. Because it was very adaptable, Gnosticism spawned many mystery religions or pagan sects, the most prominent of which was Manichaeism. Gnosticism did not exist as an organized, independent religion but, rather, attached itself to a host religion, much like a parasite. Very quickly it found sympathizers among some early Christians.

Gnosticism taught a radical form of dualism. In the *Star Wars* movies all reality was divided into the dark side and the Force; in Gnosticism all was divided into matter and spirit. The Gnostics held that the supreme god was good and a lesser god, often called the demiurge, was evil. The demiurge created the world out of matter; hence all in the world, everything containing matter, was evil. Between pure good and pure evil lay a host of intermediate beings, called Aeons. By mistake, one of them caused the demiurge to create the world. In the process, human beings were made of matter, but imbedded in this lump of matter was a spark or piece of pure good (the soul). The goal of the Gnostics was to provide the knowledge with which a Gnostic could free his true self (spark of good) and return to be with the supreme god.

Gnostic teaching was incompatible with Christianity. So when it entered the church, it had an enormous impact. Many gnostic Christians wrote new gospels whose purpose was to give the secret knowledge possessed by Jesus so that their followers could follow his example and escape evil. Those who followed gnostic teaching denied two basic biblical teachings. They denied that God had created the world. Because they denied God (the good god) any role in creation, they usually rejected most of the Old Testament. They also denied the reality of Christ's humanity. Instead, they taught that Christ appeared only as a phantom (hologram) or, at the very most, temporarily as a human being. The term *docetist* (the word means "to seem") was generally applied to them.

Obviously, Gnosticism threatened the very existence of Christianity, and it remained a threat for over two hundred years. The leaders of the early church responded quickly to the heresy by asserting the biblical teaching that Christ was fully human. Ignatius (who died as a martyr in A.D. 117) writes to the members of the church at Smyrna, ". . . Being fully persuaded as touching our Lord, that he is in truth of the family of David according to the flesh, God's Son by the will and power of God, truly born of a Virgin, baptized by John that 'all righteousness might be fulfilled by him,' truly nailed to a tree in the flesh . . ."[16]

---

[16]Ignatius, "To the Smyrnaeans," *The Apostolic Fathers*, Loeb Classical Library, Vol. 1 (Cambridge: Harvard University Press, 1970), p. 253.

Again Ignatius makes a good confession about the person of Jesus, when he writes to the Ephesians: "There is one Physician, who is both flesh and spirit, born and yet not born, who is God in man, true life in death, both of Mary and of God, first passable and then impassible, Jesus Christ our Lord."[17] Somewhat later, Melito of Sardis (d. 177), bishop of one of the seven churches to which John addressed the book of Revelation, writes just as fine a confession:

> For there is no need, to persons of intelligence, to attempt to prove, from the deeds of Christ subsequent to his baptism, that his soul and his body, his human nature like ours, were real, and no phantom of the imagination. For the deeds done by Christ after his baptism, and especially his miracles, gave indication and assurance to the world of the Deity hidden in the flesh. For, being at once God and perfect man likewise, he gave sure indications of his two natures: of his deity, by his miracles during the three years that elapsed after baptism; of his humanity, during the thirty similar periods which preceded his baptism in which, by reason of his low estate as regards the flesh, he concealed the signs of his deity, although he was the true God existing before all ages.[18]

In one sense, both these confessions are remarkable because they contained so early in Christian history a very good summary of truth about the person of our Savior. In another sense they are quite unremarkable because they simply teach what Scripture says.

Later, Origen (185?–251?) in a formal discussion with gnostic-leaning Christians, also confesses the full and real humanity of Christ: "So then, our Savior and Lord, in his desire to save the human race as he willed to save it, for this reason thus willed to save the body, just as he willed to save also the soul, and willed to save the rest of the human being: the spirit. For the whole human being would not have been saved if he had not assumed the whole human being."[19] Origen established a fundamental principle with regard to the humanity of Christ. Its classic expression was later given by Gregory of Nazianzus, "For that which he [Christ] has not assumed he has not healed; but that which is united to his Godhead is saved."[20] To put it simply, our salvation depends completely on the full and genuine humanity of Christ. Only by becoming one of us, in every way like us, could he save us. For as in Adam all humanity was ruined, so in Christ all humanity is healed, or saved.

---

[17]Ignatius, "To the Ephesians," *The Apostolic Fathers*, Loeb Classical Library, Vol. 1, p. 181.
[18]Melito of Sardis, *Remains of the Second and Third Centuries*, ANF VIII:760.
[19]Origen, *Dialogue with Heraclides*, Ancient Christian Writers, Vol. 54 (New York: Paulist Press, 1992), p. 63.
[20]Gregory of Nazianzen, *Letters on the Apollinarian Controversy*, NPNF 2:VII:218.

To deny the full humanity of Christ leads to complete disaster. Tertullian (160–220), in his usual blunt manner, demonstrates this truth:

> Since, however, Christ's being flesh is now discovered to be a lie, it follows that all things which were done by the flesh of Christ were done untruly. . . . For he suffered nothing who did not truly suffer; and a phantom could not truly suffer. God's entire work, therefore, is subverted. Christ's death, wherein lies the whole weight and fruit of the Christian name, is denied. . . . Now if his death be denied, because of the denial of his flesh, there will be no certainty of his resurrection. Similarly, if Christ's resurrection be nullified, ours also is destroyed."[21]

Basil (329–379), writing a century and a half later against a different opponent, says the same thing:

> If, then, the sojourn of the Lord in the flesh has never taken place, the Redeemer paid not the fine to death on our behalf, nor through himself destroyed death's reign. For if what was reigned over by death was not that which was assumed by the Lord, death would not have ceased working his own ends, nor would the sufferings of the God-bearing flesh have been made our gain. . . . All these boons are undone by those that assert that it was with a heavenly body that the Lord came among us.[22]

By the 300s, Gnosticism had faded as an internal threat. Later, however, by 360, another threat, equally as deadly, had emerged. It came from a most unexpected source, Apollinaris the Younger (310–390). Apollinaris had stood shoulder to shoulder with Athanasius and others who had resisted the Arian heresy (the Arians taught that Christ was only a semidivine creature). But in his old age he fell into a false teaching of his own. Apollinaris reasoned that to be human means that one is necessarily subject to change and is inevitably going to sin. If, therefore, Christ was human just as we are, he too would be subject to change and would inevitably sin. Apollinaris concluded that because Christ is also God, then God himself would be exposed to the danger of change. Apollinaris' solution was to make Christ human, but not in the full sense of that word. Apollinaris held that a human being was made up of three parts. Each human being had a body, a soul or life principle, and a spirit or

---

[21]Tertullian, *Against Marcion*, ANF III:328.
[22]Basil the Great, *Letters*, CCLXI, NPNF 2:VIII:300.

We Believe in Jesus Christ

rational soul, the ability to will and think. He taught that Christ had a human body and soul or life principle but that his spirit or rational soul was not human, but solely that of God's Son. In this way Apollinaris denied the fully humanity of Christ.

Though different in degree, this false teaching is the same in kind as that of the Gnostics/docetists. It also leads to the same consequences. For that reason, the church fathers strongly opposed Apollinaris' teaching. Gregory of Nyssa (335–394) writes: "Mind, which is man's proper nature, distinguishes him from irrational beasts. No one can define man as composed of a body, bones and senses nor judge human nature as simply the capacity to eat or be subject to change; rather, man is endowed with thought and reason. Man is necessarily rational and is not a man should he lack this capacity."[23] Scripture teaches that sin begins in the human heart (mind and will) (Mt 15:19). If Christ did not assume a human heart, then that where sin has its beginning and greatest power is not healed. Then we are hardly better off than if Christ had not come.

Cyril of Alexandria (d. 444) addresses this very point: "Clearly grace came upon us from him, as from a new rootstock, a new beginning. We must admit, of course, that the body which he united to himself was endowed with a rational soul, for the Word, who is God, would hardly neglect our finer part, the soul, and have regard only for the earthly body. Quite clearly in all wisdom he provided for both the soul and the body."[24]

Attacks on the doctrine about the humanity of Christ did not end with Apollinaris. They simply became more subtle and refined; the danger, however, remained the same. In the 400s Eutyches taught that although Christ was fully human, at the time of the incarnation his humanity was almost completely swallowed up by his divinity. The following illustration served to make his point. Christ's humanity disappeared into his divinity, just as a drop of wine would disappear into the ocean. Another favorite slogan of Eutyches' followers, who later were known as the Monophysites ("one nature"), was "Before the incarnation two natures, after the incarnation one [the divine]." For all practical purposes they denied that Jesus was fully human. This false teaching is by no means the last to attack the full humanity of Christ, but we need to look at no more, for in the end all these heresies are the same, differing only in the degree to which they deny Christ's humanity.

To lessen Christ's humanity in any way undermines our whole salvation. Nothing could be clearer. Cyril of Alexandria sets out the principle when he writes, "In short, he took what was ours to be his very own so that we might have

---

[23]Gregory of Nyssa, *Against Apollinaris*, translated by Casmir McCambley, p. 14.
[24]Cyril of Alexandria, *On the Unity of Christ*, p. 64.

---

all that was his."[25] We could not have what was his unless he were fully human. If we do not have what was his, we are quite plainly lost. Irenaeus writes:

> "Therefore, as I have already said, He caused man (human nature) to cleave to and to become one with God. For unless man had overcome the enemy of man, the enemy would not have been legitimately vanquished. And again: unless it had been God who had freely given salvation, we could never have possessed it securely. And unless man had been joined to God, he could never have become a partaker of incorruptibility."[26]

All thanks to God that Christ did become our brother.

The stairway of God

When Jacob fled for his life from his angry brother, Esau, he paused for the night at Bethel. There "he had a dream in which he saw a stairway resting on the earth, with its top reaching to heaven, and the angels of God were ascending and descending on it" (Ge 28:12). After Jacob had seen the vision and heard the words of the Lord, he exclaimed, "Surely the Lord is in this place, and I was not aware of it" (Ge 28:16). Luther believed that this vision was a picture of the incarnation. "Accordingly, the ladder is the wonderful union of the divinity with our flesh. On it the angels ascend and descend, and they can never wonder at this enough. This is the historical, simple, and literal sense."[27] What a good picture it is. The stairway reaches from heaven to earth, for Christ came down. The stairway rises from earth to heaven, for the incarnate Christ is the one mediator between God and man, and the only way to God. By this stairway alone, we who believe, travel the path to eternal life.

This is the way God chose to save us. Jesus himself tells us, "No one has ever gone into heaven except the one who came from heaven—the Son of Man" (Jn 3:13). Again he says, "The bread of God is he who comes down from heaven and gives life to the world" (Jn 6:33). By no other way can we know God and believe in God. "For the Lord taught us that no man is capable of knowing God, unless he be taught of God; that is, that God cannot be known without God."[28] Christ alone enables us to know God, for he says, "Anyone who has seen me has seen the Father" (Jn 14:9).

---

[25]Ibid., p. 59. By the words "what was ours," Cyril, in context, is not referring directly to our human nature but to our sin and its consequences of death. By inference, Christ could assume the guilt of our human sin and truly die only if he had become fully human. Again, in context, Cyril's words, "all that was his," refer not to Christ's divine nature as such but to his holiness, righteousness, and eternal life, which he possesses as the Son of God from eternity. By his words, Cyril intends to reiterate the apostle Paul's words in 2 Corinthians 8:9, which Cyril quotes immediately following his own.

[26]Irenaeus, *Against the Heresies*, ANF I:448.

[27]LW 5:223.

[28]Irenaeus, *Against the Heresies*, ANF I:468.

So we begin at the foot of the stairway, Christ in the flesh. Here God has hidden himself. Here God may be found. Luther writes in his commentary on Isaiah 61:

> It is because of His humanity and His incarnation that Christ becomes sweet to us, and through Him God becomes sweet to us. Let us therefore begin to ascend step by step from Christ's crying in His swaddling clothes up to His Passion. Then we shall easily know God. I am saying this so that you do not begin to contemplate God from the top, but start with the weak elements. We should busy ourselves completely with treating, knowing, and considering this man. Then you will know that He is the Way, the Truth, and the Life (John 14:6). So He sets forth His weakness that we may approach Him with confidence.[29]

Had God not come in weakness, hid in the flesh of Christ, we could not have endured his appearance. Irenaeus writes, "He might easily have come to us in his immortal glory, but in that case we could never have endured the greatness of the glory."[30] God taught Moses and all of us that lesson in Exodus 33. After Moses had rescued his people in the matter of the golden calf, he prayed to the Lord, "Now show me your glory" (Ex 33:18). But God replied, "I will cause all my goodness to pass in front of you, and I will proclaim my name, the LORD, in your presence" (Ex 33:19). Then the account continues, " 'But,' [God] said, 'you cannot see my face, for no one may see me and live' " (Ex 33:20). So Moses saw the back of God.

That back of God is Christ, God in the flesh. So God hides himself in Christ, who came in the form of a slave. Most do not believe it. We ourselves can scarcely believe it. Isaiah asks, "Who has believed our message and to whom has the arm of the LORD been revealed? . . . He had no beauty or majesty to attract us to him, nothing in his appearance that we should desire him" (Isa 53:1,2). This is God's way to save us. He hides himself in weakness, in weak things, which are, nonetheless, the very power of God. So God comes to us and saves us through weak things: the Word, the water of Baptism, the bread and wine of the Holy Supper, which are not weak at all, but the very power of God. The humanity of Christ, God's coming in the flesh, is typical of the way God at all times deals with us.

What could be weaker than Baptism? Many despise it. Yet through it God saves us. How contemptuously many regard Baptism. Tertullian writes, "There is nothing which makes men's minds more obdurate than the simplic-

---

[29]LW 17:331.
[30]Irenaeus, *Against the Heresies,* ANF I:528.

---

ity of the divine works which are visible in the act . . . for the simple acts it wonders at as if they were in vain."[31] Yet what a powerful thing is Baptism, the promise of God with the water. What great gifts it brings to us! "Great indeed is the Baptism which is offered you. It is a ransom to captives; the remission of offenses; the death of sin; the regeneration of the soul; the garment of light; the holy seal indissoluble; the chariot to heaven; the luxury of paradise; a procuring of the kingdom; the gift of adoption."[32] It bring such great gifts because through it we are joined to Christ.

> O strange and inconceivable thing! We did not really die, we were not really buried, we were not really crucified and raised again, but our imitation [the reference is to the practice of baptism of immersion practiced in the early church; we are reminded of Romans 6:3,4] was but in a figure, while our salvation is in reality. Christ was actually crucified and actually buried, and truly rose again; and all these things have been vouchsafed to us, that we, by imitation sharing in his sufferings, might gain salvation in reality. At the self-same moment [of your baptism], you died and were born; and that water of salvation was at once your grave and your mother.[33]

The church fathers can barely contain themselves in praise of the simple, mighty act of Baptism. "It is the carriage to God, the dying with Christ, the perfecting of the mind, the bulwark of faith, the key of the kingdom of heaven, the change of life . . . illumination [another name for baptism] is the greatest and most magnificent of the Gifts of God."[34] Through all our lives, through our doubts and fears and sorrows, we may look to our Baptism. It assures us, "You are God's own; do not be afraid; all things are yours." With it we may defy Satan and defend ourselves against all his assaults. "Defend yourself with the water; defend yourself with the Spirit, by which all the fiery darts of the wicked shall be quenched. Say to Satan, 'I am myself the image of God . . . I have put on Christ; I have been transformed into Christ by baptism; worship thou me.' Well do I know that he will depart, defeated and put to shame. . . ."[35]

So great is the desire of God to save us that he provides the gospel to us in superabundance. So great is his concern for our well-being that he gives the gospel not only in Word and in Baptism, but also in the Lord's Supper. In, with, and under the weak and simple elements of bread and wine, our Lord

---

[31]Tertullian, *On Baptism*, ANF III:669.
[32]Cyril of Jerusalem, "The Procatechesis," *Lectures on the Christian Sacraments* (Crestwood, New York: St. Vladmir's Seminary Press, 1986), p. 50.
[33]Ibid., p. 61.
[34]Gregory of Nazianzen, *Oration on Holy Baptism*, NPNF 2:VII:360.
[35]Ibid., p. 363.

gives us his very own body and blood. So he joins himself to us with the result that we are one body with him. His life is our life, our hope for life eternal. "For as the bread, which is produced from the earth, when it receives the invocation of God, is no longer common bread, but the Eucharist of God, consisting in two realities, earthly and heavenly; so also our bodies, when they receive the Eucharist are no longer corruptible, having the hope of the resurrection to eternity."[36] Though hidden to the senses, a mighty transformation takes place; the greatest gift is given.

How weak and insignificant the gospel seems. "Mere words." But we know that they are the power of God for salvation. "God was pleased through the foolishness of what was preached to save those who believe" (1 Co 1:21). His Word runs its full course. It always accomplishes the purpose for which God sends it. Of course, the power of the Word is no surprise, because it is God-breathed and Spirit-filled. Just as Jesus shouted to the dead Lazarus, "Lazarus, come out!" (Jn 11:43), so God through his Word calls us and all who hear it from death to life. More than "mere words," the Scripture is the life-giving voice of God himself.

God's love is so great that because it was impossible for us to rise to him, he came to us in the flesh. He became one with us. He remains one with us. Luther sums it up well:

> In this way we ascend into Him and are carried along through the Word and the Holy Spirit. And through faith we cling to Him, since we become one body with Him and He with us. He is the Head; we are the members. On the other hand, He descends to us through the Word and sacraments by teaching and exercising us in the knowledge of Him.[37]

Our supreme comfort

We know all too well that by Adam's sin the whole human race was corrupted, fell into and is to this very day gripped by, sin so that death has come and will come to every human being. Left to ourselves we have no means of escape. However, in his grace God provided one. He healed the whole human race from its corruption through the forgiveness of sins and from death through another who stood in the place of us all, our second Adam and our brother, Jesus Christ. "As we died in Adam, so we might live in Christ, being born with Christ and crucified with him and buried with him and rising with him."[38]

In dramatic dialogue, Cyril of Alexandria describes the gift given to us through the work of Christ:

---

[36]Irenaeus, *Against the Heresies*, ANF I:486.
[37]LW 5:223.
[38]Gregory of Nazianzen, *On the Theophany or Birthday of Christ*, NPNF 2:VII:346.

We had become accursed through Adam's transgression and had fallen into the trap of death, abandoned by God. Yet all things were made new in Christ . . . the nature of man was made rich in all blamelessness and innocence in him, so that it could now cry out with boldness: "My God, my God, why have you forsaken me?" Understand that in becoming man the Only Begotten spoke these words as one of us and on behalf of all our nature. It was as if he were saying this: "The first man has transgressed. He slipped into disobedience, and neglected the commandment he received, and he was brought to this state of willfulness by the wiles of the devil; and then it was entirely right that he became subject to corruption and fell under judgement. But you Lord have made me a second beginning for all on earth, and I am called the second Adam. In me you see the nature of man made clean, its faults corrected, made holy and pure. Now give me the good things of your kindness, undo the abandonment, rebuke corruption and set a limit on your anger. I have conquered Satan. . . ."[39]

Because Christ is our brother and the second Adam, in him and with him by faith we can begin every day in all newness, for the old has passed away.

Life and salvation are ours. "And he who gives riches becomes poor; for he assumes the poverty of my flesh, that I may assume the riches of his Godhead. He that is full empties himself; for he empties himself of his glory for a short while, that I may have a share in his fulness."[40] What a comfort! Our wealth and abundance are as inexhaustible as God himself, for God gave us all things in Christ. We can live with all boldness and confidence. We can share our abundance, for we cannot exhaust it. No matter what may come, we are always the brothers and sisters of Christ and children of God.

Our comfort is especially keen because we know that even after his return to heaven, Christ is still one of us and one with us. In him we all stand before our God and Father. It is as if he were saying to us, "I am in myself presenting all humanity to its God."[41] At the right hand of his Father and our Father, he ever intercedes for us until he brings us safely to the eternal side of his Father and our Father.

It is a great comfort that the surest pledge of our salvation and glorification is the human nature of Christ seated at the right hand of the Father where he appears before the face of God on our behalf (Heb 7:25), leading us and

---

[39]Cyril of Alexandria, On the Unity of Christ, pp. 105,106.
[40]Gregory of Nazianzen, Second Oration of Easter, NPNF 2:VII:436.
[41]Gregory of Nyssa, Against Eunomius, NPNF 2:V:113.

We Believe in Jesus Christ

joining us to the Father (Jn 17:24), in order that then we may be made to conform to his glorious body (Php 3:21). In the very nature by which we are flesh of his flesh and bone of his bones we will come to judgment, in order that we may the more eagerly love his appearing (2 Ti 4:8). By this tie and bond we shall be joined forever to God in eternal life.[42]

The hymn writer Christopher Wordsworth likewise highlights this truth:

> He has raised our human nature
> On the clouds to God's right hand;
> There we sit in heav'nly places,
> There with him in glory stand.
> Jesus reigns, adored by angels;
> Man with God is on the throne.
> By our mighty Lord's ascension
> We by faith behold our own. (CW 174:4)

While we wait, he has not left us without help. No writer expresses the daily comfort we get from the incarnation of Christ better than the writer to the Hebrews: "Because he himself suffered when he was tempted, he is able to help those who are being tempted" (2:18). Because he knows what it is to be put to the test, he stands ready to help us with timely help so that we might stand under all testing. We know we can approach him for help. "We do not have a high priest who is unable to sympathize with our weaknesses, but we have one who has been tempted in every way, just as we are—yet was without sin. Let us then approach the throne of grace with confidence, so that we may receive mercy and find grace to help us in our time of need" (4:15,16). Help is as close as a prayer, a scream, a sigh, a murmur. We do not have to beg him; he knows and understands whatever we are going through, because he is our brother. We have the sure promise, "He is able to save completely those who come to God through him, because he always lives to intercede for them. Such a high priest meets our need—one who is holy, blameless, pure, set apart from sinners, exalted above the heavens" (7:25,26). We do not have to wait until we are worthy. He has made us his own. He waits for us to ask. He often answers before we ask.

One passage gives special comfort to those who serve in the public ministry. It also speaks to all those who serve Christ in all the various offices of our congregations and churches. As he begins to write about Christ's high priesthood, the writer to the Hebrews reminds us, "Every high priest is selected from among men and is appointed to represent them in matters related to God . . . No one takes this honor upon himself; he must be called by God" (5:1,4). God chooses human beings to be his representatives. He

---

[42]Martin Chemnitz, *The Two Natures in Christ* (St. Louis: Concordia Publishing House, 1971), p. 64.

---

chooses them and us for the very reason we often find the work of that ministry so difficult. He chose us in all our weakness with all our spots, stains, and shortcomings so that "he [that is, the one called to be high priest] is able to deal gently with those who are ignorant and are going astray, since he himself is subject to weakness" (5:2). Because he has been patient with us and has loved us despite all our sin, so he trusts that we will have that same gentleness and patience with our fellow sinners and so with understanding and in tenderness call them to repent and return. For this reason too, his coming among us, his humanity, is our great comfort.

Though our Father has blessed us to this very day with great riches in Christ, the best is yet to come. The effect of Christ's incarnation and work was and will be as the apostle John described it by inspiration: "Dear friends, now we are children of God, and what we will be has not yet been made known. But we know that when he appears, we shall be like him, for we shall see him as he is" (1 Jn 3:2). Once again we shall be in paradise and walk with God. All this because the Word became flesh. We cannot treasure the incarnation enough.

> The dear fathers, I say, were amazed that the divine majesty assumed every aspect of this bag of worms, our human nature, except sin and guiltiness of death. He ate, drank, slept, waked, etc.; but He was not born in sin as we were. . . . But all this should make us meditate on the great glory that is ours. For the angels in heaven rejoice over the incarnation. . . . It would not be out of place for us still to weep for joy. Even if I should never be saved—which God forbid!—this thought would still fill me with joy: that Christ, who is of my flesh, blood, and soul, is sitting in heaven at the right hand of God the Father, and that such an honor has been conferred on my frame, flesh, and blood.[43]

Because Christ's incarnation provides us with every comfort and joy against sin, death, and hell, we can never praise or remember it enough.

> The following tale is told about a coarse and brutal lout. While the words "And was made man" were being sung in church, he remained standing, neither genuflecting nor removing his hat. He showed no reverence, but just stood there like a clod. All the others dropped to their knees when the Nicene Creed was prayed and chanted devoutly. Then the devil stepped up to him and hit him so hard it made his head

---

[43]LW 22:104,105.

---

spin. He cursed him gruesomely and said: "May hell consume you, you boorish ass! If God had become an angel like me and the congregation sang: 'God was made an angel,' I would bend not only my knees but my whole body to the ground! Yes, I would crawl ten ells down into the ground. And you vile human creature, you stand there like a stick or a stone. You hear that God did not become an angel but a man like you, and you just stand there like a stick of wood!" Whether this story is true or not, it is nevertheless in accordance with the faith (Rom. 12:6).[44]

May our joy, our hope, our strength, our song ever be: "God became our brother."

---

[44]LW 22:105.

NOW THAT GOD IS ONE OF US:
A STUDY OF THE COMMUNICATION OF ATTRIBUTES
IN THE PERSON OF CHRIST

Paul O. Wendland

South Central District Convention
Duncanville, Texas
June 8–9, 1998

"What if God was one of us?"[1] With these striking words, Joan Osborne poses for her own contemporaries one of the few questions worth asking. But as her song continues, she makes it pretty clear that she thinks he isn't. She doesn't see God anywhere in the "slobs" around her or in the other strangers on the bus trying to find their way home. We live here, she implies, in a world devoid of beauty, devoid of compassion, devoid of connection, without God and without hope.

What if God were one of us? The phrase expresses the wistful longings of Baby Boomers and Generation Xers who have largely discarded the answers of their parents and grandparents and who find themselves floating in a spiritual void. What they're experiencing is something like the feeling people had when the astronauts first showed them pictures of the earth rising over the moon's scarred surface. They saw this incredibly beautiful blue ball surrounded by the unspeakably black emptiness of space, and they thought, "Here we are, all alone."

The problem

Let us be clear about the reason why many feel so empty today. It was unbelief that caused people to banish God into some distant attic above and

---

[1] Joan Osborne, "One of Us," *Relish*, Polygram Records, 1995, compact disc.

beyond the stars, while the "natural" forces worked themselves out below. This particular strain showed up first in Europe during the Enlightenment of the 1700s, but it didn't take long before it had caused the West to forget about God almost entirely. Man was determined to fend for himself. Once God had gone away, there was no one left to judge man's actions, no one left to tell him to guard his tongue. Man had become the measure of all things. And he thought he would like it that way. He thought he would feel free at last.

But human beings, enslaved to time and change and death, could never remain sure and permanent measures of God's world. Humanity too was eventually swallowed up by the sheer size of the universe. And that is why today so many feel that there's nothing left under this vast black sky but a jumble of ill-assorted things. With God banished from the scene, there's nothing left to connect it all together, nothing left to put things into perspective, nothing left to join people to each other. All the big ideas seem to have lost their meaning. Love? Virtue? Sincerity? Truth? Whatever! Nothing but big bloated words:

> The best lack all conviction, while the worst
> Are full of passionate intensity.[2]

Most turn away from thinking entirely and devote themselves to watching television or to basking in the cold glow of their computer screens.

It's no wonder, then, that we also see some folks in headlong flight from human reason, that same human reason once welcomed as such a great light in the 1700s. People are tired of stumbling around in the fog of postmodern despair.[3] Our natural religiosity abhors a vacuum. Once reason had driven out what it thought was the evil spirit of medieval superstition, the soul was left wide open for the entry of a real demon, who has brought along with him "seven other spirits more wicked than itself" (Lk 11:26).

That is why today we see people turning to the irrational, to eastern mysticism, to New Age myth-makers, to any fool who holds out to them the hope of security in some mother ship. The great resurgence of "spirituality" that we see on every side of us is in fact the great apostasy and the turning away long predicted. These are the evil days Paul said we must experience before the very end. Thinking of our times, Jesus once asked his generation, "When the Son of Man comes, will he find faith on the earth?" (Lk 18:8).

---

[2]W. B. Yeats (1865–1939), "The Second Coming," *The Columbia Dictionary of Quotations*, compact disc.
[3]For example, in an article about Christology written for *The Atlantic Monthly*, Cullen Murphy said that "as a person who *wants* to believe" he embarked on his own "quest" for Jesus. This longing to believe in something—anything—also seems to be one of the distinguishing features of our age. For the whole article, see *http://www. theatlantic.com/unbound/cullen/cmjesus.html.*

We Believe in Jesus Christ

The answer

Come from on high to me; I cannot rise to thee.[4]

The answer to humanity's despair is found in the burning heart of God, a heart on fire with his eternal love for us poor sinners. Love begets love. God the Son is eternally begotten from the Father's heart. He is Light from Light, Love from Love, true God from true God. Now for the mystery that the apostle Paul calls "great" (1 Ti 3:16): roughly two thousand years ago, God's Son became a human being. He fully entered our space and shared our time without ceasing to be in any sense who he had always been. The eternal God was born of a woman. He became "one of us" in the person of Jesus Christ.

Although the mystery of godliness is a truth beyond all human telling, it is sufficiently and reliably described for us in the words of Holy Scripture. "In Christ all the fullness of the Deity lives in bodily form" (Col 2:9). "The Word became flesh" (Jn 1:14). Scripture has testified in language clear and plain the things our God has done for us.[5]

Despite this, from the very beginning of his earthly life Jesus has been a "sign that will be spoken against" (Lk 2:34). Who he is, and who the unbelieving world is willing to say that he is, have always been two different things (Mt 16:14). The message about Christ, the God-man, must make its way in the world not with great fanfare and success, but under constant contradiction.

Because this is so, the church has found it necessary to safeguard the truth by using a highly formal language when speaking of this subject. Over the centuries, we have learned to choose our words very carefully. At first they aren't too difficult to grasp, words like "human nature" and "divine nature." But then along comes the phrase "the communication of attributes in the person of Christ," and things start to get hazy. When finally we are presented with those terms that are a delight to every seminarian's ear—the *genus idiomaticum*, the *genus maiestaticum*, and the *genus apotelesmaticum* —our perplexity grows deeper. Are such terms really necessary? Have the theologians gone mad?

Of course the language sounds strange to us! It was forged in the heat of controversies largely unknown to us and during a time far removed from our own. In order to understand it, we have to have some sense of why believers found it necessary to talk that way in the first place. As to the importance of the subject, consider what Luther has to say about it: "Whoever wants to discuss sin and grace, law and gospel, Christ and man,

---

[4]CW 34:2

[5]Here's how Chemnitz puts it: "Although the mystery of this union far surpasses the mind, comprehension, and language of all men, yet concerning this mystery the Holy Spirit in Scripture has revealed to us as much as is necessary for us to know and believe in this life in order to be saved." *The Two Natures in Christ* (St. Louis: Concordia Publishing House, 1971), p. 68.

---

in a manner befitting a Christian, must for the most part discuss nothing else than God and man in Christ."[6]

We should also be aware that we live in an age wary of doctrine and suspicious of words being able to convey definitive truths. Folks today shy away from definition. They prefer their religion served up spiced with emotion but bland in thought. If we are impatient with doctrine, at times, it may be a symptom of the world's influence on us.[7]

At the same time, however, we must understand that it is not enough to act as if we can simply restate what has been said in previous ages. Let's face it: so often when we talk doctrine, our words sound a little musty. We sometimes fail to see that our forebears, the confessors, were speaking the truth in love to their own times and to the dilemmas people of their own generation faced. The words they hammered out were their words. For us to make a complete confession of the same truths, we also need to speak our own words, words drawn from the same clear well of God's eternal Word. This is especially necessary in our evangelism, our preaching, and our teaching. We need to speak to our own generation of Boomers, post-moderns, and Xers. "Unless dogmatics remains contemporary, it is no longer systematic but rather has become historical theology."[8]

What follows is an attempt to do that. We will take up in order, then, each one of the three genera, or "types," of passages in which Scripture speaks about the two natures of Christ and their relationship to one another. First we will briefly define them. We will then look at the historical reasons why the great teachers of the church spoke of them using the language that they did. Finally, we will try to answer the question of how these ideas speak to our own situation.

"Who do you say I am?"—The *genus idiomaticum*

When Jesus came to the region of Caesarea Philippi, he asked his disciples, "Who do people say the Son of Man is?"

Simon Peter answered, "You are the Christ, the Son of the living God."[9]

---

[6]WA 8:126,31.

[7]I've always loved C. F. W. Walther's comment in this connection. He writes, "A person may pretend to be a Christian while in reality he is not. As long as he is in this condition, he is quite content with his knowledge of the mere outlines of the Christian doctrines. Everything beyond that, he says, is for pastors and theologians. To perceive as clearly as possible everything God has revealed, that is something in which a non-Christian has no interest. However, the moment a person becomes a Christian, there arises in him a keen desire for the doctrine of Christ. Even the most uncultured peasant who is still unconverted is suddenly roused in the moment of his conversion and begins to reflect on God and heaven, salvation and damnation, etc. He becomes occupied with the highest problems of human life." *The Proper Distinction Between Law and Gospel* (St. Louis: Concordia Publishing House, 1920), pp. 12,13.

[8]David Scaer, *Christology*, Vol. VI, from the Confessional Lutheran Dogmatics series (Fort Wayne: The International Foundation for Lutheran Confessional Research, 1989), p. XIV.

[9]Matthew 16:13,16, emphasis added.

We Believe in Jesus Christ

As Peter's confession makes clear, the church has always believed that the man Jesus is the Son of God, God himself. Though he is and remains a single personality, God the Son unites in himself both a divine and a human nature. Though he is and remains true God, he has become and remains true man. Each nature is distinct and remains intact with its own unique characteristics. The humanity of Christ is not converted into his deity, nor his deity into humanity. Nor is it true to say that the two have been mixed together to become a new and composite nature—a being that is half-man, half-God. The union of the two natures is a personal one, not a substantial one.[10]

When we talk about the "communication of attributes," we simply mean: Jesus Christ is a single, undivided personality. He is not sometimes acting, feeling, or existing separately in his nature as God; nor is he sometimes acting, feeling, or existing separately in his nature as man. While each nature remains distinct, there is a genuine sharing of each nature's attributes in the one person of Christ.[11] Whatever Jesus is and does since becoming human, he is and does as a single person—the God-man![12]

In speaking this way, the confessors at Chalcedon in 451, and later at Cloister Bergen in 1577, only wished to preserve the paradoxical language of Scripture in the full weight of its true meaning. When Scripture, for example, says that the rulers of this world "crucified the Lord of glory" (1 Co 2:8),[13] it means exactly what it says. God was there on Calvary. Jesus the God-man was crucified, died, and was buried. In his single personality, he participated fully in the sufferings of his human nature. Certainly, if we are speaking in the abstract, it is not possible to say that the deity suffered, or even that it can suffer. But Christ Jesus, who was true God, *did* suffer, according to his flesh. There are not two Christs: one who suffered and the other who did not. There is only one.

Similarly, when Jesus says to the people at the synagogue at Capernaum, "What if you see the Son of Man ascend to where he was before!" (Jn 6:62), he is speaking in earnest words that are perfectly true. Certainly, if we are discussing matters in the abstract, it is not possible to say that the humanity of Christ existed essentially from all eternity. But the man Jesus is speaking as one and the same person as he who can calmly declare, "Before Abraham was born, I am!" (Jn 8:58). There are not two Sons of God, one who was born in time of Mary and the other who was begotten of the Father from all eternity.

---

[10]See Scaer's *Christology*, pp. 29ff.; Chemnitz, *Two Natures*, pp. 67ff.; Schaller's *Christology*, pp. 47ff.

[11]"The communication of attributes is a predication wherein the property which belongs to one nature is attributed to the person in the concrete." Chemnitz, *Two Natures*, p. 171.

[12]Cf. the justly famous "four adverbs of the Council of Chalcedon": The one Christ is revealed in two natures ἀσυγχύτως, ἀτρέπτως, ἀδιαρέτως, αἰχωρίστως—without confusion, without change, without division, without separation. See also FC SD VIII:11: "Since the incarnation, each nature in Christ does not so subsist of itself that each is or constitutes a separate person, but that they are so united that they constitute one single person . . . so that now . . . there belongs to the entire person of Christ personally not only his divine but also his assumed human nature."

[13]See also Acts 3:15.

There is only one. He was born in time and yet has no beginning and knows no ending.

This kind of language defies our attempts to pick it apart logically. They are unique declarations about a unique person.[14] We are not surprised to find out, then, that when people in the past *did* try to pick them apart, they only succeeded in stumbling. First there were outright unbelieving skeptics like Celsus, who lived toward the end of the second century. People like him had rid themselves long ago of any belief in the ancient myths of their people. They were far too sophisticated to believe in the gods the way that Homer had talked about them. It was a fairy tale to believe that the gods actually came down and appeared among men. To Celsus, then, the gospels seemed a self-contradictory and ridiculous patchwork, even less credible than the Greek myths![15]

There were not only denials of the truth outside the church, however, but inside it as well. One of them we probably should mention is Paul of Samosata, the third-century bishop of Antioch in Syria. His emphasis on the historical Jesus led him to divide the natures in Christ. He denied that Jesus could be God in any real sense. According to him, Jesus was only a uniquely receptive man upon whom God was able to exercise his divine influence. By responding to this influence, the man Jesus had been able to unite himself intimately with God and thus had become a fit channel through whom God worked miracles and redeemed humanity. Eventually, because of his moral excellence, Jesus achieved permanent union with God.[16] This type of false doctrine has been called Adoptionism, since it treats Jesus as if he were only the adopted Son of God—adopted because of his goodness.

I suppose we should pause to say something here about the influence Greek philosophers like Plato and Aristotle had upon the ancient world. Their ideas had become commonplace by the time of the great christological debates. Plato had emphasized the gulf separating human beings in their earthbound, physical state from a transcendent, spiritual God. He felt a person could find true happiness only by seeking out a wisdom that would free him from time and space and the material world. By cultivating such a wisdom, he would eventually be able to rise up to God. In a later section we will look at the impact this kind of thinking had on some groups called the Neoplatonists and the Gnostics. Aristotle, on the other hand, was much more down to earth. He did not deny the distance between God and the natural world. As a philosopher, however, Aristotle was much more interested in defining and classifying the world he saw around him. He was the great pigeonholer.

---

[14]*Praedicationes inusitatae* as our dogmaticians put it (Schaller, *Christology*, p. 62).

[15]"It is clear to me that the writings of the Christians are a lie, and that your fables have not been well enough constructed to conceal this monstrous fiction." Celsus, *On the True Doctrine*, R. Joseph Hoffman, trans. (Oxford: Oxford University Press, 1987), p. 64.

[16]Otto W. Heick, *A History of Christian Thought*, Vol. 1 (Philadelphia: Fortress Press, 1965) p. 148.

We Believe in Jesus Christ

It is Aristotle's mind-set that we see at work in Bishop Nestorius of Constantinople. It seems that Nestorius wanted to affirm that the Christ was both true God and true man.[17] But he was even more interested in keeping things in their proper categories and in defining things strictly. For example, while he did not object at first to simple people piously calling Mary the mother of God, he believed that "strictly speaking" it would be better in serious theological language to avoid using the term.

Nestorius thought, apparently, that if theologians took the biblical paradoxes[18] of the God-man's living and dying at face value, they would destroy the genuineness of Christ's humanity. "For him piety could never be sufficient excuse for careless exposition. . . . In his eyes, the [Mother of God] title was an outstanding example of such terminological carelessness."[19] In other words, he didn't want people to take too seriously the good news preached by the angels, "Unto you *is born* this day in the city of David a Saviour, which is Christ *the Lord*" (Lk 2:11 KJV). He felt similarly uncomfortable with saying things like "Jesus raised Lazarus from the dead" or "The Word died on the cross."[20] He believed it was much more reverent and fitting to speak of "the man Jesus" as the only subject of all human activities and of "God the Word" as the only subject of all divine activities. In this way he too wound up dividing the person of Christ by separating the human nature from the divine.

It was the great bishop Cyril of Alexandria who opposed Nestorius and who clearly enunciated the scriptural teaching of the communication of attributes for the first time. About one thousand years later, Luther confessed the same truths in the christological controversies that had erupted during the Reformation. This time it was Ulrich Zwingli, the Swiss Reformer, who had raised a question mark over the reality of the Bible's paradoxical language concerning the person of Christ. Zwingli dismissed it all as a figure of speech, calling it an *alloeosis*, that is, a figure by which "we attribute to one nature the qualities of the other."[21] Like Nestorius, he had no objection to referring to Mary as the mother of God, just so long as people understood this as a "mode

---

[17]For further reading on the subject, see John A. McGuckin's *St. Cyril of Alexandria: The Christological Controversy* (Leiden: E.J. Brill, 1994). A brief summary of Nestorius' views can be found on pages 28-39.

[18]A paradox, in the sense that I am using the word, is a seemingly contradictory statement that is nonetheless true. How can the Lord of glory die, or the Son of Man ascend to where he was before? These are seemingly impossible statements. God cannot die; man cannot speak of returning to an eternal state. Yet God did die, according to his human nature, in the person of Christ. Man did return to the state in which he had always existed, according to his divine nature, in the person of Christ. Phrases like "according to the flesh" and "according to his divine nature" are called by our dogmaticians *particulae diacriticae*. They are intended to distinguish that nature in Christ according to which the declaration of the sentence is *essentially* true. They are not at all meant to step back from the truth that these things were all experienced by one and the same subject-personality: the God-man. For examples of scriptural statements, see 1 Peter 3:18; Romans 9:5.

[19]The term θεότοκος as applied to Mary (the God-bearer)—loved by monks and Cyril, the great bishop of Alexandria, but disliked by Nestorius—was one of the matters which ignited the controversy between them. Their doctrinal debate culminated in the Council of Chalcedon of 451 and was settled there. McGuckin, *St. Cyril of Alexandria*, p. 137.

[20]McGuckin, ibid., p. 153. "The Word" (Greek: the Logos) is one of the names by which Scripture clearly affirms the divinity of Christ; see John 1:1-14.

[21]Hermann Sasse, *This Is My Body* (Adelaide: Lutheran Publishing House, 1959) p. 121.

---

of speech." Strictly speaking, she was only the mother of his human nature.[22] To this, Luther replied:

> Now if that old witch, Lady Reason, the grandmother of *alloeosis*, should say, the divinity cannot suffer or die, you should answer, That is true. Yet because divinity and humanity are one person in Christ, Scripture also, on account of such personal unity, attributes to the Godhead everything that belongs to the humanity, and in turn . . . the person who is God suffers in the humanity. In truth, the Son of God has been crucified for us; that means the person who is God.[23]

The matter did not rest at Marburg with Luther's refusal to join hands in fellowship with Zwingli. After Zwingli died, John Calvin tried to refine some aspects of Zwingli's teaching. Zwingli seemed to have been almost entirely unaware of the ancient Church's teaching of the communication of attributes. Calvin, however, was not only aware of it, but he tried to confess it, attempting to adopt a position somewhere in the middle between Zwingli and Luther. The language he used was so successful, in fact, that his teaching found many secret adherents in Lutheran Germany. Though Calvin was no doubt sincere in his desire to confess the communication of attributes, he could still speak of the divinity of Christ—after the incarnation—as existing, in part, *extra carnem* ("outside the flesh").[24] This caused those Lutherans who had remained faithful to Scripture to doubt whether Calvin genuinely believed in any communication of attributes at all. They suspected that, for Calvin, these types of statements in Scripture were mere *verbales* ("forms of speech").

This is why Article VIII of the Formula of Concord never seems to grow tired of emphasizing the reality of the biblical declarations. Over and over again, the Formula repeats words and phrases such as *vere*; *in re vere*; *propositiones non tantummodo verbales*; *neque nuda verba sine re* (truly; in actual fact; declarations that aren't a matter of mere words alone; not bare words without any substance to them). More than anything, the confessors wanted to let the scriptural statements stand at their face value: God means exactly what he says!

But were they, perhaps, pressing a point too far? Certainly they knew that the whole truth about God is a larger subject than we can ever talk about in any human language. We see, after all, only through a glass darkly. Why did they harp so on this matter? Because they wanted the scriptural statements to remain in their full force among us too! "Don't turn away from the Word!"

---

[22]Ibid.
[23]WA 26:321,19; the quotation also appears in FC SD VIII:41.
[24]Bernard Ramm, *An Evangelical Christology* (New York: Thomas Nelson Publishers) p. 62. Significantly, Dr. Ramm adds, "The debate continues today."

We Believe in Jesus Christ

they say to us through the centuries, "While the Word may not tell us every-thing, what it *does* tell us, we can be sure of." That is certainly a point worth making. As Chemnitz says:

> With reverence and care in all these questions and disputa-tions concerning this dark mystery let us turn to the light of God which shines out to us in His Word. Let us keep and restrain ourselves within the bounds of the divine revelation given us in the Scripture. With grateful minds let us be con-tent with the simplicity of the partial knowledge which is given, demonstrated, and set before us in this life by the sure and clear testimonies of Scripture, albeit in part, through a mirror, and as it were in a riddle.[25]

It is right here where Luther and Chemnitz can also help us speak scrip-tural truth to our own generation. First of all, in most of the modern scholarly discussions of this subject, there has occurred a major disconnect between the human and the divine natures in Christ. Ever since David Strauss' sour skep-ticism led him in the last century to dismiss the gospels as being largely unre-liable myths, people have lost themselves trying to "find" the historical Jesus.[26] Naturally, if the gospels themselves are perceived as unreliable, what they say must first be tested and sifted by human reason before they can be accepted as true.

Over the decades, people have used different methods to do this, too many to go into here. The basic point we need to understand is that most "Christian" scholars today have divided the man Jesus from the Christ of faith. They believe that the man can be understood, more or less, only through historical studies that adopt a critical attitude towards the Scriptures. The one whom the church believes in as divine—the Christ of faith—can only be "experienced" in community with other Christians who share the same tradition.[27] The exact connection between the two is uncertain. Some scholars who employ historical methods like these find the gospel records more reliable than others.[28] They would all, however, agree that the gospels have to be tested before they can be historically trusted.

---

[25]Chemnitz, *Two Natures*, pp. 68,69.
[26]For an excellent overview of the recent quest for the historical Jesus, see Glen Thompson's review article in the *Wisconsin Lutheran Quarterly*, "The Historical Jesus" (Summer 1995) pp. 189-197.
[27]David Tracy, as quoted by Cullen Murphy in "Who Do Men Say That I AM," *The Atlantic Monthly* (December 1986).
[28]Martin Hengel, for example, would represent the more conservative wing of this group of scholars. His recent book, *Studies in Early Christology* (Edinburgh: T & T Clark, 1995), offers a sampling of his thought. Through a study of the gospels, of Psalm 110:1, of the apostle Paul, of Christ's titles, and of early Christian songs, he advances the thesis that there is a vital connection between the messianic claims Jesus made for himself and the message believed in and proclaimed by the early church. He realizes the importance of answering the question, "Who is this one?" with the words "God became a human being in Jesus of Nazareth." Much of what he says is genuinely use-ful. However, in his willingness to classify many elements in the gospel message as mythical, he concedes too much (Foreword, p. xviii).

All this can come as no great surprise to anyone here who has ever heard about the "Jesus Seminar," where scholars vote to decide which sayings of Jesus in the gospels are real and which are bogus. Nor would it be news to any of you who might have caught the recent series on PBS' *Frontline* entitled "From Jesus to Christ."[29]

Yet while some of their language might anger us and while it certainly has caused great offense in Christendom, it would not be wise for us simply to dismiss all attempts to recreate the history of the world into which Jesus was born as being misguided and useless. Without question, we must understand Jesus within his own historical context so that we can better proclaim him to be our own. From some historical scholars we can learn a great deal; of others we should at least be aware.

What we do need to be on our guard against, and what is truly new about all these "Christologies from below," is the way these scholars drive a wedge between heaven and earth, faith and history, the man Jesus and the divine Logos. They do so by creating a gap between the language of Scripture and historical truth. On this point, there can be no compromise, and in this respect, they can teach us nothing. As Bernard Ramm puts it:

> The concept that God comes into this world by the incarnation and appears as a historical figure crashes into all our human self-sufficiencies. It is an offense to our sense of natural order, to our sense of scientific history, to our sense of our intellectual competence, and to our sense of our moral worth. *It is therefore of necessity that Christology and the human mind—wherever and whatever—clash.*[30]

Perhaps a greater problem for us, however, is what any of this can possibly mean to the postmodern generation. Why should a jaded, aging Boomer pause to consider the communication of attributes when the only kind of communication he's paid attention to for years has come to him via the television set? How can we hope to get past the cynicism and suspicion of the Xer with the absolute truth of Scripture? One self-described baby buster had this to say of himself and his generation, "Our view of religion is skeptical. Our view of commitment is wary. Our view of reality is survivalist. Our thinking is relational and feelings-oriented, not intellectual. We live in the now; we can't imagine eternity."[31]

How can we reach people like that? Well, I don't know that I would start with a dissertation on the communication of attributes. From where they're at,

---

[29]If you missed it, you can catch its major emphases online at http://www.pbs.org/wgbh/pages/frontline/shows/religion/jesus/bornliveddied.html. There is a great deal of useful information here for anyone who is interested in the history of the ancient world, despite the skeptical approach to the gospels themselves.

[30]Ramm, *Evangelical Christology* p. 22.

[31]Kevin Graham Ford, *Jesus for a New Generation* (Downers Grove: InterVarsity Press, 1995) p. 134.

We Believe in Jesus Christ

they probably can't see it as anything but dull. Reverence for the subtle textures of the gospel paradox is more likely to be engendered in one who already has faith. Once, however, the connection *has* been made with Christ, what a thrill it is to see the way Jesus replaces hard-bitten cynicism with childlike trust in every word God speaks! Then precise connections matter—whichever ones God has placed before us in the Scriptures for our contemplation. These connections matter because the person himself has become connected to him who joins everything in himself (Eph 1:10). And then a man is more than ready to get up from his couch. Now he understands in his own living experience that man does not live by ESPN alone, but by every word that comes from the mouth of God (Dt 8:3).

If I were trying to reach them, then, I would remember to tell them a story. A story that's far more compelling than the sitcoms they've been putting their minds to sleep with every night. A story that's not a cleverly invented myth like the ones they're so prone to believe. It's the first and best story, really: one that doesn't gloss over how far away we've fallen from God's glory, yet one that can still promise us a happy ending. I'd tell them how God was one of us, how he sank down into our flesh to raise us up to himself forever. To help us tell it in a truer and better way, let's have a look at the last two categories of Bible passages.

"Where can I find God?"—The *genus maiestaticum*

Anyone who has seen me has seen the Father.[32]

With the apostle Paul, the church has always joyfully confessed that "in Christ all the fullness of the Deity lives in bodily form" (Col 2:9). Note carefully the way the apostle piles up term upon term. "In Christ," that is, the one in whom we believe. "All the fullness," that is, not merely part, but the fullness, and not merely part of the fullness, but all of it. "The Deity," that is, whatever makes God to be God, all the qualities, attributes, and power of the Divine Being as it is fundamentally present in the second person of the Trinity. "Lives," that is, assumes as its permanent habitation.[33] "In bodily form," that is, in the perfectly human body and soul of the man Jesus.

The more we probe this statement, the less we understand and the more we must adore. We dare not, however, say anything less than the Scriptures say on the subject. In explicating the *genus maiestaticum*,[34] we wish to assert with the Holy Writings that Jesus' human nature, because it is united in one

---

[32] John 14:9.
[33] In the original the verb is κατοικεῖ—οἰκέω in the present tense, strengthened by the perfectivizing κατά.
[34] That is, types of Bible passages that speak of the infinite majesty of God being fully shared in by the human nature of Christ.

---

person with God the Son, has permanently received and continually "shares in the divine power, knowledge, and glory of the Son of God."[35]

When Jesus came to his disciples and said, "All authority in heaven and on earth has been given to me" (Mt 28:18), he was teaching them this truth. Even before his resurrection in glory, he declared the same thing by saying, "The Father . . . has entrusted all judgment to the Son . . . he has given him authority to judge because he is the Son of Man" (Jn 5:22,27). Here it is worth reminding ourselves of the axiom of the ancient church that states whatever Christ "received in time, he received not according to his divine nature (according to which He has everything from eternity) but . . . according to the assumed human nature."[36] To remove all doubt from his disciples' minds on the point, Jesus permitted three of them to become "eyewitnesses of his majesty" (2 Pe 1:16) as he allowed it to shine from, with, and through his human nature on the Mount of Transfiguration (Mt 17:1-9).

With the teaching of Christology it has long been true that people have troubled their minds to no good purpose in trying to unscrew the inscrutable. How can the eternal God become a timebound creature like man? Do you remember our earlier discussion of Plato and his influence on the Greco-Roman world? If ever a man had felt the gulf between God and man, none had felt it so keenly as Plato. To him God was pure, an unmoved being. He was utterly above and beyond the this-and-that, the here-and-there, the now-and-then of this world. For this reason, any involvement in the material world Plato saw as a loss of life and as a falling away from God. Naturally, it was far easier for him to describe God in negative terms—saying what he is *not*—than in positive ones—saying what he *is*. When he did, however, attempt to describe this transcendent world and the way for the human spirit to return to it, Plato resorted to metaphors and myths: "It becomes *not* a sensible man to affirm that these things are indeed *just as* I have described: but to say that . . . something *like this* is true . . . I count fitting."[37] God is indeed beyond us, he is saying, but we can tell ourselves plausible fictions that might give us some clues about him, at least.

With the repopularization of his views in the Hellenistic culture of the Roman Empire, Plato's ideas became the thinking person's credo. When Christianity was left *out* of the mix, the result has been dubbed Neoplatonism. When some ancient intellectuals tried to blend together Christianity, the Platonistic worldview, and a few mystic rites, the result was Gnosticism.

---

[35]From Professor John Jeske's 1974 essay entitled "The Communication of Attributes in the God-Man Christ Jesus." Professor Jeske's essay can be accessed under the "Library" menu at http://www.wls.wels.net/.
[36]FC SD VIII:57.
[37]Plato's *Phaedo*, as quoted in Sir Frank Fletcher's preface to his edition of Virgil: *Aeneid* VI (Oxford: Clarendon Press), p. xix.

We Believe in Jesus Christ

Anyone who attempts to describe Gnosticism is faced with the same dilemma as the seven blind men with the elephant: where does a person start? There's a simple reason for this: Gnosticism was syncretistic. It had no problem whatever discerning the deeper "truths" embedded in the myths of all religions and combining them all into their complex cosmologies. For our purposes it is enough to say that in Gnosticism, God was the one so far above us that no human could ever attain to him apart from spiritual intermediaries—angels and principalities and emanations and powers. The material world was evil, created by a malevolent deity called the demiurge. Inside some men, however, were sparks of the divine spirit, trapped within the inert "stuff" of the body.

The way out was opened for Gnostics when the Supreme God sent a redeemer to wake the elect. The elect were the ones whose material bodies contained this spark of divine spirit. They were conceived of as spiritual sleepwalkers whom the redeemer needed to rouse from the dream of life. This redeemer—and the special knowledge he brought with him—could bring these spiritual people into the light of true knowledge. He would shine on them, and they would realize their divine origin and destiny. According to the Gnostics, the man Jesus was instrumental in giving them their esoteric knowledge. He was a deeply spiritual man upon whom "the Christ" temporarily descended. This "union" was dissolved shortly before the crucifixion, an event that lacked any real significance for the sect.

Jesus, therefore, was important to the Gnostics as a teacher, as a conduit for the knowledge brought by "the Christ." But the man Jesus could never have been the Supreme God. Such a thought was inconceivable to them. Gnostics also passed along to their devotees other bits of secret wisdom, much of which was to be received through participating in mystical and magical rites. One who was thus put in the know could pass beyond the bright stars, Venus and Mars, and ascend into the realms of purest light.[38]

Neoplatonism shared Plato's definition of God as pure *Being*. The highest part within the rational soul of a human being was the closest thing to God in the world of space and time. The created world of "stuff" came into existence when the soul "fell." How that had happened in the first place was not made completely clear, but it had something to do with the passions and desires that kept people enslaved to their physical senses. People were thus trapped inside bodies which were stuck inside a material world.[39]

The way out for Neoplatonists came through the cultivation of that divine spark within. Through a study of philosophy (and maybe a little magic on the side), a wise man would turn more and more inward in thoughtful contemplation of that which *is*. (Stay with me now, and remember: the only thing that

---

[38]Heick, *A History*, p. 72.
[39]An ancient Orphic doctrine declared: σῶμα, σῆμα—the body is a tomb (for the soul).

---

purely existed was purest Mind). In this way, he could increasingly withdraw himself from the world of sight and sound and sense. If he was sufficiently skilled, he might catch a glimpse of that which *is* by means of a mystic "knowing" of God. This was the Platonic ascent to the realm of the *real*. If it all sounds like your average night on the computer, you've got it about right. Neoplatonists wanted to transcend the world of incidents and accidents, hints and allegations, to be reunited with pure Being. Neoplatonism made a deep impact on the thought of a few church fathers, including Gregory of Nyssa and St. Augustine.

We can see much that is similar in these two ancient worldviews: matter (including the physical body of a human being) is bad. God is transcendent. There is a spark of God in man (Gnostics: some men). Salvation is not *received* by faith in the God who became a human being, died, and rose again to redeem us from our sin. Instead, it is *achieved* through the reception of the correct knowledge and the willingness to put that knowledge into practice.

There is no doubt that these views were widespread in the ancient world. There is no doubt either, as we have seen, that even some ancient church fathers were influenced by some aspects of this type of dangerous thinking. Yet despite this—and with one voice—the ancient church stoutly rejected Gnosticism as heresy and affirmed the goodness of God's creation. They were firm in their confession (as we have seen) that the man Jesus *was* true God and that he was crucified, died, and was buried. The apostle John had clarified for believers what the chief issues were when he wrote against the early Gnostics of his day. He said, "The Son of God . . . came by water and blood" (1 Jn 5:5,6), which is to say Jesus was God not only when he was baptized in the Jordan river (when he passed through water) but also when he was crucified on Calvary's cross (when he endured the shedding of his blood).

The Greek church fathers plainly saw what this mythologizing and philosophical kind of separation of God from humanity would do: it would spell the end of the incarnation! If the Gnostics and Neoplatonists were right, God was not really present in Jesus in any essential and permanent way. Nor was there any need for him to be! Jesus would merely be a spiritual guide, bringing us into a better understanding of that which we pretty much knew already. The way to salvation lay outside Jesus, in making the mystic ascent to the eternal.

To clarify matters under controversy in their own time, these church fathers wanted to confess the full truth inherent in the statement "The Word became flesh and made his dwelling among us. We have seen his glory" (Jn 1:14). That is why Cyril wrote, "God the Word came down to us . . . even into the nature of man . . . [so that by this union he might] endow it with the dignities of the divine majesty. And this, far from subjecting the unchangeable God to this nature's limits, raised it up to a transcendence of its

We Believe in Jesus Christ

nature."[40] The way back up to God lay not in the mystic ascent but only through discovering God in the very physical, very human Jesus. Without attempting to explain the mystery, Cyril merely asserted that the majesty of God was shared by the human nature of Jesus without altering it essentially in any way and that the human nature was a fit organ for the eternal Word.

For Luther too the basic issue in confessing the *genus maiestaticum* was the question "Where do I find God?" His great gospel insight, his solid rock in all temptation, was that the God of love was fully found in Jesus of Nazareth *and nowhere else.*[41] We will allow him to speak more about that tremendous gospel comfort later, in our discussion of the final genus. For now it is merely necessary to emphasize this truth as Luther's biblical response to Zwingli. Zwingli, as you can well imagine, was unable to accept the thought that the human nature of Christ could so be taken up into God that it too could transcend space and time. Zwingli's logical presuppositions convinced him that a human body—in order to be genuine—had to exist in a space.[42] Luther's retort at Marburg was: "I do not admit mathematical dimensions. God is higher than all mathematicians. Christ can keep his body without space at a certain place."[43]

His deeper concern, however, is revealed in the following passage, also cited in Article VIII of the Solid Declaration of the Formula of Concord:

> Where [Christ] is, there he is as one undivided person. And when you can say, Here is God, then you must also say, Christ, the man, is also here. If, however, you were to show me a place where the divine nature is and the human nature is not, the person would be divided, because then I could say in truth, Here is God who is not man and never has become man. That is not my God![44]

Similarly for the formulators of the Formula of Concord, the problem was not Gnosticism but the *extra Calvinisticum* described earlier (see page 72). In open denial of Colossians 2:9, Calvin refused to say that the whole fullness of the Deity existed in Christ's body. Preferring Zwingli's logic concerning space and time to the logic of faith, he asserted that Jesus' body had to be locally confined in heaven, and could not transcend the limitations of human bodies as they existed in our world.[45] As a faithful reflection of his thought,

---

[40]*Scholia on the incarnation*, p. 10; McGuckin, *St. Cyril of Alexandria*, p. 304.
[41]See the discussion of Luther's views in Sasse's *This is My Body*, pp. 119,120,203; also in Sasse's *Here We Stand* (New York: Harper & Brothers, 1938) pp. 145,146. Particularly noteworthy is Sasse's quotation of the *Tischreden* (WA 1:113): *"Aut nullus est Deus aut ille est"* (Either there is no God, or he's the one!)
[42]Sasse, *This is My Body*, p. 203. This is often expressed in the philosophical axiom: *finitum non capax infiniti*. The finite can't handle the infinite. The difficulty with the axiom is, as Luther points out, it injects ideas of physical space into the notion of God's presence.
[43]Sasse, *This is My Body*, p. 206.
[44]As quoted in Sasse, *This is My Body*, p. 121.
[45]Sasse, *This is My Body*, p. 262.

the *Heidelberg Catechism* confesses that the Godhead in Christ was both *inside* and *outside* the humanity of Jesus.[46]

Now our own confessors took pains to deny that they had any thought of a spatial expansion of Jesus' humanity. To put it crudely, they didn't want anybody to believe that Jesus' humanity had been somehow inflated by Deity to the size of the whole universe like some oversized Macy's Parade balloon.[47] Christ's humanity remained essentially unchanged, while his divinity remained essentially undiminished.[48] What they wanted to affirm was the same scriptural truth Luther had confessed: *extra hunc hominem, nullus Deus reperitur* (outside this man, no God is found)![49] They wanted us to keep our eyes fixed on Christ, to understand that in him, God was "sunk deep in the flesh"[50] and that now it truly could be said, "God is one of us."

It is in this sense that Luther's famous words about approaching God "from below"[51] must be understood. In Jesus we see the love of God as nowhere else. Outside of Jesus, we who live here below can only know God in one of two possible ways. Either we must speculate, using our own reason, in which case we wander from one uncertainty to the next. The only God we find that way must be a product of our own theological imagination. Or we know him according to the law, and discover him to be a God of wrath and judgment.[52] Then we are bound to flee from him. In neither case do we really come to know the true God.

---

[46]Question 48.

[47]By quoting with approval Luther's description of the *esse ubique* of the human nature "not according to the first corporeal comprehensible mode, but according to the supernatural, divine mode" (FC SD VIII:81), a manner which by definition was completely outside human categories of space and time. As Luther said elsewhere, "You must put this essence of Christ, that He is the one Person with God, very far, far outside the creatures, as far as God is outside them; on the other hand, it must be as deep and as near in all creatures as God is in them," as quoted in Werner Elert's *The Structure of Lutheranism* (St. Louis: Concordia Publishing House, 1962) p. 234.

[48]FC SD VIII:71.

[49]FC SD VIII:81.

[50]Bernard Ramm's phrase, found in *Evangelical Christology*, p. 63. To illustrate this genus, both Cyril and Chemnitz liked to use the analogies of the twin "natures" of body and soul in man, or of fire and iron in a glowing piece of metal. Soul permeates and penetrates the body, giving it life and breath, yet with each nature—body and soul—remaining essentially what it is. Similarly the nature of fire penetrates the metal so that it glows. Yet fire remains fire, and metal remains metal with neither being converted into the other. Perhaps these illustrations no longer work as well for us who look to computer models to illustrate the relationship between mind and matter in man and whose scientific descriptions have come along way since the days when fire was thought of as one of the elemental substances of the universe. At the same time, the essential points they make—that the assumed humanity was a fit organ for the infinite Logos, and that through the humanity, the divinity shines forth—remain true and biblical.

[51]"The Scriptures begin very gently, and lead us on to Christ as to a man, and then to the one who is Lord over all creatures, and after that to one who is God. So do I enter delightfully and learn to know God. But the philosophers and doctors have insisted on beginning from above. We begin from below, and after that move upwards." As quoted by Scaer in *Christology*, p. 9.
Chemnitz shows his perfect agreement with Luther on this point in the following passage, "The person of the Logos cannot and ought not to be considered or made an object of faith outside of, without, or separate from the assumed nature, nor in turn the assumed flesh outside of and without the Logos. . . . Indeed, since for us poor sinners there is no approach open to the bare divine majesty any more than for a blade of straw to a consuming fire, the divine nature . . . assumed a nature of the same substance as ours . . . in which he placed the whole fullness of the deity personally. . . . We thus begin from the flesh of Christ and from there mount to communion with the deity of the Logos, and from there to communion with the Trinity." *Two Natures*, p. 79.

[52]Elert, *Structure*, p. 224.

We Believe in Jesus Christ

But when we come to God in Jesus and see him revealed under the face of the Suffering One, then we not only know him truly, but we also begin to love and trust in him. He who looks into the face of Christ looks into the heart of God.[53] This is why we must find God in Christ and in Christ alone: Christ is God from above come down here below. We see him revealed to us in all his glory in the trustworthy words of the Holy Scriptures.[54]

Today, sad to say, we find almost nothing but speculation as people hobble together their Christologies any way they can. We have already looked at the historicists, who have trouble dealing with the "God from above," the God who has come down from heaven and become incarnate by the Holy Spirit of the Virgin Mary. They simply dismiss from their minds, for the most part, any serious grappling with the issues of such a God-man, labeling the idea as "myth." The theologians we are most concerned with in this section, however, are those who, with Plato, have mastered the art of creating new myths. They hunger for some larger meaning in life than can be found in the spirit-shriveling materialism of modern science. So they look to Christ to provide them with larger answers. Most, however, construct their own myths from whatever materials lie close to their hand. Christ only comes into it as a pretext for talking about other things they think would invest life with greater meaning.

We might call them the contextualizers because they try to interpret the meaning of Christ within the context of some overarching, unifying concept. Theology is no longer seen as doxology—as the art of praising God by apprehending his revelation. It is rather seen as the do-it-yourself skill of building a mystery through the construction of whatever metaphor might happen to work for you. These contextualizing ideas usually spring from concerns that are current in contemporary society. "Jesus the Liberator" was—and still is— popular in South and Central America. Jesus the New Age Mystic and Spiritual Guide is another. Then there are the "theologies" and "hermeneutics" that seem to reproduce like rabbits wherever you look: Feminist, Gnostic, African-American, Reader-Response, and on and on and on. It seems as if everyone's building a mystery these days. In any case, these contexts and metaphors often act as filters for the biblical data. Whatever doesn't fit the thesis is usually strained out, leaving behind only that which does.

Now of course we all interpret Christ from within our own situation; no doubt because of the weakness of our sinful natures, some of what is there in Scripture may be hidden from our eyes. However, we also have the confidence as believers of knowing that "we have the mind of Christ" (1 Co 2:16)

---

[53]WA 2:140,36. See also Luther's thesis in the Heidelberg Disputation, *"Ergo in Christo crucifixo est vera theologia et cognitio Dei"* (Therefore a true theology and understanding of God is found in Christ crucified) (WA 1:362).
[54]Note also Paul Althaus' discussion of this same subject in *The Theology of Martin Luther* (Philadelphia: Fortress Press, 1966), pp. 182-185.

and that therefore, through the Word, the Spirit himself will open our minds to grasp even the deep things of God. Especially, we know, the Spirit will open our spiritual eyes to see the love of God as it is revealed in the face of Christ (1 Co 2:10-16; 2 Co 4:6). Precisely because of this, it is impossible for us to imagine how anyone not equipped with the spirit of faith—a faith that holds fast to the words of Scripture—will be able to say anything that's spiritually true, no matter what context he's operating with.

We are not speaking here of hardworking Christians on the frontlines of the faith who are attempting to translate the ancient story into another cultural context. We must admire the industry and ingenuity of those who grapple head-on with these issues and who make the attempt, at least, to plant the gospel into a new cultural setting. What a blessing it would be if more among us would show that same industry! (And not only abroad, but also at home to a society and a people that is rapidly changing!) Communicating in words and pictures that people can *understand* is fundamental to fulfilling the evangelical admonition to "[speak] the truth in love" (Eph 4:15).

However, there are some cross-cultural writers who *say* they want to communicate the timeless gospel but whose words are so "listener oriented" that they no longer breathe the same Spirit who speaks in Scripture. That is why the first and most basic question to ask ourselves whenever we try to communicate in this way is one suggested by Dr. E. R. Wendland, "What is truth?"[55] Pilate didn't know the answer, but we do. Truth is found in Jesus, the Son of God, and is mediated to us through the words of Scripture. To the extent that modern or cross-cultural contexts provide some useful analogies that *genuinely correspond* to the once-for-all gospel truth of Jesus, to that extent—and to that extent alone—we may press them into the service of the gospel. But where there is little or no conceptual overlap, we should avoid them. As Dr. Wendland points out in another place, "Where the attesting record of Scripture itself is ignored, or is contorted to fit the mold of some secularized methodology, it is no wonder that spiritually voided responses can predominate.[56]

This has been heavy going, I admit, so now I would like to tell you a story, a true story, actually, about the time a woman knocked on my office door in Salt Lake. I had never before met her in my life. That was one of the really neat things about working in Salt Lake: walk-ins like this to our church were not at all uncommon. She said, "I'd like to ask you a few questions about Jesus." I said, "Fine, that's what I'm here for." She began, "Now, about that time Jesus went to India . . ." "Wait a minute," I said.

---

[55]"Who Do People Say I Am?" *Africa Journal of Evangelical Theology* 10:2 (1991), p. 30.
[56]"Recent Contributions in African Christology: A Book Review Article," *Africa Journal of Evangelical Theology* 14.2 (1995), p. 121.

"Jesus never went to India!" For the next 15 minutes we went back and forth, getting absolutely nowhere. She had her book, giving her the myth she liked the best about a New Age, Gnostic Jesus. I had mine. She couldn't see why my book was any better than hers or why my book shouldn't be judged in the light of her book, instead of the other way around (as I was trying to do). She could tell I was feeling a little frustrated, so she finally said to me (with a great deal of compassion in her voice), "Look, it's fine for you if you want to believe the way you do. I'm okay with that. Your truth, my truth—what's the big deal? They're all different ways of going to the same place." And then she walked out the door, leaving me sitting there with my mouth open.

This was the first time I had realized it. Ancient Gnosticism is making a comeback in the good old USA![57] People are tired of feeling spiritually cast adrift, alone in a vast ocean of doubt and situated under a blank heaven, without God and without hope. That's where materialism and scientism have left them. They are desperately seeking spirituality. They long to be touched by an angel. So they have repopulated the middle air with new angels and demons and principalities and powers. They long to make the ascent to heaven's gate, even if it's hidden behind the misty haze of Hale-Bopp and even if they have to kill themselves to do so. They figure if there are aliens somewhere out there, then maybe they won't feel so all alone. They've also reinhabited the earth with spirit guides and channellers and mystic crystals and energy auras. They want to make a connection to God, you see. Don't tell them it doesn't make sense. It makes sense to them, and that's good enough.

What tremendously good news we have to share, if only we can be patient with them, if only we can get past their defenses, if only we can avoid blasting away at them and getting involved in some doctrinal argument that leaves behind winners and losers but no converts! We can tell them they don't need to make the ascent. That God has already touched our race with something much better than an angel. That we have something more than a spirit guide to bring us news of the world beyond. He is not far, not lost among a thousand stars. He's near, very near. They don't have to drift anymore. They don't have to wander down endless paths in search of him. Because he came looking for them. He's come down for them. See, poor and in a manger, there he lies. He is all transcendent mystery and yet all intimate love. God has sunk himself deep into the flesh, our flesh. There we can find him.

---

[57]Check out http://www.wherry.com/~gbisaga/CRJ0040A.html or http://www.wherry.com/~gbisaga/CRJ0057A.html for a couple of interesting articles on the subject which I read, unfortunately, only long after I had had this encounter. Too soon old, too late smart!

"How can I be sure?"—The *genus apotelesmaticum*

The blood of Jesus, his Son, purifies us from all sin.[58]

In some ways we have saved the best category of Bible passages for last. Certainly it's the easiest for us to understand and a great consolation to us in every trial. In fact, we can look at it as being the comfort and consolation Lutherans are trying to preserve in every one of the three types of Bible passages under our review.

The *genus apotelesmaticum* refers to those Bible passages in which the accomplishments of Jesus as our Savior, Redeemer, Mediator, Teacher, High Priest, Victor, Judge, and King[59] are described as the accomplishments of the God-man. Each nature in Christ performs in communication with the other that which is proper to it.[60] In every redemptive act of the God-man, both natures fully participate, each in communion with the other.

For example, Galatians 4:4,5 tells that "God sent his Son, born of a woman, born under law, to redeem those under law." By this Paul is telling us that the Father sent his eternal Son into the world. He was born of the Virgin Mary, and he willingly allowed himself to be placed under God's law. The purpose for God's sending—and its effect—was the redemption of all those who were under God's curse as it is pronounced in his holy law. Being born and placed under law, of course, are activities proper to the human nature. But the fact that this human nature was personally joined to the eternal Son of God lends infinite value to the fulfilling of the law and to the bearing of its curse.

Similarly, Jesus' shedding of his blood we can call an activity proper to his human nature (see 1 Jn 1:7 earlier). But John also says that Jesus' blood has the power to cleanse us from every sin. From this we can easily see that his divine nature is participating in full unity with his human nature in the work of setting us free from our sins.

> Thus our faith has the surest comfort . . . the work of our redemption is not the work of a mere man or of the humanity by itself. For thus sin would be even greater, the wrath of God heavier, and the reign of death stronger. By His own

---

[58]1 John 1:7.

[59]For an even more complete list, consult Chemnitz, *Two Natures*, p. 217. It may be observed here the important implications the modern practice of "title Christology" also has for our faith. This approach seeks to understand the various New Testament titles for Jesus within the context of the ancient world. It often assumes a "three circle" approach to the spread of Christianity: (a) first circle: Palestinian Judaism (b) second circle: Hellenistic Judaism; (c) Hellenistic Gentiles. It debates whether Jesus applied these titles to himself or whether he was only called them later by his followers. It also debates whether a particular title's origin should be traced to a Palestinian or to a Hellenistic context. To the extent that a scholar sees a basic continuity between Jesus' self-designation and the later [?] designations applied to him by his followers, these studies can be very useful. To the extent, however, that they posit a discontinuity between the two, they decline in their value (e.g. Jesus at most only saw himself as a Palestinian sage, who was later "Hellenized" into an incarnation of God). See books like Martin Hengel's, referred to in footnote 27, for a conservative approach to "title Christology." For a discussion of the subject itself, see Ramm's *Christology*, pp. 108-116.

[60]This is Chemnitz's translation of the decree of Chalcedon, *Two Natures*, p. 216. It also appears in the FC SD VIII:46.

We Believe in Jesus Christ

blood God has redeemed the Church. . . . For the power of the divine nature itself works through the obedient and suffering assumed nature and thus achieves redemption."[61]

This is what makes our hearts secure and our salvation sure. This is the point Luther was driving home with his well-known "God in the scale" illustration: "If God is not also in the balance, and gives the weight, we sink to the bottom. . . . But if 'God's death' and 'God died' lie in the scale of the balance, then He sinks down, and we rise up as light as an empty scale."[62]

We can learn a great deal from Luther, not only in what to say, but also in how to say it. Luther is someone who never grew tired of reciting the Second Article of the Apostles' Creed in his daily prayers, precisely because he knew that there he was recounting the mighty acts of the God-man, the one who had come to live, die, and rise again for you and me. "It is all ours, and concerns us," as he put it.[63] Luther was a preacher who never grew tired of retelling the simple gospel story for his people in his sermons. He did not always feel he had to chop it up into parts, with a trendy little sound bite for a theme. He was a man who opened his Bible and heard God talking.

And what he heard was all that Christ, the God-man, had done for him. Consider these words from one of his Christmas sermons:

> Look at the Child, knowing nothing. Yet all that is belongs to him, that your conscience should not fear but take comfort in him. Doubt nothing. Watch him springing in the lap of the maiden. Laugh with him. Look upon this Lord of Peace and your spirit will be at peace. See how God invites you in many ways. He places before you a Baby with whom you may take refuge. You cannot fear him, for nothing is more appealing to man than a baby. Are you frightened? Then come to him, lying in the lap of the fairest and sweetest maiden. You will see how great is the divine goodness, which seeks above all else that you should not despair. Trust him! Trust him! Here is the Child in whom is salvation. To me there is no greater consolation given to mankind than this, that this Christ became a man, a child, a baby. . . . Who is there whom this sight would not comfort? Now is overcome the power of sin, death, hell, conscience, and guilt, if you come to this gurgling Baby and believe that he is come, not to judge you, but to save.[64]

---

[61]Chemnitz, *Two Natures*, p. 221.
[62]From *On Councils and the Church*, as quoted in FC SD VIII:44.
[63]*Luther's Prayers*, Herbert F. Brokering, ed. (Minneapolis: Augsburg Publishing House), p. 60.
[64]*The Martin Luther Christmas Book*, Roland H. Bainton, ed. (Philadelphia: Fortress Press, 1948), p. 40.

In the ancient church the doctrine of Christ's saving work was certainly proclaimed, even if it was not always preached with the precision we later believers might like. Someone who looks carefully might, however, notice a different emphasis in the way Christ was presented in the West, as opposed to the way he was presented in the East. The East described the work of Christ *from its effects*: concentrating more on the way Christ cleanses, heals, and exalts our fallen natures. The West spoke of it more in terms of *its cause*: concentrating on the need for Christ to make satisfaction for our breaking of God's law. With the Reformation, greater clarity finally came on these points. Then the Reformers were able to enunciate a more biblically sound confession of both these truths—and the relationship between them—in the doctrine of justification and the doctrine of the mystic union.[65]

The primary proclamation of the church will always be the forgiveness of sins purchased by Christ and Christ's alien righteousness given to us as a gift by God's pure grace. This proclamation produces faith in us, and faith in us always holds fast to Christ-for-us. But faith in Christ-for-us is also the new life of Christ-in-us. The believer can say with Paul, "I no longer live, but Christ lives in me" (Gal 2:20). He trusts completely in God's promises to make his home in us and is fully convinced that, while outwardly we may be wasting away, inwardly we are being renewed. This is precisely the way Christ brings us at last to the eternal home he has prepared *for* us (Jn 14:23; 2 Co 4:6–5:10).

The crucial point for us to bear in mind here is that *both* the "Christ-for-us" *and* the "Christ-in-us" are the God-man. The God-man is present *to* faith as the one who loved us and who gave himself for us on Calvary's cross. The God-man is also active *in* faith, remaining with us to the very end of the age. We do not need to send our hearts soaring above, where at last we might find him (according to his human nature) sitting on a golden throne. Nor do we have to struggle in trying to come up with some mental picture of the divinity of Christ—abstracted from his humanity—as somehow being the only portion of him near to us on earth.

We rest our hope simply and always and alone in the whole Christ of the gospels. The one who has no beginning and no ending, the one who walked the dusty roads of Palestine from sunrise to sunset, the one who made all things, the one who grew tired and thirsty, the one who lives in eternal bliss, the one who shrank from the horror of death, the one who is pure, sweet goodness itself, and the one who was tempted to sin—HE IS OUR BROTHER. This God of ours has now become bone of our bones and flesh of our flesh, "like his brothers in every way" (Heb 2:17).

As our brother he lived for us. As our brother he died for us. As our brother he rose again for us. As our brother he was exalted to the heavenly

---

[65]For further reading on this subject, consult Elert, *Structure*, pp. 154-169 and FC SD VIII:78.

We Believe in Jesus Christ

realms for us. As our brother he has filled all things with his loving presence. Oh, how full of God and his love this world is now! If only our faith had eyes that were strong enough to see it that way always! As our brother he intercedes for us now. As our brother he rules all things for us now. As our brother he is present with us now. As our brother he is living out his life in us now. As our brother he is bringing us to glory now. As our brother, soon, we will see him. As our brother, he will bring us home. And then no one will take away our joy.

Now that God is one of us.

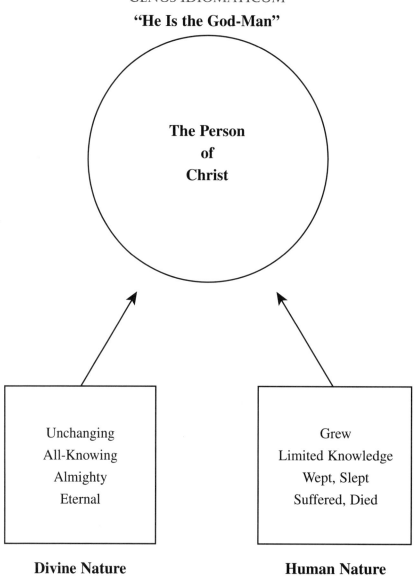

GENUS IDIOMATICUM

"He Is the God-Man"

The Person
of
Christ

Unchanging
All-Knowing
Almighty
Eternal

Grew
Limited Knowledge
Wept, Slept
Suffered, Died

Divine Nature

Human Nature

GENUS MAIESTATICUM

"In This Man, We Find God"

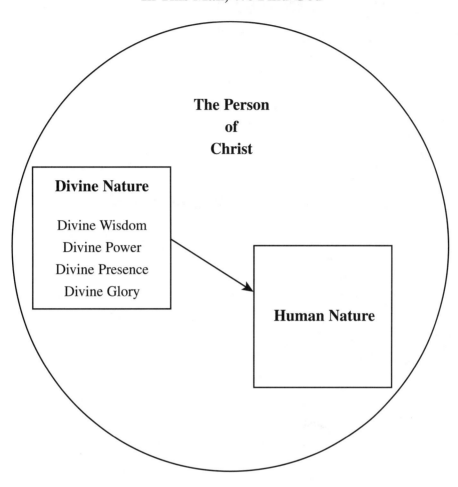

The Person
of
Christ

Divine Nature

Divine Wisdom
Divine Power
Divine Presence
Divine Glory

Human Nature

"He Is the God-Man, Our Kinsman and Redeemer"

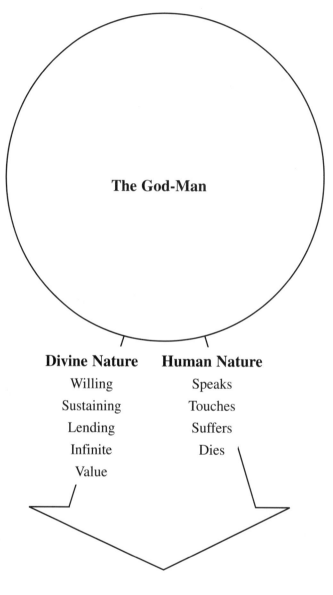

The God-Man

Divine Nature   **Human Nature**

Willing   Speaks

Sustaining   Touches

Lending   Suffers

Infinite   Dies

Value

Redeemed Us

THE OFFICE OF CHRIST

Leroy A. Dobberstein

Nebraska District Convention
Waco, Nebraska
June 15–17,1998

During these early weeks of June 1998, all of the 12 districts of the Wisconsin Evangelical Lutheran Synod have met or will be meeting in convention. The total number of pastor, teacher, and lay delegates, representing more than 1,200 congregations from all 50 states, should exceed 3,000. Each district will have its own theme. All districts and delegates will have a single purpose, to be about the business of our Lord Jesus Christ through worship, study, elections, discussions, and resolutions. After attending my own district convention last week, it is my great pleasure to be a part of the convention of your Nebraska District.

When I was asked nearly two years ago to be the essayist at this convention, your committee was considering another topic. It would have focused our attention on the end times as we move from one millennium to another, with appropriate considerations, cautions, and encouragement. I was looking forward to the assignment.

In the meantime the vice president of publishing services at Northwestern Publishing House approached the synod president and the 12 districts with a unique proposal. In order to commemorate the 2,000th anniversary of the Lord's birth, he suggested that each district plan a special convention essay on some christological topic and that a book containing all the essays be printed for presentation to all the delegates at the district conventions in 2000. This explains the topic for your convention today, chosen in consultation with your district president. Though the topic for this convention may seem to be quite different from the one originally planned, the considerations, cautions, and encouragement remain the same.

It should be noted before we begin that our district conventions and our synod convention next year stand at the threshold of not one but two momentous occasions. The one, already mentioned, is the ushering in of a new millennium. This celebration will reach far beyond the church. It is generating excitement around the world. People have been talking about it and making plans for it for years in advance. Many are planning to party and celebrate like never before. It will include celebration, I fear, that you and I want no part of. The convention essays prepared this year and to be shared at the district conventions two years from now set a far better tone for Christian thought and celebration as we reach this great event in the history of God's world.

The other momentous occasion much on our minds these days is the sesquicentennial (150th) anniversary of the founding of our Wisconsin Evangelical Lutheran Synod. This celebration will not draw worldwide attention. It will not even receive national review. It remains to be seen how many large city newspapers will even mention the occasion. I can't even imagine other Lutherans, much less other Christian denominations, getting excited about it. But it is an event that will reach around the world, in all the countries on five continents where our Lord has enabled the WELS to proclaim the gospel. Fellow Christians in 24 countries beyond the United States and Canada will join in our celebration. Praise, thanks, and glory to God will be expressed in 36 languages.

An ad hoc committee is busy making preparations for the 150th anniversary to be observed in two years, and I am sure we will be hearing more about that in the course of this convention. Meanwhile the series of essays being read at the district conventions of the synod this year also afford excellent preparation for that great occasion. What better way both to look back at what the Lord has done for the past 150 years and also look ahead to being about the Father's business than a study of the christological truths revealed to us in the sacred Scriptures. I can think of no better use of our time in this convention than to look at one facet of Christological doctrine:

The Office of Christ

Christ, appointed to office

On my desk is a ballpoint that was given to me by my son last Father's Day. It is silver, has black ink, and writes exceptionally well, even for one not known for his penmanship skills. What makes it special is the engraving on the pen. It is not something you receive as free advertisement at a hardware store, restaurant, or service station. You know the kind—name, address, telephone number, maybe a picture. That's it. This pen is different. It is as special to me as the cross, two plaques with Bible verses, a picture of my first church and parsonage painted by my wife, and a picture of classmates of my seminary graduation, all on the wall facing my desk in my study. With various print sizes and formats the pen reads: Messiah, Lord, Savior, Jesus, Son of God, Lord of Lords, Immanuel, The Way, Resurrection and Life, Alpha and Omega. All that is written on one half the pen in clear, distinct letters. It is an inscription that bears repeating. The other half of the pen reads the same. The pen is unique. It bears a unique description.

If you were an employer seeking to fill an important office in a prestigious firm, would you dare to expect anyone with such credentials? Ordinarily a detailed job description includes a list of qualifications that no single person could possibly fill. Even if a well-qualified person were able to offer something in every area described, it would only be with varying degrees of expertise. Realistically the person who most nearly matches the qualifications ends up with the job. He who is Son of God, Lord of lords, Alpha and Omega, was appointed to office, to be the Christ, the Messiah. He possesses every qualification imaginable. Immanuel, the Way, the Resurrection and the Life, only begin to describe his perfect qualifications.

God's Old Testament people had great expectations. God had promised to send a Messiah, the Anointed One. Great leaders of the Old Testament were anointed into office and served as notable types of the Messiah. They included prophets, priests, and kings. There were men like Moses, Joshua, Samuel, David, Solomon, Elijah, Elisha, Isaiah, and Jeremiah, to mention a few. All had unique qualifications for the office to which they were called, to lead and rule, teach and preach, admonish and encourage. But none was worthy of the office that he held for a brief time, much less qualified for the highest office, to be the Messiah, the Christ, the Anointed One.

None could even begin to qualify because of the nature of the work, the work of reuniting the human race with God. The fall of man into sin remains the greatest human tragedy in all of history. God had made man in his own image, in perfect harmony with his creator and God. Adam was entrusted with the noble task of naming all the creatures God had made. God placed the man and his wife in the beautiful Garden of Eden, to manage and take care of it. The trees and fruits of the garden were theirs to enjoy. As added measure of his favor God placed the tree of life in the middle of the garden and invited them to eat freely. Adam and Eve knew only happiness and bliss, which comes with knowing God's will and having willingness to live according to it. As a special token of showing their love and obedience to him, God placed the tree of the knowledge of good and evil near to the tree of life with this command: "You are free to eat from any tree in the garden; but you must not eat from the tree of the knowledge of good and evil, for when you eat of it you will surely die" (Ge 2:16,17). What God intended only as blessing became the way to man's alienation from God. Influenced by Satan, Adam and Eve abused their formal liberty. Abandoning their faith they fell into sin and under God's eternal condemnation.

With no one to rescue, no one to undo what Satan had done to man and what man had voluntarily done to himself, no one to reunite, the God of all grace and mercy said, "I will put enmity between you and the woman, and between your offspring and hers; he will crush your head, and you will strike his heel" (Ge 3:15). God came to the rescue. God promised to send a Messiah. He appointed his own Son to office. From the very beginning of the promise, the term *office*, to which God appointed himself in the person of his own Son, is to be understood as work, pure work, difficult work, demanding work, extensive work, superhuman work in the fullest sense of the term. It is the work of salvation. "God did not appoint us to suffer wrath but to receive salvation through our Lord Jesus Christ" (1 Th 5:9). The Savior himself acknowledged that appointment in his high priestly prayer on the eve of his passion: "I have brought you glory on earth by completing the work you gave me to do" (Jn 17:4). The work is none other than redemption. "When the time had fully come, God sent his Son, born of a woman, born under law, to redeem those under law, that we might receive the full rights of sons" (Gal 4:4,5).

Jesus was appointed to office, and he willingly assumed it. His willingness was stated for all to hear long in advance. "Then I said, 'Here I am, I have come—it is written about me in the scroll. I desire to do your will, O my God; your law is within my heart'" (Ps 40:7,8). At an early age the incarnate Christ was aware of his appointment to office. "'Why were you searching for me?' he asked. 'Didn't you know I had to be in my Father's house?'" (Lk 2:49). From the time he was baptized by John and publicly declared by John to be "the Lamb of God, who takes away the sin of the world!" (Jn 1:29), Jesus was consumed by the duties of his office. When his disciples attempted to call "time out" at Jacob's well in Samaria, Jesus, as tired and hungry as he was, replied, "My food . . . is to do the will of him who sent me and to finish his work" (Jn 4:34). Though the Suffering Servant called out in great agony when the guilt of the world's sins weighed heavily upon him, "My Father, if it is possible, may this cup be taken from me," his human will remained in perfect harmony with his divine will: "Yet not as I will, but as you will" (Mt 26:39).

The nature of the Savior's appointed work is expressed in the title *Mediator*, a term which is used six times in the New Testament. Paul uses this title when sharing various instructions with the young pastor Timothy: "There is one God and one mediator between God and men, the man Christ Jesus, who gave himself as a ransom for all men" (1 Ti 2:5,6). The writer to the Hebrews uses the title when speaking of the new covenant relationship God established through his Son. "For this reason Christ is the mediator of a new covenant, that those who are called may receive the promised eternal inheritance—now that he has died as a ransom to set them free from the sins committed under the first covenant" (Heb 9:15).

Until the coming of Christ, the Messiah, Moses stands as the great example of mediation. God chose Moses to lead his people out of Egypt to the Land of Promise. Through Moses God gave his law at Mount Sinai, a covenant that remained in effect for nearly 1,500 years. When the people were afraid to face God and hear his voice at Mount Sinai, they pleaded with Moses to talk to God for them. No less than seven times Moses went up to the mountain to speak to God for the people. For 40 years Moses served as mediator between God and the Israelite nation. But his mediation came to an end. The covenant God established through him also came to an end. It served only a single nation. What is more, it could not save. Christ served as mediator of a new covenant, a covenant effected for all nations, all people, a covenant that offers and freely gives eternal salvation, a covenant that has no end.

In both of the previous passages the holy writers refer to the Savior by the name that especially indicates office, the name Christ, that is, the Anointed. He is called the Anointed One already by the psalmist: "The kings of the earth take their stand and the rulers gather together against the LORD and against his Anointed One" (Ps 2:2). John the Baptist was careful not to be confused with the one of whom the psalmist had spoken: "He did not fail to confess, but he confessed freely, 'I am not the Christ'" (Jn 1:20). On Pentecost, Peter was emphatic in proclaiming Jesus of Nazareth as the one of whom the prophets had spoken: "Let all Israel be assured of this: God has made this Jesus, whom you crucified, both Lord and Christ" (Ac 2:36). To Cornelius, Peter went on to explain "how God anointed Jesus of Nazareth with the Holy Spirit and power, and how he went around doing good and healing all who were under the power of the devil, because God was with him" (Ac 10:38).

The anointing of which Peter speaks is only in Jesus' human nature.

> Since he was anointed with the oil of gladness, that is, with the Holy Spirit, by God the Father, so he was also called Christ. And he certainly was anointed not as God but as man; even though he administered the office to which he was anointed not only according to his human, but also according to his divine nature. For he is called anointed "above his fellows" (Ps 45:7), but according to his divine nature he does not have "fellows."[1]

Though Jesus' baptism by John the Baptist presents Jesus publicly as the promised Messiah, it is not the first anointing. Jesus' anointing took

---

[1]Gottfried Hoffmann, *Middler Dogmatic Notes* (Wisconsin Lutheran Seminary, 1985), p. 169.

place from the time of his conception and birth. That is the way Isaiah foretold it: "For to us a child is born, to us a son is given, and the government will be on his shoulders. And he will be called Wonderful Counselor, Mighty God, Everlasting Father, Prince of Peace" (Isa 9:6). That is the way the angel of God proclaimed it to the shepherds: "Today in the town of David a Savior has been born to you; he is Christ the Lord" (Lk 2:11). Their testimony is confirmed by the apostle Paul: "When the time had fully come, God sent his Son, born of a woman, born under law, to redeem those under law, that we might receive the full rights of sons" (Gal 4:4,5). In fact, Jesus' baptism conferred no additional spiritual power upon him. Rather, his baptism conferred the idea of unlimited imparting of the Holy Spirit upon Christ according to his human nature. It declared Jesus to be the one appointed by God to repair the damage done by Satan. "Jesus replied, 'Let it be so now; it is proper for us to do this to fulfill all righteousness.' Then John consented. And a voice from heaven said, 'This is my Son, whom I love; with him I am well pleased'" (Mt 3:15,17). It confirmed his qualifications to reunite the human race with God.

Just as Jesus' anointing took place from the time of his conception and birth, so also his circumcision and presentation in the temple were already part of his mediatorial work for the salvation of mankind. "On the eighth day, when it was time to circumcise him, he was named Jesus, the name the angel had given him before he had been conceived" (Lk 2:21). By his circumcision he fulfilled the law not for himself but for sinners. Luke declares the same for his presentation. "When the time of their purification according to the Law of Moses had been completed, Joseph and Mary took him to Jerusalem to present him to the Lord (as it is written in the Law of the Lord, 'Every firstborn male is to be consecrated to the Lord')" (Lk 2:22,23).

He who is the Son of God, Lord of lords, Alpha and Omega, was appointed to office, to be the Christ, the Messiah. He possesses every qualification possible for this high office, Immanuel, the Way, the Resurrection, and the Life. Though some have spoken of a twofold office of Christ, Priest and King, it is customary for us to speak of a threefold office, Prophet, Priest, and King.

> As many as are the divisions in which it is possible to refer the names which are ascribed to the office of Christ by the mind, and the teaching of Scripture which are spoken concerning the office of Christ, so many parts stand to the office of Christ. . . . Because of the ignorance of the mind through the introduction of sin, we stood in need of a teacher or prophet. Because of sin and the punishment of sin we were in need of a priest, reconciling us to God; making satisfaction for us and interceding before the tribunal of God. Because of

the infirmity of the will we were in need of a king leading and defending us.[2]

The Old Testament declared him to be such. "I will raise up for them a prophet like you from among their brothers; I will put my words in his mouth, and he will tell them everything I command him" (Dt 18:18). "The LORD has sworn and will not change his mind: 'You are a priest forever, in the order of Melchizedek'" (Ps 110:4). "I have installed my King on Zion, my holy hill" (Ps 2:6). The New Testament reveals him in his offices. That will comprise the remainder of this study.

Before we begin this study, we must reflect on the importance of what we have said up to this point. The office of Christ has come under direct attack over the centuries. One must expect that many will continue to oppose it in the new millennium and as we move beyond the 150-year mark of our synod's history.

As soon as Christ had presented himself to John to be anointed publicly into office, Satan was there to resist him: "If you are the Son of God, tell these stones to become bread" (Mt 4:3). "If you are the Son of God . . . throw yourself down. For it is written: 'He will command his angels concerning you, and they will lift you up in their hands, so that you will not strike your foot against a stone'" (Mt 4:6). "All this I will give you . . . if you will bow down and worship me" (Mt 4:9). Satan also knows Scripture. He knows it but does not believe it. He knows just enough about Scripture to twist it and use it for his own cunning devices. Satan's misuse of God's Word goes all the way back to the beginning, when he said to Eve: "Did God really say, 'You must not eat from any tree in the garden'?" (Ge 3:1). Eve correctly quoted God's Word concerning the trees in the garden but in such a way that Satan found an opening to proceed from a question intended to raise doubt to a bold-faced lie, "You will not surely die" (Ge 3:4), and the rest is history.

Christ, Eve's offspring promised in the garden, met Satan's temptations in the wilderness by an exemplary use of Scriptures. "It is written: 'Man does not live on bread alone, but on every word that comes from the mouth of God'" (Mt 4:4). "It is also written, 'Do not put the Lord your God to the test'" (Mt 4:7). "For it is written: 'Worship the Lord your God, and serve him only'" (Mt 4:10).

Satan's attacks against the doctrine of Christ have not abated over the centuries: Arianism, Nestorianism, enthusiasm, rationalism, modernism, humanism, both ancient and present. Doubts concerning Christ's divine person, two natures, virgin birth, miracles, vicarious death and glorious resurrection and ascension persist. The church's defense against all heresies, big and small, is

---

[2]Johann Gerhard, *Middler Dogmatic Notes*, p. 170.

one: "It is written." It is the only way to doctrinal integrity, staunch confessionalism, a united voice.

It is only by God's grace that the WELS became a truly confessional church body. It took most of two decades to rid ourselves of unionistic tendencies. It has remained a confessional Lutheran church—for 150 years. During that time it has witnessed a steady erosion of Lutheran doctrine and practice all around. It has witnessed the demise of the Synodical Conference. Two thirds of all Lutherans in the United States and Canada have compromised one doctrine after another as they seek a wider fellowship, which now includes several Reformed churches and overtures to the Roman Catholic Church. Our former sister synod in the Synodical Conference has fallen into the very unionistic practices from which it helped free us in our early history.

One hundred and fifty years is a long time. It is especially long when we consider what has happened to most of Lutheranism in America and throughout the world as well. One hundred and fifty years exceeds the time between the writing of the Formula of Concord (1580) and the end of the age of orthodoxy in the land of the Reformation. It nearly equals the time from the writing of the first of the Lutheran Confessions, the Augsburg Confession, to the end of the age of orthodoxy.

The battle to remain a confessional Lutheran church has not been easy. We remain a confessional church only by God's grace and with a great sacrifice of time and energy. There are a few among us today who lived through the battle to save the Synodical Conference. It virtually consumed the leadership of our church body for most of two decades. It left deep scars on families, congregations, and the synod. At the same time, contending for the truth has made us stronger and will continue to make us stronger whenever it sends us back to the Scriptures, to say with our victorious Lord, "It is written."

It has not been easy. It won't get any easier. Satan has found the doctrine of Scripture to be the Achilles heel in the religious world today. *Sola Scriptura* is relegated to putting one's faith in a book. An inerrant Scripture is labeled unscientific. Truth is relative. Doctrinal integrity is living in the past. Staunch confessionalism is being close minded, arrogant, proud. It seems there has never been a time when so many within the pale of the visible church have had such a low view of Scripture. Even during the dark days before the Lutheran Reformation, there was a much higher view.

The stakes are high. Doctrines under the headings of theology, anthropology, soteriology, and eschatology all hang in the balance to the doctrine of Scripture. These include the church's teaching on origins, creation, angels and demons, the fall into sin, man's present state, faith, means of grace, justification, conversion, sanctification, church and ministry, fellowship, life and death, heaven and hell, and the final judgment. All, properly taught and believed, are sacred truths. None can endure in the hearts and lives of Christians without a correct doctrine of Scripture. But at greatest risk of all is the study of Christology, teachings concerning Christ, his person, office, and work. Without the latter, the former have no basis.

One hundred and fifty years of being a confessional church body means nothing for the future if we do not remain committed to the Scriptures and the Lutheran Confessions. "It is written" must remain the battle cry as we step into the 21st century. I doubt that anyone would stand in this place today and predict what will be the next battle that will have to be fought in order to remain true to the doctrine of Christ and all the teachings of Scripture. Even as we approach this milestone in our synod's history, we continue to contend for pure teaching on church and ministry, church fellowship, and the role of man and woman, to name those that have fallen into complete disfavor and disarray in the church bodies around us and that we have restudied intensively in recent years.

As we pass from one century and one millennium to the next and as we prepare to celebrate 150 years as a synod, may we go with firm conviction in the Savior's words: "If you hold to my teaching, you are really my disciples. Then you will know the truth, and the truth will set you free" (Jn 8:31,32). May every step of preparation and celebration be fully in tune with the words of the sainted WELS pastor Kurt J. Eggert:

> Not unto us, not unto us be glory, Lord;
> Not unto us but to your name be praise;
> Not unto us but to your name all honor be giv'n
> For matchless mercy, forgiveness, and grace. (CW 392:1)

Christ, the Prophet

What is the measure of a man? Is it the offices he holds, the number of offices, a certain combination of offices, or the importance of any one of those offices? Occasionally I tune in to a television program on current, usually controversial, political events, called *One on One*. The leader, John McLaughlin, regularly provides a profile of the guest or guests on his show. Without fail, the profiles are long. At times the profiles seem as long as, and more impressive than, the discussion to follow. The profile does not always seem to be the true measure of the person. My listening may not last much beyond the profile.

The offices of Christ are a true measure of the man. Whether the number of offices, a combination of offices, or the importance of any one of those offices—Christ is incomparably great on all counts. Christ is Prophet, Priest, and King. Each office was prominent among God's people. At times a man functioned in a combination of these offices. A priest, by the very nature of his office, both made sacrifices upon the altar and taught the people. Therefore one can easily combine the offices of priest and prophet into a single office. David served as both king and prophet but always with distinct limitations. Only in Christ are all three offices combined. Combination of offices aside, it is impossible to do justice to the threefold office of Christ without looking at each office individually, though Christ filled each office routinely and perfectly at the same time.

As we had already begun to note, Christ was declared to be a prophet. "The LORD your God will raise up for you a prophet like me from among your own brothers. You must listen to him" (Dt 18:15). In numerous places the Old Testament Scriptures spell out the prophetical work of the Lord's anointed. We cite a couple of the more familiar ones from the prophet Isaiah. "Here is my servant, whom I uphold, my chosen one in whom I delight; I will put my Spirit on him and he will bring justice to the nations. He will not shout or cry out, or raise his voice in the streets. A bruised reed he will not break, and a smoldering wick he will not snuff out. In faithfulness he will bring forth justice" (Isa 42:1-3). "See, I have made him a witness to the peoples, a leader and commander of the peoples. Surely you will summon nations you know not, and nations that do not know you will hasten to you, because of the LORD your God, the Holy One of Israel, for he has endowed you with splendor" (Isa 55:4,5).

What the writers of the Old Testament foretold, the New Testament Scriptures announce repeatedly. After the raising of the young man at Nain (Lk 7:16), at the Feast of the Tabernacles (Jn 7:40), and at the entrance of Jesus into Jerusalem on Palm Sunday (Mt 21:11), the people concluded that Jesus was a prophet. The Samaritan woman (Jn 4:19) and the Emmaus disciples (Lk 24:19) could come to no other conclusion but that Jesus is the Prophet whom Scripture foretold.

On almost every page of the writings of the evangelists, Jesus is busy doing the work of a prophet. "From that time on Jesus began to preach, 'Repent, for the kingdom of heaven is near'" (Mt 4:17). Such is the case in the instances cited. In Judea, Samaria, and Galilee and beyond, in the cities and out in the country, on the mountain, in the temple, in their synagogues, by the side of a pool, in a Pharisee's house, wherever he went and while he was on the way, he taught the people. He chose 12 disciples in order that he might teach them and prepare them for teaching others. When the crowd pressed down on him, he taught from a boat (Lk 5:3). When they stayed with him too long and lost track of time, he fed multitudes with a minimum of provisions (Jn 6:1-15; Mt 15:29-39). Even an interruption of his privacy and rest became an opportunity to teach (Mk 6:31).

Jesus proclaimed himself to be the Prophet. At the synagogue of his hometown, he applied to himself the well-known words of Isaiah: "The Spirit of the Lord is on me, because he has anointed me to preach good news to the poor. He has sent me to proclaim freedom for the prisoners and recovery of sight for the blind, to release the oppressed, to proclaim the year of the Lord's favor" (Lk 4:18,19). During that week of weeks, when the hour of his death was just days away, he told the unbelieving Jews: "I did not speak of my own accord, but the Father who sent me commanded me what to say and how to say it. I know that his command leads to eternal life. So whatever I say is just what the Father has told me to say" (Jn 12:49,50). To the glory of his Father's name and for the comfort of his disciples who were still by his side, Jesus prayed to his Father in his high priestly prayer: "I gave them the words you gave me and they accepted them. They knew with certainty that I came from you, and they believed that you sent me. I have given them your word and the world has hated them, for they are not of the world any more than I am of the world. I have made you known to them, and will continue to make you known in order that the love you have for me may be in them and that I myself may be in them" (Jn 17:8,14,26).

Inasmuch as Jesus was anointed into office from his conception and birth, it follows that he should be called a prophet from birth. "Before I formed you in the womb I knew you, before you were born I set you apart; I appointed you as a prophet to the nations. 'Ah, Sovereign LORD,' I said, 'I do not know how to speak; I am only a child.' But the LORD said to me, 'Do not say, "I am only a child." You must go to everyone I send you to and say whatever I command you. Do not be afraid of them, for I am with you and will rescue you,' declares the LORD" (Jer 1:5-8). Though the prophet speaks of his own prophetic office, Jesus is all the more the Prophet from birth.

Unlike all the prophets who preceded his coming and pointed to him, Christ spoke with divine authority. When Jews at the Feast of the Tabernacles had challenged Jesus authority, he answered: "My teaching is not my own. It comes from him who sent me. If anyone chooses to do God's will, he will find out whether my teaching comes from God or whether I speak on my own. He who speaks on his own does so to gain honor for himself, but he who works for the honor of the one who sent him is a man of truth" (Jn 7:16-18). The temple guards who were then ordered by the chief priests and Pharisees to arrest Jesus returned empty handed and explained, "No one ever spoke the way this man does" (Jn 7:46). On the next day Jesus continued his authoritative teaching: "If you hold to my teaching, you are really my disciples. So if the Son sets you free, you will be free indeed. I am telling you what I have seen in the Father's presence, and you do what you have heard from your father" (Jn 8:31,36,38).

Jesus' message as Prophet did not change. From the beginning of his ministry, Jesus preached, "Repent, for the kingdom of heaven is near" (Mt 4:17). Acknowledge sin and believe the good news! Jesus' message was both law and gospel.

Jesus also preached law to make sinners conscious of sin and guilt:

> On one occasion an expert in the law stood up to test Jesus. "Teacher," he asked, "what must I do to inherit eternal life?"

"What is written in the Law?" he replied. "How do you read it?"

He answered: " 'Love the Lord your God with all your heart and with all your soul and with all your strength and with all your mind'; and, 'Love your neighbor as yourself.' "

"You have answered correctly," Jesus replied. "Do this and you will live." (Lk 10:25-28)

Jesus also preached the law as a guide for Christian living (Mt 5). But always Jesus' preaching of the law was his "other" work. "Do not think I will accuse you before the Father. Your accuser is Moses, on whom your hopes are set" (Jn 5:45).

Jesus' real work was always the gospel. "The law was given through Moses; grace and truth came through Jesus Christ" (Jn 1:17). From his headquarters in Capernaum, Jesus announced, "I must preach the good news of the kingdom of God to the other towns also, because that is why I was sent" (Lk 4:43). Even when he speaks of "doing" the will of God and "obeying" his word, Jesus is urging sinners to believe in him and live accordingly. "We know that God does not listen to sinners. He listens to the godly man who does his will" (Jn 9:31). "Whoever has my commands and obeys them, he is the one who loves me. He who loves me will be loved by my Father, and I too will love him and show myself to him" (Jn 14:21).

The purpose of his message is to enlighten and convert sinners. "I tell you the truth, a time is coming and has now come when the dead will hear the voice of the Son of God and those who hear will live" (Jn 5:25). "I am the light of the world. Whoever follows me will never walk in darkness, but will have the light of life" (Jn 8:12). "My sheep listen to my voice; I know them, and they follow me. I give them eternal life, and they shall never perish; no one can snatch them out of my hand" (Jn 10:27,28).

Jesus, the Prophet of Galilee, is the Prophet of the entire world. It is true, during his state of exinanition, his teaching was limited to Israel. "I was sent only to the lost sheep of Israel" (Mt 15:24). He sent out his disciples with the firm instructions "Do not go among the Gentiles or enter any town of the Samaritans" (Mt 10:5). Christ had come as a "servant of the Jews on behalf of God's truth, to confirm the promises made to the patriarchs" (Ro 15:8). Yes, Christ was a Savior first to the Jews, but never to the exclusion of the rest of the world, as Paul assured the Romans: "I am not ashamed of the gospel, because it is the power of God for the salvation of everyone who believes: first for the Jew, then for the Gentile" (Ro 1:16). Even during his time of exinanition, Jesus showed himself to be the Savior of Gentiles when he reached out to save a Roman centurion (Lk 7:1-10), a Canaanite woman (Mt 15:21-28), and a Samaritan woman at Jacob's well (Jn 4:1-26).

We Believe in Jesus Christ

Not only is Jesus' message good news for a dying world; it is the only message for the entire world. "Salvation is found in no one else, for there is no other name under heaven given to men by which we must be saved" (Ac 4:12). Other religions may contain elements of truth to the extent that they are based on the natural knowledge of God. But what is not of Christ is of works of man. What is of works always leaves sinners without peace, without comfort, without hope in this world and the life to come.

The office of Christ as Prophet has lost none of its importance as we move toward another milestone in our synod's history and as we step into another millennium. Christ continues to be the Prophet. He continues to do his work. He continues to proclaim the message that is able to save. Today he does his work through his church. Two thousand years ago he said to his disciples, to believers, to his church, to us, Go, preach, be my witnesses, baptize and teach . . . into all the world, to all nations, to all creation, to the very end of the age (Mk 16:15; Mt 28:18-20; Ac 1:8).

Christ's office as Prophet has urgency written all over it. It proclaims the love and mercy of a gracious God to condemned sinners. It offers and gives peace where there is complete separation (Ro 5:1), comfort where there is only distress (2 Co 1:5), light where there is utter darkness (Jn 1:5), and hope where there is abject despair (Eph 2:12,13).

We cannot claim that the work of Christ's prophetic office is any more urgent today than it was two thousand years ago, unless we are thinking of the growing world population and the fact that judgment day is drawing closer with each passing day. The work was no less urgent when Christ gave the divine commission. Souls were no less precious to the Savior. Souls today have the same eternal value. The urgency continues.

One could build a valid case for greater urgency, however. With the turning away from God's Word of Truth to lofty human opinions, views on the church's mission and the building of Christ's church in today's world is changing. Sin is no longer sin. Sin is no longer considered man's great dilemma. Sin is purely a temporal matter. Sin is more and more something that others commit against me instead of that which I commit against God. Sin is, for the most part, that which causes human suffering. Sin no longer has any real eternal consequences.

If sin is no longer sin, if it has no eternal consequences before a holy and just God, the gospel is no longer gospel. The moral betterment of man and society becomes the mission of the modern church. In order to realize any moral improvement, the church must become more sensitive to man's felt needs, whatever the individual might perceive them to be. The person in the pew is conditioned to look to the church for anything that makes him feel good and offers some temporal advantage for the shorter or longer haul.

As we move from millennium to millennium, from one century to another, from one decade to another, from one district convention to another, we must recognize the urgency of our mission. We do not exist merely as a guardian of Christian doctrine. Our mission statement does not stop at the exit sign of our church parking lot or the boundary line of our property, church, or home. The church's mission has not changed: "Go into all the world and preach the good news to all creation" (Mk 16:15). The gospel message is intended for all of those for whom Christ died. Regardless of race, culture, nationality, social status, the gospel is "the power of God for the salvation of everyone who believes" (Ro 1:16). True, there are many other churches with a message to share, but so many offer little more than a social gospel. There are many other churches that have ambitious outreach programs but are compromising precious truths of Scripture. That unfortunate combination only intensifies the need for us to take to heart the Lord's Great Commission.

We need to rid ourselves of any notion that confessionalism and mission-mindedness are somehow incompatible or that being a confessional church body takes away some of the urgency to reach out with the gospel. Looking back in the history of our synod, it may seem that there were times when love for truth and mission outreach were mutually exclusive. There was the struggle to become a confessional church body. There were battles fought, and by God's grace won, to remain true to God's Word. Mission outreach during this time, especially the first one hundred years, might seem pale when compared to the last 30 to 40 years. But immigration of German Lutherans to the Midwest provided a genuine mission field. There were ambitious building programs to provide places for worship and the Christian training of the children. A sound system for training future workers was established. To this day we reap the harvest of this solid work. Besides, there were extenuating circumstances. The typical WELS family was far less affluent. Many were starting over in a new country. There were two world wars and a great depression.

But love for truth and love for missions were not incompatible then. They are not incompatible now. There is no better example with which to reassure ourselves of this than the life and ministry of the apostle Paul. No one is able to question Paul's missionary zeal. Paul himself could not have realized the impact of the Lord's response on his life and the lives of others when Paul asked: "What shall I do, Lord?" (Ac 22:10). No amount of opposition and persecution were able to prevent this world's greatest missionary from preaching the gospel from city to city, country to country, and finally in a prison cell. Love, love for his Savior, love for the truth of the gospel, and love for souls, set him on a course that would consume his life and end in an untimely death.

It was both a love for missions and a love for the truth. Paul's love for the truth may be seen from the manner in which he dealt with error and false teachers. There was no compromise. False teachings were immediately condemned, as can be noted in Paul's epistles to the Galatians, the Corinthians,

We Believe in Jesus Christ

and the Colossians. False teachers were exposed, sometimes even identified by name (2 Ti 2:17). Paul warned believers to have nothing to do with the false teachers and to separate themselves from those who taught or tolerated false teaching (Ro 16:17; Tit 3:9-11).

Paul's love for the truth is apparent in various exhortations found in his pastoral epistles. "He [an elder] must hold firmly to the trustworthy message as it has been taught, so that he can encourage others by sound doctrine and refute those who oppose it" (Tit 1:9). "Preach the Word; be prepared in season and out of season; correct, rebuke and encourage—with great patience and careful instruction. For the time will come when men will not put up with sound doctrine" (2 Ti 4:2,3). "If you point these things out to the brothers, you will be a good minister of Christ Jesus, brought up in the truths of the faith and of the good teaching that you have followed" (1 Ti 4:6).

We have a message to proclaim. It is a message the world desperately needs to hear. The WELS is a community of Christians that has been richly blessed. We are spiritually blessed. A deep love for the truth of the gospel is included in the long list of spiritual blessings. And we are temporally blessed. America is a prosperous country. WELS Christians share in that wealth. Any affluence our forefathers may have lacked has been poured out upon us. We have the means to reach out with the gospel such as no generation before us. There is no reason for hard choices between home projects and mission outreach, between thorough Christian training of the young and church planting throughout our country, between thorough training of future workers in the public ministry and world missions. The Lord has given us the means to do it all and do it well. He has given us a love for the truth. May he also give us the resolve, the will, and the eagerness to sacrifice our time, our treasure, and our talents to share the truth that sets men free.

> O faithful love—that shepherded through faithless years;
> Forgiving love—that led us to your truth;
> Unyielding love—that would not let us turn from you
> But sent us forth to speak pardon and peace. (CW 392:3)

Christ, the Priest

The gospel which Christ proclaims as Prophet He Himself established as Priest. His prophetic message is dependent on His priestly work. If He as Priest produced a partial salvation, He can as Prophet proclaim only a partial salvation. If He produced a conditional justification, He can as Prophet do no more than announce the condition. As Priest He did not provide a justification which we receive only after meeting certain conditions, He provided a justification complete in every

respect, which He proclaims as a ready blessing and which we
receive as such through faith.[3]

The office of Christ as Prophet is important. Our eternal salvation is
linked directly to it. We will note the same for his office as King. We must
insist, nevertheless, that the office of Christ as Priest is critical. Without his
office as Priest, his offices as Prophet and King leave us destitute, separated
from God, under wrath and judgment. It is the office of Priest that has been
and continues to be the most difficult for people to acknowledge and accept.

When Jesus proclaimed himself the Prophet of Galilee, not everyone
was ready to accept him. Many were doubtful, some even furious with him
(Lk 4:28,29). Members of his own family thought him to be out of his mind
(Mk 3:20,21). The opposition of the chief priests and Pharisees is well
known. But the fact is that multitudes did turn out to see him, stayed with
him for days at a time, and followed him from place to place (Jn 6). Granted,
some did it for the wrong reasons; some were more interested in the miracles, in temporal advantages. Most turned away in the end. But many did
hear and were impressed by his teaching. They were ready to say that he was
a prophet, comparable to any of the great prophets of old (Mt 16:13-28).

One could make a similar claim for Jesus' office as King. The people of
Jesus' day had high millennialistic hopes. They longed for a king to come and
deliver them from social and political oppression. Many were waiting for
Jesus to make his move and claim himself a national hero. Jesus' own disciples held to fuzzy notions concerning the nature of Jesus' kingdom and cov-
eted and quarreled over positions of importance (Mt 20:20-28). It comes as no
great surprise when the crowds proclaimed him king as he entered Jerusalem
on Palm Sunday.

But priest—at least the kind of priest Jesus claimed to be—was out of the
question, not a matter for serious consideration. Not that the office of priest
was unfamiliar. It was the most familiar from their Old Testament worship.
The priesthood, with the office of the high priest, was the one constant office
for them. The age of kings had passed. Prophets came and went. The priest
was usually there, in the temple, doing his assigned work. So also the high
priest. He was their spiritual leader. The priest offered the daily sacrifices in
the temple. He spoke the prayers and offered the incense. He presided on the
festival days and offered more sacrifices.

Jesus came as Priest, and they missed it. They missed it then, and until
this day people are more easily excited with the idea of a prophet or a king
than they are with a priest. They missed it because Jesus had so much more
to offer than any priest before him. As Priest (as also Prophet and King for

---

[3] John P. Meyer, *Middler Dogmatic Notes*, p. 173.

We Believe in Jesus Christ

that matter), Jesus is one of a kind. He is the great High Priest. "We have a great high priest, who has gone through the heavens, Jesus the Son of God" (Heb 4:14). He never sacrificed a lamb or a bull, a dove or grain offering. He sacrificed himself. John the Baptist had it right: "Look, the Lamb of God, who takes away the sin of the world!" (Jn 1:29). He was both Priest and Lamb, Sacrificer and Sacrifice. These words of John at the very beginning of Jesus' ministry bring immediately to mind Isaiah's description of God's Suffering Servant (Isa 53).

How difficult was it for the people to accept the idea of Christ as Priest? Jesus' own disciples had their problems. Repeatedly Jesus announced that he must suffer and die, but they could never quite accept the idea. We recall the occasion when Peter took his Lord aside and said: "Never, Lord! . . . This shall never happen to you!" (Mt 16:22). Peter earned Jesus' sternest rebuke for his well-intentioned notion: "Get behind me, Satan! You are a stumbling block to me; you do not have in mind the things of God, but the things of men" (Mt 16:23). To this day it goes against man's human nature to be told that he needs such a Priest, that he must depend upon another, Christ, for his salvation. Tell him he must look within himself, be religious, prove himself worthy, do something, deny himself, and man will believe it.

We cannot stress too much the importance of Jesus' high priestly work. The importance of Jesus' office as Priest is apparent from both the names and descriptions of his office. Already the psalmist called him Priest: "You are a priest forever, in the order of Melchizedek" (Ps 110:4). The prophet Zechariah linked Jesus' priestly office with his office as King: "It is he who will build the temple of the LORD, and he will be clothed with majesty and will sit and rule on his throne. And he will be a priest on his throne. And there will be harmony between the two" (Zec 6:13). The writer to the Hebrews links it with his prophetical office. "Therefore, holy brothers, who share in the heavenly calling, fix your thoughts on Jesus, the apostle and high priest whom we confess" (Heb 3:1). The same writer, who speaks at length of Jesus' high priestly office, captures the uniqueness of the office when he states, "For this reason he had to be made like his brothers in every way, in order that he might become a merciful and faithful high priest in service to God, and that he might make atonement for the sins of the people" (2:17).

Since the purpose of the priesthood is to restore communion between the sinner and the God whom he has offended, Christ's priestly office is referred to by still other names. We noted two of these previously in passing. One is *mediator*: "To Jesus the mediator of a new covenant, and to the sprinkled blood that speaks a better word than the blood of Abel" (Heb 12:24). Another is *Lamb of God*. "You know that it was not with perishable things such as silver and gold that you were redeemed from the empty way of life handed down to you from your forefathers, but with the precious blood of Christ, a lamb without blemish or defect" (1 Pe 1:18,19). This passage refers to yet another name, *Redeemer.* "This is what the LORD says—Israel's King and Redeemer, the LORD Almighty: I am the first and I am the last; apart from me there is no God" (Isa 44:6).

In keeping with these names—Mediator, Lamb of God, and Redeemer—priestly functions such as sacrifice, intercession, and benediction are ascribed to Jesus. He himself is the supreme sacrifice. "How much more, then, will the blood of Christ, who through the eternal Spirit offered himself unblemished to God, cleanse our consciences from acts that lead to death, so that we may serve the living God! Then Christ would have had to suffer many times since the creation of the world. But now he has appeared once for all at the end of the ages to do away with sin by the sacrifice of himself" (Heb 9:14,26). As a true priest he made intercession for his people. "During the days of Jesus' life on earth, he offered up prayers and petitions with loud cries and tears to the one who could save him from death, and he was heard because of his reverent submission" (Heb 5:7). Blessing was his parting high priestly act. "When he had led them out to the vicinity of Bethany, he lifted up his hands and blessed them. While he was blessing them, he left them and was taken up into heaven" (Lk 24:50,51).

Many times the priestly office is expressed in terms of obedience. "When the time had fully come, God sent his Son, born of a woman, born under law, to redeem those under law, that we might receive the full rights of sons" (Gal 4:4,5). Though it was a real submission to the law, it was first and foremost a submission to his Father's will. "I have come down from heaven not to do my will but to do the will of him who sent me" (Jn 6:38). It was a free and full submission to the law, yet all the while he remained Lord of the law, "who, being in very nature God, did not consider equality with God something to be grasped. . . . And being found in appearance as a man, he humbled himself and became obedient to death—even death on a cross!" (Php 2:6,8).

The obedience of which Scripture speaks is active. Christ acted not as a boss or a foreman standing at a distance, supervising or giving orders. He was on the job, working, sweaty, with callused hands, dirty fingernails, and all. "Do not think that I have come to abolish the Law or the Prophets; I have not come to abolish them but to fulfill them" (Mt 5:17). And Christ's obedience is passive: "By that will, we have been made holy through the sacrifice of the body of Jesus Christ once for all" (Heb 10:10). Active or passive, his obedience was always vicarious, not for himself but in the place of others, as the substitute for sinners.

> Since we have now been justified by his blood, how much
> more shall we be saved from God's wrath through him! For
> if, when we were God's enemies, we were reconciled to him
> through the death of his Son, how much more, having been

reconciled, shall we be saved through his life! Consequently, just as the result of one trespass was condemnation for all men, so also the result of one act of righteousness was justification that brings life for all men. For just as through the disobedience of the one man the many were made sinners, so also through the obedience of the one man the many will be made righteous. (Ro 5:9,10,18,19)

The vicarious nature of Christ's obedience is set forth in a variety of ways, with the use of prepositions. "Just as the Son of Man did not come to be served, but to serve, and to give his life as a ransom for many" (Mt 20:28). "You do not realize that it is better for you that one man die for the people than that the whole nation perish" (Jn 11:50). It is called a sacrifice, as we have already noted under priestly functions, and a ransom, as noted in the previous passage.

Scripture holds up the high priestly work for our review when it states the blessed results of his high priestly work. Though it does not use the word *satisfaction*, it assures with many passages that all the demands of God's righteousness have been fully met. "It is because of him that you are in Christ Jesus, who has become for us wisdom from God—that is, our righteousness, holiness and redemption" (1 Co 1:30). It is called a *propitiation*, or a covering for sin. "He is the atoning sacrifice for our sins, and not only for ours but also for the sins of the whole world" (1 Jn 2:2). Another term, which is very close to the thought of satisfaction and propitiation, is *reconciliation*. "All this is from God, who reconciled us to himself through Christ and gave us the ministry of reconciliation: that God was reconciling the world to himself in Christ, not counting men's sins against them. And he has committed to us the message of reconciliation" (2 Co 5:18,19). Yet another term is *peace*. "He himself is our peace, who has made the two one and has destroyed the barrier, the dividing wall of hostility. He came and preached peace to you who were far away and peace to those who were near" (Eph 2:14,17). All these terms express a similar idea. All can be used interchangeably. Yet each one adds its own dimension to underscore the grand result of Christ's work.

When speaking of the blessed results of Jesus' high priestly work, we must also stress the completeness of that work. It is a very popular notion within visible Christianity to think in terms of a Savior who helps man on the way to salvation. The opinion of the law *(opinio legis)* is strong within the human heart. It is the notion that man must do something to merit, earn, win, in order to be sure of his salvation. Roman Catholicism insists on it with its teaching of a free will in natural man that is able to choose the good, a justification by faith that is never alone, cooperation in conversion, sacrifice of the Mass, and sacramental system (seven sacraments). Reformed theology undermines the completeness of Christ's high priestly work with its teaching of limited atonement (Calvinism), decision theology (Arminianism), and emphasis on sanctification at the expense of justification. Each in its own way stresses the "Christ in us" in place of the "Christ for us."

The salvation won for us by Christ is complete in every respect. It is complete intensively. All sins have been paid for; a perfect righteousness has been procured.

> If it is preached that Christ has been raised from the dead, how can some of you say that there is no resurrection of the dead? If there is no resurrection of the dead, then not even Christ has been raised. And if Christ has not been raised, our preaching is useless and so is your faith. More than that, we are then found to be false witnesses about God, for we have testified about God that he raised Christ from the dead. But he did not raise him if in fact the dead are not raised. For if the dead are not raised, then Christ has not been raised either. And if Christ has not been raised, your faith is futile; you are still in your sins. Then those also who have fallen asleep in Christ are lost. If only for this life we have hope in Christ, we are to be pitied more than all men.

> But Christ has indeed been raised from the dead, the first-fruits of those who have fallen asleep. (1 Co 15:12-20)

The salvation Christ won is complete also extensively. The extent of Christ's high priestly work is as common as the word *all.* "Consequently, just as the result of one trespass was condemnation for all men, so also the result of one act of righteousness was justification that brings life for all men" (Ro 5:18). "Christ's love compels us, because we are convinced that one died for all, and therefore all died" (2 Co 5:14). ". . . through him to reconcile to himself all things, whether things on earth or things in heaven, by making peace through his blood, shed on the cross" (Col 1:20). The "all" that Paul refers to is also expressed with words such as *world, people, sinners, lost,* and even *many.* "God so loved the world" (Jn 3:16). "Christ was sacrificed once to take away the sins of many people" (Heb 9:28). "Christ Jesus came into the world to save sinners" (1 Ti 1:15). "The Son of Man came to seek and to save what was lost" (Lk 19:10)." "The Son of Man did not come to be served, but to serve, and to give his life as a ransom for many" (Mt 20:28).

The offices of Christ are unique, not only for what Christ has done but also for what he continues to do for his church. As Prophet, Christ not only preached the everlasting gospel but he continues to equip his church for the work of the ministry. As Priest, Christ offered up himself as the sacrifice for sin once and for all. "Unlike the other high priests, he does not need to offer sacrifices day after day, first for his own sins, and then for the sins of the people.

He sacrificed for their sins once for all when he offered himself" (Heb 7:27). Following this completed work, our great High Priest assumed again the glory that was his from eternity. Nevertheless, Christ continues to serve as our great High Priest. At the Father's right hand he carries on his sacerdotal work by making intercession for us. "Because Jesus lives forever, he has a permanent priesthood. Therefore he is able to save completely those who come to God through him, because he always lives to intercede for them" (Heb 7:24,25).

Even in his state of humiliation Christ made intercession for sinners—for his enemies: "Jesus said, 'Father, forgive them, for they do not know what they are doing'" (Lk 23:34); for his disciples: "I have prayed for you, Simon, that your faith may not fail. And when you have turned back, strengthen your brothers" (Lk 22:32); and for his church: "My prayer is not for them alone. I pray also for those who will believe in me through their message" (Jn 17:20).

Though nothing is revealed about the manner of his intercession in his state of exaltation, the intercession is real. "My dear children, I write this to you so that you will not sin. But if anybody does sin, we have one who speaks to the Father in our defense—Jesus Christ, the Righteous One" (1 Jn 2:1). The apostle Paul ties Christ's present work of intercession directly to his completed work of redemption. "Who is he that condemns? Christ Jesus, who died—more than that, who was raised to life—is at the right hand of God and is also interceding for us" (Ro 8:34). Christ died. Christ rose. Christ intercedes for us.

Christ's intercession complements in every way the tender care of the third person of the Holy Trinity. On the evening before his death, Christ comforted his troubled disciples: "I will ask the Father, and he will give you another Counselor to be with you forever. But the Counselor, the Holy Spirit, whom the Father will send in my name, will teach you all things and will remind you of everything I have said to you" (Jn 14:16,26). The counsel of the Holy Spirit is invaluable as he testifies about Christ (Jn 15:26), searches the hearts of the saints (Ro 8:27), helps us in our weakness, and intercedes for us with groans that words cannot express (Ro 8:26). All the while that the Holy Spirit comes to us and comforts our hearts by the gospel, Christ, according to both natures, intercedes for us from his exalted throne in heaven. His intercession will continue all the way to judgment day, when his mediatorship will have achieved its purpose. "Then the end will come, when he hands over the kingdom to God the Father after he has destroyed all dominion, authority and power" (1 Co 15:24). The fruits of his intercession for us will endure forever. "He is able to save completely those who come to God through him, because he always lives to intercede for them" (Heb 7:25).

We have discussed the result of Christ's high priestly work. We have noted terms used by the Scriptures and Lutheran dogmaticians to describe those results: satisfaction, propitiation, reconciliation, atonement. Granted, these words require some definition, explanation, even illustration when we use them in our preaching and teaching. But they are words that are essential when discussing and holding fast to everything that is involved and included in Christ's high priestly work. Another word that must be mentioned is *justification.*

Justification, more than any other, is the doctrine upon which the church stands or falls. It is this doctrine, above all others, that identifies Dr. Martin Luther's reformation. Luther called this doctrine the head and cornerstone of the church and went on to say that without it the church of God cannot subsist for one hour. The dogmatic notes of sainted Professor John P. Meyer are still used at Wisconsin Lutheran Seminary. In them Professor Meyer identifies justification as the central doctrine of the gospel and goes on to describe the relation of justification to other doctrines:

- to law and sin, necessitating it
- to God, in love preparing it
- to Christ and his work, laying the foundation
- to the church—the congregation of the justified
- to Word and sacraments, proclaiming and sealing it
- to sanctification (in all its ramifications)—the fruit
- to the salvation of man and the glory of God—its end[4]

Justification is rightly called the chief doctrine of the Lutheran church. When someone asks what the difference is between Lutherans and other Christian denominations, one could very well begin with a discussion of the doctrine of justification.

On this basis alone one has to say that any discussion of Christ's high priestly work would be incomplete without some discussion of the doctrine of justification. It is all the more important, even critical, for our discussion as we look ahead at this historic time in the history of the New Testament church and the milestone of our Wisconsin Evangelical Lutheran Synod. Most Lutherans today have drifted away from this important doctrine. Any departure from this doctrine severely devaluates Christ's work as Priest.

Justification is a term that takes us into the courtroom. It is a judicial, a forensic, term. We speak of the courtrooms of our land, on all levels—local, state, and federal—as halls of justice. In the courtroom, when all is said and done, it falls to the judge to find—declare—accused persons innocent or guilty. Whenever the innocent are declared innocent and set free or the guilty are declared guilty and punished in a manner relative to the crime committed, we would say that justice has been served. A judge who regularly does so, as far as humanly possible, is worthy of his office. A judge who fails to do so deserves impeachment.

---

[4]Meyer, *Senior Dogmatic Notes* (Wisconsin Lutheran Seminary, 1985), p. 117.

We Believe in Jesus Christ

The doctrine of justification takes us into the courtroom of God. But it is unlike any other courtroom. Sinners are the accused, and there is not an innocent one among them. "All have sinned and fall short of the glory of God" (Ro 3:23). God is holy and just. He must punish sin. He cannot overlook a single sin. To the amazement of everyone, God declares sinners righteous, innocent. Unbelievable!

It can't be. Sin must be punished. God's law demands it. "The soul who sins is the one who will die" (Eze 18:20). But the fact is, sin has been punished. God, who is gracious and merciful and does not desire the death of the sinner, made Christ, the great High Priest, to be sin in the sinner's place. "All have sinned and fall short of the glory of God, and are justified freely by his grace through the redemption that came by Christ Jesus" (Ro 3:23,24).

Which sinners did God declare righteous? When did the verdict take place? Genuine Lutherans have taught that God declared all sinners righteous. This took place at the resurrection of Jesus Christ, our Lamb and our Priest, from the dead. "He was delivered over to death for our sins and raised to life for our justification" (Ro 4:25). This we call universal and/or objective justification. A couple of the key passages for the when and whom of God's act of justification have already been noted. "Consequently, just as the result of one trespass was condemnation for all men, so also the result of one act of righteousness was justification that brings life for all men. For just as through the disobedience of the one man the many were made sinners, so also through the obedience of the one man the many will be made righteous" (Ro 5:18,19). Because of Adam's sin, a verdict of condemnation was passed upon all men. In the same way, because of our Priest's one act of righteousness, a verdict of acquittal was pronounced on all men.

> All this is from God, who reconciled us to himself through Christ and gave us the ministry of reconciliation: that God was reconciling the world to himself in Christ, not counting men's sins against them. And he has committed to us the message of reconciliation. We are therefore Christ's ambassadors, as though God were making his appeal through us. We implore you on Christ's behalf: Be reconciled to God. God made him who had no sin to be sin for us, so that in him we might become the righteousness of God. (2 Co 5:18-21)

The word used now is not *justification.* It is *reconciliation,* but it describes the very same act of God. The word speaks of a change, not in God, for God does not change, nor in man, for man remains ever the sinner. The change is in man's status before God. Again, reconciliation includes all. God reconciled the world to himself. He no longer counts men's sins against them. Again the cause for such reconciliation, for the world's justification, is clear. God made

Christ to be sin for us. Suffering and death as the substitute for sinners was part of the office. It was his great high priestly work.

Universal justification is objective. All cause for man's justification is found outside of man. Objective justification is universal. All, believers and unbelievers, have deserved God's wrath and eternal punishment. Christ was anointed as the substitute for all sinners. He died in the place of every sinner. When Jesus died, every sinner died. When Jesus rose, he rose as the substitute for every sinner. By his resurrection God declared sinners, all of them, righteous, reconciled. This is the message of the gospel. There are no words sweeter than the words "Your sins are forgiven; go in peace." No conditions are tied to the message. Not even faith is a condition to be met. Scripture promises: God does not count your sins against you. All sins are paid in full. Christ, the great High Priest of sinners, died in your place. Such is the message of universal, objective justification.

This is the message with which Christ sent his apostles into the world. In his high priestly prayer Jesus said of his disciples: "I gave them the words you gave me and they accepted them. They knew with certainty that I came from you, and they believed that you sent me" (Jn 17:8). Three days later Jesus commissioned them and his church for all time: " 'Peace be with you! As the Father has sent me, I am sending you.' And with that he breathed on them and said, 'Receive the Holy Spirit. If you forgive anyone his sins, they are forgiven; if you do not forgive them, they are not forgiven' " (Jn 20:21-23). "Then the disciples went out and preached everywhere, and the Lord worked with them and confirmed his word by the signs that accompanied it" (Mk 16:20).

Through this announcement objective justification becomes subjective. On the strength of God's promises in the doctrine of justification, Paul and Silas could say to the jailer at Philippi, "Believe in the Lord Jesus, and you will be saved—you and your household" (Ac 16:31). Writing to the Christians at Ephesus, Paul reminded them of their response when they first heard the message of reconciliation: "You also were included in Christ when you heard the word of truth, the gospel of your salvation. Having believed, you were marked in him with a seal, the promised Holy Spirit, who is a deposit guaranteeing our inheritance until the redemption of those who are God's possession—to the praise of his glory" (Eph 1:13,14). Luther captures the nature of the announcement of objective justification in his explanation of the Third Article of the Apostles' Creed:

> I believe that I cannot by my own thinking or choosing believe in Jesus Christ, my Lord, or come to him.
>
> But the Holy Spirit has called me by the gospel, enlightened me with his gifts, sanctified and kept me in the true faith. In the same way he calls, gathers, enlightens, and sanctifies the

whole Christian church on earth, and keeps it with Jesus Christ in the one true faith.

In this Christian church he daily and fully forgives all sins to me and all believers.

Through faith in the redemptive work of Christ, the great High Priest, sinners overcome the consciousness of divine wrath. God still hates sin. The law still condemns sinners to hell. And even Christians still need to hear God's law because of the old Adam, which clings to them and always tries to get the upper hand. But the one who has faith in Christ and his righteousness is no longer under law. "Christ is the end of the law so that there may be righteousness for everyone who believes" (Ro 10:4). "For sin shall not be your master, because you are not under law, but under grace" (Ro 6:14). Through faith in Christ's priestly work, Christians have the full rights of sons. "When the time had fully come, God sent his Son, born of a woman, born under law, to redeem those under law, that we might receive the full rights of sons" (Gal 4:4,5). The fear of law and punishment have been removed.

What, then, shall we say in response to this? If God is for us, who can be against us? He who did not spare his own Son, but gave him up for us all—how will he not also, along with him, graciously give us all things? Who will bring any charge against those whom God has chosen? It is God who justifies. Who is he that condemns? Christ Jesus, who died—more than that, who was raised to life—is at the right hand of God and is also interceding for us. Who shall separate us from the love of Christ? Shall trouble or hardship or persecution or famine or nakedness or danger or sword? As it is written: "For your sake we face death all day long; we are considered as sheep to be slaughtered." No, in all these things we are more than conquerors through him who loved us. For I am convinced that neither death nor life, neither angels nor demons, neither the present nor the future, nor any powers, neither height nor depth, nor anything else in all creation, will be able to separate us from the love of God that is in Christ Jesus our Lord. (Ro 8:31-39)

That is the gospel's message. No strings attached. No conditions. By grace alone. By faith alone. It is all wrapped up in Christ's high priestly work and the doctrine of justification. Sadly, the doctrine of justification has not fared well these latter days. The midpoint of the second millennium saw a return to the doctrine of justification through the Lutheran Reformation, after justification was eventually compromised during the first millennium. For most of the next two centuries there was a strong loyalty to Scripture and its teaching on justification. Throughout the 18th and 19th centuries, pietism, rationalism, and modernism took turns undermining one doctrine after another in the churches, including the Lutheran church. These centuries saw almost a complete loss of orthodox Lutheranism in the European churches. Today 60% of all Lutherans live in these European countries, and almost all of them belong to the Lutheran World Federation (LWF), which from the beginning was not able to agree on the doctrine of justification. In recent years the LWF has turned away completely from any kind of doctrinal unity or integrity and committed itself entirely to outward unity and the social gospel.

Considering the state of Lutheranism in the European countries, it is a miracle of God's grace that confessional Lutheranism was able to take root on North American soil. The early history of our synod was followed closely by the formation of the Synodical Conference, which represented an unwavering commitment to the Scriptures and the Lutheran Confessions, including the doctrine of justification. Even then, most of the Lutherans in the United States remained outside the Synodical Conference.

During the present century, modernism and ecumenism have taken a heavy toll on Lutheranism in America. Two-thirds of the Lutherans are represented by the Evangelical Lutheran Church in America (ELCA), which is also a member of the LWF. Lutherans in ELCA have never held to the doctrine of objective justification. Long ago they settled for unity with diversity, for outward unity with doctrinal diversity. Forty years ago the Synodical Conference became history. Confessional Lutheranism, never representing a majority of Lutherans in America, has dwindled to about 5% of those who confess to be Lutheran.

The purpose of this brief history is not to question the faith of those who are members of other Christian denominations, much less of other Lutherans. Nor is it to extol the virtues of the WELS. The WELS is what it is only by the grace of God. May God keep us from using this moment in history to congratulate ourselves. The purpose of these reminders to this convention is to encourage us to praise and thank our God for his grace and mercy. He alone has enabled our fathers to become and remain a confessional church body. He alone can keep us faithful to the Scriptures and the Lutheran Confessions.

Also, I cite this history to impress upon ourselves the great responsibility that falls upon confessional Lutherans today. "'Let the prophet who has a dream tell his dream, but let the one who has my word speak it faithfully. For what has straw to do with grain?' declares the Lord" (Jer 23:28).

Notice the two words that deserve emphasis. The one has already received attention. It bears repeating. It is the word *faithfully*. It directs attention first to the message. In one word, the message is justification. God has declared all sinners righteous in Christ. In two words, the message is law and gospel, sin and grace. Law is a vital part of every lesson to be taught, every sermon to be preached. It lays bare man's greatest need. It reveals sin and God's wrath against all who sin. It condemns sinners to hell. It works contrition. Until the law has done its work, the heart is unprepared for the gospel. The vital part of each lesson and sermon is the gospel. Once the law has done its work, the sinner needs only to hear the gospel. The gospel declares forgiveness through Christ, forgiveness of all sins, forgiveness to all who sin.

Faithfulness to this message must be the concern of every pastor and teacher, veteran or recent graduate of Wisconsin Lutheran Seminary and Martin Luther College. It must be the concern of every congregation, from the oldest and largest to the smallest and most recent mission. God's Word must be handled carefully, spoken faithfully. When handling the Scriptures we are not dealing with modern or ancient research, opinion polls, rules of logic, or human expectations. We are entrusted with a sacred text, God's inspired, infallible Word.

The other word to catch our eye is the word *speak*. It directs our attention to the messengers, to those who preach and teach the message. Preparation for the public ministry in the WELS requires both sound doctrine and good methodology. The WELS has a rich history of good teaching and preaching. Classroom to classroom, pulpit to pulpit, our people have come to expect quality work. One can step into any one of approximately 1,800 Lutheran elementary school classrooms and expect to hear a rich portion of God's Word in the form of Bible history and/or catechism to begin each day. One can attend any one of more than 1,200 congregations in the United States and Canada on any given Sunday and expect to hear an edifying sermon based upon a sacred text. It is my firm opinion that preaching and teaching in the WELS is second to none.

Having said that, one would have to insist that nothing is done so well that it cannot be done better. It is to be expected that a new teacher in the classroom and a new pastor in the pulpit will grow immeasurably during the first years of their ministry. Each added experience has the potential to make one a better teacher, a better preacher. But that need not be true only during the early years of one's ministry. It can be—we hope that it would be—the case long after one has realized 5, 10, 15, 20, or 25 years in the ministry. Thorough preparation of sermons and lessons has no substitute. Lessons and sermons that have been prepared well deserve to be delivered to the best of one's ability. Any improvement begins with self, a desire to improve and the willingness to make the necessary effort. Improvement is no farther away than the advice or encouragement of a brother or sister in the ministry.

Both Martin Luther College and Wisconsin Lutheran Seminary have an ongoing continuing education program for teachers and pastors respectively. For 27 years the seminary has offered three-week summer quarter courses.

Pastors' institutes have been held for an even longer time. More than one hundred pastors will be on campus at Mequon the next three weeks, choosing from 14 courses being offered in this year's summer quarter. Since its 1992–1993 self-study, the seminary has intensified its efforts to offer extension courses for these programs. Most of the districts have responded to the offer, including the Nebraska District. A pastors' institute was held earlier in the year and a summer quarter course will be conducted right here at Waco from July 20 to 24. Courses are scheduled or planned in six additional districts as more and more congregations are encouraging and enabling their pastors to take advantage of these opportunities.

A new century and a new millennium, along with a new period in our synod's history, await us. Are we ready to meet all of the challenges of a changing world, to seize the opportunities as the Lord opens doors, and to counterattack the assaults of Satan and an ungodly world? According to God's abundant grace, we have the message. May God's grace grow in our hearts so that we may proclaim that message faithfully.

> Amazing grace—that chose us e'er the worlds were made;
> Amazing grace—that sent your Son to save;
> Amazing grace—that robed us in your righteousness
> And taught our lips to sing glory and praise. (CW 392:2)

Christ, the King

If the people of Christ's day had been given a choice, which title would they have chosen for their Messiah: Prophet, Priest, or King? They had considerable interest in a prophet. Following the midpoint of his three-year ministry, Jesus asked his disciples, "Who do people say the Son of Man is?" (Mt 16:13). Without hesitation the disciples responded: "Some say John the Baptist; others say Elijah; and still others, Jeremiah or one of the prophets" (Mt 16:14). The idea of a prophet, a great prophet, fit comfortably into their way of thinking.

As noted earlier, the idea of a priest proved to be more remote from their idea of the Messiah, at least a priest who had come to offer up himself as a sacrifice for their sins. The Jewish leaders, along with many of the people, preferred to hear law, not gospel. Like the rich young man, they wanted to hear what man must do to become right with God (Mt 19:16-30). As long as Jesus performed miracles, healed diseases, fed thousands, even raised the dead, they were for the most part content to stand back and observe—as long as he did not do it on the Sabbath Day. The idea of their Messiah forgiving sins was another matter. They demanded to know by what authority he did this (Mt 9:1-8). Instead of rejoicing in the fact that he led sinners to repentance, they openly criticized him for having any contact with tax collectors and sinners (Mt 9:11).

We Believe in Jesus Christ

Jesus' own disciples reflect the general misunderstanding in connection with Christ's office as Priest. To the question "Who do you say that I am?" (Mt 16:15), Peter, speaking for the disciples, made a fine confession: "You are the Christ, the Son of the living God" (Mt 16:16). This fine confession lost some of its luster when Jesus proceeded to inform his disciples that he must go to Jerusalem and suffer and die and rise again (Mt 16:21). Peter wanted to hear no more of that kind of talk and earned the Lord's stern rebuke: "Get behind me, Satan! You are a stumbling block to me; you do not have in mind the things of God, but the things of men" (Mt 16:23). Peter's response, no matter how well intended, showed a lack of understanding for his Lord's high priestly office.

Jesus' office as King proved to be more popular among the people. The only real objection we hear to Christ's office as King is raised early Good Friday morning. In response to Pilate's question, "Shall I crucify your king?" the people responded, "We have no king but Caesar" (Jn 19:15). Even then their response may say more about their frustration with Jesus' priestly office. Or at least it reflects their disappointment that Jesus did not fulfill their millennialistic dreams of a Messiah-King.

The idea of a Messiah-King was firmly rooted in the writings of the Old Testament prophets. It was frequently identified with the kingdom of David, but always a ruling that surpassed anything David or those who ruled after him had accomplished. Some of the most powerful and delightful prophecies speak of the Messiah-King. David spoke of his royal son: "The Lord will extend your mighty scepter from Zion; you will rule in the midst of your enemies" (Ps 110:2). Isaiah identified the Messiah specifically with David's throne:

> For to us a child is born, to us a son is given, and the government will be on his shoulders. And he will be called Wonderful Counselor, Mighty God, Everlasting Father, Prince of Peace. Of the increase of his government and peace there will be no end. He will reign on David's throne and over his kingdom, establishing and upholding it with justice and righteousness from that time on and forever. The zeal of the Lord Almighty will accomplish this. (Isa 9:6,7)

Jeremiah echoes the sentiments of Isaiah: "'The days are coming,' declares the Lord, 'when I will raise up to David a righteous Branch, a King who will reign wisely and do what is just and right in the land. In his days Judah will be saved and Israel will live in safety. This is the name by which he will be called: The LORD Our Righteousness'" (Jer 23:5,6). Following the Babylonian captivity, Zechariah revived the hopes of a Messiah-King. "Rejoice greatly, O Daughter of Zion! Shout, Daughter of Jerusalem! See, your king comes to you, righteous and having salvation, gentle and riding on a donkey, on a colt, the foal of a donkey" (Zec 9:9). The fulfillment of these words on Palm Sunday most closely identifies the people's hope for a Messiah-King. When the crowds heard that Jesus was on his way to Jerusalem for the Passover Feast, they wasted no time to go out and meet him and proclaim him their king (Jn 12:12-19).

Though the people longed for a king, their idea of a king left much to be desired. After the feeding of the five thousand on the hillside in Galilee, the crowds attempted to take Jesus by force and make him a bread king (Jn 6). Failure to be the kind of Messiah they wished him to be accounts greatly for the fact that Jesus' popularity in Galilee dissipated almost as quickly as it had appeared (Jn 6:66). Though crowds were eager to acclaim him king on Palm Sunday, the only crowd we find five days later is the one gathered before Pilate, demanding that he be crucified (Jn 19:1-16). Jesus' own disciples harbored strange notions concerning the nature of Jesus' kingdom when James and John requested, "Let one of us sit at your right and the other at your left in your glory" (Mk 10:37). As late as his ascension into heaven, the disciples asked, "Lord, are you at this time going to restore the kingdom to Israel?" (Ac 1:6).

Disappointment with Christ's office reflects a deeper misunderstanding concerning the nature of his kingdom. Before Pilate, Jesus reaffirmed himself to be the king of the Jews but quickly added: "My kingdom is not of this world. If it were, my servants would fight to prevent my arrest by the Jews. But now my kingdom is from another place" (Jn 18:36). For the Messiah-King, *kingdom* means "activity, the exercise of kingly authority, the carrying out of kingly prerogatives." Christ, our mediator according to both natures, governs and controls all things in heaven, on earth, and even in hell.

Christ the Prophet had done nothing to contribute to the false notions the people held concerning his kingdom. When some of the people questioned by what authority Jesus cast out demons, his response spoke of the true nature of his kingdom: "If Satan is divided against himself, how can his kingdom stand? I say this because you claim that I drive out demons by Beelzebub. But if I drive out demons by the finger of God, then the kingdom of God has come to you" (Lk 11:18,20). On a later occasion the Pharisees came to him with questions concerning the kingdom. Jesus responded, "The kingdom of God does not come with your careful observation, nor will people say, 'Here it is,' or 'There it is,' because the kingdom of God is within you" (Lk 17:20,21). On the strength of these words of the Savior, the apostle Paul could say what he did of Christ's kingdom: "The kingdom of God is not a matter of talk but of power" (1 Co 4:20). "The kingdom of God is not a matter of eating and drinking, but of righteousness, peace and joy in the Holy Spirit" (Ro 14:17).

This kingdom was given to Christ according to his human nature. According to his divine nature he possessed it from eternity. David spoke of his installation: "I have installed my King on Zion, my holy hill" (Ps 2:6). Daniel

We Believe in Jesus Christ

says the same, along with a brief description of the kingdom given to him: "He was given authority, glory and sovereign power; all peoples, nations and men of every language worshiped him. His dominion is an everlasting dominion that will not pass away, and his kingdom is one that will never be destroyed" (Da 7:14). The exalted Christ cites the kingdom as a gift when he commissioned his disciples and his church of all times: "All authority in heaven and on earth has been given to me. Therefore go and make disciples of all nations, baptizing them in the name of the Father and of the Son and of the Holy Spirit, and teaching them to obey everything I have commanded you. And surely I am with you always, to the very end of the age" (Mt 28:18-20).

The kingdom was given to Christ from the time of his conception and birth. God's angel announced it: "You will be with child and give birth to a son, and you are to give him the name Jesus. He will be great and will be called the Son of the Most High. The Lord God will give him the throne of his father David, and he will reign over the house of Jacob forever; his kingdom will never end" (Lk 1:31-33). The infant was called a king: "Where is the one who has been born king of the Jews? We saw his star in the east and have come to worship him" (Mt 2:2). The suffering Savior also tied his office as King directly with his birth: "'You are a king, then!' said Pilate. Jesus answered, 'You are right in saying I am a king. In fact, for this reason I was born, and for this I came into the world, to testify to the truth. Everyone on the side of truth listens to me'" (Jn 18:37).

The manner of Christ's ruling varies with the attitude, or state, of the persons to whom it extends. Therefore we are accustomed to speak of Christ's kingdom as a kingdom of power and of grace and of glory. Frequently Scripture calls attention to the power and authority of the Messiah's ruling. Daniel foretold the extent of it:

> He was given authority, glory and sovereign power; all peoples, nations and men of every language worshiped him. His dominion is an everlasting dominion that will not pass away, and his kingdom is one that will never be destroyed. Then the sovereignty, power and greatness of the kingdoms under the whole heaven will be handed over to the saints, the people of the Most High. His kingdom will be an everlasting kingdom, and all rulers will worship and obey him. (Da 7:14,27)

The Savior claimed it: "All authority in heaven and on earth has been given to me" (Mt 28:18). The apostle Paul confirmed it: "By him all things were created: things in heaven and on earth, visible and invisible, whether thrones or powers or rulers or authorities; all things were created by him and for him. He is before all things, and in him all things hold together" (Col 1:16,17).

Christ's power extends freely over his enemies. "The LORD says to my Lord: 'Sit at my right hand until I make your enemies a footstool for your feet.' The LORD will extend your mighty scepter from Zion; you will rule in the midst of your enemies" (Ps 110:1,2). "He must reign until he has put all his enemies under his feet" (1 Co 15:25).

Always Christ exercises his power in the interest of his church. He promised as much when he stated in the presence of all his disciples, "I tell you that you are Peter, and on this rock I will build my church, and the gates of Hades will not overcome it" (Mt 16:18). Again the inspired apostle confirms it: "God placed all things under his feet and appointed him to be head over everything for the church" (Eph 1:22). Christians of all times, especially during evil days, times of pain or loss, trouble or persecution, have drawn endless comfort from the words of the same apostle, Paul: "We know that in all things God works for the good of those who love him, who have been called according to his purpose" (Ro 8:28). Who can count the number of times these words have been spoken in the pulpit, at the hospital bed, and at the death of a loved one? One might wonder if we have overused these words. One might wonder, but only for a moment—for how could words so profound and so comforting as these ever be used too much?

Whereas Christ rules the world with his power, his kingdom of grace has an entirely different end. In this kingdom Christ conveys spiritual blessings on those who are his. "The kingdom of God is not a matter of eating and drinking, but of righteousness, peace and joy in the Holy Spirit, because anyone who serves Christ in this way is pleasing to God and approved by men" (Ro 14:17,18). The means by which he exercises this kingdom is the gospel. "This gospel of the kingdom will be preached in the whole world as a testimony to all nations, and then the end will come" (Mt 24:14). The precious fruit of Christ's kingdom of grace is saving faith. "I am not ashamed of the gospel, because it is the power of God for the salvation of everyone who believes: first for the Jew, then for the Gentile. For in the gospel a righteousness from God is revealed, a righteousness that is by faith from first to last, just as it is written: 'The righteous will live by faith'" (Ro 1:16,17).

Because the fruit of Christ's kingdom of grace is faith born of the gospel (which is specifically the work of the Holy Spirit), the kingdom is known only to God. "I have revealed you to those whom you gave me out of the world. They were yours; you gave them to me and they have obeyed your word. I have given them your word and the world has hated them, for they are not of the world any more than I am of the world. Sanctify them by the truth; your word is truth" (Jn 17:6,14,17). For the same reason Christ's church is called invisible. Though *kingdom of God* and *church* are not identical, *kingdom of God* being the broader term, the two terms have been used interchangeably by the church.

The members of Christ's kingdom of grace, united to him by faith, enjoy a rich measure of spiritual gifts. "In him you have been enriched in every way—in all your speaking and in all your knowledge—because our testimony about

Christ was confirmed in you. Therefore you do not lack any spiritual gift as you eagerly wait for our Lord Jesus Christ to be revealed" (1 Co 1:5-7).

For the building of his kingdom, Christ our King also supplies special gifts. "In the church God has appointed first of all apostles, second prophets, third teachers, then workers of miracles, also those having gifts of healing, those able to help others, those with gifts of administration, and those speaking in different kinds of tongues" (1 Co 12:28).

Christ's kingdom of grace is real, It is the greatest of all realities. It unites hearts to him by faith. It confers upon believers all spiritual blessings. It blesses with spiritual gifts. It shall continue to the end of time. "Surely I am with you always, to the very end of the age" (Mt 28:20). It does not preclude, however, a lifelong struggle against the enemies of Christ's kingdom.

> Our struggle is not against flesh and blood, but against the rulers, against the authorities, against the powers of this dark world and against the spiritual forces of evil in the heavenly realms. Therefore put on the full armor of God, so that when the day of evil comes, you may be able to stand your ground, and after you have done everything, to stand. Stand firm then, with the belt of truth buckled around your waist, with the breastplate of righteousness in place, and with your feet fitted with the readiness that comes from the gospel of peace. In addition to all this, take up the shield of faith, with which you can extinguish all the flaming arrows of the evil one. Take the helmet of salvation and the sword of the Spirit, which is the word of God. And pray in the Spirit on all occasions with all kinds of prayers and requests. With this in mind, be alert and always keep on praying for all the saints. (Eph 6:12-18)

All millennialistic thought, past or present, with its teaching of a thousand-year rule of Christ upon the earth with temporal peace and utopian existence for his church, is a travesty of Christ's kingdom of grace. It sells short the perfect redemption Christ has won for his church. It robs from the perfect peace given through the gospel. It distracts from the priceless spiritual blessings of the kingdom, which are already ours as members of his church. It raises false hopes for those who are members of the church militant. The eyes of believers are directed to look for betterment upon the earth instead of the perfect home awaiting in heaven. It leads to speculation about the manner of Christ's return on the Last Day.

When we speak of Christ the King, we also speak of his kingdom of glory. The exalted Christ already sits at the right hand of the Father and shares the glory that is his from eternity. "In a loud voice they sang: 'Worthy is the Lamb, who was slain, to receive power and wealth and wisdom and strength and honor and glory and praise!' Then I heard every creature in heaven and on earth and under the earth and on the sea, and all that is in them, singing: 'To him who sits on the throne and to the Lamb be praise and honor and glory and power, for ever and ever!'" (Rev 5:12,13).

This rule includes the resurrection and the final judgment on the Last Day.

> Just as the Father raises the dead and gives them life, even so the Son gives life to whom he is pleased to give it. Moreover, the Father judges no one, but has entrusted all judgment to the Son, that all may honor the Son just as they honor the Father. He who does not honor the Son does not honor the Father, who sent him. Do not be amazed at this, for a time is coming when all who are in their graves will hear his voice and come out—those who have done good will rise to live, and those who have done evil will rise to be condemned" (Jn 5:21-23,28,29). All who are in the grave will come out. His glory will be revealed for all to see. "Father, I want those you have given me to be with me where I am, and to see my glory, the glory you have given me because you loved me before the creation of the world. (Jn 17:24)

Only those who are members of his kingdom of grace will enjoy it and participate in his kingdom of glory. "The King will say to those on his right, 'Come, you who are blessed by my Father; take your inheritance, the kingdom prepared for you since the creation of the world'" (Mt 25:34). "He will wipe every tear from their eyes. There will be no more death or mourning or crying or pain, for the old order of things has passed away" (Rev 21:4). At that time Christ's church militant shall become the church triumphant. "Those he predestined, he also called; those he called, he also justified; those he justified, he also glorified" (Ro 8:30).

> Not unto us but to your name be glory, Lord,
> For grace so rich, so wide, so high, so free.
> Abide with us till trav'ling days are over and done,
> And pilgrim feet lead us home, Lord, to you. (CW 392:4)

Conclusion

As it often is in our lives, we have spent much time during this essay looking back. We would be remiss if we did not. The entire Christian life is a time of looking back to our Lord in his office as Prophet, Priest, and King. In our worship we continually look back. We look at the Prophet of Galilee, who revealed himself in word and deed to be our Savior. We look back to the Savior's perfect obedience and holy passion, to the altar of the cross, where our sins were nailed and remitted. We look back to our victorious and glori-

We Believe in Jesus Christ

fied King, who established the holy Christian church, of which we are privileged to be members for life, life now and in eternity. Christians are "guilty" of living in the past.

We have also spent some time looking back at the history of the WELS. During the next two years I expect all of us will be doing more of this. Yes, we will remember our leaders, men faithful to their Lord, faithful to the Scriptures and faithful to those whom they were privileged to serve. But especially we will remember our Lord, who gave us these leaders, who took fallible men and made them faithful to his infallible Word, weak men and made them strong to do his will, ordinary men and made them eager to use their talents and abilities in extraordinary ways for the preaching and teaching of the gospel and salvation of souls. Christians, and especially WELS Christians, have every right and reason and a divine obligation to live in the past. God grant that, in the sense of which we have spoken, we will continue to do so.

Christ, however, who served as our Prophet, Priest, and King in the past, continues to be Prophet, Priest, and King. These offices have no end. They continue for time and eternity. He continues to serve in his notable offices until the end of time. As much as Christians long for the end of the world, to join the church triumphant, and to live with all the saints in glory, we remain in this world. And these are momentous days, a great time to be alive. We live at the very end of the second millennium, A.D. Most of us, God willing, will step into a third millennium in a matter of months. At the very same time we will be celebrating 150 years as a church body, 150 years under God, blessed by God, and by his grace, faithful to Scripture and the Lutheran Confessions.

Our horizon during these waning days of this century and this millennium, however, has to stretch farther, much farther, well beyond this brief time of celebration. It needs to include the opportunities God has placed before us to reach out with the gospel in order to gather in the elect. The mere mention of this brings to my mind enough thoughts for another entire essay. Allow me, in the remaining time for this essay, to touch upon two areas that are of great concern to me and, I trust, also to you.

One is manpower, especially the pastoral ministry. There is every indication that at the very time we step into the 21st century and the next half century of our synod's history, we will be in the early years of a growing vacancy problem. This problem will be compounded by another, a wonderful "problem" to have—no end of opportunities to expand our home and world mission fields.

During the 150 years of our synod's history, manpower problems have come and gone. So has the need for greater financial support. One constant during this entire time has been opportunities. The Lord has continued to open doors, and more doors, in order to preach the gospel to more people in more places. May we never see these opportunities as problems but as blessings from our God.

These blessings make it all the more urgent that we face our real problem. The best way I know how to face it is to "ask the Lord of the harvest" (Mt 9:38). Pray the Lord of the harvest to inspire young men to prepare for the pastoral ministry. Pray the Lord of the harvest that every Christian find ways to encourage young men to prepare to become pastors, and stand ready to lend support. Our synodical schools have stepped up what has been an intensive recruitment effort. At the same time, we realize that pastors and teachers, parents and grandparents, and leaders in the congregations remain the best recruiters. You may recall reading in the March 1998 issue of the *Northwestern Lutheran* the comment by our former seminary president that no one has more influence in encouraging a child to prepare for the ministry than the mother. Mother, father, teacher, pastor, whoever, "ask the Lord of the harvest."

With such a fervent request to our God, let us not fail to add prayers of deep gratitude to him for the workers he has given us. Other church bodies face greater problems just to fill existing pulpits than we do in filling existing pulpits and at the same time expanding our mission outreach. Another area of blessing is the quality of men enrolling year after year in our seminary. I know of no other seminary our size or larger that is so blessed. Most seminaries throughout the land have come to depend upon mostly second-career candidates, who have little or no training in the biblical languages and often few models for ministry. After teaching at the seminary for 16 years, I continue to be amazed at the qualifications class members bring to the seminary. They are the products of strong Christian homes. They are equipped and ready to do independent work in the biblical languages. They have had many excellent role models for ministry in their extensive Christian training. They know what it is to be Lutheran and much about being a shepherd in a Christian congregation. Except for training in the languages of the Bible, the same can be said of the young men and women who attend Martin Luther College in order to become teachers in our Lutheran elementary schools. Thank the Lord of the harvest. Pray for more of such workers.

The other area of my concern is related, but different. It is related because it also has to do with that which is dear to all the delegates at this convention, ministry. It is different in that it is not something that changes from time to time, such as manpower and funding. It is something that is constant. It is the thought that comes to mind when I see so many delegates gathered in one place, even though for a few days. It struck me as I was privileged to stand in the pulpit at the opening service of this convention. It is the thought that lingers when the work of this convention is over and each of us returns to our respective ministries. The concern, the thought, may also be expressed in the form of a prayer: Lord, keep us faithful to you and to the ministry entrusted to us.

I am not saying anything new when I suggest that the work Christ has given to his church has not gotten easier over the years. It is a challenge; it has always been a challenge; it always will be. The demands upon ministry today are great. As never before we pray that the Lord will fill our hearts with the same fire that filled our hearts when we began to serve: love for the Savior, love for the truth, love for souls, and the willingness to sacrifice for the sake of the gospel. May we return to our respective congregations committed to use our strength and our talents to the best of our abilities, never as doing our job and putting in our time, but in service to our Prophet, Priest, and King. Even during those more difficult times, "bad" days, and frustrating moments in our ministries, may we be able to say, "What a privilege it is to be able to do this, to serve God's people with the gospel."

Nor am I saying anything new when I suggest that behind every faithful pastor and teacher there is a supportive family and a dedicated laity that stands ready to assist. A church with a strong laity is a church richly blessed. A congregation is only as strong as the laity within it. Though it might be somewhat of an overstatement, it has been suggested that a congregation is only as strong as the weakest member within. True or not, it serves to remind us of the need on the part of called workers and laity alike to grow in faith and to be ready to encourage and strengthen one another. When I think back to my days in the parish ministry, I remember fondly those brothers in the ministry nearby and the support and encouragement we were able to give one another. Next I remember dedicated laypeople who had a deep love and respect for the work of the ministry and a great vision for the building of Christ's church.

The year 2000 looms just ahead, the end of the second millennium. Or does it end at 2001, as some have argued? The 150th anniversary of the WELS is upon us. Should we be celebrating it on the day our fathers met to organize our fellowship or a year later to make it a full 150 years? It really doesn't matter. Solving these questions doesn't prepare us for what is beyond. Readiness depends upon looking back and looking ahead with a proper focus. We look back daily to the cross of our Prophet, Priest, and King. That is where it all began. We look ahead to the crown of glory that awaits us. That is where it all reaches fulfillment. While we wait for the crown, we eagerly search out the opportunities God gives us to serve in his kingdom. With a single voice we pray to the Lord of the harvest for workers in the harvest field. We pray for faithful workers. We pray for dedicated leaders in our congregations and throughout our church body. In each instance, may the prayer begin with me.

JESUS CHRIST IS THE SAME YESTERDAY AND TODAY AND FOREVER.

THE ACTIVE AND PASSIVE OBEDIENCE OF JESUS CHRIST

Richard D. Balge

North Atlantic District Convention
Elizabethtown, Pennsylvania
June 9–10, 1998

All the work of Jesus Christ as our representative before God can be characterized as obedience. The subject deals with our eternal salvation, with the eternal life that is ours as God's gift in Christ Jesus. To treat the subject of his obedience, therefore, is to preach the gospel. This doctrine derives from God's Word, which is the record and interpretation of God's mighty and gracious works. With this study we are dealing with history—time, place, events, significance of events.

The author of Hebrews, citing Psalm 40:7, declares that the Messiah was foreseen in prophecy as the obedient Servant of the Lord: "Then I said, 'Here I am—it is written about me in the scroll—I have come to do your will, O God'" (Heb 10:7). The "evangelist of the Old Testament," Isaiah, also speaks in the voice of the coming Messiah: "The Sovereign LORD has opened my ears, and I have not been rebellious; I have not drawn back" (Isa 50:5).

The apostle Paul writes in Romans 5:18,19, "Just as the result of one trespass was condemnation for all men, so also the result of one act of righteousness was justification that brings life for all men. For just as through the disobedience of the one man the many were made sinners, so also through the obedience of the one man the many will be made righteous." Notice that Adam's trespass (fatal for us all) is equated with disobedience. Notice how the one act of righteousness (resulting in justification) equates with "the obedience of the one man [Christ]."

It is only appropriate, then, that our church's great confession of 1577 identifies and equates Jesus' righteousness with his obedience: "The righteousness which is imputed to faith or to the believer out of pure grace is the obedience, suffering, and resurrection of Christ, since He has made satisfaction for us to the Law, and paid for our sins."[1]

No explicit distinction between Christ's active obedience and his passive obedience is made in Scripture. Neither does the Bible use those terms. They are theological shorthand for what the Scripture says about all of Jesus' saving work. We distinguish between what he did (active) and what he suffered (passive), between his living the perfect life of love (active) and his suffering punishment for the sins of the world (passive). When we speak of the active obedience, we must not overlook the fact that long before his crucifixion he *suffered* the pain of circumcision, hunger pangs, and fatigue. When we speak of the passive obedience, we must not forget that in his passion he acted voluntarily. He set his face toward Jerusalem, submitted to arrest, and went the way of the cross.

The Formula of Concord does not make a formal distinction between active and passive obedience, but it includes both without the formal terminology. For example: "Christ covers all their sins . . . for the sake of [his] obedience (which [he] rendered the Father for us from His birth to His most ignominious death upon the cross). . . ."[2] "From his birth to his most ignominious death" summarizes all that he did and all that he suffered under the term *obedience.*

The God-man Christ Jesus submitted to God's law and kept it perfectly for us (active obedience).

What we were obliged to do and never could do, Jesus Christ, the God-man, did in our place.

We do not measure up to what God had in mind when he created man in his own image. "All have sinned and fall short of the glory of God" (Ro 3:23). In Romans 2:10, Paul gives assurance—to the moral Jew and the Greek lover of wisdom alike—of "glory, honor and peace for everyone who does good: first for the Jew, then for the Gentile." The problem is that there is no one who does good by God's standards: "All have turned away, they have together become worthless; there is no one who does good, not even one" (Ro 3:12). Not only have we inherited a sinful nature from our first parents, but we have also been active sinners, rebels, of no use to God, a definite danger to one another. The spiritually blind cannot respond to the Light; the spiritually deaf cannot listen to God's instruction or his good news; a spiritual corpse cannot take a step toward God or make a decision to accept and follow Jesus. Human nature, when it comes to the things of the Spirit of God, is not only weak and sickly—it is dead.

---

[1]FC SD III:14.
[2]FC SD III:22.

We Believe in Jesus Christ

All mankind fell in Adam's fall;
One common sin infects us all.
From one to all the curse descends,
And over all God's wrath impends. (CW 378:1)

More than a man was needed to do what God required of human beings. The prophet Jeremiah gave the coming Messiah a name that belongs only to God. He writes, "In his days Judah will be saved and Israel will live in safety. This is the name by which he will be called: The LORD Our Righteousness" (23:6). In his good time, God would send a man to do his saving work. That man would be more than a man. He would bear the name of the God of free and faithful grace, that special name of God that in English we spell with four capital letters, LORD. It also has four letters in Hebrew, and it is the name we transliterate as Yahweh, or Jehovah.

God was faithful to all his promises concerning the one whom he would send. "When the time had fully come, God sent his Son, born of a woman, born under law, to redeem those under law, that we might receive the full rights of sons" (Gal 4:4,5). In the days of the Vietnam War, a picket sign appeared at a union convention: "War is good business; invest your son." That was a sobering and even shuddery thought. It is what God did. He made it his business to conquer Satan and establish peace with a race that was at enmity with him. He invested his only Son in that war.

More than a man was needed. Though Jesus, the Messiah, had willingly submitted to the law, he also declared that he was above the law: "The Son of Man is Lord of the Sabbath" (Mt 12:8). He is the Lord of the Sabbath because he is the Lord who established the Sabbath. On the seventh day God rested. By his word he made all things, seen and unseen. Jesus is that Word made flesh, and there is none greater. He calls himself the Son of Man. That does not mean he is the "ideal man" or the "flower of humanity." It means he is God come in the flesh to destroy the works of the devil. It means he came to win "the endless Sabbaths of the blest" (TLH 7:4) for us through his perfect obedience.

"When the time had fully come, God sent his Son, born of a woman" (Gal 4:4). "The Lord Our Righteousness" came as a baby, fully human. "We do not have a high priest who is unable to sympathize with our weaknesses, but we have one who has been tempted in every way, just as we are—yet was without sin" (Heb 4:15). Truly God and truly man, the divine and human are united in one person.

> We Christians should know that if God is not in the scale to give it weight, we, on our side, sink to the ground. I mean it this way: if it cannot be said that God died for us, but only a man, we are lost; but if God's death and a dead God lie in the balance, his side goes down and ours goes up like a light and

empty scale. . . . But he could not sit on the scale unless he had become a man like us, so that it could be called God's dying, God's martyrdom, God's blood, and God's death. For God in his own nature cannot die; but now that God and man are united in one person, it is called God's death when the man dies.[3]

"When the time had fully come, God sent his Son, born of a woman, born under law, to redeem those under law, that we might receive the full rights of sons" (Gal 4:4,5). *Law* here does not refer only to the Mosaic complex, the cradle-to-grave system of laws that God gave Israel. It refers to God's holy and unchanging will, everything that God demands of all people. He was acting for all people, not only his own Jewish people. He accepted the requirement to live as a human being in perfect love for God and unselfish love for his neighbor. He did so simply by becoming a human being. As a creature he was subject to the First Commandment. As Mary's son he was subject to her and Joseph under the Fourth Commandment.

"Such a high priest meets our need—one who is holy, blameless, pure, set apart from sinners, exalted above the heavens" (Heb 7:26). Not only according to his divine nature but also according to his human nature, he was holy, not polluted by sin. He was blameless; every kind of evil was foreign to him. He was undefiled, not stained by any sin. He was set apart from sinners—not aloof from our human struggles, but not partaking of our sinful nature. That he has measured up to the law's requirements is clear from the fact that God has exalted him.

Christ's victory over the old evil foe did not come without a struggle. "We do not have a high priest who is unable to sympathize with our weaknesses, but we have one who has been tempted in every way, just as we are—yet was without sin" (Heb 4:15). Not only did our Savior withstand the day-to-day assaults of the tempter. At the beginning of his public ministry, he was "led by the Spirit into the desert to be tempted by the devil. After fasting forty days and forty nights, he was hungry. The tempter came to him and said, 'If you are the Son of God, tell these stones to become bread.' Jesus answered, 'It is written: "Man does not live on bread alone, but on every word that comes from the mouth of God"'" (Mt 4:1-4).

Materialism has been a temptation to believers in every age. Whether a person is full or hungry, he will be tempted to that form of unbelief which in a variety of ways believes man *does* live on bread alone. Even baptized children of God know the temptation to "take the cash and let the credit go." In the Garden of Eden, where there was plenty to eat, the devil overcame Adam.

---

[3]LW 41:103,104.

We Believe in Jesus Christ

He did it by questioning God's goodness. In the desert, addressing a man who had been fasting for more than a month, he tries to get Jesus to doubt his Father's grace and providence. Also, to prove his own deity by a miracle. Basically, to do the tempter's bidding.

In our place and on our behalf, Jesus obeyed his Father's will, refusing to do the devil's bidding. In perfect obedience he feared, loved, and trusted God above all things. In our stead and on our behalf, Jesus said: "It is written. . . ." The weapon of his warfare was, as ours must always be, the reliable written Word of God.

As he has proved for thousands of years, and especially in the last two thousand, Satan is not a quitter. "Then the devil took him to the holy city and had him stand on the highest point of the temple. 'If you are the Son of God,' he said, 'throw yourself down. For it is written: "He will command his angels concerning you, and they will lift you up in their hands, so that you will not strike your foot against a stone."' Jesus answered him, 'It is also written: "Do not put the Lord your God to the test"'" (Mt 4:5-7).

Like the temptation in Paradise, like the first temptation of Jesus, like all temptations, this one was at bottom a temptation to unbelief. Challenge God to see whether he will really do what he has promised. Test whether he means what he says. Also, it was a temptation to self-aggrandizement. Prove your identity and your authority by doing the spectacular. Forget God's painful plan and take the easy way to glory.

Again, the reliable Word of God was Jesus' weapon of choice: "It is written. . . ." Again, he was keeping the law in our stead to remedy our lack of righteousness.

The adversary came back and offered easy terms on a grand bargain. "Again, the devil took him to a very high mountain and showed him all the kingdoms of the world and their splendor. 'All this I will give you,' he said, 'if you will bow down and worship me.' Jesus said to him, 'Away from me, Satan! For it is written: "Worship the Lord your God, and serve him only"'" (Mt 4:8-10). As usual, the devil was promising what he could not possibly deliver. Why shouldn't he try? It had worked with the first Adam, and with millions after him—and usually with promises much less grand. Here is the offer of kingship without the cross. Instead of the long agonizing road, one little gesture. Instead of enduring an ignominious, shameful death, bow down and worship God's archenemy, the first revolutionary. Instead of the bitter cup, only a single obeisance.

Here as always, Jesus put God first—his name, his will, and his kingdom. Here again, Scripture is the weapon of Jesus' warfare. He knew it, meditated on it, relied on it, lived it. Finally, he overcame with it. His victory is ours.

The outcome was never in doubt, since Jesus is truly God and could not sin. Yet, the battle was real, not a charade. The inner turmoil and the appeal of "another way" were a real test. The athlete who faces a lesser adversary and is bound to win still needs to make a real effort. Jesus was up against a wily opponent of long experience and many successes, and the struggle was real.

In his ministry our Lord not only avoided the negative, the things prohibited by God's law, but also lived the positive, motivated by and always demonstrating the love that is the sum and substance of the law. As a human being, he was required by God's unchanging will to honor, serve, and obey his parents: "Then he went down to Nazareth with them and was obedient to them" (Lk 2:51). As a Jewish baby boy, he was circumcised at the age of one week (Lk 2:21). As a Jewish youth, he was observant of the feast days and made the most of the opportunity to learn: "They found him in the temple courts, sitting among the teachers, listening to them and asking them questions. Everyone who heard him was amazed at his understanding and his answers" (Lk 2:46,47). As a subject of the Roman Empire, he honored and obeyed the government and paid taxes: "Give to Caesar what is Caesar's, and to God what is God's" (Mt 22:21). He gladly heard and learned God's Word: "He went to Nazareth, where he had been brought up, and on the Sabbath day he went into the synagogue, as was his custom" (Lk 4:16). He prayed (Lk 6:12). He gave thanks (Jn 6:11).

He made sure his mother would be taken care of after he was gone. Even when he was giving up his life to pay for the sins of the world, he was not too busy to provide for her (Jn 19:26,27). To the end, he was perfectly fulfilling God's law in our stead.

Active and positive in his love, he helped and befriended those in need: "News about him spread all over Syria, and people brought to him all who were ill with various diseases, those suffering severe pain, the demon-possessed, those having seizures, and the paralyzed, and he healed them" (Mt 4:24).

During his trial, under more provocation than any mere human being could bear, he responded in a loving way that did not divert him from his assignment or make him mistrust the one who had assigned his work. "'He committed no sin, and no deceit was found in his mouth.' When they hurled their insults at him, he did not retaliate; when he suffered, he made no threats. Instead, he entrusted himself to him who judges justly" (1 Pe 2:22,23). Under hideous torture Jesus said, "Father, forgive them, for they do not know what they are doing" (Lk 23:34). Human beings at their worst had subjected him to cruel treatment. He made intercession for the sinners who were torturing him, for ignorant unbelievers. He might have prayed for justice. Instead, he prayed that his Father would give these murderers time and grace and knowledge to repent of what they had done in ignorance, and to receive the pardon of a forgiving God. A schoolboy was asked, "When was Jesus at his greatest?" His answer: "When he prayed for his enemies, because I couldn't have done that."

"In him is no sin" (1 Jn 3:5).

Christ came and has God's anger stilled,
Our human nature sharing.
He has for us the law obeyed
And thus the Father's vengeance stayed
Which over us impended. (from CW 390:4)

That is to say . . .

Jesus' active obedience was for our salvation.

In Romans 5, Paul compares the "two Adams" and the results of their activity: "Just as the result of one trespass was condemnation for all men, so also the result of one act of righteousness was justification that brings life for all men. For just as through the disobedience of the one man the many were made sinners, so also through the obedience of the one man the many will be made righteous" (Ro 5:18,19). What the first Adam and the second Adam did affects all human beings. They are not merely representative types. Adam's act is charged against the whole human race. Christ's act is credited to the whole human race.

The "one trespass" was Adam's, eating the forbidden fruit. The offense of Adam consisted in breaking the law. Adam grasped at equality with God, ate the forbidden fruit, and thus brought guilt and death upon himself and all his descendants.

The righteousness of Christ consisted in his perfect obedience to the law. He was acting in our stead, obeying as our substitute, and so God has credited that righteousness to us. Jesus Christ, the Son of God, "being in very nature God, did not consider equality with God something to be grasped, but made himself nothing, taking the very nature of a servant, being made in human likeness. And being found in appearance as a man, he humbled himself and became obedient to death—even death on a cross!" (Php 2:6-8). Through that humble obedience "the many will be made righteous." "Many" does not mean some. It means all. The same "many" who were made sinners in Adam's sin are declared righteous in Christ's obedience.

The 1577 confession of our church interprets and applies Romans 5:18,19 in this way: "Our righteousness before God is that God forgives us our sins out of pure grace, without any work, merit, or worthiness of ours preceding, present, or following, that He presents and imputes to us the righteousness of Christ's obedience, on account of which righteousness we are received into grace by God, and regarded as righteous."[4]

---

[4]FC Ep III:4.

O the sweet exchange, O the inscrutable creation, O the unlooked-for benefits, that the sin of many should be put out of sight in one Righteous Man, and the righteousness of one should justify many sinners![5]

The God-man Christ Jesus willingly suffered the punishment for our sin (passive obedience).

"No man can redeem the life of another or give to God a ransom for him—the ransom for a life is costly, no payment is ever enough" (Ps 49:7,8). What we were obliged to do and could not do, Jesus Christ the God-man did. He bore the punishment for our sin. Our Redeemer took upon himself the punishment for our failures to love God and our neighbor. Christ, who willingly accepted the obligation to keep the law in our stead, also accepted the obligation to bear the punishment that the law demanded.

Quoting the Old Testament Scriptures, quoting psalmists and prophets, Paul characterizes the human race. He begins and ends with First Commandment sins, mentioning sins of the tongue and of hatred in between:

"All have turned away,
    they have together become worthless;
there is no one who does good,
    not even one."
"Their throats are open graves;
    their tongues practice deceit."
"The poison of vipers is on their lips."
    "Their mouths are full of cursing and bitterness."
"Their feet are swift to shed blood;
    ruin and misery mark their ways,
and the way of peace they do not know."
    "There is no fear of God before their eyes."

Now we know that whatever the law says, it says to those
who are under the law, so that every mouth may be silenced
and the whole world held accountable to God. (Ro 3:12-19)

In 1536–1537 Dr. Martin Luther wrote in the Smalcald Articles: "All in us is nothing but sin. . . . For there is nothing left with which we can think of any good thing to pay for sin, but there is only a sure despairing concerning all that we are, think, speak, or do."[6]

"We all, like sheep, have gone astray, each of us has turned to his own way; and the Lord has laid on him the iniquity of us all" (Isa 53:6). There was

---

[5]Epistle to Diognetus ix.5 (mid-2nd century).
[6]SA III,III:36.

a way that God had chosen for his foremost creatures. It was the way of life. It was a way of peace and joy in following his will and living in harmony with him. But we knew better; we thought that somehow God was trying to hold out on us, to keep us from really living. We have gone our own way. As Augustine said, we were one great *massa perdita*, "damned mass." Ignorant and helpless, like a flock of foolish sheep, unaware that we had gone astray and were straying blindly toward our damnation. We followed our urges, impulses, and desires, giving no thought to the dangers of eternal death that surrounded us.

We have gone astray. Like sheep, not very bright. Following blind impulse, false leaders, our own selfish will. Looking for greener pastures, looking for grass on the wrong side of the fence, wandering away, always farther from the real source of life. Finally getting lost in the desert, where there is no food and water, no shade or safety. In trying to find our way back to God, in trying to know him again and be like him, we were confused and ignorant. We were incapable of knowing or choosing him—or even wanting to.

Everyone devises his own path to God, and no one finds God's path to life. Like sheep, not smart. This was a universal condition, including the whole human race. Criminals and solid citizens, thieves and statesmen, tax collectors and Pharisees, selfish swingers and humanitarians—all lost sheep. And where does that lead? It leads to a miserable eternity of regret, of rage, of doing the same hateful and stupid things over and over again, forever and ever. When a human being keeps saying to God, "Let me alone; let me go my own way," there finally comes a time when God lets that person go his own way. And that is the way to hell.

> Some . . . are slaves to riches, honors, pleasures, and the powers of this world. But others . . . are zealous for their own righteousness, virtue, and wisdom, having deserted the righteousness and obedience of God in their spiritual pride.[7]

God did not leave us to go to hell. He did not leave us in our spiritual slavery. "Since the children have flesh and blood, he too shared in their humanity so that by his death he might destroy him who holds the power of death—that is, the devil—and free those who all their lives were held in slavery by their fear of death" (Heb 2:14,15). Flesh and blood is subject to death. Death was there waiting for us when we were born. It did not get us then, but it is waiting for another time, even if it has to wait a hundred years.

In taking on our humanity and obeying to the full, the Son of God subjected himself to death. He did that for a special and glorious purpose. He has rendered the devil, "who holds the power of death," ineffective. Jesus, who

---

[7]LW 25:226.

The Active and Passive Obedience of Jesus Christ

shared in our humanity, has neutralized the devil's ultimate weapon. He did this by satisfying God's justice and paying the ransom price for our deliverance. The devil still exists and people still die, but death has lost its power to terrify those who trust the Savior.

"Christ redeemed us from the curse of the law by becoming a curse for us, for it is written: 'Cursed is everyone who is hung on a tree'" (Gal 3:13). Lecturing on this passage, Luther says:

> The Law did everything to Him that it did to us. It accused us and terrified us. It subjected us to sin, death, and the wrath of God; and it condemned us with its judgment. And it had a right to do all this, for we have all sinned. But Christ "committed no sin, and no guile was found on His lips" (1 Peter 2:22). Therefore He owed nothing to the Law. And yet against Him—so holy, righteous, and blessed—the Law raged as much as it does against us accursed and condemned sinners, and even more fiercely. It accused Him of blasphemy and sedition; it found Him guilty in the sight of God of all the sins of the entire world; finally it so saddened and frightened Him that He sweat blood (Luke 22:44); and eventually it sentenced Him to death, even death on a cross (Phil. 2:8).[8]

"We all, like sheep, have gone astray, each of us has turned to his own way; and the LORD has laid on him the iniquity of us all. He was oppressed and afflicted, yet he did not open his mouth; he was led like a lamb to the slaughter, and as a sheep before her shearers is silent, so he did not open his mouth" (Isa 53:6,7). Sin has to be somewhere. It can't be swept away or removed with a snap of the finger. It can't be ignored or removed with a cheap miracle. It has to be somewhere, on someone. "The LORD has laid on him the iniquity of us all."

Old Testament Israel was commanded to celebrate, once each year, the Great Day of Atonement. A lamb was chosen, a yearling without any spot or blemish, any scar or flaw. The lamb was observed for 14 days, to make sure it met the requirements. Then, on the great day, the high priest of Israel placed his hand on the animal, symbolically transferring the sins of Israel to that spotless lamb. The lamb's throat was cut, and it was offered as a burnt sacrifice.

That lamb, and all those lambs through all the years, was a type, or foreshadowing, of Christ. It pictured what God would finally do for the sins of the world. Christ Jesus, who was without sin, became the bearer of the whole

---

[8]LW 26:370.

world's sin. There were two possible places for our sin to reside and for the punishment of our sin to fall: on us, or on him. "The LORD has laid on him the iniquity of us all." "All" does not leave anyone out.

> In this text all the apostles have attacked the religions and the Law itself. *All we have gone astray.* The religions through their own rules and their own way want to load our sins on us and say, "If you will observe these things, you will be free from your sins." . . . *On Him,* not on us, contrary to every law and order, where whoever sins is punished.[9]

Our Lord's suffering and death was not a mere human tragedy, not an accident of fate, not simply a prime example of man's inhumanity to man. It was "God's Great Exchange." "God made him who had no sin to be sin for us, so that in him we might become the righteousness of God" (2 Co 5:21). Our sin on him who had not experienced sin. His perfect obedience credited to us. For that the Son of God was treated like the greatest sinner, accursed, and godforsaken. Where we should have been—under the load of sin, bearing its guilt and punishment—he was. He traded places with us. There was no reason he should die. He had no sin, knew no sin, committed no sin. He was not inclined to sin, had not experienced it, and was untouched by it. God made him to be sin for us. God treated him like Sin personified. God punished our sins in him.

Recall all the wrongs you have suffered, all the hurtful things that were ever done to you. All of it together cannot begin to compare to the wrong you and I have done to the just and loving God. He charged it all to his Son. "The deepest stroke that pierced him was the stroke that Justice gave" (CW 127:2). Jesus was not a sinner, but he was treated as the sinner. When he cried out because God would not look at him, because God had turned his back on him, he was where we should have been. He was there so that you and I will never have to be there and know what that is like. To be where God is not, where there is no sense of his loving presence, to be godforsaken and *know that God is justly angry with me*—that is hell.

He was the one who loved his Father perfectly and lived the perfect life of love, and God has credited that to us, "that in him we might become the righteousness of God" (2 Co 5:21). Where Christ is, there is his righteousness, and through faith we are in him. Where righteousness is, there is forgiveness and life and salvation, and they are ours in him.

"For you know that it was not with perishable things such as silver or gold that you were redeemed from the empty way of life handed down to you from your forefathers, but with the precious blood of Christ, a lamb without blemish or defect" (1 Pe 1:18,19). God did not do something cheap

---

[9]LW 17:225,226.

when he rescued us. He did not use things that can be stolen, that no one can keep forever. He did not redeem us with something undependable, like money, which gets lost or devalued. "Not with perishable things such as silver or gold . . . but with the precious blood of Christ." That was a tremendous price. The blood of Christ, the Lamb of God. That was the price of our redemption.

"The next day John saw Jesus coming toward him and said, 'Look, the Lamb of God, who takes away the sin of the world!'" (Jn 1:29). From many a modern pulpit we hear of God's fatherly heart. We are assured that we do not have to be afraid of God. We are urged to stop being angry with him and to be at peace with one another. None of this has any foundation or substance apart from the blood of the Lamb of God.

In the Old Testament, in the religion of John and Jesus, lambs died. When Abraham was taking Isaac to the mountain of sacrifice, the boy asked where the lamb was. When Moses led Israel out of Egyptian slavery, a lamb was killed for every Jewish household. The blood of the lamb was smeared on the door posts of every Jewish house. When the angel of death moved through the land of Egypt, slaying the firstborn of every house and palace in Egypt, the firstborn of Israel were spared. Once a year, on the Great Day of Atonement, when the high priest of Israel made sacrifice, first for his own sins and then for the sins of the people, it was the lamb that died instead of the people of Israel. Lambs were for dying, for sacrifice, for taking the place of sinners. John the Baptist said of Jesus: "Look, the Lamb of God, who takes away the sin of the world!"

The whole world must include you and me. I can say, "Christ died for me." You can say it too, because it was for all.

That is the ground of our faith. That is the gospel. This Lamb was sacrificed, and our sins are atoned for. That is the plain language of the Bible. It does not need more explanation and it must not be explained away.

> If we allow sin to remain in our conscience and try to deal with it there, or if we look at sin in our heart, it will be much too strong for us and will live on forever. But if we behold it resting on Christ and [see it] overcome by his resurrection, and then boldly believe this, even it is dead and nullified. Sin cannot remain on Christ, since it is swallowed up by his resurrection. Now you see no wounds, no pain in him, and no sign of sin. Thus St. Paul declares that "Christ died for our sin and rose for our justification" [Rom. 4:25]."[10]

---

[10]LW 42:12,13.

"Christ redeemed us from the curse of the law by becoming a curse for us, for it is written: 'Cursed is everyone who is hung on a tree'" (Gal 3:13). How could the sinless Son of God be subjected to God's curse? Paul solves the difficulty for us with one expression: "for us." "Redeemed" means he paid the price to set us free. He settled our account with the law by taking our place. Our sins became the sins of Christ as though he himself had committed them, and God treated him as Sin personified: "God made him who had no sin to be sin for us" (2 Co 5:21).

The crucified Jesus was more than a victim of man's inhumanity to man. He was the victim of God's justice. Someone once said with a sneer, "Depending on your view of Jesus of Nazareth, God is either a sadist or a masochist. He loves to torture, or he loves to be tortured. If Jesus is only a man, then God is a sadist for letting an innocent man suffer that way. If Jesus is God, then God is a masochist for letting himself be tortured that way." That bit of brilliance does not take into account that when a crime is pardoned, someone must still take the consequences. When a debt is canceled, someone must still absorb the loss. A hurt that is forgiven is still a hurt. That is reality. That is justice. That was the way of the cross, and that was the only way for the simple reason that it was the way God did it.

The innocent God-man endured the consequences and paid the debt and suffered the hurt, *willingly*: Through the prophet Isaiah, the pre-incarnate Christ said, "The Sovereign Lord has opened my ears, and I have not been rebellious; I have not drawn back" (Isa 50:5). He feared the baptism with which he was to be baptized. He trembled and agonized and sweat blood. But he willed the Father's will; he willed to do what was necessary to redeem the world; he did it. This means that he was not merely passive in his passion. In his voluntary suffering he was actively obeying the law: loving God and loving man.

> Seek whom you may to be your stay;
> none can redeem his brother.
> All helpers failed; this man prevailed,
> the God-Man, and none other.
> The Servant-Lord our life restored.
> We're justified, for he has died,
> the guiltless for the guilty. (CW 395:2)

The benefits of Christ's obedience are ours through faith alone, in Christ alone.

"Since in the wisdom of God the world through its wisdom did not know him, God was pleased through the foolishness of what was preached to save those who believe" (1 Co 1:21). The philosophy of the Greeks, the gods of the barbarians, the legalism of the Roman world, did not help anyone to find

God or his salvation. Paul says that in his wisdom God did not want the world to know him by its own wisdom. What would happen to people who weren't smart enough to find him that way? Besides, why should God do anything for people who can do it themselves? Why should Christ pay such a price for the self-sufficient?

"God was pleased through the foolishness of what was preached to save those who believe." It is not by precise argumentation or accurate syllogisms but by preaching the fact of Christ's perfect obedience in our stead and on our behalf. Those who believe that objective truth have the righteousness of Christ, the salvation he came to earn for us.

The world still calls it foolishness. It has never been possible for man by his thinking or willing to believe. Church membership has been respectable in some times and some places. Some standard of morality seems like a good idea to almost everyone. Jesus the Teacher is generally respected. Paul, however, knew very well what human reason thinks of the message that a Jewish carpenter was the Son of God, that he died like a criminal only to have God raise him from the dead, and that this Jesus is the world's only hope of salvation. It is still true, however, as it was in the first century: "Faith comes from hearing the message, and the message is heard through the word of Christ" (Ro 10:17).

> God . . . has His divine eternal Law and His wonderful plan concerning our redemption . . . publicly preached; and by this collects an eternal Church for Himself from the human race, and works in the hearts of men true repentance and knowledge of sins, and true faith in the Son of God, Jesus Christ.[11]

It has been said that quoting the familiar John 3:16 to a knowledgeable congregation is tantamount to inviting them to think about other things. If, however, you can get them to wonder where your emphasis is going to be on that particular day, they might listen: "God so loved the world that he gave his one and only Son, that *whoever believes in him* shall not perish but have eternal life." Believing is trust, reliance, banking all on the object of one's faith. Believing in God's one and only Son does not mean loving my neighbor as myself. I have not lived up to that. Believing is not experiencing the "inner light," a feeling somewhat like an electrical shock, making a decision for Christ. Nor is it merely assenting to a dogma. It is relying on Jesus Christ, who was obedient in life and death as the substitute for every human being, whom God raised from the dead as the beginning of a great crop of people who will be raised to everlasting life.

---

[11]FC SD II:50.

Paul writes to the believers at Rome, "We maintain that a man is justified by faith apart from observing the law" (Ro 3:28). He also demonstrated that salvation, or justification, has always been through faith. Citing Genesis 15:6 he asks, "What does the Scripture say? 'Abraham believed God, and it was credited to him as righteousness.' Now when a man works, his wages are not credited to him as a gift, but as an obligation. However, to the man who does not work but trusts God who justifies the wicked, his faith is credited as righteousness" (Ro 4:3-5). Not on the basis of his own obedience was Abraham righteous in God's sight. No, Genesis 15:6 says, "Abraham believed the Lord, and he credited it to him as righteousness." He was not righteous in himself, this "father of all believers." Nor was his faith some virtue or meritorious act that God recognized as righteous. A gracious God simply credited faith to him as righteousness.

What Paul does not say in these verses but is implicit in his argument is that Abraham's faith rested on God's promise, in the Descendant who was the object of God's promise. It was the object of faith, Christ with his righteousness (obedience), that was credited to Abraham. From that Paul generalizes regarding "the man [any person] who does not work but trusts God." Like Abraham, "his faith is credited as righteousness."

Paul writes to the believers at Ephesus, "It is by grace you have been saved, through faith—and this not from yourselves, it is the gift of God—not by works, so that no one can boast" (Eph 2:8,9). God's grace is not something he gives us to enable us to become righteous. God's grace is that he regards us with unconditional love and unmerited mercy. Grace is not a subtle concept for philosophers and theologians. It is what God demonstrated when he worked out the salvation of all sinners. It is not a private thought in the Lord's mind. It is there to see in what he did to redeem the human race.

By God's grace and through faith we have been saved. Like grace, faith is the gift of God. Faith is not a self-conscious, deliberate decision to accept God's salvation. Just as we did not decide to accept physical life from our parents but simply received it as a gift, so faith is a gift and not the result of a decision on our part.

Strictly speaking, it is not faith that saves us, but the Savior. It is not faith that justifies us, but God. Faith only trusts that he has done it. Without the cross, without the empty tomb, without the Savior's obedient living and dying for us, faith would be without any foundation. The drowning person does not concentrate on his hand or the strength of his grip. He focuses on the life buoy. So faith does not examine itself, measure itself, rely on itself. It focuses on Christ, who is strong to save. Do not ask, "Do I have faith?" Rather, ask, "Do I have a Savior?" The answer to the first question is always yes when you know that the answer to the second question is yes.

Even if my faith is feeble, I still have the selfsame treasure and the selfsame Christ that others have. There is no difference. Faith in Him makes us all perfect, but works do not.[12]

God gave me faith and forgiveness in Baptism. He nourishes and strengthens my faith with the assurance of forgiveness in his Supper. He does these things daily in his Word.

We thank our Savior for his obedience with a life of joyful obedience.

We did not elect him King of kings and Lord of lords, and he is not subject to recall or impeachment. He will continue in office whether we acknowledge him or not. We were, however, redeemed to live under his rule. Every sin is an act of disloyalty; every denial is an act of treason. Every time the Lord turns us again, calls us back, and forgives us, he calls us to renewed faithfulness: "But be sure to fear the LORD and serve him faithfully with all your heart; consider what great things he has done for you" (1 Sa 12:24). As we remember Christ's obedience for us, we will "serve him faithfully with all [our] heart."

"He died for all, that those who live should no longer live for themselves but for him who died for them and was raised again" (2 Co 5:15). It is at this point that David Valleskey writes in his People's Bible commentary on 2 Corinthians, "Christians today who weary of service in the kingdom, who sense a decline in the fervency of their love for Christ, would do well to come back again and again to the fountain, to the source of a Christian's love and service. We need to return to Calvary and view again the love Christ demonstrated for us where one died and therefore all died. And then, with Christ, we rise to newness of life, living a 'borrowed life,' his life, to his glory."[13]

"You know the grace of our Lord Jesus Christ, that though he was rich, yet for your sakes he became poor, so that you through his poverty might become rich" (2 Co 8:9). Our Lord Jesus Christ was rich. That is a very understated way of saying that he was the Lord from eternity. The holy and all-powerful God came to become a part of our human race. He did not stop being what he has been from eternity, but he became what he had not been, one of us. He became poor when he did that. He was laid in a borrowed manger; he preached from a borrowed boat; he entered Jerusalem on a borrowed donkey; he was buried in a borrowed tomb. He made himself of no reputation, took on a servant's form, humbled himself, and died the death of the cross.

Because he did that, we are rich. We have in our possession the most wonderful and most necessary thing there is: salvation. For his sake, God

---

[12]LW 23:28.
[13]David J. Valleskey, *2 Corinthians*, The People's Bible (Milwaukee: Northwestern Publishing House, 1992), pp. 88,89.

regards you and me as forgiven, saints, his children, heirs of eternal life. His grace was stronger and more abundant than our sin. His gospel declares this, and even while the gospel is declaring it, this truth is the power to convince us of it. When we trust this truth, we already have what it promises, salvation (Ro 1:16; 10:17).

God's grace in Christ is not cheap, for he paid a terrible price. It is, however, free. It is a fact that the Lord has added many riches to this great gift. He has given most of us abundant material blessings. He also gives us grace to share those riches.

"Those who belong to Christ Jesus have crucified the sinful nature with its passions and desires" (Gal 5:24). Notice the indicative. Paul does not say "should crucify" or "must crucify," but "have crucified." Paul gives us more encouragement and motivation in stating what is the case and what has occurred than in telling us what ought to occur. Luther also used the indicative in discussing the same subject: "The saints are certainly not without the flesh, but they repress their carnal impulses, lest they break out in action."[14]

In the Christian's life of faith there is no thought of fixing up the old sinful nature, giving up a few bad habits, and cultivating a few virtues. Get rid of it, Paul says: "You were taught, with regard to your former way of life, to put off your old self, which is being corrupted by its deceitful desires; to be made new in the attitude of your minds; and to put on the new self, created to be like God in true righteousness and holiness" (Eph 4:22-24). "Put on the new self." This new self is a creation of God. It is the restored image of God. It is the renewal of what was lost when man fell into sin. It is true righteousness and holiness. As God created them, our first parents were capable of knowing and willing and doing what God wanted. From the moment of their first disobedience, however, from the moment of the Fall, they lost God's image. You and I were born in their image, not God's. When Paul speaks of the old self, he is speaking of the sinful ego that we inherited from Adam. He is speaking of all the thoughts, motives, emotions, impulses, and desires in us that oppose God. When God speaks the word of forgiveness, based on Christ's perfect life and innocent death and assured by his glorious resurrection, he creates a new self. He says to us, Put off the old; put on the new.

Paul gives an example of putting off the old self and putting on the new: "Each of you must put off falsehood and speak truthfully to his neighbor, for we are all members of one body" (Eph 4:25). Put off lying. Put on the truth. We are no longer subject to the father of lies. God is a God of truth. We are created anew to be truthful. A Christian who lies not only injures the person to whom he lies, whether that is a fellow Christian or not, but also injures the circle of his fellow Christians. He gives them a bad name and sets them a bad

---

[14]LW 6:97.

---

example. The new self is responsive to God and responsible for the body of believers. The Christian will not want to enter a relationship or an occupation that involves lying or dishonesty.

"Be imitators of God, therefore, as dearly loved children and live a life of love, just as Christ loved us and gave himself up for us as a fragrant offering and sacrifice to God. But among you there must not be even a hint of sexual immorality, or of any kind of impurity, or of greed, because these are improper for God's holy people. Nor should there be obscenity, foolish talk or coarse joking, which are out of place, but rather thanksgiving" (Eph 5:1-4). In speech, posture, and attitudes, children imitate their parents. So are God's children to imitate him. The apostle urges us, "Live a life of love."

Imitating God also means abhorring what he abhors: "Among you there must not be even a hint of sexual immorality." It should be so far removed from us that no thought of its presence among us would occur to anyone. Furthermore, the gift of speech is for praising our Creator and Redeemer, not for dirt or smut or double entendres: "Nor should there be obscenity, foolish talk or coarse joking, which are out of place, but rather thanksgiving."

In Colossians 3:12,13, Paul addresses God's chosen, holy, dearly loved people. "Clothe yourselves," he says, and names a five-piece outfit. That is, he mentions five virtues. They do not constitute an exhaustive list, but we are not likely to wear out these five by overuse. "As God's chosen people, holy and dearly loved, clothe yourselves with *compassion, kindness, humility, gentleness* and *patience*. Bear with each other and forgive whatever grievances you may have against one another. Forgive as the Lord forgave you" (Col 3:12,13). Maybe the five virtues aren't always so apparent in your fellow believers, especially those you know best. Still, "bear with each other." Let forgiveness be your continuing and characteristic attitude. Not when forgiveness is asked for or when apologies are offered, but before—as God did. Not if your neighbor meets you halfway, but being ready to go all the way—as God did. Not bringing up the past, but forgetting it—as God did.

"Finally, brothers, we instructed you how to live in order to please God, as in fact you are living. Now we ask you and urge you in the Lord Jesus to do this more and more. For God did not call us to be impure, but to live a holy life" (1 Th 4:1,7). The Christian lifestyle is a developing thing, not a finished product. We are justified through faith in Christ our Redeemer. Justification is complete and perfect; there is nothing to improve or develop there. Our sanctification, the holy living to which God has called us and for which he has made us new, is still imperfect and will be until the Lord takes us to himself. His apostle calls on us to live more and more according to what pleases God.

The Christian lifestyle is a practical thing. That means learning and living God's standards and not those of the unbelievers. "God did not call us to be impure."

As Paul did, so Peter also sums up the Christian life: "Finally, all of you, live in harmony with one another; be sympathetic, love as brothers, be compassionate and humble" (1 Pe 3:8). One Sunday per month, I think, our pastor says, "Brothers and sisters, go in peace. Live in harmony with one another. . . ." What does it mean to live in harmony with one another? It means to "be sympathetic." Feel for your fellow Christians in good times and bad. When your fellow believer has reason to be sad, be sad with him. When he has reason to be happy, rejoice along with him. Resist the temptation to be jealous. "Love as brothers." Remember that we are all members of the same family, because we all have the same Father and because his Son became our brother. "Be compassionate." Let your heart go out to those who are in need, and act accordingly, in their best interest. Be "humble." Let someone else have the credit for what is done in the congregation. Be willing to let someone else have the place of honor. In church or family or community, be willing to take the role of a servant, remembering what our Lord Jesus did not come for and what he did come to do.

Peter continues in verse 9, "Do not repay evil with evil or insult with insult, but with blessing, because to this you were called so that you may inherit a blessing." It may be easy enough to keep from using our fists or reaching for a weapon, but sometimes it is difficult to keep our mouths shut. Peter writes, "Do not repay . . . insult with insult." How hard it is sometimes to keep from heaping verbal abuse on someone who has wronged us, to snap back, to trump someone's ace with a cruel remark. Repay evil and insult with blessing, says Peter. It is what our Lord taught in the Sermon on the Mount.

"Dear friends, now we are children of God, and what we will be has not yet been made known. But we know that when he appears, we shall be like him, for we shall see him as he is" (1 Jn 3:2). We are in the position of heirs who have not yet come into the full use of their inheritance. God has not publicly displayed the glory that belongs to his children. "What we will be has not yet been made known." Our life in Christ is like a diamond still uncut. "But we know that when he appears, we shall be like him, for we shall see him as he is." God does not plan to spend eternity by himself. Because of Jesus' perfect obedience in our stead, when he comes we will not be disappointed in what we can glimpse only vaguely now.

"Everyone who has this hope in him purifies himself, just as he is pure" (1 Jn 3:3). John uses the indicative; he states a fact. Since we live in the hope of being like Christ, of seeing him as he is, we will pursue purity of living. A Christian life that is not charted and motivated by the sure hope of eternal life is inconceivable. Conversely, it is inconceivable that those who live in this hope should live anything but a life of joyful obedience to him who willingly obeyed in our place.

CHRISTOLOGY AND JUSTIFICATION: A VITAL LINK

John C. Jeske

Western Wisconsin District Convention
Watertown, Wisconsin
June 8–9, 1998

The Christian church claims to have answers to the deepest questions that have ever occupied the human mind. Do I exist by accident or by design? If by design, by whose design? By whose order do I occupy a space on this planet, using up some of its natural resources and contributing to its landfill? Is life worthwhile? What's it for—just to pay your bills and stay out of jail? What are people for? Where am I headed, and how can I be sure I'll end up where I hope to? If the church is to have answers to important questions like these, we need not only a God who exists; we need a God who has spoken. And we have such a God.

When God spoke to a sinful world, he did not first conduct a public opinion poll to learn what people wanted to hear. Speaking through prophets and apostles at many times and in various ways, God gave us the message of heaven in the language of earth. He even gave it to us in written form. And then, after speaking through prophets and apostles, God gave us his final revelation through his Son.

The things Jesus Christ has to say to us are different from what any other religious teacher ever said. He says: "I am the truth. If you want to find out the truth about God, you'll have to come to me to find it out. If anything hinders you whatsoever from hearing what I have to tell you, throw it away. If it's your eye, gouge it out. If it's your hand or your foot, cut it off."

Realize what a drastic, shocking claim it is that Christ makes for himself in those words. The minute you hear them, you can understand how when Jesus spoke, people said, "No one ever spoke the way this man does!" The words Jesus speaks to us are radically different from what any other religious teacher ever told his followers. The people who first heard Jesus speak such words came to very different conclusions about Jesus of Nazareth.

When Jesus preached and taught, some of his countrymen said, "He is out of his mind" (Mk 3:21). In plain English: "He's mad!" Others took an even more unflattering view: "You are demon-possessed," they told Jesus (Jn 7:20). In other words, "You're in league with the devil; you're evil." But God saw to it that there were others who recognized Jesus for what he claimed to be. The disciple Thomas was one of those. "My Lord and my God!" he confessed a week after Easter (Jn 20:28). These are the only three realistic options a person has when seeking to evaluate the words and the work of Jesus Christ. He's either mad, or he's bad, or he's God.

I.

The topic assigned for this convention essay takes for granted that there is a vital link between what God has told us about Jesus' human/divine nature (Christology) and God's not guilty verdict on the sinner (justification). The purpose of this convention essay is to explore the link between the two.

Before we can do that, however, there's a question we must ask. The question may strike your ears as harsh, but we must ask it: "What qualifies Jesus of Nazareth to save anybody?"

The Christology taught unanimously by both Old and New Testaments is that *in Jesus Christ a human and a divine nature are inseparably joined.* Seven centuries before Christ was born, the prophet Isaiah called him *Immanuel,* a Hebrew name meaning "God with us." Think of it: God joined with us humans! Jesus is the only Savior for sinful mankind because he is one-of-a-kind, both God and a human being—the God-man.

That Jesus is a real human being is obvious even to a Sunday school kid. He spent nine months as an unborn baby. He was born of a human mother. He ate and drank. He grew from infancy to childhood to teen to grown man. He got tired, he cried real tears, he bled when he got a cut, he died. For you. The Bible calls Jesus human. Nobody has difficulty recognizing him as such.

It's a different matter, however, when it comes to recognizing Jesus' divine nature. Many nominal Christians are willing to call Jesus "the Son of God" but back off when it comes to calling him "God." They will acknowledge his human nature but refuse to recognize his divine nature. We will not identify any link between what the Bible teaches about Christology and what it teaches about the sinner's justification if we refuse to listen here: *the Bible calls Jesus "God."*

Listen carefully. In Psalm 45 the psalmist David addresses the Messiah and says, "Your throne, *O God,* will last for ever and ever" (v. 6). Seven hundred years after the prophet Isaiah foretold that the virgin would give birth to a child who would be Immanuel ("God with us," remember?), the angel Gabriel appeared to the virgin Mary. He gave her this information about the child she would bear: "The holy one to be born will be called the Son of *God*" (Lk 1:35). In describing the high privileges the ancient Israelites enjoyed, the apostle Paul comments, "Theirs are the patriarchs, and from them is traced the human ancestry of Christ, who is God over all, forever praised!" (Ro 9:5). The opening chapter of the epistle to the Hebrews emphasizes how superior Christ is to the angels of God. They are merely God's "servants" (v. 7). "But about the Son he says [quoting Psalm 45], 'Your throne, *O God,* will last for ever and ever'" (v. 8).

The human nature and the divine nature of the God-man don't exist side by side, like two boards glued together, two pieces of lumber that have absolutely no connection to each other. Christ's two natures are more like the body and soul in a human being. Christ's divine nature so permeates and penetrates his human nature that the two together make one person. *In Jesus Christ a human nature and a divine nature are inseparably joined.* This is biblical Christology.

To the casual observer of religion in America, this may seem to be one of the finer points of Christian doctrine. Is this pretty remote from the beating heart of everyday Christian life? If it is, why should we devote a large block of convention time this morning to this topic?

Satan knows something that casual observers of religion in America don't know. This basic teaching about the person of our Lord is the bedrock on which Christian faith and hope rest. Church history makes it clear that the teaching of the personal union of the two natures in Christ (the human and the divine) was one of the first teachings to be attacked by the opponents of Christ and his church. The attacks started while Jesus was still on earth. When he told the religious leaders of ancient Jerusalem, "I and the Father are one" (Jn 10:30), they picked up stones to stone him dead. In biblical times, that was the penalty for blasphemy, for mocking God.

About four centuries later, Arius, a church leader in Alexandria, Egypt, carried half of the church with him when he denied that Jesus of Nazareth had a divine nature. This Arius taught that Jesus Christ was only a man—so perfect that his followers called him "divine," but only a man. A hundred years later, Nestorius, bishop of Constantinople, denied that a divine and a human nature were united in the person of Jesus Christ. Nestorius argued—very logically, I might add—that the divine nature cannot share its attributes with a human being. He explained: "I cannot worship a God who was born, who died, and who was buried." How many Americans would echo Nestorius' thought, even though they couldn't say or spell his name? Nestorius' solution to the problem was to teach that the Son of God was one person, the Son of Man another person.

A century later, a new attack was made on the teaching of the personal union of the two natures in Christ. This time it came from Eutyches, like

Arius, a prominent leader in the Christian church in Alexandria, Egypt. He began to teach that at Bethlehem the two natures were mingled into one single essence. According to this heresy, Christ no longer has a human nature and a divine nature.

Perhaps more familiar to us is the time of the Reformation. The teaching of the union of two natures in Christ again came under heavy barrage, this time from Ulrich Zwingli and John Calvin. These men are the founders of the Reformed church on your street. They denied that Christ's two natures are inseparably joined, since, as they saw it, Christ's human nature is not capable of divine power and wisdom. Their mantra was *"Finitum non est capax infiniti."* Even if you don't read Latin, you should be able to figure that one out. "The finite is not capable of the infinite." A finite human nature is not capable of having real communion with the infinite divine nature.

As Zwingli and Calvin saw it, Christ's human nature could not receive divine attributes without being annihilated, like a light not wired for all the electricity flowing into it. They argued, for example, that the minute you ascribe omniscience to a human being, he's no longer a human being. Calvin was a lawyer, and Calvin was above all logical. Of course, that's fine—until the Bible disagrees with your logic. Then you must do as Dr. Siegbert Becker used to say: "Take off your hat in the presence of the Holy Spirit, and give him credit for being more learned than you are."

It was to counteract religious lies such as the ones just described that our Lutheran fathers drew up Article VIII of the Formula of Concord. They had this to say about the personal union of the two natures in Jesus Christ:

> We believe, teach, and confess that the Son of God,
>   although from eternity He has been
>   a particular, distinct, entire divine person,
> and thus, with the Father and the Holy Ghost, true,
>   essential, perfect God,
> nevertheless,
> in the fullness of time assumed also human nature into the
>   unity of His person,
> not in such a way that there now are two persons or two
>   Christs,
> but that Christ Jesus is now in one person
> at the same time true, eternal God, born of the Father from
>   eternity,
> and a true man, born of the most blessed Virgin Mary. . . .
>
> We believe, teach, and confess that now, in this one
>   undivided person of Christ,
> there are two distinct natures,
> the divine, which is from eternity,

We Believe in Jesus Christ

and the human, which in time was assumed into the unity of
> the person of the Son of God;
[these] two natures in the person of Christ are never
either separated from,
or mingled with, one another,
or changed the one into the other.[1]

Christ is and remains to all eternity
God and man in one undivided person,
which, next to the Holy Trinity, is . . . the highest mystery,
upon which our only consolation, life, and salvation
> depends.[2]

(This last phrase means that to be saved eternally, we need to know this, agree with this, and trust this.)

Since errors in Christology are usually of three different kinds, the response of the Lutheran Church (in Article VIII of the Formula of Concord) has been a threefold one.

We emphasize, first of all, that since *both* natures belong to the same person in Christ, *attributes belonging essentially to only one nature of the God-man* (for example, omnipotence and omniscience of the divine, or being born and dying of the human) *are always ascribed to his whole person.*

> If . . . Dame Reason, . . . would say, Yea, divinity cannot
> suffer or die; you shall reply, That is true; yet, because in
> Christ divinity and humanity are one person, Scripture . . .
> ascribes also to divinity everything that happens to the
> humanity, and vice versa.[3]

That means the Bible will often name the Savior according to *one* of his natures (either the divine or the human) and ascribe to him attributes of his *other* nature. This works two ways.

In 1 Corinthians 2:8, for example, Paul makes the striking statement that *the Lord of glory* was *crucified.* Now, it surely cannot be said that one of the characteristics of the divine nature is the ability to die. God is the same yesterday, today, and forever; he cannot change. And yet Paul states that the Lord of glory was crucified. He designates Christ according to his *divine* nature and then says something about him which properly applies to his *human* nature. (The Holy Spirit may do this; it's his book.)

The reverse is also true. The Scripture often designates Christ according to his *human* nature and says things about him which actually and essentially

---

[1] FC SD VIII:6,7.
[2] FC Ep VIII:18.
[3] FC SD VIII:41.

---

apply only to his *divine* nature. For instance, Jesus once said to his opponents, "What if you see the Son of Man ascend to where he was before!" (Jn 6:62). Here Jesus is named according to his human nature, but something is said about him which properly is not true of his human nature—that he existed as a person of the Holy Trinity prior to his becoming a human being. Again, *an attribute which belongs essentially only to one nature is always ascribed to the whole person of the God-man.*

Are you wondering if this kind of speaking is going to get a believer into hot water? The moment we teach this, we have opened the door to all kinds of questions and to apparent contradictions. The Bible tells us that Christ is *without a beginning,* yet he *was born* of a human mother. He was *born* of a woman, and yet remains the *Maker* of the woman. He gives food to all, yet must be fed by his mother. He is the Shaper and the Shaker of the universe, yet must be carried about on Joseph's arm. He is omniscient, yet he grew in wisdom. In the beginning was the Word, yet as a boy he had to learn his Bible passages.

Lutheran Christology simply *states* the truth God has revealed to us about the God-man without *trying to explain* that truth. It's enough for us to know that it makes sense to God. We're reminded once again that God is a hidden God, who has told us no more about himself than he feels we need to know. Is he under obligation to us to provide a rational explanation for everything he tells us? He doesn't owe us an explanation. He doesn't owe us a nickel. "Blessed . . . are those who hear the word of God and obey it" (Lk 11:28).

At the time of the Reformation, Luther's Reformed opponents, Zwingli and Calvin, maintained that Christ's human nature is not capable of divine power and wisdom. "The finite is not capable of the infinite." Admittedly that viewpoint makes sense to our human reason. The fathers who drew up the Lutheran confessions, however, saw this as false Christology, because the Scripture speaks otherwise. *Christ's human nature shares in the divine power, knowledge, and glory of the Son of God.* When the Son of God assumed human nature, he communicated divine majesty to it. Referring to the Word who had become flesh, St. John tells us, "We have seen his glory, the glory of the One and Only, who came from the Father" (Jn 1:14). When the disciples looked at the lowly Son of Man, they saw all the excellence and majesty which his divine nature shared with his human nature. St. Paul assured the Colossians, "In Christ all the fullness of the Deity lives in bodily form" (2:9).

On the pages of the Scripture we learn that God's chosen leaders often performed miracles. They opened up a path through the Red Sea, made an ax-head float, and restored the dead to life. But they performed these miracles through a power not their own. By contrast, the Carpenter-Teacher from Nazareth spoke of his divine power as his very own. "Destroy this temple, and I will raise it again in three days," he told the religious leaders in ancient Jerusalem (Jn 2:19). He could say that because *his human nature shares in the divine power and glory of the Son of God.* The Formula of Concord puts it this way: "The entire fullness of divinity dwells in Christ . . . bodily, as *in its own body,* so that it shines forth with all its majesty, power, glory, and efficacy in the assumed human nature . . . as the soul does in the body and fire in glowing iron."[4]

Because of this communion of the two natures, Jesus Christ had this divine majesty at his birth. St. Paul explains, however, that for most of his life Christ laid it aside. He kept it concealed, so that if you and I had walked the streets of Nazareth and Capernaum two thousand years ago, it's very possible we could have seen but never recognized God himself walking on our planet.

Christology as taught by the Reformed Church has consistently denied that Jesus of Nazareth possessed divine power. "Finitum non est capax infiniti," remember? The heirs of Zwingli and Calvin are willing to admit that Jesus had great power and wisdom, but insist that human nature is not capable of divine power and wisdom without being destroyed. The motives of Reformed theologians may be noble; they believe themselves to be safeguarding Christ's glory and sovereignty. In effect, however, they deny that in Jesus of Nazareth all the fullness of the Deity lives in bodily form.

Their denial actually goes one step further. Reformed Christology denies that Jesus' redemptive acts (all the verbs in the Second Article of the Creed: conceived, born, suffered, crucified, died, buried, descended, rose, ascended) were shared by both of his natures. The Formula of Concord addresses this error by emphasizing that *Christ performs all his official acts according to both natures,* each nature contributing its proper share to the act in intimate communion with the other. What Jesus accomplished in his work as our Priest, Prophet, and King may not be ascribed to either of his natures to the exclusion of the other, but must be ascribed to both natures together.

Who was it who came under the law, so he could obey God's Commandments perfectly, thereby providing the perfect obedience God *demands* of us but never *received* from us?

Was it the man-child born of the virgin Mary? St. Paul says no. "When the time had fully come, God sent his Son, born of a woman, born under law, to redeem those under law, that we might receive the full rights of sons" (Gal 4:4,5).

Who was it who was conceived of the Holy Spirit, born of the virgin Mary, suffered under Pontius Pilate, was crucified, died, and was buried? Again, was it the man Jesus? For centuries Christians have confessed, "I believe in Jesus Christ, *[God's] only Son, our Lord*, who was conceived . . . , born . . . , suffered . . . , was crucified, died, and was buried." For more than four and a half centuries, Lutheran children have learned to say, with Martin Luther, "I believe that Jesus Christ, *true God* . . . and also *true man,* . . . is my Lord. He has redeemed me."

---

[4]FC SD VIII:64.

Let's say it again. Our faith needs to hear it again. Christ performed all of his official acts according to both natures. Destroying Satan and his murderous plan was not performed by Christ's divine nature independently of his human nature; it was performed through his human nature. The writer to the Hebrews makes this crystal clear: "Since the children have flesh and blood, he too shared in their humanity so that by his death [there's the human nature] he [namely, the Son of God] might destroy him who holds the power of death—that is, the devil" (2:14). In every step of Christ's redemptive work, his two natures did not act independently of each other. There was a communication, a sharing of the divine and the human natures, in each of Christ's official acts.

Reformed theology aggressively disagrees. According to that lawyer-like belief system, to say that the Son of God could suffer and die changes God into a human being. Foolish! Blasphemous! Zwingli and Calvin consistently denied that the *Son of God* shed his blood. They also taught that Christ's human nature must be excluded from all cooperation in works of almighty power, because that would exceed its capability.

The simple Christian asks, "What do the Reformed books do with those clear Bible passages that ascribe Christ's redemptive work to both of his natures?" From the time they could talk, we taught our kids to pray at bedtime: "The blood of Jesus, [God's] Son, purifies us from every sin" (1 Jn 1:7). "When we were God's enemies, we were reconciled to him through the *death of his Son*" (Ro 5:10). Zwingli readily admitted that many Scripture passages speak of the sacrifice of God's Son, but he insisted these must be understood as referring exclusively to Christ's human nature. He called this an *alloeosis,* a figure of speech by which one nature is named, but the other one is meant.

Can you guess that Martin Luther had no kind words for the alloeosis? He labeled it a device of human reason that gives no credit at all to the Saviorhood of Christ or to the clarity of Scripture. Luther added:

> Now if the old witch, Lady Reason, alloeosis' grandmother, should say that the Deity surely cannot suffer and die, then you must answer and say: That is true, but since the divinity and humanity are one person in Christ, the Scriptures ascribe to the divinity, because of this personal union, all that happens to humanity, and vice versa. And in reality it is so. Indeed, you must say that the person (pointing to Christ) suffers, and dies. But this person is truly God, and therefore it is correct to say: the Son of God suffers. Although, so to speak, the one part (namely, the divinity) does not suffer, nevertheless the person, who is God, suffers in the other part (namely, in the humanity).[5]

---

[5]LW 37:210. (Quoted in FC SD VIII:41,42.)

II.

Take a breath. From what we've studied so far today, you can sense how the Lutheran church has struggled to remain faithful to how the Bible speaks about Jesus Christ and at the same time to respond to attacks made on it. The language used in Article VIII of the Formula of Concord is technical and theological. Maybe that was really necessary back in the 16th century. But perhaps more to the point, as the Christian church approaches its 2,000th anniversary, how important is the doctrine of Christ's two natures? Have the lengthy explanations and the careful definitions and the technical terminology we have reviewed been mere battles about words? The title assigned for this convention essay asks us to address the question, What connection is there between biblical Christology and the sinner's justification? Does it really matter?

In the opinion of many, Jesus Christ was a Jewish carpenter-teacher who taught beggar and king alike that there's a whole lot to be said for loving your neighbor. They see in him a heroic martyr who was willing to put other people first. I pray that our review of biblical Christology has reminded us that Jesus is God in human form.

From the time the LORD God called "Adam, where are you?" we have been called to hear our Lord's voice. But to whom are we listening when we hear Jesus Christ speak to us from the pages of his Word? We were reminded earlier that because of the union of the two natures in Christ, his human nature shared in all the majesty and power of God. Contrast this with the statement of the eminent Reformed theologian Charles Hodge: "Omniscience is not an attribute of which a creature can be made the organ."[6] (Can you hear echoes of *"Finitum non est capax infiniti"*?) Do you see how Hodge's statement debases all of Christ's teaching? If what Hodge said is true—if our great Prophet is not omniscient—then Christ's ministry is reduced to the level of the prophets of ancient Israel. No offense to Jeremiah there, but our certainty of where we stand with God depends on knowing that *because Jesus is both God and man, when Jesus speaks to us, God speaks to us.*

It's important to maintain the union of the two natures in all of Christ's work as our *Prophet* and our *King*. But it's absolutely critical to see clearly on this teaching when we study and proclaim Christ's redemptive work, his work as our *Priest*. That's the focus of the concluding portion of this essay.

You will recall that once early in his Galilean ministry, Christ was in a house preaching. Some people brought a paralyzed man on a mat and tried to place him before Jesus. When this was impossible because of the crowd, they

---

[6]Charles Hodge, *Systematic Theology*, Vol. 2, 1997 edition (Grand Rapids: Wm B. Eerdmans Publishing Company, 1872), p. 417. Also quoted by Francis Pieper, *Christian Dogmatics*, Vol. 2 (St. Louis: Concordia Publishing House, 1951), pp. 167,243,253,259.

---

removed some roof tiles and lowered their friend right into the crowded room, in front of Jesus.

Jesus knew the man lying before him was suffering from a disability that made his life difficult and unpleasant. But Jesus knew also that the man suffered from another problem infinitely and eternally more serious than his paralysis. And so the first thing Jesus said to him was, "Friend, your sins are forgiven" (Lk 5:20). The Pharisees (those stalwart defenders of the law of Moses) and the teachers of the law who were in the house began thinking to themselves, "Who is this fellow who speaks blasphemy? Who can forgive sins but God alone?" (v. 21).

Today people don't accuse Christ of *blasphemy* when he announces forgiveness of sins, but of *irrelevance.* The age we live in has an easy conscience about sin. I'm reminded of the answer the American poet Walt Whitman gave when somebody asked him, "Have you made your peace with God?" He responded, "Why, I didn't know God and I were on the outs!"

Back to Jesus' treatment of the paralyzed man. What would've been the use of giving him two sound legs to walk on if the man didn't know where he was going and had nothing to live for? Augustine had it right when he said, "Lord, you have made us for yourself, and our heart is restless until it finds its rest in you."[7] I dare not forget that I am a creature of God. I'm dirt plus the breath of God. The Bible teaches that I have been designed to live under God in a master-servant relationship. Your life, my life, have absolutely no value in and of themselves. We and everything we call our own are valuable and worthwhile only when we have found our way back into friendship and fellowship with the God who created us. And that will happen only when you and I have heard the message of how the son of Mary and Son of God traded places with us in life and in death, so that God could pronounce us not guilty.

With pathetic pride, church leaders today pronounce this message irrelevant for people who have greater concerns as they prepare to enter the 21st century. But was this message irrelevant for the 1st century Jews and Greeks to whom Jesus and the apostles preached? There were social problems in Christ's day—plenty of them—but he still thought it necessary to bring people the message of sin and grace, of law and gospel. There were plenty of people in Bible times who didn't have enough to eat. Jesus dealt with a man born blind, with a woman arrested in the act of adultery, and with a five-time divorcee. In Palestine there was racial hatred between Samaritans and Jews. Onesimus was a runaway slave. In Ephesus a labor union caused Paul a lot of trouble. In Rome there was anti-Semitism. Why do we think that our problems today are so different or that we need a new message for the people whom God has called us to serve?

---

[7]Augustine, Confessions I:1.

You will remember that when God gave his law to his human creatures, he said basically two sorts of things. He said something about *obedience,* and he said something about *disobedience.* The one he demands; the other he forbids. He still says these things to every human being.

God says first of all: I want obedience, and I insist on it. "Obey me and do everything I command you, and you will be my people, and I will be your God" (Jer 11:4). But the moment God announces his requirements to his creatures, he has to spell out what will happen if they fail to meet his requirements. God does not say, "If you break my law, well, I disagree, but you have to do what's right for you." What God does say is, "I don't want disobedience, and I forbid it." "Cursed is the man who does not uphold the words of this law by carrying them out" (Dt 27:26).

Our Savior, therefore, had a double job to do in order to ransom and rescue us and to restore us to a place in God's family. As our substitute he first of all had to provide that perfect obedience to the word and will of God, which God demanded—but never got—from us. The one who had no place to lay his head was not permitted to mope or to covet a comfortable cottage by the lake. We call this Christ's *active obedience*—doing what we had not done.

The other half of Christ's assignment was to undo what we had done. On that awful Friday we call "Good," he suffered the curse God had announced on our sinfulness. "It was the LORD's will to crush him and cause him to suffer" (Isa 53:10). This work we call Christ's *passive obedience.* He provided this by suffering a substitutionary death, letting God's anger crush the very life out of him, suffering the ultimate torment of the damned in hell. Stop and think. Our God is a righteous God, a God who is true to his principles: I am the God who punishes every sin; I am the God who forgives every sin (cf. Ex 34:6,7). Because of Christ's active and passive obedience, this God could—without compromising his principles—pronounce a worldful of guilty sinners not guilty.

Now what does the doctrine of Christ's two natures have to do with this cardinal doctrine of Christianity—justification? Everything, that's what! Imagine for a moment that you were perfect, without stain of sin. What could the heavenly Judge say to you when you stand before his judgment throne? What else than "Come, my child, your place is ready. Enter the joy of your Lord." But what if in that moment you were to ask God, "May I take my family along with me?" The Judge would have to answer, "Your holiness is sufficient for you, but not enough for you and them. They'll have to stand before me on their own."

Do you sense the frightful implications of that Reformed Christology—that God cannot die, that death is incompatible with deity, that Jesus Christ died only according to his human nature? What if Christ obeyed God's law only according to his human nature? What if he died only as a man? Then you and I don't have a Savior. *It's Christ's divine nature personally united with his human nature* that elevates his work to count for you and all of your fellow sinners. If I write you a check for $100,000, don't get your hopes up; my checking account doesn't hold that kind of money. But if you get a $100,000 check signed by Bill Gates, take it to the bank.

The psalmist said it well: "No man can redeem the life of another or give to God a ransom for him—the ransom for a life is costly, no payment is ever enough" (Ps 49:7,8). The deliverance only God can give is not for sale; even if it was, you couldn't afford it. But Jesus Christ is no mere human being, either. *He, the God-man, came to earth as the only one in all of history who could be holy and remain holy.* He did this so that God might credit the holiness of his Son as a free gift to all. What God demands, he has given to us in his Son, who became our substitute. The God whose holiness will not permit him to accept me for what I am is a God whose mercy has accepted me for what Christ is.

> Surely he took up our infirmities
> > and carried our sorrows,
> yet we considered him stricken by God,
> > smitten by him, and afflicted.
> But he was pierced for our transgressions,
> > he was crushed for our iniquities;
> the punishment that brought us peace was upon him,
> > and by his wounds we are healed.
> We all, like sheep, have gone astray,
> > each of us has turned to his own way;
> and the Lord has laid on him
> > the iniquity of us all.
> He was oppressed and afflicted,
> > yet he did not open his mouth;
> he was led like a lamb to the slaughter,
> > and as a sheep before her shearers is silent,
> > so he did not open his mouth. (Isa 53:4-7)

Because of the union of the two natures in Christ, *the God-man's death on Calvary was actually not a single death, but one death for every sinner who ever lived.* He who had no sin became what he was not—he became sin for us. He traded places with you under the judgment of your righteous God. He intercepted and absorbed in his holy body the fiery bolts of God's white-hot anger over your sinful heart and hand. On the skull-shaped hill, Jesus was damned by his Father; he experienced hell for you. And now a righteous God can justly consider the penalty for sin to have been paid for a whole world of sinners.

Here is the vital link between Christology and justification. Because the God-man lived the life we owed, and died the death we had coming, he reconciled a whole world of sinners to God. Martin Luther wrote many beautiful

We Believe in Jesus Christ

prayers, but none more beautiful than the one incised in marble at the base of his statue on the campus of Wisconsin Lutheran Seminary:

> Lord Jesus, you are my righteousness, just as I am your sin.
> You have taken upon yourself what is mine and have given to
>   me what is yours.
> You have taken upon yourself what you were not and have
>   given to me what I was not.[8]

Might you want to memorize that?

Dr. Martin Luther once made the perceptive comment that if it's only the human nature of Christ that died for me, then Christ is a mighty poor savior. "We Christians should know that if God is not in the scale to give it weight, we, on our side, sink to the ground. I mean it this way: if it cannot be said that God died for us, but only a man, we are lost; but if God's death and a dead God lie in the balance, his side goes down and ours goes up like a light and empty scale."[9] If Christ died only as a human being, then he was no more than one of the many great human benefactors who have died in a noble cause. *But if it's the God-man who lived a perfect life and who died an innocent death, a world of sinners is saved.* That means I am saved. And then life is worth living, and death is worth dying. "I love you, O LORD, my strength" (Ps 18:1)!

Think of what the biblical doctrine of the two natures of Christ means to you as you live out your life in a world that's hostile to Christianity. The Scripture has assured us that Christ ascended to heaven not merely as some sweet saint, but as the all-powerful and ever-present God-man. The LORD is my Rock, my Fortress, and my Deliverer. When Christ was on earth, in the words of St. Paul, he "made himself nothing, taking the very nature of a servant" (Php 2:7). During the thirty-some years Jesus spent on earth, he kept his divine nature under wraps; he didn't always use it. In what we call his *state of humiliation,* he chose to be in only one place at a time. If he was in Perea, east of the Jordan River, then he wasn't in Bethany, where Martha later complained, "Lord, . . . if you had been here, my brother would not have died" (Jn 11:21). But Christ is no longer in his state of humiliation. The Ascension festival we celebrated three weeks ago promises that he has ascended far above all heavens. He rules as God-man from sea to sea, to the ends of the earth—at your kitchen table, in the hospital corridors, on the runway, over the Oval Office and the Kremlin.

Do you sense the implications of this statement for you? Little five-year-old Sarah was afraid to be alone. Her mother told her, "But, Sarah, God is with you." To which the little girl responded, "But I want somebody with skin

---

[8]LW 48:12. (Letter to George Spenlein, April 8, 1516.)
[9]LW 41:103. (Cf. also FC SD VIII:44.)

---

on." The helper whom God sent us is a helper "with skin on." The One who is seated at the video monitor of the universe is the eternal God—yet who in the womb of the virgin Mary wrapped himself in your flesh and blood. He is like us in every respect except that he is without sin. And do you recall he never laid aside his human nature? He may not always have *used* it, but he *retained* it and still retains it. It's our brother who is alive today in a resurrected and glorified body of flesh and blood who rules the world. He knows your pain, your loss, your broken heart, your homesickness, and he has promised us that nothing in all of creation will separate you from his love. You just have to love the Holy Scriptures!

It seems to me that *those of you who have been called into the public ministry* have additional reason to remind yourself exactly who this omnipresent Lord of the church is. The Lord of the lampstands, the One who guides and oversees the work of his church, who is he? Is it enough to answer: "The Lord of the church is God?" I confess I find that a disturbing thought. If the one who observes and evaluates my ministry is only God, majestic and perfect, then I must know that his holiness is to my ministry what fire is to kindling. I'm toast, and my work is of no consequence. That's as grim as it gets. That's the bleakness which moves desperate people to go out in a blaze of meaningless gunfire. And then, really, what man is there among us who will dare to say with Isaiah, "Here am I. Send me!" (6:8)? We'll more likely want to say with Moses, "Here am I; send Aaron!" (cf. Ex 3:4–4:17).

The God-man, my Savior and my brother, has promised his Christians

> that not only His mere divinity would be with them, . . . but that He, He, the man who has spoken with them, who has tried all tribulations in His assumed human nature, and who can therefore have sympathy with us, as with men and His brethren,—He will be with us in all our troubles also according to the nature according to which He is our brother and we are flesh of His flesh.[10]

Jesus—my brother—sympathizes with me! It almost brings tears to your eyes. What a Savior!

Many people feel God is far away and aloof and disinterested. It's hard to understand a God who is remote. Just try to love a God like that. But our brother has said, "Anyone who has seen me has seen the Father" (Jn 14:9). Because the God-man permitted his Father to become his Judge, we can look upon him who is our Judge as our loving Father. We can talk to him as dear children talk to a loving father. We know the Father to whose house we are going.

---

[10]FC SD VIII:87.

In Jesus Christ, God entered life on this planet. This God-man experienced our hurts, wept our salty tears. He loved people and served the weakest of his creatures. We have no reason to suspect that this has changed now that Immanuel, the God-man, has ascended. Let me tell you of a widow who has been in a sitting position for five long, weary, painful years. Think about it: five years, unable to stretch, unable to lie down. She wrote, "I have spent many a day alone, but never a lonely day—because of Jesus." Disciples of Christ, this matters! As we live out the lives God has cut out for us, we can rejoice, as the Formula of Concord puts it, that "our flesh and blood is placed so high at the right hand of the majesty and almighty power of God."[11]

Enough of "*Finitum non est capax infiniti*"! Accept in simple faith what the Scripture teaches about the union of the human and the divine natures in Christ. Today we have identified the vital link between Christology and justification. And we have something solid to live for, to work for, to die for—something to share. And having that, we have all we need.

"To him who loves us and has freed us from our sins by his blood, and has made us to be a kingdom and priests to serve his God and Father—to him be glory and power for ever and ever! Amen" (Rev 1:5,6).

---

[11]FC SD VIII:96.

CHRIST IN US:
THE PLACE OF THE DOCTRINE OF SANCTIFICATION
IN REFORMED AND LUTHERAN TEACHING

Paul M. Janke

Arizona-California District Convention
Mesa, Arizona
June 15–17, 1998

"When the Son of Man comes, will he find faith on the earth?" (Lk 18:8). Jesus asked that question after he told the parable of the persistent widow. The Savior provided the answer to his question when he promised in Matthew chapter 16 that the gates of hell would not overcome his church. "[Christ's] Church shall endure," says the hymn.[1] The fact that Jesus asked the question, however, implies that there will be a falling away from the faith. The Lord told us in Matthew chapter 24 that when he returns he'll find apostasy, false prophets, and the love of most grown cold. But he also promised us, "He who stands firm to the end will be saved" (Mt 24:13).

The next time this assembly of Lutheran pastors, teachers, and congregational delegates gathers, God-willing, will be in June of the year 2000. Perhaps the millennium fever will have subsided by then. Or perhaps King Jesus will already have returned and there won't be the need for another of these conventions. Whatever the case, in view of the Savior's warnings about apostasy and in love for his truth, it's always appropriate for us to ask, Are we as a body of Lutheran believers remaining faithful to our coming King? We ask the question not simply on account of some parochial desire to see the Lutheran church sustained as an institution or merely as a nameplate. The

---

[1] CW 536:1, "Lord Jesus Christ, the Church's Head."

question deserves to be asked because it is our conviction that the Evangelical Lutheran church has historically, by the grace of God, borne faithful witness to the Son of Man and exalted his name by its faithful adherence to his teaching. Are we remaining faithful?

On the eve of a new millennium, there are troubling trends in the largest Lutheran church body in our country. The Evangelical Lutheran Church in America's adoption of a "Joint Declaration on the Doctrine of Justification" at its 1997 Church Assembly and its approval of "full communion" with Reformed Churches at the same convention are just the latest signals that not all those who bear the name Lutheran are standing firm in Christ's teaching. Approval of full communion with Reformed churches indicates that the long-held belief that there are substantive doctrinal differences between Reformed and Lutheran theology is evaporating. This would not be the first time that has happened. Lutherans fled Prussia in the previous century to escape a king who believed that Lutheran-Reformed doctrinal differences were inconsequential. The problem is that when Reformed and Lutheran churches enter full communion, it will not be that Reformed churches begin teaching Lutheran doctrine but that Lutheran churches begin to adopt Reformed doctrine.

While differences between Lutherans and the Reformed regarding the sacraments, particularly the Lord's Supper, are perhaps better known and more easily recognized, differences between the two on the doctrine of sanctification also exist. The difference is sometimes expressed in this way: the Reformed emphasize "Christ in us," while Lutherans emphasize "Christ for us." That is, in Reformed theology, sanctification ("Christ in us") is often emphasized at the expense of justification ("Christ for us").

Harold Senkbeil writes that in Reformed theology "Christ's action in me is held to be of more importance than Christ's action *for me*."[2] "Lutheran theology correctly views man's problem to be the guilt of his sin," writes Robert Koester. "The gospel is nothing other than that in Christ, God has justified the world. Reformed theology is skewed in the direction of making the goal of Christianity the *remaking* of people into more moral individuals."[3] This difference in emphasis was noted earlier by E. Arnold Sitz, who writes, "The Calvinist is less concerned about doctrine, theology, and knowledge, more insistent upon life, piety, and doing. He looks more to the holiness of God, less to the love of God; more to the law, and less to the gospel."[4]

---

[2] Harold Senkbeil, *Sanctification: Christ in Action* (Milwaukee: Northwestern Publishing House, 1989), p. 113.
[3] Robert Koester, *Law and Gospel: Foundation of Lutheran Ministry* (Milwaukee: Northwestern Publishing House, 1993), pp. 33,34.
[4] E. Arnold Sitz, "Calvinism: Its Essence and Menacing Impact Upon American Lutheran Doctrine and Practice," *Our Great Heritage*, Vol. 3, Lyle W. Lange, editor (Milwaukee: Northwestern Publishing House, 1991), pp. 641,642.

One Lutheran theologian described the consequences of Lutherans adopting Reformed views on sanctification this way:

> Through the process of intellectual infiltration, theological transfusion, religious exposure, and direct ingestion and imbibing, the authentic Lutheranism of Luther and the Confessions is lost and views inimical to the heart of our theology are held. Past history shows that, whereas Calvinism and Arminianism have never reached the point of extinction, Lutheranism frequently has. Sanctification is an area where Lutherans are vulnerable to Protestant influences and can be, have been, and still are overtaken by outside influences.[5]

This essay is written in the belief that if we are to be found faithful on the day our Lord returns, we must emphasize in our teaching not sanctification but justification, not "Christ in us" but "Christ for us." It is not that "Christ for us" and "Christ in us" are to be split or separated, with justification being treasured and sanctification being discarded. Sanctification is taught in Scripture. Sanctification flows from justification. But if the doctrine of justification is what the Apology to the Augsburg Confession says it is, namely, "the main doctrine of Christianity,"[6] then that is where the emphasis should lie in our teaching, preaching, and practice.

First, there is the matter of definitions. In this essay the term *Reformed* will be used to refer to "all Protestantism in this country outside the Lutheran."[7] While grouping all of Protestantism together like this ignores many obvious distinctions in theology, it is still true that the various segments of Protestantism can trace their origins back to the Swiss Reformation and fathers of the Reformed churches, such as Ulrich Zwingli and John Calvin.[8] Protestant churches also have a great deal in common in this matter of "Christ in us."

When we speak of justification in this essay, we refer to the Bible's teaching that God, by grace, for Christ's sake, has declared all people not guilty of sin. "God was reconciling the world to himself in Christ, not counting men's sins against them" (2 Co 5:19). This verdict of not guilty becomes ours when the Holy Spirit works through the gospel to cause us to believe

---

[5]David P. Scaer, "Sanctification in the Lutheran Confessions," *Concordia Theological Quarterly*, Vol. 53, No. 3 (July 1989), p. 172.

[6]Ap IV:2, Tappert, p. 107.

[7]Sitz, p. 605.

[8]In a sense, Lutherans were among the earliest to "protest" the doctrinal errors of the Roman Catholic Church. However, Lutherans are not merely Protestants. "The Lutheran Church has not the slightest theological interest in this antithesis between Catholicism and Protestantism. It does not know to which side it belongs. If only there were a clear-cut contradiction between true and false doctrine in the antithesis! But this does not happen to be the case. For there are heresies in Protestantism which are just as dangerous as those of Catholicism." Hermann Sasse, *Here We Stand: Nature and Character of Lutheran Faith*, p. 110.

that the righteousness of Christ has been given to us. "To the man who does not work but trusts God who justifies the wicked, his faith is credited as righteousness" (Ro 4:5).

When we use the term *sanctification* in this essay, it will normally be in the narrow sense of the word, that is, referring the Spirit-wrought hatred of sin and the accompanying desire to live a holy life filled with good works. The apostle Paul was referring to sanctification in its narrow sense when he wrote, "God did not call us to be impure, but to live a holy life" (1 Th 4:7). While justification through faith in Jesus is instantaneous, perfect, and complete; sanctification, on account of our continuing struggle with the sinful nature, is progressive, imperfect, and incomplete.

Placing the emphasis on "Christ in us" (sanctification) over "Christ for us" (justification) is not necessarily something that the Reformed deny doing. In an article titled "The Reformed Family Today," Alan P. F. Sell wrote,

> It would therefore seem that there are not ten or twenty—or even FIVE—doctrines that are Reformed in the sense that they are nobody else's. The Reformers, let us recall, had catholic intentions: they were in quest of a biblically based account of the gospel of God's grace. Thus, if they *emphasized*, as they did, the priority of the regenerating work of God the Holy Spirit; if they *emphasized*, as they did, the inescapability of the church and the duty of raising the banner of Christ's lordship over the whole of life—then they made these emphases not because they were Reformed but because they were scriptural.[9]

Another Reformed author quotes the Westminster Larger Catechism at the place where it answers the question, Wherein do justification and sanctification differ?

> Although sanctification be inseparably joined with justification, yet they differ, in that, God in justification, imputeth the righteousness of Christ; in sanctification, his Spirit infuseth grace, and enableth to the exercise thereof; in the former, sin is pardoned; in the other, it is subdued; the one doth equally free all believers from the revenging wrath of God, and that perfectly in this life, that they never fall into condemnation; the other is neither equal in all, nor in this life perfect in any, but growing up to perfection.

---

[9]Alan P. F. Sell, "The Reformed Family Today: Some Theological Reflections," *Major Themes in the Reformed Tradition*, Donald K. McKim, editor (Grand Rapids: Wm B. Eerdmans Publishing Co., 1997) p. 435.

We Believe in Jesus Christ

Then he adds, "This is a remarkably balanced statement. In practical life, however, Calvin and the Reformed tradition often failed to maintain the tension and overemphasized sanctification."[10]

The emphasis on sanctification in Reformed writings

This overemphasis on sanctification can be seen in a devotional for men called *Promises to Keep: Daily Devotions for Men Seeking Integrity*. Though the book wasn't published by the Promise Keepers organization, it is designed to be a resource "for men in search of spirituality."[11] The format of the book is that the devotions are usually selections from books by writers as diverse as Christopher Columbus, John Grisham, Orel Hershiser, Tom Landry, Abraham Lincoln, Martin Luther, Roger Staubach, and Jim Ryun. For the most part, though, the authors come from a Reformed background and many of them have been associated with the Christian men's movement. There are contributions to the book by Tony Evans, Gene Getz, Jack Hayford, Robert Hicks, Bill McCartney, Gary Smalley, and Stu Weber. A Scripture passage that was seen to have some connection with the author's topic was then positioned at the beginning of the devotion. So, for the most part, the devotions are not expositions of a Bible passage.

As the title of the book implies, this devotional aims to be a collection of promises for Christian men to keep. It does very well at achieving that goal. With rare exceptions, the book is a daily dose of "do this" and "don't do that." Here's just a partial list of the exhortations: *Do* . . . be courageous, commit yourself completely to God, say your prayers, be a good father, be a devoted husband, have a heart for excellence, be thankful, get some exercise, be patient, show affection to your wife, exercise self-discipline, keep your promises, and make appropriate physical contact with your child. The other side of "Do!" is "Don't!" *Don't* . . . gamble, be a racist, watch pornographic movies, be a workaholic, break your promises, or be afraid to cry.

Much of what is being urged on Christian men in these devotions can be supported from the Scriptures. And the gospel is not completely absent. It can be found in some of the devotions. The reading for January 1 was written by Coach Tom Landry. In it he says, "As a Christian I believe my past is forgiven; I can start over with a clean slate."[12] Not a bad thought at all on which to start a new year. It's just that the law is so prominent in the remainder of the book that any gospel that is present is pushed into the background and overshadowed.

The law that is so overwhelmingly present in *Promises to Keep* is almost always what we would call the third use of the law, and hardly ever the sec-

---

[10]John H. Leith, "The Ethos of the Reformed Tradition," *Major Themes in the Reformed Tradition*, p. 11.
[11]Nick Harrison, editor, *Promises to Keep: Daily Devotions for Men Seeking Integrity* (San Francisco: Harper, 1996), jacket copy.
[12]Tom Landry, "Tom Landry: An Autobiography," *Promises to Keep*, p. 1.

---

ond use of the law. As the Formula of Concord describes it, there are three uses of God's law: "(1) to maintain external discipline against unruly and disobedient men, (2) to lead men to a knowledge of their sin, (3) after they are reborn, and although the flesh still inheres in them, to give them on that account a definite rule according to which they should pattern and regulate their entire life."[13] If the *Promises to Keep* devotions had employed the law more in its second use, to arouse a consciousness of sin, then there might also be more gospel content in the book in order to comfort sinners. As it is, the book comes off as more of a manual on how to find fulfillment and satisfaction in life as a Christian man.

Consider this excerpt from a devotion written by Bill McCartney, the former head coach of the University of Colorado football team and one of the founders of Promise Keepers. Speaking of a conference for Christian athletes that he attended, McCartney says,

> For the first time I was confronted with whether or not I had actually surrendered control of my life to Jesus Christ. I understood that if I would submit to Christ, Almighty God would take dominion in my heart and take over the direction of my life. *Then my life would start to gain some real satisfaction and fulfillment.* That really appealed to me because in my work I had just entered into an arena where it was extremely competitive and I wasn't feeling good about myself.[14] [emphasis mine]

Notice the preoccupation with the law. As McCartney sees it, Christ confronts us with a demand that we surrender control of our lives to him. That means, I assume, that we agree to start living by his law. But where is the consciousness of sin? Where is the despairing of man's power to comply with the law, like we hear in the apostle Paul: "For what I want to do I do not do, but what I hate I do" (Ro 7:15)? Jesus comes across not so much as a Savior from sin, but as a top-notch lifestyle coach who will direct us to ways of living that are more wholesome, healthy, and fulfilling.

The Bible then becomes a how-to manual with specific directions for those interested in making their lives more satisfying.

> So if God and heaven and eternal life be absolute verities and if it be true that heaven is as certainly prepared for those who prepare for it, as the opportunity to practice medicine or surgery, to say nothing of a successful practice thereof, depends on thorough preparation, how important that we pre-

---

[13] FC Ep VI:1, Tappert, pp. 479,480.
[14] Bill McCartney, "What Makes a Man?" *Promises*, p. 29.

We Believe in Jesus Christ

pare for heaven by the study and the practice of the principles laid down in the only Text-book ever given to point out the way to accomplish that preparation."[15]

Daniel Webster apparently had a similar view of the Scriptures, though he does allow that the Bible prepares us for death. "This is the Book. I have read the Bible through many times, and now make it a practice to read it through once every year. It is a book of all others for lawyers, as well as divines; and I pity the man who cannot find in it a rich supply of thought and of rules for conduct. It fits a man for life—it prepares him for death."[16]

All this emphasis on "rules for conduct" and "the practice of principles" makes it a bit ironic that *Promises to Keep* also contains a devotion excerpted from a book titled *Grace Works*, by Dudley Hall. He writes, "I spent many years seeking to discover all [God's] principles and to live by them. I wanted to become an expert in understanding the ways of God." But, he says, "I reached a point when the principles I was discovering turned out to be too many, and I realized I just did not have the mental capacity to decipher the multifaceted wisdom of Almighty God." Hall says it was at that point that he came to the realization that God is "very big and very good." That's a rather vague statement of God's grace, but Hall says it caused a transformation in him. "The point is: I began to be free of inner turmoil not when I focused on the complexity of God's principles, but when I perceived the awesomely simple truth of who he is. And that change of perspective dramatically changed the way I looked at everything else in life."[17] You have to wonder if a statement like that doesn't negate most of the rest of the book.

R. Kent Hughes is the senior pastor of College Church in Wheaton, Illinois. He has written a book titled *Disciplines of Grace: God's Ten Words for Vital Spiritual Life*. Hughes is well known in evangelical circles. A selection from his book *Disciplines of a Godly Man* appeared in *Promises to Keep*. Obviously, Hughes is big on discipline. The title *Disciplines of Grace* intrigued me because it refers to the Ten Commandments as grace, not as law.

Hughes is exactly right when he refers to the Commandments and says, "In point of fact, the Law was *founded* on God's grace." He's right again when he says that Exodus 20:2 is "the preamble of grace."[18] The passage reads, "I am the LORD your God, who brought you out of Egypt, out of the land of slavery." The People's Bible volume on Exodus quotes August Pieper, who said of this verse, "There is no purer, more heartwarming gospel in the whole

---

[15]James Anderson, "Thoughts That Breathe," *Promises*, pp. 198,199.
[16]Ibid., p. 177.
[17]Dudley Hall, "Grace Works," *Promises*, pp. 311,312.
[18]R. Kent Hughes, *Disciplines of Grace: God's Ten Words for a Vital Spiritual Life* (Wheaton, Illinois: Crossway Books, 1993), p. 17.

Scripture than this verse with its promise."[19] One might even be able to understand Hughes correctly when he says, "Law and grace are not antithetical or the least bit opposed,"[20] if he resolved the huge apparent contradiction between law and grace at the foot of the cross. In places he seems to do that. He speaks of the need to preach the law in such a way that people are brought first "to Sinai, the mount of doom and the consuming fire of God's holiness." Then, he counsels, people are to "be led to Calvary, the mount of grace and the consuming love of God."[21] Hughes even takes issue with the fact that "the evangelical presentation of Christ as Savior" often centers on his being able "to enrich life" or make one "complete" or, though it is not so crassly stated, to add Christ as "a mere religious component of one's self-actualization."[22]

But then the early promise dissipates when Hughes says, "Fittingly, meditation upon God's Law invites its keeping by the believer. It is quite simple: Jesus *authored* the Law, Jesus *kept* the Law, Jesus *indwells* believers, and Jesus sends His Holy Spirit to indwell believers and to enhance His life in them."[23] This, I believe, is where Hughes attributes to the law a power that it does not have, namely, to invite the keeping of the law. He quotes Psalm 19 to buttress his position, including verse 7—"The law of the LORD is perfect, reviving the soul"—apparently believing that the law as we find in the Decalogue has the capability to bring new life to men's souls. It's true that the new man delights in God's law (Ro 7:22), but we are also possessed of an old self, which chafes and balks and rebels at the thought of obeying the law. What will invite us to keep the law, then? Not more reading of the law, but the gracious word of forgiveness for Christ's sake, of which the Ten Commandments have not a one. As for the Psalm 19:7 reference, the psalmist uses the Hebrew word *torah* (translated "law") here in the sense of "teaching," which can include both law and gospel. The torah in verse 7 must be the gospel, since only the gospel has the power to breathe life into souls that were dead in sin.

Hughes says a bit later, "I am convinced that for the Christian, the understanding of God's Ten Words, the Decalogue, coupled with a determination to live them out by God's Spirit, will invite God's grace and will free his children to soar above the ignorance, moral relativism, and ethical desolation of our culture."[24] At the end of his introduction, he reveals his bias quite clearly when he exhorts, "Discipline yourself, for these are Ten Words of Grace!"[25] Hughes is so confident of the power of discipline that the summary chapter on this extensive review of the Ten Commandments contains no

---

[19]Ernst Wendland, *Exodus*, The People's Bible (Milwaukee: Northwestern Publishing House, 1984), p. 133.
[20]Hughes, p.17.
[21]Ibid., p. 19.
[22]Ibid., p. 19.
[23]Ibid., p. 20.
[24]Ibid., p. 22.
[25]Ibid., p. 23.

assurance of the forgiveness we have in Christ for our failures to keep the Commandments. Rather, the author insists, "If one knows Christ, it is possible, through discipline, to live within the spiritual parameters, the borders, of the Law" because "Jesus Christ fulfilled the Law, and because we are in Christ and *he is in us.*"[26] In *Disciplines of Grace* the gospel is once again buried under a mountain of law.

The Goal of the Gospel: God's Purpose in Saving You was written by two Missouri Synod pastors, Philip Bickel and Robert Nordlie. It was published by Concordia in 1992. The book created a minor stir because of the authors' assertion that Lutheran churches are frequently guilty of "sanctiphobia," which the authors define as the "malady of fearing to challenge people to live courageously for their Lord."[27] The authors' thesis is that "[God] redeemed us in order to restore us to his image, so that we may live at the very center of his will, experiencing his perfect goodness. This is the goal of the gospel."[28]

One chapter of the book features a conversation between a husband and wife in which the wife expresses concern about the devotional booklet the couple has been using (apparently a Lutheran publication). "I don't feel like I'm being challenged by these devotional readings," she says to her husband. "Almost every day they remind us once again that Jesus is our Savior and that our sins are forgiven through faith in him." The husband is at first puzzled by his wife's concern. So she explains, "We do need to be reminded of those precious truths; but it seems that the readings rarely go beyond reminding us that we are saved. It's sort of like we are always being pointed back to square one in the Christian life but are not given much encouragement or guidance about all the steps that come after that." The husband grasps his wife's point and suggests they borrow a devotional booklet from a friend named Charlie, who attends the Community Church. Their use of that booklet was a success at first, but after a time left the couple feeling burdened "with the continual stress on all the things that I ought to be doing as a Christian."[29] Ultimately, they hit upon a solution, which was to use both books, as if one were to read devotions alternately from *Meditations* and *Promises to Keep*, I suppose.

The book is carefully researched and interesting to read. If the authors' thesis is correct—that we Lutherans often suffer from "gospel myopia," that "we have a tendency to lift great Gospel verses right out of a sanctification section without seeing beyond them"[30]—then it is a matter of concern. The preaching of the law is necessary, not only to arouse an awareness of sin but also to guide us in living lives that please God.

---

[26]Ibid., p. 187, (emphasis mine).
[27]Philip M. Bickel and Robert L. Nordlie, *The Goal of the Gospel: God's Purpose in Saving You* (St. Louis: Concordia Publishing House, 1992), p. 97.
[28]Ibid., p. 24.
[29]Ibid., p. 96.
[30]Ibid., p. 73.

It's one thing to make a case for continuing to preach sanctification. It's another thing, however, to do as Bickel and Nordlie do in stressing the importance of obeying God's law, and say, "Do you want concrete evidence of your salvation? Look at your life. Are you obedient to Christ's command to love?"[31] In support of the direction to peer inside ourselves for the proof of our salvation, they cite 1 John 3:18-20: "Dear children, let us not love with words or tongue but with actions and in truth. This then is how we know that we belong to the truth, and how we set our hearts at rest in his presence whenever our hearts condemn us."

It would have been good if Pastors Bickel and Nordlie could have sat in as Professor Siegbert Becker, formerly a member of their synod, expounded the true meaning of 1 John 3:20. In preaching on this text he said, "We make a great mistake when we look for the certainty of our salvation in our own heart in any way."[32] He pointed out that 1 John 3:20 wasn't written for people who live in false security. "Our text speaks especially to people whose hearts condemn them," he said. When our hearts condemn us and tell us that our sins are too great to be forgiven, it is then that "God is greater than our hearts" (1 Jn 3:20). "When our heart tells us one thing and God tells us another, we have no business listening to this heart of ours."[33] The authors of *The Goal of the Gospel* show how easy it is to go from a valid concern—that the preaching and teaching of sanctification are sometimes neglected—to the error of emphasizing sanctification so much that believers are even encouraged to find the assurance of their salvation in their own sanctified living.

As to Bickel and Nordlie's insistence that sanctification is the goal of the gospel, the late Professor Donald Deffner set the matter straight when he wrote, "In sum, in our teaching we do not proclaim the Gospel's *purpose* as the production of good works. Good works are preaching's *result*. But *justification* remains the Gospel's only purpose."[34]

The emphasis on sanctification in Reformed preaching

The Ministers Manual "has for more than half a century remained the most trusted and comprehensive preaching and resource book available," say the publishers.[35] The book consists of sermons and worship aids, including benedictions, prayers, quotes, and illustrations. "Hundreds of original sermons from the nation's leading preachers" is how the resource describes itself. The editor is James W. Cox, a senior professor of homiletics at the

---

[31]Ibid., p. 91.
[32]Siegbert W. Becker, *The Word Goes On: Sermons by Dr. Siegbert Becker*, compiled by James P. Becker (Milwaukee: Northwestern Publishing House, 1992) p. 131.
[33]Ibid.
[34]Donald L. Deffner, "Moralism" in *Concordia Pulpit Resources*, Vol. 5, No. 4, p. 14.
[35]*The Ministers Manual*, James Cox, editor, 1997 edition (San Francisco: Harper, 1996).

Southern Baptist Theological Seminary in Louisville, Kentucky. I read through the sermons in the book to try to get a handle on what it is that distinguishes Reformed preaching from Lutheran preaching, at least the Lutheran preaching practiced in our synod.

The sermons in *The Ministers Manual* don't appear to be full-length sermons that a minister could preach just as they appear in the book. Most of them seem too short for that. They are written out, however, rather than being presented in outline form. The book contains no direction to personalize the sermons or flesh them out or, for that matter, to add some gospel.

The gospel is not entirely absent from this collection of sermons. Not every sermon proclaims "Christ for us," but some do. In a sermon on Hebrews 2:6—"What is man that you are mindful of him, the son of man that you care for him?"—the author says, "God's estimate of human worth can be seen in the crucifixion. Nowhere is God's love for mankind more clear than at Calvary. God loved us so much that he gave his Son Jesus for our sins."[36] In a sermon on the baptism of Christ, the preacher states "that at this moment of his baptism in water [Jesus] was being ordained to that sacrificial ministry that would end with his baptism in his own blood 'shed for us.' "[37] In a sermon for Easter Sunday, William Richard Ezell says, "The point is that Jesus died and rose again for you."[38] And later, speaking of Christ's Easter victory, he writes, "You can know that you have that victory because of Jesus' resurrection."[39] In a sermon called "The Clothes of Christ," based on Luke 2:7 and Revelation 1:13, Robert Shannon writes, "Now we see the most wonderful thing of all. . . . He put his robe on them: his robe or righteousness—his robe of purity, his robe of sinlessness. He put his robe on them! He put his robe on us!"[40] In one place a Lutheran, Richard Andersen, finds his way into the collection and says that Baptism is a sacrament in which we "are rinsed clean of sin's stain."[41]

Having noted a few places where the gospel can be found, though, it must also be said that many sermons are entirely devoid of gospel. The first sermon in the book, based on Psalm 91, never mentions the *name* of Jesus, to say nothing of the gospel of Jesus. The theme of the sermon is "Depending on God." The author cites Ben Franklin, of all people, as someone who depended on God. Franklin stood up at the Constitutional Convention and said, "The longer I live, the more convincing proofs I see of this truth; that God governs in the affairs of men."[42] While that statement may be considered a break-

---

[36]Ibid., p. 26.
[37]Ibid., p. 21.
[38]Ibid., p. 248.
[39]Ibid., p. 249.
[40]Ibid., p. 248.
[41]Ibid., p. 111.
[42]Ibid., p. 18.

---

through for Franklin, his well-documented rejection of Jesus as his Savior makes him a strange choice for illustrating dependence on God.

In a sermon on Jeremiah 33:12-16—a text which includes the prophecy, "I will make a righteous Branch sprout from David's line" (v. 15)—there is no clear statement that Jesus Christ is the righteous Branch, the one in whom that prophecy is fulfilled. Nor is there any statement that through faith in Jesus, God credits Christ's righteousness to us. Instead, the sermon limps to a close on this note: "Salvation comes to this—truth and honesty and fairness before God are still expected even when all else is going up in flames. God wants a commitment to righteousness from us even under widespread conditions of unrighteousness. The behavior of others is no excuse for our misbehavior."[43] Like many of the sermons in the book, this one is not expository, that is, it really doesn't attempt to set forth the meaning of the text on which it purports to be based.

The sermon for Palm Sunday, listing Matthew 21:1-11 as the text, is a good example of the problem with many of the sermons in *The Ministers Manual*. Taking off on the way the cheering Palm Sunday crowds deserted Jesus just five days later, the preacher calls for increased commitment to Christ. "We are all aware that Lent is a time for reflection and repentance and renewal. But it can also be a time of deepening our commitment to Christ's cross, at the same time allowing his Spirit to deepen our Christian character."[44] Nowhere is there any mention that Jesus came to Jerusalem to die for us. That note is missing from the vast majority of the sermons in the book. In its place there is frequently a call for commitment to Christ, a rather vague call. In the sermon above it seemed to mean "broadening the base of Christ-like compassions."[45] After hearing that call often enough, you want to shout, "Why? Why should I be more committed to Christ? Tell me what he's done for me!" But in most of the sermons, a specific declaration of Christ's meritorious work on our behalf is absent.

One of the biggest disappointments in the book is the sermon for Christmas, based on the song of the angels in Luke 2:14, "Glory to God in the highest, and on earth peace to men on whom his favor rests." What the angels presented as an accomplished fact, this preacher characterizes as a dream, the dream of peace.

> The secret is that this God who has come in Christ will bring peace, if we will let him use us. But can it be? We dream of it. If only everybody would love God, what a nice world this would be! But in order for that to happen we have got to give

[43]Ibid., p. 255.
[44]Ibid., p. 240.
[45]Ibid.

glory to God, and that means you and I have got to take God seriously. You and I have to believe in his way of life. You and I have got to put him first in our lives.[46]

Also disappointing is a sermon for the Easter season, with the text taken from Luke chapter 24, the story of the two disciples on the road to Emmaus. The theme of the sermon is "Take a Stranger to Lunch." It turns out that's not just a catchy theme. The preacher actually means it. The preaching value he found in that appearance of the risen Savior was an injunction to demonstrate hospitality. Take a stranger to lunch and "you could experience the power of the universe working through you."[47]

Preachers in our circles are sometimes criticized for a lack of creativity in proclaiming the gospel. Sunday after Sunday, the accusation goes, it's the same lines of gospel promise; John 3:16 repeated *ad drowsium*; the gospel by boilerplate, fashioned with all the freshness and variety of a paralegal slapping together a $75 will. And it could be that more than just occasionally the criticism hurts because it's true. But I must say that after reading through so many sermons that never mention the gospel of "Christ for us," the shopworn cadences of gospel clichés would be welcome relief.

Chuck Colson, the former Nixon aide and Watergate conspirator, now the president of Prison Fellowship, has a sermon in *Best Sermons 2*, also edited by James Cox. The text for the sermon is Matthew 5:13-16, from the Sermon on the Mount, where Jesus speaks of believers as the salt of the earth and the light of the world. "What can a fellow believe in anymore?" Colson asks. After speaking about the self-centeredness of our culture, he lists "six points on what I think the responsibility of the church is today in modern American culture. The first point is to get serious in your own life with God."[48] When Colson explains what he means by that, he says, "What's involved is a recognition that Jesus Christ died on the cross for your sins and your forgiveness and that you come to him and ask forgiveness of those sins. . . ." So far, so good. But then he continues, ". . . and surrender your life to him and commit yourself to live under his lordship and make a difference in the world." All of that. The gospel and then law, lots of law. The second point is to be repentant people. The third point is to take a stand on the holy Word of God. The fourth point is to think as Christians. Then to "learn that the heart of Christian life is obedience."[49] The last point is "be holy." To his credit, he sums up the points by asking the same question, "What can a fellow believe anymore?" and he answers with, "The good news that Jesus came and died on that cross for your

---

[46]Ibid., p. 254.
[47]Ibid., p. 64.
[48]James W. Cox, editor, *Best Sermons 2* (New York: Harper, 1988), p. 8.
[49]Ibid., p. 14.

Christ in Us: The Place of the Doctrine of Sanctification

177

sins." Colson's text would certainly dictate that the sermon was going to deal extensively with sanctification—and he did speak of Jesus and the forgiveness we have through him. But to say that the heart of the Christian life is obedience places the emphasis of the Christian message on sanctification rather than on justification, where it really belongs.

It's much easier to keep the emphasis in our preaching on "Christ for us" when we follow the kind of guidance that was a big part of the homiletics training at Wisconsin Lutheran Seminary. First, follow the church year. The church calendar is divided into two parts. The Advent-to-Pentecost festival half of the year regularly directs us in its appointed readings to what Christ has done for us. "Christ in us" isn't neglected, though, because the non-festival half of the church year focuses more on the Christian life.

Second, preach the pericopes, choosing a text from the appointed Scripture lessons, whether the series is the ILCW, the Historic, or something else. The readings have been selected to give the preacher and his congregation a well-balanced diet based on the whole counsel of God. Free texts aren't absolutely forbidden, but too much of that poses an increased risk that the preacher will be back on his hobbyhorse each Sunday, and it probably won't be a gospel hobbyhorse either.

Then, preach the text. In some of *The Ministers Manual* sermons, there was beautiful gospel in the text, but the preacher never mentioned it because he wasn't preaching the text. When a preacher reads a text to a congregation, the people have a right to expect that the sermon is going to be based on that text. In the great majority of the texts found in the ILCW, the gospel is there explicitly. If not, then it's there by implication. Either way, the gospel is to be "proclaimed to the joy and edifying of Christ's holy people." A sermon that fails to use "the power of God for salvation" is going to be shooting blanks.

Finally, preach Christ. That, after all, is why we pastors and teachers are in the ministry. That is why our congregations exist. Christian teachers and pastors are servants of the gospel of Jesus Christ. From front to back, Jesus and the salvation we have through him are the message of the Bible. Even when it's an Old Testament text where the names Jesus or Christ aren't mentioned, the Old Testament Scriptures still testify about Jesus. Whether the text is Old Testament or New Testament, the preacher will want to make a beeline for Jesus.

Martin Luther is on record as having believed that a sermon which proclaims only law is insufficient in both departments: justification and sanctification.

> Ancient teachers said that there are four things a preacher
> should keep in mind in all his sermons; he should give con-
> sideration to vices and virtues, to punishments and rewards.
> And they did well to give this advice, provided that they

We Believe in Jesus Christ

retained Christ. For the Law concerns itself with these four things: vices contrary to the Law, virtues in accordance with the Law, punishments in accordance with the Law, and rewards in accordance with the Law. But this doctrine does not produce Christians. It is the doctrine of the Law, which does not bring about perfection. The Gospel of grace must be joined to this doctrine of the Law! Then at last the Christian is made complete.[50]

In another place Luther wrote,

> If you preach faith, people become lax, want to do no good, serve and help no one. But if you do not preach faith, hearts become frightened and dejected and establish one idolatrous practice after another. Do as you please; nothing seems to help. Yet faith in Christ should and must be preached, no matter what happens. I would much rather hear people say of me that I preach too sweetly and that my sermon hinders people in doing good works (although it does not do so) than not preach faith in Christ at all; for then there would be no help for timid, frightened consciences.

> I see and experience this: Here is a man who is lax and lazy, who falsely boasts of faith and says that he relies on the grace and mercy of God and that these will no doubt help him even though he clings to sins. But as soon as death comes to him, it appears that he has never really grasped and believed the grace and mercy of God. Therefore one will have enough to do to cheer and comfort him, even though he has not practiced any particular idolatry. But when the message of faith has been extinguished and the heart is completely swamped by sadness, there is neither counsel nor help. Say something about grace to such a heart, and it will answer: You preach much to me about grace and mercy; but if you felt what I feel, you would speak differently. So a frightened, inconsolable heart goes on. I have heard people speak like this when I tried to comfort them. Therefore I should like to have the message of faith in Christ not forgotten but generally known. It is so sweet a message, full of sheer joy, comfort, mercy, and grace. I must confess that I myself have not yet fully grasped it. We shall have to let it happen that some of our people turn the

---

[50]LW 3:132,133.

---

message into an occasion for security and presumption; but others, the work-righteous, slander us on this account and say that we make people lazy and thus keep them from reaching perfection. Christ Himself had to hear that he was a friend of publicans and sinners (Luke 15:2), that he broke the Sabbath, etc. We shall not fare any better.[51]

The emphasis on the law that we find in Reformed theology is due, in the case of Calvinistic Reformed, to their belief in the so-called "limited atonement." John Calvin (1509-1564), a Frenchman educated as a Catholic priest, fled to Switzerland in 1535 after openly espousing the Protestant cause. In 1536 he wrote *The Institutes of Christian Religion*, an explanation of his theology, which stresses the sovereignty of God and reposes great confidence in human reason. It has been said, "Luther stresses the glory of God's love; Calvin stresses God's love of glory."[52] The Five Points of Calvinism, a brief summation of Calvin's teaching, include (1) total depravity, (2) unconditional election, (3) limited atonement, (4) irresistible grace, and (5) perseverance of the saints.

Calvin's theology has been expressed in this century by the writings of Reformed theologian Louis Berkhof. Like Calvin, Berkhof teaches a limited atonement. "In distinction from [Lutherans and others] the Reformed Churches believe in a limited atonement. They maintain that it was the intention of both the Father and the Son to save only the elect, a purpose that is actually accomplished."[53] This statement makes it hard to know what the Holy Spirit had in mind when he caused the apostle Paul to write, "This is good, and pleases God our Savior, who wants all men to be saved and to come to a knowledge of the truth" (1 Ti 2:3,4). St. Paul even asserts that Jesus "gave himself as a ransom for all men" (v. 6). In 2 Corinthians 5:19 the same apostle writes that "God was reconciling the world to himself in Christ, not counting men's sins against them." The Reformed must also reckon with the apostle Peter, who writes, "[The Lord] is patient with you, not wanting anyone to perish, but everyone to come to repentance" (2 Pe 3:9). And there are the familiar words of Jesus, "God so loved the world . . . " (Jn 3:16).

The Reformed belief in limited atonement fits hand in glove with their belief in double predestination. Berkhof writes about election this way: "[Election] may be defined as God's eternal purpose to save some of the human race in and by Jesus Christ." Then, with a deduction that sounds eminently logical but that is scripturally inaccurate, Berkhof goes on to say, "The doctrine of election naturally implies that some of the human race were not

---

[51]Martin Luther, *What Luther Says*, Vol. 3, #3603, p. 1128, (from an Ascension Day sermon on Acts 1:1-11 and Psalm 68:18).
[52]Erwin L. Lueker, *Lutheran Cyclopedia* (St. Louis: Concordia Publishing House, 1975) p. 125.
[53]Louis Berkhof, *Manual of Christian Doctrine* (Grand Rapids: Wm B. Eerdmans Publishing Co., 1933), p. 216.

elected. If God purposed to save some, he also purposed not to save others."[54] You see in that statement how the application of human reason results in the undermining of the truth of Scripture.

Diagram:[55] The Approaches of Luther and Calvin to Theology

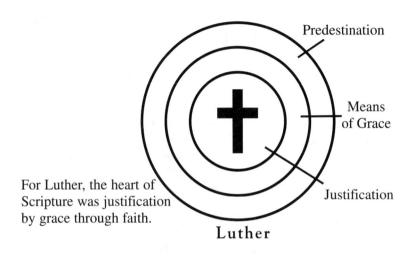

Predestination

Means
of Grace

For Luther, the heart of
Scripture was justification
by grace through faith.

Justification

Luther

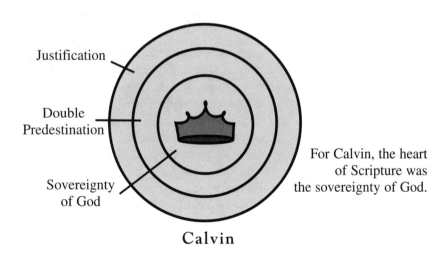

Justification

Double
Predestination

Sovereignty
of God

For Calvin, the heart
of Scripture was
the sovereignty of God.

Calvin

---

[54]Ibid., p. 91.
[55]John Moldstad, Jr., *Predestination: Chosen in Christ*, People's Bible Teachings (Milwaukee: Northwestern Publishing House, 1997), p. 76. Used by permission.

The Calvinist teaching that "God purposed not to save" some people is called reprobation, "the decree of God whereby he has determined to pass some men by with the operation of his special grace and to punish them for their sin to the manifestation of his justice."[56] In other words, "the horrible decree": God in all eternity predestined some people to eternal damnation.

The key question, then, among those who adopt this belief in double predestination is, "Am I one of the elect?" If you're one of the elect, then Christ died for you. How can a person know that he's one of the elect? To answer that question, unfortunately, people are sometimes advised by Reformed teachers to look inward. Look at your life. Is there evidence in your life that Christ is living in you? A Reformed theologian by the name of Strong said, "The only conclusive evidence of perseverance is a present experience of Christ's presence and indwelling, corroborated by active service and purity of life."[57]

Over against this answer the Lutheran theologian Francis Pieper declared,

> This is the cure for these cases—the objective, universal, perfect grace of God, which is not based on Christ's indwelling and on the holy life of the suppliant, but has been gained by Christ's vicarious satisfaction for all men, is offered in the Gospel to all, with the object of bringing them to faith in it. Universal grace (which is an objective reality and is offered in the objective means of grace), and not "Christ in us" and our virtuous life, is "the grace of God that brings salvation" (Titus 2:11).[58]

Classical Calvinism, however, is actually rather rare in this country. Much more common than Calvinism is Arminianism, named after Jacob Arminius (1560–1609). Arminius, who was from Holland, opposed the Five Points of Calvinism with what came to be known as the Five Points of Arminianism. They are (1) God from all eternity predestined to eternal life those of whom he foresaw as remaining steadfast in faith to their end, (2) Christ died for all mankind, not only for the elect, (3) man cooperates in his conversion by free will, (4) man may resist divine grace, and (5) man may fall from divine grace.[59] While Lutherans would heartily agree with several of the elements of this list, Point 1, with its espousal of election "in view of faith," and Point 3, with the bold statement of cooperation in conversion (synergism), are quite obviously at odds with the Bible's truth that our salvation is by grace alone. Arminianism teaches that man does at least this much: he uses his free will to

---

[56]Berkhof, p. 91.
[57]Quoted by Francis Pieper, *Christian Dogmatics*, Vol. 3 (St. Louis: Concordia Publishing House, 1950), p. 90.
[58]Ibid.
[59]Lueker, p. 49.

---

cooperate in his conversion and then keeps himself steadfast in the faith. Any credit, however, is too much for people who were dead in sin, blind to spiritual truth, and enemies of God. Scripture clearly teaches that our salvation is due to the grace of God in Christ Jesus and to that alone.

The adherents of Arminianism end up emphasizing the law because their definition of faith commonly includes so much more than a simple trust in the promises of God. For many Arminians, faith includes good works. (See Chuck Colson's explanation of "getting serious about your life with God" on page 177 above.) "The Arminians look upon justifying faith as obedience to the entire Word of God, also the Law," wrote Pieper.[60] Justification is then based, at least in part, on some accomplishment of man. Hence the emphasis on "Christ in us."

As we stated earlier, it's our contention that the emphasis in Scripture is on "Christ for us" rather than on "Christ in us," on justification rather than on sanctification. Can that be supported from the Scriptures? It can. Listen to the apostle John as he sums up the message of his gospel: "Jesus did many other miraculous signs in the presence of his disciples, which are not recorded in this book. But these are written that you may believe that Jesus is the Christ, the Son of God, and that by believing you may have life in his name." (20:30,31). In the prologue to his gospel, John had written earlier, "From the fullness of his grace we have all received one blessing after another. For the law was given through Moses; grace and truth came through Jesus Christ" (1:16,17).

John the Baptist was a stern preacher of the law who called upon people to "produce fruit in keeping with repentance" (Mt 3:8). Yet all his preaching of the law was designed to show people their sins and thus also their desperate need of a Savior. When John saw Jesus coming he said, "Look, the Lamb of God, who takes away the sin of the world!" (Jn 1:29).

The invitation to believe in Jesus rings clearly throughout John's gospel, nowhere more famously than in the third chapter. "For God so loved the world that he gave his one and only Son, that whoever believes in him shall not perish but have eternal life. For God did not send his Son into the world to condemn the world, but to save the world through him. Whoever believes in him is not condemned, but whoever does not believe stands condemned already because he has not believed in the name of God's one and only Son" (3:16-18). In the aftermath of the healing of the invalid at the pool of Bethesda, Jesus said, "I tell you the truth, whoever hears my word and believes him who sent me has eternal life and will not be condemned; he has crossed over from death to life" (5:24). Later in the same chapter, Jesus told the Jews, "You diligently study the Scriptures because you think that by them you possess eter-

---

[60]Francis Pieper, *Christian Dogmatics*, Vol. 2, p. 12.

---

nal life. These are the Scriptures that testify about me, yet you refuse to come to me [that is, believe] to have life" (v. 39).

After Jesus fed the five thousand, some of the people asked him, "What must we do to do the works God requires?" (Jn 6:28). Jesus' answer was plain and simple: "The work of God is this: to believe in the one he has sent" (v. 29). A little later Jesus told the same group, "This is the will of him who sent me, that I shall lose none of all that he has given me, but raise them up at the last day. For my Father's will is that everyone who looks to the Son and believes in him shall have eternal life, and I will raise him up at the last day" (vv. 39,40).

While he was in Jerusalem attending the Feast of Tabernacles, Jesus said, "If anyone is thirsty, let him come to me and drink. Whoever believes in me, as Scripture has said, streams of living water will flow from within him" (Jn 7:37,38).

In addition, each of the I AM statements of Christ in John's gospel is an invitation to faith: "I am the light of the world. Whoever follows me will never walk in darkness, but will have the light of life" (8:12); "I am the gate; whoever enters through me will be saved" (10:9); "I am the good shepherd. The good shepherd lays down his life for the sheep" (10:11). And Jesus said to his grieving friend Martha, "I am the resurrection and the life. He who believes in me will live, even though he dies; and whoever lives and believes in me will never die. Do you believe this?" (11:25,26).

In John 12:36 we hear Jesus invite us to "put your trust in the light while you have it, so that you may become sons of light." Later in the same chapter, the Savior said, "When a man believes in me, he does not believe in me only, but in the one who sent me. When he looks at me, he sees the one who sent me. I have come into the world as a light, so that no one who believes in me should stay in darkness" (vv. 44-46).

In his 1535 commentary on Galatians, Dr. Luther contended that justification by faith was also the theme of the book of Acts:

> The entire book of Acts speaks of nothing else but that Jews as well as Gentiles, the righteous as well as the unrighteous, are justified only by faith *(sola fide)* in Christ Jesus, without the Law and works. The sermons of the apostles, Peter, Paul, Stephen, Philip, and others show this, as well as the examples of the Gentiles and the Jews. For just as God by the preaching of the Gospel gave the Holy Spirit to the Gentiles, who lived without the Law, so He gave Him also to the Jews, not through the Law, not through the ceremonies and sacrifices prescribed in the Law, but through the preaching of faith alone. Now if the Law had been able to justify, and the righteousness of the Law had been necessary for salvation, then

We Believe in Jesus Christ

the Holy Ghost would certainly not have been given to the Gentiles, who had not kept the Law.[61]

The emphasis on the gospel, on faith in what Jesus has done for us, is also to be found in the New Testament epistles. As it is well known, the apostle Paul clearly emphasizes Christ for us. Paul is "not ashamed of the gospel, because it is the power of God for the salvation of everyone who believes" (Ro 1:16). He told the Corinthians, "We preach Christ crucified" (1 Co 1:23). Scorning worldly wisdom, Paul told the Corinthians, "I resolved to know nothing while I was with you except Jesus Christ and him crucified" (1 Co 2:2). This truth—that Jesus is the Christ, the Son of God who died for us—is the basis of our faith. There is no substitute. "No one can lay any foundation other than the one already laid, which is Jesus Christ" (1 Co 3:11).

Paul has plenty to say to the Corinthians regarding their sanctification, but at the beginning of his great resurrection chapter he writes, "What I received I passed on to you as of first importance: that Christ died for our sins according to the Scriptures, that he was buried, that he was raised on the third day according to the Scriptures, and that he appeared to Peter, and then to the Twelve" (1 Co 15:3-5).

After he had preached the law in such a way that all, Jew and Gentile, were included under sin, Paul shared the unsurpassed comfort of the gospel of "Christ for us." "But now a righteousness from God, apart from law, has been made known, to which the Law and the Prophets testify. This righteousness from God comes through faith in Jesus Christ to all who believe. There is no difference, for all have sinned and fall short of the glory of God, and are justified freely by his grace through the redemption that came by Christ Jesus. God presented him as a sacrifice of atonement, through faith in his blood" (Ro 3:21-25).

The little word *for* speaks repeatedly of the reconciliation that Jesus effected by taking our place under the law and at the cross. "Christ redeemed us from the curse of the law by becoming a curse for us" (Gal 3:13). "Christ loved us and gave himself up for us as a fragrant offering and sacrifice to God" (Eph 5:2). "Husbands, love your wives, just as Christ loved the church and gave himself up for her" (Eph 5:25). "There is one God and one mediator between God and men, the man Christ Jesus, who gave himself as a ransom for all men" (1 Ti 2:5,6). Writing to Titus, Paul speaks of "the glorious appearing of our great God and Savior, Jesus Christ, who gave himself for us to redeem us from all wickedness" (2:13,14).

The apostle John teaches "Christ for us" too. "My dear children, I write this to you so that you will not sin. But if anybody does sin, we have one who

---

[61]Luther, *What Luther Says*, Vol. 2, #2189, p. 702.

---

speaks to the Father in our defense—Jesus Christ, the Righteous One. He is the atoning sacrifice for our sins, and not only for ours but also for the sins of the whole world" (1 Jn 2:1,2). And later in the same epistle: "This is how we know what love is: Jesus Christ laid down his life for us" (3:16). And finally, "This is love: not that we loved God, but that he loved us and sent his Son as an atoning sacrifice for our sins" (4:10).

The Apology of the Augsburg Confession speaks of the beautiful comfort of the "Christ for us" gospel in its article on justification. When the central truth of "Christ for us" is in the preeminent place, then good works will follow too. Justification results in sanctification. Sanctification flows from justification.

> The Gospel is, strictly speaking, the promise of forgiveness of sins and justification because of Christ. Since we can accept this promise only by faith, the Gospel proclaims the righteousness of faith in Christ, which the law does not teach. And this is not the righteousness of the law. For the law requires our own works and our own perfection. But to us, oppressed by sin and death, the promise freely offers reconciliation for Christ's sake, which we do not accept by works but by faith alone. This faith brings to God a trust not in our own merits, but only in the promise of mercy in Christ. Therefore, when a man believes that his sins are forgiven because of Christ and that God is reconciled and favorably disposed to him because of Christ, this personal faith obtains the forgiveness of sins and justifies us. In penitence and terrors of conscience its consoles and encourages our hearts. Thus it regenerates us and brings us the Holy Spirit, so that we can finally obey God's law, love him, truly fear him, be sure that he hears us, and obey him in all afflictions. It mortifies our lust. By freely accepting the forgiveness of sins, faith sets against God's wrath not our merits of love, but Christ the mediator and propitiator. *This faith is the true knowledge of Christ, it uses his blessings, it regenerates our hearts, it precedes our keeping of the law.*[62]

The authors of the Formula of Concord cited the Augsburg Confession and quoted Luther in pronouncing the doctrine of justification to be the central message of the Scriptures:

> In the words of the Apology, this article of justification by faith is "the chief article of the entire Christian doctrine," "without which no poor conscience can have abiding comfort

---

[62]Ap IV:43-46, Tappert, p. 113, (emphasis mine).

---

or rightly understand the riches of the grace of Christ." In the same vein Dr. Luther declared: "Where this single article remains pure, Christendom will remain pure, in beautiful harmony, and without any schisms. But where it does not remain pure, it is impossible to repel any error or heretical spirit."[63]

On Friday evenings of the school year from September 1884 to November 1885, Dr. C. F. W. Walther of Concordia Seminary lectured to the student body on a subject that was close to his heart and of vital importance for the ministries of those pastors-in-training: the proper distinction between law and gospel. In the last of 25 theses that he set forth on the topic, Walther stated, "The Word of God is not rightly divided when the person teaching it does not allow the Gospel to have a general predominance in his teaching."[64] In explaining this thesis, Walther went on to say, "For we are told in this thesis that Law and Gospel are confounded and perverted for the hearers of the Word, not only when the Law predominates in the preaching, but also when Law and Gospel, as a rule, are equally balanced and the Gospel is not predominant in the preaching."[65] A bit later he would say, "The very finest form of confounding both [Law and Gospel] occurs when the Gospel is preached *along with* the Law, but is not the predominating element in the sermon."[66] The law has its purpose, that is, to crush stony hearts, "but that is merely preparatory work. The waters of grace cannot penetrate a stony heart. But the Law is merely an auxiliary doctrine; it is not the real doctrine of Christ."[67] The remedy for sad-faced preachers and sleepy Sunday morning churchgoers is not less gospel, but more of it. The cure for congregations that seem to be asleep rather than active in joyful sanctified living is not a resort to the law, but continued preaching of the sweetness of the gospel.

Dr. Walther in his day noted what can still be seen in Reformed writing and preaching today: a scarcity of the gospel.

> You can observe this in some of the sectarian spirits, who have learned from us to speak of Christ and of faith, *how rarely they treat this doctrine, yea, how cold and inept they are whenever they have to treat this chief point of doctrine,* and how they rush over such texts as these and merely skim their surface, regarding this matter as a paltry thing that everybody is able to do quite well.[68]

---

[63]FC SD III:6, Tappert, p. 540.
[64]C. F. W. Walther, *The Proper Distinction between Law and Gospel* (St. Louis: Concordia Publishing House), p. 403.
[65]Ibid.
[66]Ibid., p. 406.
[67]Ibid., p. 405.
[68]Ibid., p. 409.

Preach the law, then, to trouble the comfortable, but don't linger before presenting the gospel. Comfort those who are troubled by their sins. Point people to Christ. Assure them of forgiveness through faith in the Lamb who was slain for us. This alone changes hearts and produces fruit in the lives of believers.

If it is the intention of preachers and their congregations to allow the gospel to have predominance in their public services, they will be greatly assisted by the use of the Lutheran liturgy. Since the time of Luther it has been a principle of Lutheran worship that the gospel should be clearly proclaimed through the liturgy. While non-liturgical worship is conveniently structured to allow for an emphasis on law and moral instruction, the liturgy repeatedly proclaims Christ and his gospel. Consider, for example, the canticle "O Lord, Our Lord" in the Service of Word and Sacrament in *Christian Worship.* There we sing, "Almighty God, merciful Father, you crown our life with your love. You take away our sin; you comfort our spirit; you make us pure and holy in your sight. You did not spare your only Son, but gave him up for us all."[69] The Verse, the Creed, the Seasonal Sentences, the Sanctus, and the Agnus Dei all in various ways join in proclaiming "Christ for us."

The role of the doctrine of sanctification in Lutheran teaching

None of the foregoing, however, should be understood to say that preaching and teaching that is truly Lutheran will ignore or neglect the teaching of sanctification. How could it, if we claim to teach what the Bible teaches? Professor J. P. Koehler once said, "The one great calling of the Christian is sanctification. It permeates his entire life with all its actions and enters into consideration at every instance when it comes to judging whether what we do or the manner in which we do it is of faith or not."[70]

We heard earlier how the authors of *The Goal of the Gospel* charged that fellow Lutheran pastors sometimes pluck gospel promises right out of a context that spoke of sanctification, thereby ignoring sanctification. In the eyes of some of the Reformed, Lutheranism is guilty of "onesidedness,"[71] of "an arbitrary exaggeration of one side of the divine revelation *(the gospel)* at the expense of the other *(the law).*"[72] Have we reduced the message of the Scriptures to the gospel alone? The Lutheran Confessions deny the validity of that charge:

> We also reject and condemn as offensive and as subversive of
> Christian discipline that bald statement that good works are
> detrimental to salvation.

---

[69]*CW*, p. 28.
[70]J. P. Koehler, "Sanctification Is Not Hurrah," *The Wauwatosa Theology*, Vol. 2, p. 394.
[71]Sasse, p. 150.
[72]Ibid., p. 129.

Especially in these last times, it is just as necessary to exhort people to Christian discipline and good works, and to remind them how necessary it is that they exercise themselves in good works as the evidence of their faith and their gratitude toward God, as it is to warn against mingling good works in the article of justification. Such an Epicurean dream concerning faith can damn people as much as a papistic and Pharisaic confidence in one's own works and merit.[73]

It is beyond question that the inspired writers of the Scriptures do frequently place exhortations to sanctification side by side with the gospel's proclamation of what Christ has done for us. Ephesians 2:8-10 is perhaps the most well known example. Verses 8 and 9 are sure to be familiar: "It is by grace you have been saved, through faith—and this not from yourselves, it is the gift of God—not by works, so that no one can boast." But then Paul continues in verse 10: "For we are God's workmanship, *created in Christ Jesus to do good works*, which God prepared in advance for us to do." While some have argued that a better translation would be "We are created in Christ Jesus on the basis of [his] good works,"[74] the argument isn't convincing. The final phrase in verse 10 is literally "that we should walk in them." The word for "walk" is περιπατέω, a word that Paul commonly uses to speak of the Christian's life.

Later in Ephesians, Paul will write, "You were once darkness, but now you are light in the Lord" (5:8). Then, on the heels of the good news of who we are in Christ, he encourages, *"Live as children of light (for the fruit of the light consists in all goodness, righteousness, and truth) and find out what pleases the Lord"* (vv. 9,10).

Romans chapter 6 is the classic passage for showing how justification leads to sanctification. Paul has just finished saying at the end of chapter 5, "Where sin increased, grace increased all the more, so that, just as sin reigned in death, so also grace might reign through righteousness to bring eternal life through Jesus Christ our Lord" (vv. 20,21). Chapter 6 then begins with four questions in quick succession: "What shall we say, then? Shall we go on sinning so that grace may increase? By no means! We died to sin; how can we live in it any longer? Or don't you know that all of us who were baptized into Christ Jesus were baptized into his death? We were therefore buried with him through baptism into death *in order that, just as Christ was raised from the dead through the glory of the Father, we too may live* (περιπατέω) *a new life"* (Ro 6:1-4).

---

[73]FC Ep IV:17,18, Tappert, p. 477.
[74]See *Wisconsin Lutheran Quarterly*, Vol. 92, No. 1 (Winter 1995), p. 51.

In Philippians chapter 2 Paul's beautiful statement regarding Christ's humiliation and exaltation ("And being found in appearance as a man, he humbled himself and became obedient to death—even death on a cross!" [v. 8]) is prefaced by a call to forsake selfishness: "Your attitude should be the same as that of Christ Jesus," Paul says (v. 5).

We find the same pattern in the writings of the apostle Peter: "You are a chosen people, a royal priesthood, a holy nation, a people belonging to God, *that you may declare the praises of him who called you out of darkness into his wonderful light*" (1 Pe 2:9). Later in the same chapter, Peter writes, "To this you were called, because Christ suffered for you, leaving you an example, that you should follow in his steps. 'He committed no sin, and no deceit was found in his mouth.' When they hurled their insults at him, he did not retaliate; when he suffered, he made no threats. Instead, he entrusted himself to him who judges justly. He himself bore our sins in his body on the tree, *so that we might die to sins and live for righteousness;* by his wounds you have been healed" (vv. 21-24).

John speaks the same way in his first letter: "This is how we know what love is: Jesus Christ laid down his life for us. *And we ought to lay down our lives for our brothers. If anyone has material possessions and sees his brother in need but has no pity on him, how can the love of God be in him?*" (3:16,17).

This is just a cursory look at a phenomenon that occurs time and again in the Scriptures: justification and sanctification situated adjacent to each other. The gospel is proclaimed; then comes the law in its third use.

Another way to examine the interplay between justification and sanctification in the New Testament epistles is to look at the context surrounding the little adverb *therefore*. The word occurs at a significant juncture in Romans, at the beginning of chapter 12. "Therefore, I urge you, brothers, in view of God's mercy, to offer your bodies as living sacrifices, holy and pleasing to God—this is your spiritual act of worship." The *therefore* at the head of the sentence comes after the doctrinal section has been completed. The practical portion of the letter is now to begin. What Paul is about to encourage in chapters 12 to 16 is based on the gospel he had proclaimed in chapters 1 to 11. The body of the Christian offered as a living sacrifice is the appropriate response to a God who "demonstrates his own love for us in this: While we were still sinners, Christ died for us" (Ro 5:8).

At the end of his great resurrection chapter Paul writes, "Therefore, my dear brothers, stand firm. Let nothing move you. Always give yourselves fully to the work of the Lord, because you know that your labor in the Lord is not in vain" (1 Co 15:58). The call to be steadfast is based on more than 50 verses of resurrection gospel, including the victorious taunt, "'Where, O death, is your victory? Where, O death, is your sting?' The sting of death is sin, and the power of sin is the law. But thanks be to God! He gives us the victory through our Lord Jesus Christ" (1 Co 15:55-57). Then comes the *therefore*.

Galatians chapter 5 begins with a bold declaration of freedom: "It was for freedom that Christ set us free." Then comes the exhortation: "Therefore keep standing firm and do not be subject again to a yoke of slavery" (5:1 NASB). Ephesians chapter 5 commences with "Be imitators of God, therefore, ..." In the context Paul has reminded his readers that "in Christ God forgave you" (4:32) and that they are "dearly loved children" (5:1) through faith in Jesus. The humiliation-exaltation of Christ passage in Philippians chapter 2, of which we spoke earlier, resolves into the apostle saying, "Therefore, my dear friends, as you have always obeyed—not only in my presence, but now much more in my absence—continue to work out your salvation with fear and trembling, for it is God who works in you to will and to act according to his good purpose" (vv. 12,13).

Writing to the Colossians, Paul speaks of the crushing defeat that Christ handed Satan: "When you were dead in your sins and in the uncircumcision of your sinful nature, God made you alive with Christ. He forgave us all our sins, having canceled the written code, with its regulations, that was against us and that stood opposed to us; he took it away, nailing it to the cross. And having disarmed the powers and authorities, he made a public spectacle of them, triumphing over them by the cross" (2:13-15). Then, the transition to sanctification: "Therefore do not let anyone judge you by what you eat or drink" (v. 16). A chapter later, Paul draws an inference from the resurrection of Christ: "Since, then, you have been raised with Christ, set your hearts on things above, where Christ is seated at the right hand of God" (v. 1). And in the middle of the chapter he admonishes, "Therefore, as God's chosen people, holy and dearly loved, clothe yourselves with compassion, kindness, humility, gentleness and patience" (v. 12).

The author of Hebrews, under the Spirit's inspiration, follows the same procedure. "Therefore, since the promise of entering his rest still stands, let us be careful that none of you be found to have fallen short of it" (4:1). The opening verses of chapter 13 are really a restatement of the second table of the Decalogue. These verses are preceded by the final two verses of chapter 12, where it says, "Therefore, since we are receiving a kingdom that cannot be shaken, let us be thankful, and so worship God acceptably with reverence and awe, for our 'God is a consuming fire.'"

Then, one last sample, this time from the writings of St. Peter. After assuring his fellow believers that they had been "born again, not of perishable seed, but of imperishable, through the living and enduring word of God" (1 Pe 1:23), Peter advises, "Therefore, rid yourselves of all malice and all deceit, hypocrisy, envy, and slander of every kind. Like newborn babies, crave pure spiritual milk, so that by it you may grow up in your salvation, now that you have tasted that the Lord is good" (2:1-3).

Anyone with a passing familiarity with Luther's Small Catechism will recognize that Dr. Luther also regularly went—in a way that seems completely natural—from proclaiming the gospel to encouraging sanctified living. In his explanation to the First Article of the Apostles' Creed, he listed the extensive blessings that we receive richly and daily from our Creator. Then he concluded, "For all this I ought to thank and praise, to serve and obey him. This is most certainly true."[75] Similarly in the explanation of the Second Article, Luther tells how Christ redeemed us and then proceeds to tell us why we were redeemed: "All this he did that I should be his own, and live under him in his kingdom, and serve him in everlasting righteousness, innocence, and blessedness, just as he has risen from death and lives and rules eternally. This is most certainly true."[76]

Clearly, the call to sanctification never occurs in a vacuum. The gospel either precedes or follows such calls to sanctification. Often the gospel both precedes and follows. Without the gospel there is no hope that sinful people could ever produce works that please God. It was because they understood how justification results in sanctification that the Lutheran princes could say to Emperor Charles V:

> Consequently this teaching concerning faith is not to be accused of forbidding good works but is rather to be praised for teaching that good works are to be done and for offering help as to how they may be done. For without faith and without Christ human nature and human strength are much too weak to do good works, call upon God, have patience in suffering, love one's neighbor, diligently engage in callings which are commanded, render obedience, avoid evil lusts, etc. Such great and genuine works cannot be done without the help of Christ, as he himself says in John 15:5, "Apart from me you can do nothing."[77]

The power for producing these good works does not reside in the law. Nor is it something we can bring to fruition through our own powers of persistence or through our concentrated efforts at self-discipline. As the Augsburg Confession says, "great and genuine works cannot be done without the help of Christ." This is the place at which to speak of "Christ in us." Jesus said, "I am the vine; you are the branches. If a man remains in me and I in him, he will bear much fruit; apart from me you can do nothing" (Jn 15:5). Writing to the Galatians, the apostle Paul also attributes his ability to live for God to the indwelling of Christ: "I have been crucified with Christ and I no longer live, but Christ lives in me. The life I live in the body, I live by faith in the Son of God, who loved me and gave himself for me" (2:20).

---

[75]Martin Luther, *Luther's Small Catechism*, 1997 edition (Milwaukee: Northwestern Publishing House, 1979), p. 5.
[76]Ibid., p. 6.
[77]AC XX:35-39, Tappert, p. 46.

The union of the triune God with his believers is known in theology as the mystical union. God establishes this union when he bestows on us the gift of saving faith. "This indwelling follows the preceding righteousness of faith, which is precisely the forgiveness of sins and the gracious acceptance of poor sinners on account of the obedience and merit of Christ."[78]

August Pieper explained the relationship between the mystical union and the believer's sanctified living this way:

> From the Lutheran standpoint, in the justified person faith, bringing with it the *unio mystica*, is such a unity of the human subject with the divine that he finds in himself the norm and stimulus for his actions. He no longer needs to receive this from outside. Because he has been given the Holy Spirit, he is an independent source of a divine manifestation in his life and his activity. The law, therefore, does not stand over him anymore as something *foreign* to his will, but it *has passed over into his will* as the impulse of love, inflamed by the Holy Spirit. But in this life faith is never present in such ideal perfection.[79]

That is why the law still needs to be preached: because even the believer still has a sinful nature "waging war against the law of my mind and making me a prisoner of the law of sin at work within my members," as St. Paul says in Romans 7:23.

> On account of this Old Adam, who inheres in people's intellect, will, and all their powers, it is necessary for the law of God constantly to light their way lest in their merely human devotion they undertake self-decreed and self-chosen acts of serving God. This is further necessary lest the Old Adam go his own self-willed way. He must be coerced against his own will not only by the admonitions and threats of the law, but also by its punishments and plagues, to follow the Spirit and surrender himself a captive.[80]

But where the Lutheran says that the Christian, as a Christian, needs no law, the Reformed insist that the Christian, as a Christian, still has need of the law. In fact, as a believer he has an even greater need of the law. August Pieper characterized the Reformed position this way:

> But the norm for faith and the will which is carried along by faith, in individual situations always is the divine will *as*

---

[78] FC SD III:54, Tappert, p. 549.
[79] August Pieper, "The Difference Between the Reformed and the Lutheran Interpretation of the So-Called Third Use of the Law, *The Wauwatosa Theology*, Vol. 2, p. 108, (emphasis mine). (Hereafter cited as "The Difference").
[80] FC Ep VI:4, Tappert, p. 480.

---

something still standing over it, demanding the particular action. The *"you must"* has not yet been overcome, but rather sharpened. Only now does the believer begin to understand the law in its spiritual nature. Its commands and promises, as well as its threats and prohibitions, become more penetrating because they are now understood in faith.

So, just *because* faith has been kindled, *for that reason* the law is necessary, which urges one on to action. It is precisely the regenerate person who needs the law for his development, his perfection, his positive progress, his manifestations of obedience, and his good works, which should glorify God. By no means does he need the law only to control and discipline the unregenerate part in him.[81]

Herman Sasse took note of this marked difference between Lutherans and the Reformed on law and gospel, and concluded that there is a vast difference between the two traditions:

The difference lies in the fact that the Reformed believe that both Law and Gospel are parts of Christ's real work, and consequently are essential functions of the church; the Lutheran Church, on the other hand, teaches that the preaching of the Law is the "strange," and the preaching of the Gospel is the "real," work of Christ, and that accordingly, although the church must also preach the Law—how else could it proclaim the Gospel?—the only thing which is essential to its nature as the church of Christ is that it is the place, the only place in the world, in which the blessed tidings of forgiveness of sins for Christ's sake are heard. At first glance these differences seem to be insignificant. To the layman they must appear to be theological distinctions which are of no particular consequence. In fact, the two views are so close to each other that the difference, at this point, between the two evangelical churches was frequently not observed at all in the Age of the Reformation. But the nearness is only an apparent one. These views of the relation of Law and Gospel stand side by side at first, like two railroad tracks that lie next to each other and seem to be headed toward the same place, until it turns out, later, that they are going in entirely different directions.[82]

---

[81]August Pieper, "The Difference," pp. 108,109, (emphasis mine).
[82]Sasse, p. 129.

What makes Christianity unique is not the law or the morality prescribed there. We can find the same moral principles outlined in the teachings of many non-Christian religions. Jews, Mormons, Jehovah's Witnesses, and Muslims would all be in favor of the sort of things *Promises to Keep* encourages: courage, total commitment to God (or in this case, *god*), prayer, being a loving father and devoted husband, thankfulness, patience, self-discipline, loyalty. We can probably assume that those same non-Christian religions speak against drug abuse, racism, and pornography. What sets Christianity apart is not the law, but the gospel: Jesus Christ is the way, the truth, and the life. That's why it ought to be unthinkable that a *Christian* minister could offer as a model for preaching a sermon that fails even to mention the *name* of Jesus.[83] What does such a sermon offer that one could not also hear in a Unitarian meeting house? By the same token, molding men of integrity by serving them huge doses of the law may succeed in the short term, but it is bound to fail in the long run. Neither the adrenaline surge of a revival in a jam-packed football stadium nor the most insightful multimedia presentation of principles for Christian living can come close to matching the power of the gospel. The gospel, and the gospel alone, is God's power for salvation.

Certainly there is room for rejoicing that even if the law dominates the message heard in many Reformed churches, the gospel is still being proclaimed to some degree. Nor is it the case that every preacher or teacher of a Reformed background is oblivious to the fact that law without gospel is a dead end. But as this brief study has demonstrated, the law does dominate Reformed preaching and teaching. The reason for that is rooted in Reformed theology. The differences are not superficial. "Dividing Lutherans and Protestants is not simply a different sacramental perspective, but an essentially different world view. For Lutherans the kingdom of God comes in the preaching of the gospel and the administration of the sacraments, not in the moral improvement of the individual and society."[84]

But what about that complaint that the Lutheran church is a sleeping giant?[85] What will we do when a member tells us he's leaving our church because he wants to be "fed" and from now on he's going to be taking his meals at a church that specializes in imparting seven principles and a promise? What shall we do about low voters' meeting attendance, indifference to Bible study opportunities, and depressing rates of inactivity among young people just three or four years after confirmation? Forsake the gospel?

---

[83]See page 175 above.

[84]Scaer, "Sanctification," p. 172.

[85]The authors of *The Goal of the Gospel* report that Billy Graham and others have referred to the Lutheran Church–Missouri Synod as a "sleeping giant" (p. 14).

Accordingly, the cure for our lack of works does not consist in this, that we become more legalistic in our Christianity and adopt something of the Reformed spirit, but in this, that we, in a genuinely Lutheran spirit, apply the law in its sharpness as a mirror to our lazy flesh, that we allow ourselves to be judged and condemned by it, that we become alarmed at our lack of energy because of which we neglect God's kingdom and poor souls, and that we flee again to grace and from its fullness and fervor, which surpasses all human thought, acquire for ourselves new, *free*, spiritual willpower.[86]

Our heritage as Lutherans is a bias for the gospel, a ministry "not of the letter but of the Spirit" (2 Co 3:6). True, to prepare the ground for the gospel we will, as we should, preach the law with such sharpness and clarity, so that no one, least of all the preacher, can escape its convicting and condemning thunder. We will also use the law to guide believers as they seek to serve the triune God, not coercing their compliance with the law but allowing it to flow from the "free and merry spirit"[87] of one who has discovered forgiveness and freedom in Christ Jesus. What we delight in, what we live for, what makes us truly "evangelical," therefore, is to comfort the wounded consciences of sinners with the gracious words of the absolution won for us by Christ. "You were washed, you were sanctified, you were justified in the name of the Lord Jesus Christ and by the Spirit of our God" (1 Co 6:11).

Lord, keep us steadfast in your Word;
Curb those who by deceit or sword
Would seek to overthrow your Son
And to destroy what he has done.

Lord Jesus Christ, your pow'r make known,
For you are Lord of lords alone;
Defend your Christendom that we
May sing your praise eternally.

O Comforter of priceless worth,
Send peace and unity on earth.
Support us in our final strife,
And lead us out of death to life. (CW 203)

---

[86]August Pieper, "The Difference," p. 110.
[87]FC SD VI:17, Tappert, p. 566.

HOW DOES OUR CHRISTOLOGY IMPACT OUR DAILY LIVES?

Forrest L. Bivens

Southeastern Wisconsin District Convention
Mequon, Wisconsin
June 9–10, 1998

Introduction

We believe in one Lord, Jesus Christ, the only Son of God,
>   eternally begotten of the Father,
>   God from God, Light from Light, true God from true
>   God,
>   begotten, not made,
>   of one being with the Father.
Through him all things were made.
For us and for our salvation, he came down from heaven,
>   was incarnate of the Holy Spirit and the virgin Mary,
>   and became fully human.
For our sake he was crucified under Pontius Pilate.
He suffered death and was buried.
On the third day he rose again in accordance with the
>   Scriptures.
He ascended into heaven
>   and is seated at the right hand of the Father.
He will come again in glory to judge the living and the dead,
>   and his kingdom will have no end.[1]

---

[1]This is the Nicene Creed, Second Article, as it appears in *Christian Worship*. This translation is based on a translation of the Nicene Creed prepared by the English Language Liturgical Consultation (ELLC) in 1988.

This is a statement of what we believe concerning Jesus Christ. It is a confession of our Christology. *Christology* most narrowly defined means "the study of Christ." But in frequent usage the term also refers to the teaching or doctrine of Christ, that which is believed and confessed concerning him. Our Christology tells what we hold to be true regarding who Christ is (his person) and what he does (his work).

All 12 of the WELS district conventions this year are giving attention to one or more aspects of our Christology. Essays and studies are being prepared and presented to focus on those truths we draw from Scripture regarding the second person of the triune God. Briefly stated, we hold that Jesus is true God, coeternal, coequal, and one in essence with the Father and Spirit, and that he became fully human at the incarnation without for a moment ceasing to be God. The divine and human natures are most intimately and permanently united in the person of Christ, the God-man. We also believe that in Christ the attributes or inherent characteristics of each nature are communicated to or shared with the other nature. Characteristics, emotions, and activities that are normally peculiar to either nature are shared with the other in the person of Christ.[2] As the God-man and for our salvation, Christ did not always make full use of the divine powers and attributes he possessed, but he humbled himself to carry out the work of redemption. He voluntarily did this to serve us, obeying the law of God perfectly in our place and also dying as our substitute to ransom us sinners from guilt and death. As a result of this work, often referred to as his active and passive obedience on our behalf, the whole world of sinners has been declared forgiven. Upon the completion of this aspect of his work for us, Christ again took up the full use of his divine powers and prerogatives, and in this exaltation he continues to serve us. His descent into hell, bodily resurrection, ascension, current activities, and approaching return in glory for judgment are aspects of his exaltation. To describe Christ's work, the Bible often refers to him as the ultimate and eternal Prophet, High Priest, and King who functions in these capacities. More than anything else, assurances are given that Christ, by his substitutionary obedience, has achieved reconciliation between this world of sinners and the righteous God. His redemptive work is perfect and complete and applies to all mankind. Jesus Christ is the only Savior and Lord of mankind.

Our assigned task at this convention is not to review any of these aspects of our Christology specifically, but to consider what impact our overall teachings about Christ have in our daily lives. We hold that the relationship between belief and behavior is basically a relationship between cause and

---

[2]Not all characteristics of each nature, of course, are communicated reciprocally. The Bible frequently and freely speaks of the human nature being enriched with the endowment of divine attributes, but the already perfect divine nature as such could not be enriched—or impoverished—with creaturely attributes of the human nature. To clarify such biblical distinctions, a thorough study is needed. This present essay cannot provide that study.

We Believe in Jesus Christ

effect. If a person believes what is correct, that person's behavior will tend to be correct. But if someone clings to what is false, what that person does will reflect and express what is untrue. In short, what we believe has great impact on how we live from day to day. In the study that follows, we will consider how our Christology influences the way we think (the mind), the way we feel (the emotions), and the way we make decisions (the will). But before we do this, an important point should be stated.

Our Christology is not everyone's Christology

As stated above, a Christology is a statement telling who Jesus is and why he is important or significant. Not all professing Christians agree on these points. There are several kinds of Christologies that are competing for attention and acceptance. As in the ancient church, the biblical view of Christ's person and work continues to face opposition. Further, it is not uncommon to find two or more Christologies combined and declared compatible as though each contributes a valid part of the whole truth about Christ. To make you aware of at least some of the jargon used today, we report that some schools of thought provide us with mystical, existentialist, and dialectical approaches to Scripture and to Christ, while others give us functional, humanitarian, and evolutionary approaches to Jesus.[3] Aside from the always elusive but never correct "historical Jesus" of the Jesus Seminars, we have serious and scholarly urgings to recognize a Jesus who endorses feminist, neoorthodox, liberationist, and process theologies. Those who choose a theology of hope or a theology of religions also construct a Christ after their image and invite us to follow him. Twenty-five years ago historian Paul L. Maier wrote this description of what he called "The Jesus Game."

> Anyone can play the Jesus game, although it helps if you're a scholar. The rules are simple enough. First you read the New Testament Gospels and draw a general sketch of Jesus. Then distort that sketch as much as you please, add clashing colors, paint in a bizarre background, and if the surviving Christ resembles anything in the Gospels, you lose. But if you come up with a radically different—above all sensational—portrait of Jesus, you win. The prizes are maximum

---

[3]The limited time and assigned focus of this essay prohibit the giving of details on the Christological types mentioned in this and the next sentences. The reader should be aware of at least three general tendencies that prevail in modern Christologies: (1) The felt need to interpret Christ pluralistically and inclusivistically, finding value in him also for those who have not and do not possess explicit knowledge of and faith in him; (2) the blatant use of Christ to endorse social and political issues with little or no meaningful focus on the relation of mankind to God; and (3) the almost inevitable use of Christ as model or example coupled with an absence or downplaying of his role as substitute and mediator between God and mankind. Students who desire to read more on specific approaches mentioned here may refer to *The Blackwell Encyclopedia of Modern Christian Thought* (Cambridge, MA, Blackwell Publishers Ltd., 1993) pp. 80-92, or *Jesus Christ* by Donald G. Bloesch (InterVarsity Press, Downers Grove, IL, 1997), pp. 19-23.

---

coverage in the nation's news media, frowns from the faithful, and plaudits from everyone else.[4]

Our Christology is noticeably different because our approach to Scripture is different. Our conviction that the Bible is God's verbally inspired and inerrant message of unchangeable truth leads us to limit ourselves to what is revealed there about the identity and characteristics of Christ, his purposes, and the nature of his work. It is this kind of Christology, a *biblical* one, that has a profound effect on the way we think, feel, and exercise our will.

Our Christology influences the way we think

In basing our doctrine of Jesus Christ solely on Scripture, we assume more than its authority, truthfulness, and trustworthiness. We also assume that the words given and the thoughts expressed there are understandable and are designed to tell us something definite. So when the disciple Thomas refers to Jesus Christ as "my Lord and my God" (Jn 20:28) and Jesus accepts the statement, we maintain that Jesus is really God. Since the Bible also says "there is one God and one mediator between God and men, the man Christ Jesus, who gave himself as a ransom for all men" (1 Ti 2:5,6), we believe Jesus is fully human and worked for the good of all humanity. When Paul speaks of "the church of God, which he [God] bought with his own blood" (Ac 20:28), we conclude that Christ's human characteristics, like his blood, may be used with reference to his deity as well as his humanity. To us this is reality, truth, and factual information. No matter if we are unable to grasp *how* this was brought about or is maintained by God, we cling to *what* is revealed as it is revealed. We are told in unmistakable language that "God was reconciling the world to himself in Christ, not counting their [the world's] sins against them" (2 Co 5:19), so the universality of Christ's work is to us a historical and reliable reality. That is the way we think because that is how the Bible leads us to think. Frequently the Scriptures stress the necessity of reading, understanding, and pondering God's written revelation. We are repeatedly urged to be eager, diligent, and to make every effort to obtain a correct understanding of the Word of Truth and to cherish it with utmost confidence. The idea is that we can and should know the truth of God through his revelation. Really. This is not to say that saving faith is to be equated with intellectual comprehension. The creation of saving trust in the heart is a work of the Holy Spirit, distinguishable from mental knowledge. But alongside our God-given faith we receive intellect and the ability to receive God's thoughts communicated through words and language that mean what they say. Our Christology reinforces and expresses this way of thinking in us.

---

[4]*Eternity* magazine (December 1973), p. 17.

We Believe in Jesus Christ

We believe Christ who said, "If you hold to my teaching, you are really my disciples. Then you will know the truth, and the truth will set you free" (Jn 8:31,32). By the grace and power of God, we are able to learn, know, and hold to the truth from Christ and about Christ. And how does this impact our lives? Consider these sample effects:

- *We enjoy stability of doctrine.* The Christ of Scripture is not drawn from subjective opinion nor is he subject to fluctuations of human thought. He does not change. "Jesus Christ is the same yesterday and today and forever" (Heb 13:8). What we hold to be true now is perpetually true, not subject to revision.

- *We learn to subject our reason and logic to divine revelation.* St. Paul stated as a part of the apostolic ministry the demolition of human arguments and "every pretension that sets itself up against the knowledge of God" and to "take captive every thought to make it obedient to Christ" (2 Co 10:5). In love God brought this about among us. With the gift of reason and the ability to understand revealed knowledge, sinful humans often fall prey to the temptation to exalt reason above revelation and to manufacture so-called knowledge to usurp the place of divine truth. Our Christology fully admits that there are things about Christ's person and work that go beyond our ability to really understand, but it also teaches us to be content with what God has revealed. We ask questions about the mechanics of the virgin birth and wonder what it really means for the full godhead or deity to dwell in Christ in bodily form. We ponder how it is possible for God to die at Christ's crucifixion and wrestle with Christ's real temptations to sin coupled with his equally real inability to sin. We often frame acceptable, though not absolutely authoritative, answers. Perhaps more than anything else, we learn humility and are trained to limit ourselves to God's level of self-revelation.

- *We learn to trust the biblical message of Christ.* "We preach Christ crucified" for the same reason Paul did: the message is God's reasonable and reliable instrument to save souls, despite people's opinion that it is foolishness (1 Co 1:18–2:16). We do not keep the sword of the Spirit in its sheath simply because scoffers say it is an unworthy weapon. We have learned otherwise about this message of wisdom centered in Jesus.

- *We derive comfort from the reasonableness of what we believe.* No, we don't believe in Christ because it appeals to our reason. We believe because the Spirit of God has brought us to embrace Jesus. But with faith we also enjoy the ability to see how our Christology is grounded in history rather than built on speculative philosophy. We share Paul's conviction that what we say and believe is "true and reasonable" and cheerfully note that what Christ did was done for the world to see rather than "in a corner" (Ac 26:25,26). We mentally note that the gospel is sensible and intellectually defensible, worthy of thoughtful appreciation by all. When Jesus appealed to his miracles as evidences of his identity (Jn 14:11) or exposed the fallacy of his opponents who said he was using satanic powers (Lk 11:17-26), he demonstrated the fundamental reasonableness of his claims and work. A part of our rich theological heritage in Christ is this way of thinking about the truth.

We who are here assembled likely take these points for granted and accept them as a matter of course. The danger, however, is precisely in taking this way of thinking for granted and then assuming that it requires no special attention. One would think that among professing Christians, despite sweeping changes in other aspects of theology, the identity and work of Christ would remain fairly constant. In the 18th century, however, there began in the church a frontal assault on classic, biblical Christology, and the 20th century has taken this movement to extremes. The supernatural God-man portrayed in the Bible and confessed in the long-standing creeds was assigned an obscure position in the realm of superstition and ignorance. The Christ revealed in clear words of Scripture is now deemed ambiguous or an absurdity. The popular and often quoted theologian Dietrich Bonhoeffer wrote that "Christ's deeds are not sinless, but ambiguous. One can and should see good and bad in them."[5] Yet Bonhoeffer is consistently held to be a 20th-century thinker who maintained a significantly high view of Christ. At the heart of all this confusion, of course, is the fact that modern religious thinkers have adopted various approaches to the biblical text and the message there presented. Any study of these Christologies will demonstrate at least two cardinal presuppositions of modern theologians: (1) The supernatural, historical Christ of the Bible text is impossible and patently false, and (2) our ability to know anything truly or objectively about Christ is likewise impossible. As you might guess, a person's subjective ideas about Christ then become the significant and important thing, at least for that person.

---

[5]Dietrich Bonhoeffer, *Christ the Center* (New York: Harper and Row, 1966), p. 113.

We Believe in Jesus Christ

Church historians have sometimes labeled the 13th century the Age of Faith and the 18th century the Age of Reason. The 20th century, in the opinion of thoughtful observers, may well be called the Age of Irrationalism or Anti-intellectualism. In previous centuries the vast majority of religious and secular philosophers have generally believed that definitive knowledge is possible to mankind. That idea has largely been abandoned. What might be called a radical skepticism regarding objective truth and reality has filtered down from prominent philosophers and theologians to penetrate our culture, from television to art to literature. There are evidences of an overwhelming cultural consensus, sometimes stated explicitly but more often simply implied, that mankind does not and cannot know anything truly or with certainty.[6] Regarding our topic this means we cannot know that the Bible is the Word of God, that Christ is true God, or that he died in our place or that he is alive today. So modern theology is largely content cataloging theological and christological differences without scrutinizing causes for them and not worrying about the rightness or wrongness of them. To people who approach Christ and the Bible in this way, however, true Christianity becomes nonsensical, for it claims to be knowledge.

A related tragedy is that of wholesale ignorance about the content of the Bible. Over 40 years ago Herman Gockel observed that modern man "is so far removed from the thought-world of the Bible that it is almost a miracle if he can still understand the kind of things the Bible speaks about."[7] There is little or no evidence to indicate things have improved in this regard over the last several decades. The Bible words and message are largely meaningless to millions. Sadly, this is acceptable to most of them. Their ignorance is cynically declared to be bliss.

We are the ones who are considered abnormal. Our way of thinking is indicted as impossible, even absurd in a scientific age. If objective knowledge is not possible to mankind, for example, it is silly to argue points of doctrine. Subjective opinions, variable yet held to be equally valid, become the intellectual standard to be gained and maintained. Needless to say, Bible statements about Christ and his work are also considered subjective human testimonies that stem largely from inner longings of the soul and find expression in "hyperbole of the heart." Elements of myth, legend, and poetic inaccuracies are assumed to be present in all christological accounts. Obviously our Christology and other Christologies are in conflict.

We now turn our attention to an influence on daily living that is more powerful than our thoughts. Human emotions invariably impact behavior and

---

[6]For a treatment on this subject the reader is pointed to "The Crisis of Our Time," a brief treatise by John W. Robbins appended to the book *The Atonement* by Gordon H. Clark (Jefferson, Maryland: The Trinity Foundation, 1987), pp. 167-175. It may also be mentioned that theological or religious irrationality and intellectual skepticism are often included in current definitions of theological *postmodernism*, a term being used more and more.

[7]Herman W. Gockel, *The Cross and the Common Man* (St. Louis: Concordia Publishing House, 1955), p. vi.

lifestyle more than mere knowledge does. Our Christology feeds the heart as well as the head to make profound differences in daily life.

Our Christology influences the way we feel

"When they saw the star, they were overjoyed. . . . They saw the child with his mother Mary, and they bowed down and worshiped him" (Mt 2:10,11). "Praise be to the Lord, the God of Israel, because he has come and has redeemed his people" (Lk 1:68). "Then the man said, 'Lord, I believe,' and he worshiped him" (Jn 9:38). "He showed them his hands and side. The disciples were overjoyed when they saw the Lord" (Jn 20:20). This small sampling of passages has something in common: it describes how people responded to Christ with strong emotions, even though no explicit command to do so was given at the time. Christ's incarnation, ministry, and resurrection from the dead, with the implications they bring, breed strong feelings. We will also find no shortage of Bible passages that explicitly command, invite, and urge us to respond to Christ and his work with love, gratitude, awe, humility, joy, courage, comfort, zeal, peace, and many other appropriate feelings. Our Christology impacts our emotions. "We love because he first loved us" (1 Jn 4:19).

When our emotions flow from the truth of Christ and his atoning work on our behalf, we feel the way God wants us to feel. Due primarily to time limitations, we cannot now mention, or list in depth, ways in which our Christology influences the way we feel. But we can highlight a sampling of emotions that are to be found in our daily lives.

- *We grieve over our sin as we behold Christ taking its guilt and consequences upon himself.* We learn also in this way to take our sinfulness most seriously. (Yes, this is certainly the "strange," or "foreign," work of Christ's deeds, for they here function more as divine law in exposing and clarifying our sinfulness. It is not the primary focus of the gospel events, of course, yet a real one that impacts our emotions.)

- *We are overjoyed with the reliable news that our sins are truly removed, divine justice is truly satisfied, and life rather than death is truly our inheritance.* Despite the ongoing accusations of the devil, the law, and our consciences, we find refuge in Christ who "has appeared once for all at the end of the ages to do away with sin by the sacrifice of himself" (Heb 9:26). He is utterly faithful to his promises and cannot deny himself. We are forgiven.

- *We find comfort in his being the eternal, almighty Lord as well as our human brother.* Daily we wrestle with our creaturely weaknesses and dependency on forces beyond our

We Believe in Jesus Christ

control. And daily we look to the all-sufficient Savior, who directs our destinies and in all things works for our good. We are able to view the here and now from the perspective of the hereafter. "In this world you will have trouble. But take heart! I have overcome the world" (Jn 16:33).

- *We find comfort because Jesus is our sympathetic brother.* "We do not have a high priest who is unable to sympathize with our weaknesses, but we have one who has been tempted in every way, just as we are—yet was without sin" (Heb 4:15). His experiences while he laid aside the full use of his powers are particularly comforting as we live out our lives with extremely limited powers. So we confidently approach the throne of grace to receive mercy and grace to help in times of need.

- *We face the future cheerfully*, fully able to react to dreadful and unpleasant signs of the end by lifting up our heads in anticipation rather than apprehension (Lk 21:28). Our optimism rests on Christ's power and promises and serves as the perfect antidote for whatever pessimism would otherwise result from viewing current events purely from our human perspective.

Again, lest we take these and related blessings for granted, let us pause to note that if true Christology does not influence our emotions, false views regarding him will. At the heart of false Christologies is something deeper than wrongheadedness. There is human emotion. Terrifically subjective and variable, feelings are nevertheless powerful. When divorced from or pitted against truth or objective reality, emotions can do great damage. False teachings about Christ amply demonstrate this tragedy.

It has been argued that many who succumb to false Christologies at least wish they could have some of the same emotional reactions that we do. Perhaps most people who have heard the Christmas story, for example, genuinely like the idea of believing it even as they conclude it is impossible. It is attractive and beautiful, though incredible. It revives nostalgic memories of childhood, stimulates thoughts of an ideal "peace on earth, good will toward men," and it presents a most likable concept of God, somehow identifying himself with humankind. But in the end these emotions usually fail to make any lasting impact on lives, because they evaporate in the presence of skepticism. The false intellectualism previously mentioned claims many victims in this way. Since its biblical basis is despised as uncertain, the whole concept of the incarnation is easily dismissed as lacking any foundation of reality.

But there is a deeper reason, an emotional one, why most people reject a truly biblical Christology. It is their natural hatred of the meaning and purpose of the incarnation as defined in Scripture, which center in the message of human sin and Christ's atonement for sin. The person and work of Christ simply cannot be adequately understood or appreciated without an accompanying understanding and acknowledgment of human sinfulness and its consequences. "When Christ came into the world, he said: 'Sacrifice and offering you did not desire, but a body you prepared for me. . . . I have come to do your will, O God.' And by that will, we have been made holy through the sacrifice of the body of Jesus Christ once for all" (Heb 10:5,7,10). Here there are no stars leading wise men, nor Christmas trees, nor any easily misunderstood "peace on earth." Without the Holy Spirit, people cannot and do not see themselves as so sinful that they need such a Savior as described in the Bible. So to them there is nothing attractive about the cross of Christ.

People of this world understand and emotionally react to human weaknesses and the failure to be or act as one ought to. But to speak of failing to live up to one's full potential, shirking of responsibility, or trashing relationships through ethical lapses is not the same as understanding or endorsing the Bible concept of sin. False Christologies are invariably linked to false, inadequate appraisals of sin, its source, and its seriousness in the eyes of God. Wrong appraisals of the cross of Christ are sure to follow. Liberationist and feminist theologies, for example, see in Christ a model of resoluteness against social and political powers of oppression. Christ is no longer portrayed or proclaimed as Savior from sin but as political activist and social reformer. Similarly, many contemporary comforters present a Christ who supposedly leads us to deal with feelings of guilt by coming to terms with our inner selves through self-analysis, not by getting right with God through his work. That kind of Christ has a distinctly different kind of impact on human emotions than the kind we enjoy.

Another intense and pervasive emotional source of false ideas about Christ and salvation is the hatred of the idea of divine punishment. Human standards of justice usually find it cruel to threaten condemnation for those who remain ignorant of Christ or who lack faith in his saving work. To really understand false christological systems that are gaining in popularity, one must know the pluralistic and inclusivistic moods that are linked to the rejection of any claims of absolute truth. Even if Christianity is viewed as superior and unique among other religions (as inclusivism usually allows), the tendency to be optimistic about the salvation of those who do not know or trust Christ is still strong. This optimism does not enjoy a biblical foundation, but it expresses well the emotions of people who seek to appear loving, compassionate, and tolerant of non-Christian belief systems. The concept of a guaranteed salvation for all is also quite acceptable to Americans in particular because of cherished democratic ideals like equal opportunity, equal rights, and equal standing before the law for everyone. Even though the idea that all religions are basically the same lacks intellectual integrity because of their mutually exclusive teachings regarding God and salvation, the idea is nevertheless embraced. Emotions override reason.

If emotions are stronger than intellectual reasoning, there is yet another, stronger force that determines the way people live. We refer to the human will. Our Christology also touches and transforms us in our exercise of the will and in this way impacts our daily lives.

Our Christology influences the way we choose to live

The biblical and real Christ told his first disciples: "If you love me, you will obey what I command. Whoever has my commands and obeys them, he is the one who loves me. . . . If anyone loves me, he will obey my teaching" (Jn 14:15,21,23). Those who by grace possess correct knowledge of Christ and embrace him in faith and grateful love understand this truth. "If anyone is in Christ, he is a new creation; the old has gone, the new has come!" (2 Co 5:17). "We are God's workmanship, created in Christ Jesus to do good works, which God prepared in advance for us to do" (Eph 2:10).

Any talk of the new life of a Christian must take into account the continuing existence and influence of the sinful nature that opposes all that Christ and the Christian seek to enjoy and express. The struggle between old and new is fierce and continuous. Two opposing wills are in conflict within every follower of Christ. In saying that our biblical Christology influences the way we choose to live, we do not mean that the sinful nature has been rendered totally inactive. It is still casting its ballot against what is the good, pleasing, and perfect will of God. We do mean, however, that the message of Christ and his saving work on our behalf brings ongoing renewal and a genuine desire to do God's revealed will despite the contrary will of the sinful nature. The petition of everyone who has been given life in Christ echoes that of David: "Show me the way I should go, for to you I lift up my soul. Teach me to do your will, for you are my God; may your good Spirit lead me on level ground" (Ps 143:8,10). The confession of Paul expresses reality for each of us: "In my inner being I delight in God's law" (Ro 7:22).

What does this mean for our daily lives? Again, with no attempt to give an exhaustive list of ways our lifestyles are impacted by our Christology, we cite the following:

> • *We resolve to follow Jesus in faith and to imitate him.* "To this you were called, because Christ suffered for you, leaving you an example, that you should follow in his steps" (1 Pe 2:21). A year ago a book was published with the title

WWJD?: The Question Everyone Is Asking.[8] The popularity of the book and the greater popularity of bracelets, T-shirts, and other merchandise bearing the acronym *WWJD* bear witness to the number of people who have apparently joined the "What would Jesus do?" movement. As Thomas a Kempis did in 1427 with his *The Imitation of Christ* or Charles Sheldon did in 1896 with his *In His Steps*, so people today recognize Christ is the perfect role model and pattern for godly living. Our Christology leads us to appreciate the general sentiment expressed when people strive to deal with a situation, problem, or dilemma by pondering how Jesus would respond and then resolving to imitate him. Our doctrine of Christ does more than that. Since it highlights the substitutionary nature of his obedience, it helps us maintain the primacy of "Christ for us" that empowers us to appreciate and rightly use "Christ in us." It keeps us from separating what we would call a sanctification emphasis from the more important justification emphasis in Christ's work. We resolve to use the Bible as more than a manual for behavior modification.

• *We are willing to bear the cross chosen for us.* The words of Jesus to Simon Peter in John 21:19 are interesting and instructive: "Jesus said this to indicate the kind of death by which Peter would glorify God. Then he said to him, 'Follow me!'" Jesus enables us to follow him despite inevitable cross bearing. "Everyone who wants to live a godly life in Christ Jesus will be persecuted" (2 Ti 3:12), yet this does not dim our resolve to follow or our willingness to suffer. In joyful response to Christ's love and labors on our behalf, we do not crave what may be called a false triumphalism in our Christian lives, but rather follow the general pattern established by Christ. This is the pathway to glory that takes us through the cross to the crown.

• *We want to share the truth of Christ with everyone.* "This gospel of the kingdom will be preached in the whole world as a testimony to all nations, and then the end will come" (Mt 24:14). This is a remarkable statement since the preaching described will take place during days more and more characterized by lovelessness and hostility, hatred and

---

[8](Santa Ana, California: Bob Siemans Designs, 1997).

We Believe in Jesus Christ

betrayal, persecution and apostasy in the religious community. Christ enables his people to desire and to carry out what pleases him (Php 2:13) and what is really beneficial for our neighbor.

What a contrast there is between those who enjoy the true Christ and say "Your will be done" and those who embrace a false Christology as an expression of their own will. In departing from the Christ who reveals himself on the pages of Scripture, they choose a nonexistent Christ, one of their own devising. Without the enlightenment of the Holy Spirit, they are unable to do anything else. By nature they despise the real Christ of history, find his cross offensive, and consider his gospel foolishness. In blindness and rebellion against truth, they manufacture a Christ that is compatible with their own self-chosen social or political agenda.

The unwillingness to assent to the biblical identity of Jesus Christ normally involves a redefining or downplaying of his saving work. Attacks on his person, that is, on the union of the divine and human natures in the person of Christ, ultimately bring a negative impact on the significance of his redemptive work. The early church fathers recognized this in their resistance to all definitions, or descriptions, of Christ that failed to uphold his full humanity, full deity, and the union between the two. As Luther so graphically phrased it, the devil attacks Christ "in three lines of battle. One will not let him be God, another will not let him be man, and the third will not let him do what he has done. Each of the three wants to reduce Christ to nothing."[9] Unbelieving scholars today still refer to a "divinity" and a "humanity" of Jesus but do so in vague terms and with the purpose of highlighting mankind's assumed ability to ascend to the divine. What Friedrich Schleiermacher wrote almost two hundred years ago is pretty much assumed by modern religious thinkers: "As certainly as Christ was man, there must reside in human nature the possibility of taking up the divine into self, just as did happen in Christ."[10] When all is said and done, false teachers invariably tell us that we must duplicate or complete Christ's work to be saved. Christ is thus a pattern or example, stimulator and pathfinder, but not really Savior in the biblical sense of the word.

Deliberate rejection of Bible truth does not erase familiarity with—or the use of—Bible vocabulary. False teachers must define words like *Savior* and *salvation* in ways that twist the biblical emphasis. The rescue from the guilt and condemnation from sin, the reconciliation between the Holy God and sinful mankind, and the giving of spiritual and eternal life to replace death is no longer the focus. Salvation from various economic, ethical, social, political, and psychological maladies is made the primary purpose and goal of Christ's

---

[9]LW 34:210.
[10]Quoted by Bloesch, p. 19.

---

words and deeds. It is not uncommon for modern theologians to use a "salvation" vocabulary without distinct meaning, just as our society in general does. You are perhaps aware of the recent strong and negative reactions to the blockbuster movie *Titanic*. Religious reviewers have often condemned the movie as satanic, evil, godless, and so forth. A case can be made for this appraisal, of course, as it can for probably 90% or more of all movies made and marketed by major filmmakers and studios. But the furor over *Titanic* focuses less on the almost obligatory fornication portrayed or the failure to use the 1912 sudden tragedy to urge spiritual preparedness than it does on one line in the movie's script. The heroine speaks the words as she declares that the hero "saved" her "in every way that a human being can be saved." With this mention of salvation without the mention of Christ, the film almost invites critics to look for the cloven hoof, sniff for brimstone, and assail the moviemakers for attacking Christianity.[11] If taken seriously as a thoughtful and purposeful theological assertion, the words are blatantly anti-Christian and reflect a totally inadequate view of Christ and salvation. It is more likely, however, that the sentence, in the context of the movie plot, probably referred to a "salvation" from a potentially bad marriage, from a social haughtiness and prejudicial class consciousness, and from a basically boring voyage on the part of the heroine. Viewed in the light of known religious ideas of contemporary Hollywood writers and producers, the words may more accurately be described as a silly overstatement or somewhat of a cultural cliché that uses words that have become largely vague and meaningless in society despite having a rich biblical meaning. One gains the same impression when reading what many major contemporary theologians and scholars have to say about Christ's saving work. They show themselves unwilling and therefore incapable of taking sin and salvation from sin seriously.

Conclusion

It might have been sufficient for this essay simply to highlight the impact of a true, biblical Christology in our daily lives. Serious thought was given to concentrating entirely on stating and describing only positive effects that our doctrine establishes and maintains among us. But an approach to the assigned topic that included brief looks at false Christologies was chosen. The decision to do this was made quite consciously, with the hope that this material will prove profitable in a number of ways.

First, may the contrasting look at true and false ideas regarding our Savior stimulate us to ask God for continued wholesome thinking. Love for divine truth is always to be accompanied by watchfulness over against false-

---

[11]A number of appraisals and critiques that take this approach were included in the April 13 and April 27, 1998 issues of *Christian News*.

hood. We are sometimes tempted to view false doctrines as relatively impotent formulations of theologians who dwell mostly in ivory towers. Yet there is ample evidence that the ivory tower is often "the control tower of a civilization" as John Robbins phrased it.[12] Recognized scholars, despite (and perhaps often because of) the sheer nonsense of their conclusions, usually get good press and are usually assumed to be authoritative by the religious laity. We should not underestimate the influence of false teachers and their ideas on the way people think.

On the emotional level, may our love for the Lord Jesus Christ and our hatred for everything that denies or obscures him remain strong. "All error, heresy, idolatry, offense, misuse, and evil in the church originally came from despising or losing sight of this article of faith in Jesus Christ. And if one looks at it correctly and clearly, all heresies do contend against this dear article of Jesus Christ."[13] With these words Luther wisely observes that to fall prey to errors regarding Christ and faith in Christ is to lose all we need for life and salvation. The impact on our daily lives would be massive and deadly. So let us cherish the treasure of truth that God has so graciously preserved among us.

May our resolve to share the truth with our neighbor also grow and express itself vigorously. It is a major part of our Christian calling to reach out to those still enslaved by ignorance and error and to seek their release. We have what they need. We have what is fully able to change the way they think, feel, and make decisions as surely as it can change their eternal destiny. Jesus is true God and true man. Jesus is the only Savior from sin, death, and the devil. His life and death have won forgiveness of sins for the world. His resurrection assures us of this fact. This is the heart of true Christology. This is the saving gospel of Jesus Christ.

---

[12]Robbins, "Crisis," *The Atonement*, p. 172.
[13]LW 34:207,208.

A LIVING, ACTIVE, POWERFUL CHRIST FOR THE CHURCH OF THE NEXT MILLENNIUM

Eric S. Hartzell

Pacific Northwest District Convention
Des Moines, Washington
June 12–14, 1998

Some computer folks speak in doomsday terms about the year 2000. That's when they say all computers will go into shock and electronic fibrillation. Time as they were programmed to think of it won't exist any more. There will be that strange number 2 and all those zeroes, and computers will balk, and life as we know it on the planet will come to an end.

As believers in Jesus, we are not afraid of the year 2000—for whatever reason. We just hope that it doesn't come. We hope that Jesus will come back before the zeroes of the new millennium roll over. It is not only a distinct possibility; it is what we should expect because our Savior has told us, "Yes, I am coming soon." And we take seriously what Peter said when he encouraged us, "You ought to live holy and godly lives as you look forward to the day of God and speed its coming" (2 Pe 3:11,12). So we look forward to Jesus' coming more than we look forward to another thousand years of time passing. We say with the apostle John, "Amen. Come, Lord Jesus" (Rev 22:20).

But the Lord in his love and patience might delay a few more years, and the next millennium might come. We have more to look forward to than the possible debacle with the computers. We can gather together this afternoon and peek through the keyhole of these last months of the 20th century and actually peer into the 21st century. That is the hope of the title before us: A Living, Active, Powerful Christ for the Church of the Next Millennium.

We can only speculate as to what the new millennium will bring for the church in the way of changes and challenges in outward things and in its work. The 20th century went from horseback to rocket ships, from quill pens to computers. The only web sites people knew at the turn of this century were those of spiders in their own basements. Who could even guess what the 21st century will bring in the way of changes to life on the planet? God only knows that. It would be pure conjecture and foolishness to try and see what physical changes or moral changes or any other changes the next millennium will bring.

But when we consider the living, active, powerful Christ for the church of the next millennium, we are considering something that we can know. We can know exactly how Christ will be in the next millennium because he has promised us that he doesn't change. So what he is today—which is what he was yesterday—is what he is going to be in the new millennium. If Jesus does come before the year 2000, our work today will not have been in vain. We will have been obedient to the command, "Finally, brothers, whatever is true, whatever is noble, whatever is right, whatever is pure, whatever is lovely, whatever is admirable—if anything is excellent or praiseworthy—think about such things" (Php 4:8). And in thinking about Jesus as being living and active and powerful and the Christ, we will have calmed our nerves and received the strength to live and work, and the reason to look ahead.

That must be the intent of this essay: not to be a prophecy of how Christ will be in the next millennium but to be a proclamation of how he is—yesterday, today, and forever.

To help us deal with the topic in an orderly way, we will consider it along the following lines of thought:

1. Jesus is living.
2. Jesus is active.
3. Jesus is powerful.
4. Jesus is still Christ, the chosen one of God.
5. What Jesus was in the past and is in the present he still will be in the future.

1. Jesus is living.

There are many religious road-kill victims along the highway of life. All the gods of mankind have been squashed flat by the passing of time. They are dead. They haven't been able to get out of its way. Goliath pranced back and forth in front of God's people in the Valley of Elah. When the shepherd stepped forward to do battle with his sling, "the Philistine cursed David by his gods" (1 Sa 17:43). One of those gods was dubbed Dagon. He had a temple at Ashdod, and dead though he was, he supposedly lived there. One day the Philistines who had captured the Ark of God carried it in triumph into Dagon's temple. And then the Scripture tells us the rest of the story: "But the following morning when they rose, there was Dagon, fallen on his face on the ground before the ark of the LORD! His head and hands had been broken off and were lying on the threshold: only his body remained. That is why to this day neither the priests of Dagon nor any others who enter Dagon's temple at Ashdod step on the threshold" (1 Sa 5:4,5). We thank God that when we enter our church to worship our living Jesus, we don't have to sidestep the threshold in the narthex because that is where we saw the grisly remains of his head and his hands.

All the gods of history are dead. Buddha is dead. You can climb up into one of his lifeless statues in Kamakura, Japan, and look out one of his vacant eyes at the people down below who are worshiping, praying, and leaving sake in little cups and tidy piles of oranges and rice cakes. The awful god of the hammer and sickle in our world's recent experience is dead. There are still some who worship at his altar, but they will finally also be disappointed. He— by his name, Communism—promised to share all good things with his worshipers, but it hasn't happened, and it won't. Only the living Jesus we celebrate in Communion shares all good things with those who follow him and claim him and have him living with them.

The prophets of the Old Testament called idols "worthless" and "detestable" and "abominable." And the idols' worst crime was that they were dead. Isaiah said, "They know nothing, they understand nothing; their eyes are plastered over so they cannot see, and their minds closed so they cannot understand" (Isa 44:18). The plight of those who worship something dead is horrible. To stop this terrible abomination from happening, our hands are driven deep into our pockets and our missionaries are driven in love and concern to leave their homes and familiar places to preach to those still bowing down to dead things. And all of us say with the apostles who witnessed Easter, "We cannot help speaking about what we have seen and heard" (Ac 4:20). Jesus is alive. He will be in the new millennium too.

It seemed for a while that Jesus was dead. That's what those defeated and sad lumps-of-clay human beings were doing as they moved slowly on the first Easter morning: going to worship a dead and cold Jesus with the rich poverty of their collected spices and ointments and tears. The angel voices echoed in his tomb as they reminded, "Why do you look for the living among the dead? He is not here; he has risen! Remember how he told you . . ." (Lk 24:5,6).

We worship a living Jesus. In this 20th century since he rose from the dead, we have been worshiping a living Jesus. In the 21st century we will worship a living Jesus too. It won't happen in these next two years that we will gather at some heaped up hole in the ground to watch our Jesus and our faith lowered slowly out of sight by green canvas belts. Reality and truth make us entertain the possibility that even some of those who are now listening to this essay will be members of the church triumphant before New Year's Eve

1999 comes. But Jesus will still be with his living and struggling believers in the church militant because he lives.

And all the illegitimately conceived baby gods and philosophies and gods not yet born will quickly grow old and die, some even before the new millennium comes. The "God is dead" philosophy of the 1970s died, but Jesus is still alive. The so-called New Age Movement is really the same old attempt to convince people that God is a benign being somewhere who doesn't really care and didn't really say what he said. So New Agers get interested in channeling spirit guides and crystals and divination. The next millennium is billed to bring the New Age heaven on earth. It is hoped that at about the year 2000 there will finally be so many people doing good that they will sway the remainder to do good too, and the so-called "Quantum Leap" will happen when by mutual example everyone will save himself. But it won't be a quantum leap that will happen. Things will continue toward demise and destruction. If the New Age lingers until the year 2000, we know that its sickness is terminal.

But Jesus will live on.

Every Sunday, every time we worship our God, we celebrate life. His! Ours! We celebrate and give thanks for being in the living church, gathered around the Word of God that is "living and active" (Heb 4:12). We are the only ones out of all religions who are not doomed to holding services in man-made mortuaries. The Philistines didn't realize when they made the temple for Dagon at Ashdod that it would house the remains of their dead hopes, but Dagon being dead on the doorstep was entirely predictable.

Sometimes in our home mission work, WELS Lutheran churches have their first worship services in mortuaries and funeral chapels. The facilities are available, and they are nice. There might even be the chance to use the organ with its "good" vibrato sound. But it hasn't happened yet, when the ability came to move to a church building of its own with its promise of growth and life, that the mission congregation chose to stay in the mortuary. We don't like even a whiff of death to be associated with our worship. Our Jesus is living!

To understand that Jesus is living is to understand our purpose as a church—and our privilege! We try as WELS Lutherans to get people out of the mortuaries of their dead gods. All religions without the living Jesus are doomed to mortuary worship. Pity if nothing else should fire our mission zeal. Jesus is living!

2. Jesus is active.

Jesus also is active. Ozymandias, the proud "king of kings," was not; or at least he is no longer active. The poet Shelly immortalized the human inability to stay active when he saw the toppled statue and read the inscription lying there in the desert sand:

'My Name is Ozymandias, king of kings:
Look on my works, ye Mighty, and despair!'
Nothing beside remains. Round the decay
Of that colossal wreck, boundless and bare
The lone and level sands stretch far away.[1]

There is a "King of kings," and it is not Ozymandias. We read of this King and his followers in John's Revelation, "They [God's enemies] will make war against the Lamb, but the Lamb will overcome them because he is the Lord of lords and King of kings—and with him will be his called, chosen and faithful followers" (17:14). Listen to this King. "This is what the Lord says—Israel's King and Redeemer, the Lord Almighty: I am the first and I am the last; apart from me there is no God. Who then is like me? Let him proclaim it. Let him declare and lay out before me what has happened since I established my ancient people, and what is yet to come—yes, let him foretell what will come. Do not tremble, do not be afraid. Did I not proclaim this and foretell it long ago? You are my witnesses. Is there any God besides me? No, there is no other Rock; I know not one" (Isa 44:6-8). It is the active Christ who makes this claim for his ancient people and modern people and "what is yet to come."

Jesus our King is active. He is quick. We believe in the living Christ, and he proves he is alive by being active. He does things: he made all things; he preserves all things; he saved all things; he prepares a place for us according to his promise! This is activity that Jesus is involved in right now, not just with his eye on the next millennium, but on eternity.

Jesus' love is active. He can imagine no other kind of love. You know this when you listen to his encouragement that you love him "with all your heart and with all your soul and with all your mind" (Mt 22:37). Love with a soul in it is active love, love with life, love with a pulse. That is how you tell if the still person lying there on the bed is alive or not. Is there some movement? Is there warmth? Is there a pulse? If there is still a soul there, those manifestations of the soul will be there too. God's love has a soul in it. It has activity. It always has, and it always will.

When Jesus encourages us to love him with our souls, he wants us to look for the evidence of that soul in our love. Is our love active like his? Few would be comfortable with a cadaver stretched out in their living room. No one could live very long with a corpse. Mary and Martha, even though they loved their brother, were the first to tell Jesus not to take the stone from Lazarus' grave. Lazarus was "inactive." Lazarus stunk in his inactivity. God is not happy having a dead and inactive love lying in state in his parlor, even

---

[1] *The New Oxford Book of English Verse,* chosen and edited by Helen Gardner (New York and Oxford: Oxford University Press, 1972), p. 580.

---

if it be yours or mine. Any love that is inactive, that doesn't prove life by warmth and activity and action, is not God's kind of love. The Christ is active in his love, and he wants us to be that too as we consider the next millennium.

Paul's prayer for Philemon is what we want for ourselves: "I pray that you may be active in sharing your faith, so that you will have a full understanding of every good thing we have in Christ" (v. 6). The inspiration and the motivation for that kind of activity comes from God's love to us. It is soul-love. God's love is warm and moving. We can hear its soul's strong pulse even now if we listen. We hear it in mercies new to us every morning. We hear it when we stand shoulder to shoulder at the Communion rail and God says, "Depart in peace." We hear the pulse of God's active love in every benediction and every blessing from Christian friends who say, "God bless you!" We feel the heartbeat when we stand at the grave of a loved one and hear God say, "Precious in the sight of the Lord is the death of his saints" (Ps 116:15). And it is a God with living and active love—and hands—that we trust when we confess, "My times are in your hands" (Ps 31:15).

This active love of Christ will be with us in the next millennium as well, because this Christ of God does not change and will not change.

We enter the millennium with the machine of this activity: God's Word. "The word of God is living and active. Sharper than any double-edged sword, it penetrates even to dividing soul and spirit, joints and marrow; it judges the thoughts and attitudes of the heart. Nothing in all creation is hidden from God's sight. Everything is uncovered and laid bare before the eyes of him to whom we must give account" (Heb 4:12,13).

With this love and with this Word, we know something about the church in the next millennium. Believers are going to continue to be inspired in their love for Christ. The love of Christ is truly going to constrain them. It will propel them too. When the century dawned, the Wisconsin Synod was doing mission work among the Apaches in Arizona. Solo mission work was at that time a new endeavor, only seven years old. As the century's sun sets, Christ's active love has drawn our church into 19 foreign countries. That translates into 56,049 baptized members, 61 missionaries, 64 national pastors, 99 seminary students, and 489 congregations.[2] Just imagine the possibilities that exist for active love in mission work in the next hundred years if Christ delays his coming that long! Our century has seen God's active love motivate Christians to establish Kingdom Workers and Builders for Christ. Active love works with the elderly; the hearing impaired, vision impaired, and mentally impaired; those in prison. Christ's active love

---

[2]Statistical Report of the Wisconsin Evangelical Lutheran Synod for 1997, p. 117.

inspires us to go beyond cultural boundaries in our own country. Christians from our midst give aid to those who suffer natural disaster, and the gifts are significant. The People's Bible series puts God's Word into the hands of the laity in simple and clear words. The Christ-Light religion curriculum offers a whole new vista and era of coordinated Bible instruction for our children and for the members of our synod. Our educational facilities have grown and are wonderfully appointed through the gifts of love that support them. Special gifts and special giving to do special things in ministry and mission abound. And really, most of the things described here have made their appearances in our church in this century. Just think of the optimism we should have as we contemplate the further flurry of activity in the new millennium with the active Christ and his love!

The love of many will grow cold. We are warned of this. But just as this is true, so it is also true that the love of the active Christ will never grow cold, nor will the love of those who feel themselves loved by him.

3. Jesus is powerful.

Jesus is powerful. His Father chose him—anointed him—to do the most difficult of all tasks: save every man, woman and child. King David, who had some power residing in his sturdy and ruddy frame, said, "One thing God has spoken, two things I have heard: that you, O God, are strong, and that you, O Lord, are loving" (Ps 62:11,12). And what Jesus has been is what he will continue to be for the church in the next millennium. Powerful!

We are certain of Jesus' power because we have heard the angels sing about it in John's Revelation: "Then I looked and heard the voice of many angels, numbering thousands upon thousands, and ten thousand times ten thousand. They encircled the throne and the living creatures and the elders. In a loud voice they sang: 'Worthy is the Lamb, who was slain, to receive power and wealth and wisdom and strength and honor and glory and praise!' Then I heard every creature in heaven and on earth and under the earth and on the sea, and all that is in them, singing: 'To him who sits on the throne and to the Lamb be praise and honor and glory and power, for ever and ever!'" (Rev 5:11-13). The Greek language has many words for power and strength describing different facets of the phenomenon. Virtually every word in the Greek language for power is used in these words the angels sing.

We like power. We will pay for power if we can. Ask teenage boys about power when they look for their first car. We see advertisements for it—multi-valved, fuel injected, "rules have changed" kind of power. And we want it. We admire power in chiseled and defined bodies. We even like power in our vacuum cleaners and can openers.

We Christians are of all people most blessed when it comes to power. We sing about a powerful Christ. We recognize with David that our God is strong and that he is loving, and actually, he is the one because of the other. His love for his church is strong and will continue on powerfully into the next millennium. Consider some of the ways. . . .

Jesus is powerful. He has a crushing handshake and grip, the bulldog tenacity to hang on to his people, those resting in the palm of his hand. "No one can snatch them out of my hand. My Father, who has given them to me, is greater than all; no one can snatch them out of my Father's hand" (Jn 10:28,29).

Jesus is powerful to overcome and conquer opposition against his church. This is his dynamite power. (The Greek word used in the following verse is the origin for our word *dynamite*.) "They [God's enemies] marched across the breadth of the earth and surrounded the camp of God's people, the city he loves. But fire came down from heaven and devoured them" (Rev 20:9). Notice the short work Jesus' power makes of the enemies of his church of believers. "Then the end will come, when he hands over the kingdom to God the Father after he has destroyed all dominion, authority and power" (1 Co 15:24). As we look to the future, we need to know this power. "I pray also that the eyes of your heart may be enlightened in order that you may know the hope to which he has called you, the riches of his glorious inheritance in the saints, and his incomparably great power for us who believe. That power is like the working of his mighty strength, which he exerted in Christ when he raised him from the dead and seated him at his right hand in the heavenly realms, far above all rule and authority, power and dominion" (Eph 1:18-21).

Don't you see how it will be with Jesus' power in the next millennium?

Jesus is powerful to destroy what is wrong, and he will do this. This is the tidal wave of Jesus' power. Who will be able to stand against this power? The psalmist observed, "The kings of the earth take their stand and the rulers gather together against the Lord and against his Anointed One" (Ps 2:2). But the psalmist also knew of the portentous power of God when he continued, "Therefore, you kings, be wise; be warned, you rulers of the earth. Kiss the Son, lest he be angry and you be destroyed in your way" (Ps 2:10,12).

Evildoers will not get away with it. The impunity of the impious will be dealt with. This is atomic bomb kind of power, the deadly mushroom cloud of God's judgment in the sky. "[Abraham] looked down toward Sodom and Gomorrah, toward all the land of the plain, and he saw dense smoke rising from the land, like smoke from a furnace" (Ge 19:28). We surely don't speak with glee over the prospects, but this power stands waiting in the wings of this next millennium.

Jesus has power over the mind and actions of all, forcing even enemies to do his will. It was Nebuchadnezzar's nightmare. "In the visions I saw while lying in my bed, I looked, and there before me was a messenger, a holy one, coming down from heaven. He called in a loud voice: 'Cut down the tree and trim off its branches; strip off its leaves and scatter its fruit. Let the animals flee from under it and the birds from its branches. But let the stump and its roots, bound with iron and bronze, remain in the ground, in the grass of the field. Let him be drenched with the dew of heaven, and let him live with the animals among the plants of the earth. Let his mind be changed from that of a man and let him be given the mind of an animal, till seven times pass by for him'" (Da 4:13-16). The living and active Christ has power over men's minds.

The Christ has power over those philosophical giants who belly laugh when someone believes Jesus and his Word. In their awful obstinacy, as they wield their awesome influence, God still has power over them. "For this reason God sends them a powerful delusion so that they will believe the lie and so that all will be condemned who have not believed the truth but have delighted in wickedness" (2 Th 2:11,12).

We hear the boulders roll and churn in the flash flood of God's justice. "Let justice roll on like a river" (Am 5:24). And this happens in full view of our court system, with its all-too-frequent mockery of justice. Think of the power needed to straighten out our world of jurisprudence. Some of the greatest and most powerful machines this world knows are made to make roads. Isaiah knew of this coming power of the Christ in the new millennium when he said in the 7th century B.C., "The crooked roads shall become straight, the rough ways smooth. And all mankind will see God's salvation" (as quoted in Lk 3:5,6). Jesus has power over all things, even those crooked and perverted.

Jesus has power to crush. "The stone the builders rejected has become the capstone. He who falls on this stone will be broken to pieces, but he on whom it falls will be crushed" (Mt 21:42,44). Isaiah 53:5 speaks of God's power to crush—even his own Son: "He was crushed for our iniquities." God warns through Amos of this pressure of his power: "I will crush you as a cart crushes when loaded with grain. The swift will not escape, the strong will not muster their strength, and the warrior will not save his life" (2:13,14).

We think of the power of the Wind of God, his Spirit, to move where it will and level before it all the flimsy structures of man's resistance and reason. You and I cannot change people's minds about much. Try changing someone's mind even about their football team, let alone changing their lifelong cache of religious beliefs. Jesus called Nicodemus' attention to this power: "The wind blows wherever it pleases. You hear its sound, but you cannot tell where it comes from or where it is going. So it is with everyone born of the Spirit" (Jn 3:8). This is the power of the Spirit of Jesus to convert, to change old men like Nicodemus into babies in faith. This wonderful change and rebirth comes only through great power, the unstoppable power of God's Spirit Wind.

Jesus has power to control the work his servants do in his church. It takes power to keep them sometimes from doing pet projects they think are necessary to his kingdom. Such was God's power with the apostle Paul: "When they came to the border of Mysia, they tried to enter Bithynia, but the Spirit of Jesus would not allow them to" (Ac 16:7). We pray for Jesus to powerfully overcome our best intentions as a church in the next millennium if those intentions do not square with his wisdom and will. Because Jesus doesn't change, we can be sure that he will use his power in this way.

Jesus is powerful to save. This power is the rainbow of his mercy and salvation struck across the storm clouds. "Whenever the rainbow appears in the clouds, I will see it and remember the everlasting covenant between God and all living creatures of every kind on the earth" (Ge 9:16). Mercy is a great power. The eternal mercy in God's covenant of grace and his unending commitment to that covenant calls for great and ongoing power.

Jesus is God's Son, and God's Sun. He is that incredible radiation of power and light and heat which supports life itself. "In him was life, and that life was the light of men. The light shines in the darkness, but the darkness has not understood it" (Jn 1:4,5). If you look at the footnote for this verse in the NIV, you will see that what is translated "understood" can also be translated "overcome." The darkness has not *overcome* the light. It can't. It doesn't have the power.

Hannah admired the power of her God and of his Anointed when she said, "He will give strength to his king and exalt the horn of his anointed" (1 Sa 2:10). The ultimate evidence of this power is when God the Father empowered his Son to be this world's strongest man: all-powerful to obliterate sin, to forgive all wrong, to love all love, to carry all anxiety. Twice in her song of praise to the God who honored her with a son, Hannah spoke of this horn. The Hebrews knew the horn as a symbol of strength, the very point where the significant strength of a bull or goat was focused. God is going to "exalt the horn of his anointed" indeed! He did it. This is the powerful Jesus who will be with his church in the next millennium.

Jesus is powerful to make his people into something they could never be by themselves. This power transformed David the shepherd into David the warrior and David the poet and David the king. This power made David into someone who was after God's own heart. "So Samuel took the horn of oil and anointed him in the presence of his brothers, and from that day on the Spirit of the LORD came upon David in power" (1 Sa 16:13). He is going to continue to use this power to equip and empower his special leaders in the church of the next millennium.

And in all of this, we think of our God's name *Pantokrator* (παν-τοκράτωρ), the all-powerful one, the one light-years beyond any character in C. S. Lewis' *The Space Trilogy* in strength, the very maker of the stars himself. He is the one who breathes hoarsely through fiery nostrils, striking out with the sword of his mouth and saving all those who strike their own colors to march under his blood-red banners. "We give thanks to you, Lord God Almighty, the One who is and who was, because you have taken your great power and have begun to reign" (Rev 11:17).

We Believe in Jesus Christ

It takes great power. It takes great power to save us. It takes great power for Jesus to overcome our sin and weakness. Our weakness is the abysmal lack of any power to do anything good. We sing about God's power—the angels sing about God's power—in the vacuum of our power shortage and power outage. As we approach the new millennium, we pray like Solomon did—with our hands stiff and empty, still upturned. "Nothing in my hand I bring, simply to thy cross I cling" (from CW 389:3). Still. And on into the future. Lord we do believe. Help our unbelief. Empower us with your power.

It takes great power. It takes power to overcome your and my objections to God. As our minds and thoughts pursue ever more sophisticated ways as they step into the next millennium, it will take power to rein them in and tame them and bring them under the control of the foolishness of preaching. It will continue to take power to overcome all man's intelligence and knowledge, to give us simple and childlike faith. It will take power to keep our approach to sinners the same simple gospel and not to rely on more "reasonable" ways to reach people. "I am not ashamed of the gospel, because it is the power of God for the salvation of everyone who believes" (Ro 1:16). The power of Jesus' gospel—and that power alone—will continue to work the miracle of faith.

It takes power to raise someone from the dead, to get a body up or a hope up or a faith up when it is dead. The best science is going to do in the new millennium is push back the hands a little on the clock that ticks for each person—perhaps. (They hope that by the year 2025, the average life-expectancy per resident of the globe will be 73 years. It is 66 now.) And perhaps for all the efforts to extend life, a new and deadly virus strain will strike, and a new Black Death will come in spite of all the hospitals and medicines. Death still gives up with terrible reluctance. It takes power to make him give up. "[The body] is sowed in weakness, it is raised in power" (1 Co 15:43). "The last enemy to be destroyed is death" (v. 26).

It takes power for the crushed and broken to hear and believe the gospel, but Jesus comes with this power. "He has sent me to bind up the broken-hearted" (Isa 61:1). It takes power to comfort the afflicted. It also takes great power to afflict the comfortable, those who don't think anything is wrong and those who have a high opinion of their own goodness. But Jesus comes with this power too, as Mary acknowledges in her great song: "He has performed mighty deeds with his arm; he has scattered those who are proud in their inmost thoughts" (Lk 1:51).

In all of these ways and for all of these reasons, Jesus has power.

Batteries run out of power. Batteries die. Batteries stand useless and dead. It takes power to get the batteries to have life again. It takes power from outside the battery. Dead batteries just supply the lack of spark, the absence of current, the uselessness and the hopelessness of ever doing anything on their own. But there is a source of power, and if the battery stays connected to that source, after a time it comes to life again. The longer the battery stays connected to the power, the stronger its current is. And in the new millennium, if the world stands, throughout the darkness the lights will continue to go on in people's lives. In electrical terms, we will be able to say that Jesus and his Spirit will truly turn the power on.

We enter the new millennium with great optimism. Not that the world is going to get better but that our Jesus is going to be up to the challenge. He continues to have power. All things are possible.

4. Jesus is still Christ, the chosen one of God.

Jesus is the Christ. Jesus is the Messiah. In whatever language you speak, Jesus is the chosen one of God.

We continue to recognize the importance of the words *Christ* and *Messiah*. Those words tell us that Jesus is still the one, and if we see the arrival of the next millennium, he will be the one for that time too. He is the real thing. All the fullness of the Godhead continues to rest in him. There is no other. God still says, "This is my Son, whom I love; with him I am well pleased. Listen to him!" (Mt 17:5).

Jesus still is the chosen one of God. When we step into the next millennium, he will be real. "The reality, however, is found in Christ" (Col 2:17). Christ is the real thing. In all of religious life, the only real, real thing is Jesus. So the teenager exclamation "Get real!" is not a bad reminder for our worship and our preaching as we get close to the next millennium. We will continue preaching Christ crucified. That will be the only thing that will continue to be real. It is a comfort to pastors and teachers to know that they can present Jesus to their people not in virtual reality but in actual reality. The blood is real. The sins died for are real sins. The Savior is not only a Savior who looks like a Savior, but is a Savior who feels like a Savior and speaks like a Savior and is a Savior. WELS Lutherans find great comfort in this reality in the Lord's Supper—the *real* presence of Jesus' body and blood, given and shed for them.

We can still hear our Father say, "This is my Son, whom I love; with him I am well pleased. Listen to him!" We will still listen to the Christ of God in our Bible studies. The message will be forever relevant. The truth of it will still be objective and propositional. "Jesus Loves Me, This I Know" will still be a good song to sing and to teach our children no matter how sophisticated our world becomes.

Jesus said, "If anyone loves me, he will obey my teaching. My Father will love him, and we will come to him and make our home with him. He who does not love me will not obey my teaching. These words you hear are not my own; they belong to the Father who sent me" (Jn 14:23,24). This is our hope! And this is God's direction as to how he will truly be with his people in the future: through the words, through the teaching of those words that belong to the Father. If our synod is going to continue to be part of God's church of

We Believe in Jesus Christ

believers, if Jesus and his Father are going to continue to make their home with us, it is only going to be through the practiced study of God's Word. Our leadership has put this before our eyes and must continue to do it. (*The Adult Bible Study Handbook* put out by the Commission on Adult Discipleship is one example of this effort.)

The living, active, powerful Christ will be with his church in the next millennium. That is a fact with no variables. The variable comes in who will follow this fact. "From this time many of his disciples turned back and no longer followed him" (Jn 6:66). And in view of this terrible variable, Peter said what we still want to say: "Lord, to whom shall we go? You have the words of eternal life" (v. 68).

5. What Jesus was in the past and is in the present he still will be in the future.

We started by saying that to know the living, active, and powerful Christ in the next millennium is to know this same Christ in the closing years of this millennium. Some things truly don't change and won't change. Jesus will stay the same. And our worship of him will essentially stay the same.

This is the hope that we have as we live in the world teetering on the brink of the year 2000.

The passing of time affects our earthly homes. Things change and make us feel sad. But though this does happen and must happen to our earthly home, it doesn't and can't happen in our church home. The building might change. The staff might change. The hymnbooks might change. But the essence remains the same. And we can truly sing,

> Now thank we all our God with hearts and hands
> and voices,
> Who wondrous things has done, in whom his world
> rejoices,
> Who from our mother's arms has blessed us on our way
> With countless gifts of love *and still is ours today.*
> (CW 610:1)

In the 20th century some things have changed in our churches. The black suit is almost extinct among Sunday worshipers. Veils and hats on our womenfolk have flown away. Ties have expanded and contracted through all possible measurement known to man. Women no longer sit on one side of the church and men on the other. The hymnal abbreviation is CW and not TLH. Some congregations may sing the Psalm responsively. Padded pews are common (no more Puritan hardness to endure). Some pastors stand behind freestanding altars; very few make their way with their sermon up narrow steps into cloistered pulpits towering over their waiting parishioners. Some parishioners sit tethered to hearing devices—and hear every word of the sermon for the first time in years. There is now a WELS Web site. And not far from the chancel of every (almost every?) church, a computer lurks on a desk, eager to serve with a Bible program or an e-mail or a connection to the Internet.

But even though some things have changed, we enter the next millennium counting on the fact that there will be no change in our worship of Jesus. What he was in the past and what he is in the present is what he will be in the future. And those who worship him will continue to do it in spirit and in truth.

As we come face-to-face with this noteworthy step in time, we can't help but sing along with the hymnist,

> Swift to its close ebbs out life's little day;
> Earth's joys grow dim; its glories pass away.
> Change and decay in all around I see;
> O thou who changest not, abide with me! (CW 588:2)

Jesus Christ—the same yesterday, today, and forever. He is our global positioning unit that brings us back unerringly to the very spot we need to be, in this millennium or the next.

Ernst H. Wendland

Minnesota District Convention
New Ulm, Minnesota
June 16–18, 1998

The topic assigned to me for presentation at this convention is about as timely as it can get. Another change of a millennial year is just around the comer. When this convention meets again, the year 2000 will be upon us.

This is not only a matter of special interest to people with computers, who worry that their two-digit abbreviations for years will not be able to cope with dates after December 31, 1999. Many other interests are involved at this particular time, when another millennium is upon us. "Futurism," *Newsweek* magazine tells us, "has become the trendiest profession." Changes that boggle the mind in business ventures and scientific discoveries are being predicted for the coming millennium. Many sales procedures as we know them, futurists say, will cease to exist. Huge department stores, for example, will be a thing of the past, since many people will do their shopping by computer. Advanced technology, they claim, will be able to produce genetically engineered people who can work with greater precision than ordinary human beings. Microbugs and robotic snakes will be developed that are capable of crawling into buildings in order to detect nuclear, chemical, or biological weapons of mass destruction. NASA officials are proposing the launching of a satellite that can produce a global image of weather patterns, so that in the future we will be able to protect ourselves from the destructive changes of nature. Optimism concerning the future knows no bounds.

As the third millennium A.D. nears, however, religious prognosticators are less optimistic. Hard-core evangelists are increasing their dire warnings about "Armageddon" and the end of "Planet Earth," calamities so "awesome" that

227

they can't even be described. "It's in the Scriptures," they declare. We hear about asteroids that will strike the earth. Apocalyptic visions have already led to mass suicides by the members of Heaven's Gate in California, and to the inferno at the Branch Davidian complex in Waco, Texas.

With millennialism on the rise, and so many strange notions being proposed concerning the future, it is good that we sharpen up on our study of "the last things," known theologically as *eschatology* (*eschata* [Greek], "last things"). Indeed, the topic assigned for this convention is certainly timely. Rather than being led astray, let us as Christians find greater assurance and hope in the precious truth that

Jesus Is Coming Again

I. Let's be sure of it
II. Let's be informed about it
III. Let's be ready for it

I. Let's Be Sure of It

Anyone who takes the Bible seriously doesn't need much convincing to know that Jesus must surely be coming again.

In the New Testament

It is Jesus himself who provides the most familiar Bible passages for such assurance. One passage that occurs to us immediately is that beautiful promise recorded in John 14, where Jesus tells his disciples that he will go to prepare a place for them in his heavenly Father's house. Then he declares: "I will come back and take you to be with me that you also may be where I am" (v. 3). What greater assurance would anyone want?

The Lord's chief eschatological statements pertaining to his second coming are found in what is called the "Olivet Discourse," spoken on the Mount of Olives shortly before his death, recorded in Matthew 24, Mark 13, and Luke 21. Here Jesus refers to himself as "the Son of Man," a Messianic title occurring 81 times in the gospels, emphasizing that he is true God in human form. He speaks openly of his coming at the end of the world and of the many signs that will precede his coming, stating that there will be *one* final return, *one* final bodily resurrection of all people, *one* final judgment. This Olivet Discourse is basic, providing us with the *sedes doctrinae*, as the dogmaticians express it, of all theology that looks to the last things.

We find this same assurance in the first chapter of Acts, which tells of Christ's ascension into heaven. The disciples are told by two men dressed in white, "This same Jesus . . . will come back in the same way you have seen him go into heaven" (v. 11).

The absolute certainty of Christ's return can be found in frequent references in the epistles. In his letter to the Philippians, the apostle Paul writes that "our citizenship is in heaven," and that "we eagerly await a Savior from there, the Lord Jesus Christ" (3:20). In 1 Thessalonians Paul writes of the Lord's return, of the glorious resurrection of believers: "and so will we be with the Lord forever" (4:17). Facing a martyr's death, that same apostle could look forward to a "crown of righteousness," which the Lord would award to him and to "all who have longed for his appearing" (2 Ti 4:8). The apostle Peter refers emphatically to the Lord's coming again, when heaven and earth will be destroyed, encouraging believers to look forward to "a new heaven and a new earth, the home of righteousness" (2 Pe 3:13). The apostle John's book of Revelation, from the very first to the last chapter, deals with visions that assure Christians of their Lord's second coming. We'll have more, much more, to say about these visions of John in the second part of this paper.

In the Old Testament

The Old Testament is no less reassuring about Christ's second coming. How often haven't we heard of suffering Job's song of praise to his Redeemer, his *goel*, who lives, who in the end will stand upon the earth, whom he will see "with [his] own eyes" (19:27). The Psalms not only tell of the Lord's return in judgment (58:11; 75:7; 96:13), but also in promise (2:8; 102:25-27).

All the prophets from Isaiah to Malachi refer in some way to "the last days," or "the great day of the LORD." They do not always distinguish between his first coming in humility and his second coming in glory, foretelling these related events without separating them in different perspectives of time. Professor Gawrisch explains, "Reading them is therefore like looking from a distance at two mountain peaks without seeing the valley that lies between them."[1] We can be sure, however, that the Old Testament prophecies of the "day of the LORD" and the "end of all things" point clearly to the time of New Testament fulfillment, as declared by Jesus and his apostles. Ezekiel, Daniel, and Zechariah are especially similar to the book of Revelation in imagery, with the same purpose of assuring the redeemed children of God of their final victory, when the Lord, the God of free and faithful grace, will return.

In our Lutheran Confessions

We remind ourselves of Christ's second coming every time we confess our faith in one of the ecumenical creeds. In each of these we express in almost identical words that Jesus Christ, the Son of God, is coming again in

---

[1] Wilbert R. Gawrisch, "Eschatalogical Prophecies and Current Misinterpretations," *Wisconsin Lutheran Quarterly* (Mequon, Wisconsin: Wisconsin Lutheran Seminary, 1989), p. 14.

---

glory, coming from the right hand of the Father, coming to judge the living and the dead, and that his kingdom will have no end. Again we stress through our Lutheran Confessions that there will be only one second coming of Christ, one final resurrection of the dead, one final judgment, one eternal life in the glory of heaven, one eternal punishment in hell.

The Augsburg Confession (A.D. 1530), Article XVII, entitled "Of Christ's Return to Judgment," clearly teaches that "Christ will appear for judgment, and will raise up all the dead; He will give to the godly and elect eternal life and everlasting joys, but ungodly men and the devils He will condemn to be tormented without end."[2]

In this article the Anabaptists are condemned, "who think that there will be an end to the punishments of condemned men and devils."[3] Also condemned are "others, who are now spreading certain Jewish opinions, that before the resurrection of the dead the godly shall take possession of the kingdom of the world, the ungodly being everywhere suppressed."[4] What a succinct way, in one simple sentence, of censuring those who at that time were spreading millennialistic teachings!

Our Wisconsin Synod's confessional statement *This We Believe*, under Article IX, "Jesus' Return and the Judgment," declares: "We reject every form of millennialism, since it has no valid scriptural basis and leads Christians to set their hopes upon the kingdom of Christ as an earthly kingdom."[5]

These eternal truths, stated so emphatically in Scripture and in our Lutheran Confessions, are contrary to mankind's entire cultural thought-patterns relating to the future, concepts that people have set for themselves according to their own natural thinking.

African culture

African natural religion has perhaps the simplest way of avoiding the issue of an endless hereafter with a future accountability before a mighty God. African tradition expresses a belief in a higher power, a *Mulungu, Unkhulukhulu, Mvami, Leza*, or however their languages may designate this mysterious "High God." It teaches that man's entire life on earth is a sort of religious drama, enacted from birth to death. He celebrates every new phase of life in one way or other—birth, puberty, maturity, marriage, death. His beliefs about life, however, are entirely *man-centered*.

According to John S. Mbiti, one of the keenest analysts of African traditional religion, the concept of time has a long "past," an actual "present" in which all human life is centered, but only a potential "future." Time must be

[2] AC XVII:1-3.
[3] AC XVII:4.
[4] AC XVII:5.
[5] *This We Believe* (Milwaukee: Northwestern Publishing House, 1980), p. 24.

experienced in order to be real. His language, Mbiti states, reflects a "short future," which is merely an extension of the past and the present, but having no verb tense expressing a "distant future." There is no concept of history moving toward a distant climax, such as the end of the world. When a person dies, he exists in the community of the 'living-dead," but only as long as he is remembered in the present. To him the idea of an eternal future is totally foreign.[6]

Euro-American culture

The traditional beliefs of Europeans and Americans may seem to be expressed in more complicated ways, but reflect similar concepts. A distant past, based on rather vague scientific theories, leads to a dominant present, and from there to an inconclusive future.

Theories of evolution have long been with us, finding expression in books like Charles Darwin's *Origin of Species*. According to this thought-pattern, the world has come into existence by some kind of evolutionary process going back billions of years, presumably developing gradually toward something better. Mankind has no real destiny beyond death. At best, perhaps, his more enduring hopes lie in the fact that his accomplishments will have somehow contributed toward making this earth a better place in which to live, and that he will somehow be remembered.

A recent issue of *National Geographic* magazine (January, 1998) offers to "make sense of the MILLENNIUM" in a series of articles on topics that "will shape human destiny into the next thousand years." If one wishes to experience personally the extent to which the theory of evolution is generally accepted by our society, one can go to any national park or any museum, or read any modern textbook of science or history used in our educational systems. Theories dealing with billions of years are simply set forth as facts. One doesn't even seem to question anymore why there should be such a great variation in these estimates. To disagree with or even call them into question puts one somewhere back in the Dark Ages.

The sad thing is that much of present-day religion in Europe and America, nominally "Christian," has accommodated itself to these evolutionary views. Religious leaders such as Paul Tillich, John A. T. Robinson, and Rudolph Bultmann refer to Bible stories as "myths," denying the facticity of Christ's visible ascension and his visible return.

The *Social Gospel Movement*, so prominent in the many church bodies joined in the World Council of Churches, seems more concerned about the improvement of social, economic, and political conditions in this world rather than preparing Christ's people for the life to come.

---

[6]John S. Mbiti, *African Religion and Philosophy*, second edition (Portsmouth, New Hampshire: Heinemann Educational Books, Inc., 1990), pp. 24-26.

One of the most extreme examples of an activist religion claiming to be "Christian" is known as *Liberation Theology*. It promotes as its greatest eschatological purpose the rescue of the poor and underprivileged from oppressive governments. We paraphrase Gustavo Gutierrez, a Peruvian priest and one of its most articulate voices, "In today's society everything has a political flavor. A Christendom which remains aloof from political involvement is out of touch with reality. This applies especially to a situation where by passive silence the church lends legitimacy to oppressive governments. Consequently the building of a just society today is a salvific work in which the church must be involved."[7] Such "involvement" includes the active overthrow of oppressive governments. Roman Catholic missionaries from Maryknoll, New York, are the chief representatives of liberation theology in Latin American countries.

These examples are cited to show how not only mankind's natural thinking but even much of that which goes under the name of "Christianity" today has become captured by mankind's humanistic philosophies. It has "adapted itself," become earthbound, man-centered, having lost sight of a primary purpose and the destiny that lies with the Lord Jesus in eternity.

Man's natural wisdom, culture, and tradition, whether it finds its expression in a bush village in Africa or in a sophisticated classroom in Europe or America, is devoid of any living hope beyond the grave. Death ends it all. Nothing lies beyond this final curtain. No matter how mournful our wails and our cries, no matter how complimentary our eulogies to cover our many failings, no matter how we try to hide behind impressive ceremonies, if there is no hope beyond the grave, then even Christians, as the apostle Paul declares, "are to be pitied more than all men" (1 Co 15:19).

To imagine that this earthbound, man-centered philosophy does not constitute a real danger to the Christian faith of our people today is being naive. As Christians, we are living in a world steeped in natural thought-patterns entirely different from our own. An African is surrounded by such traditions from the cradle to the grave. Our young people here in America, continuing their studies in most every field of secondary education, are being saturated with humanistic ideas that are the exact opposite of whatever they may have learned in their earlier years in a Sunday school. Man's natural wisdom in matters relating to the end of all things totally contradicts the revealed wisdom of God.

The apostle Paul was keenly aware of cultural differences and knew that there were reasons for cross-cultural adaptations when dealing with people of other cultural backgrounds. Yet culturally sensitive Paul could say to the Corinthians, "We preach Christ crucified: a stumbling block to Jews and fool-

---

[7]Gustavo Guitierrez, *A Theology of Liberation* (Maryknoll, New York: Orbis Press, 1973).

---

ishness to Gentiles, but to those whom God has called, both Jews and Greeks, Christ the power of God and the wisdom of God. For the foolishness of God is wiser than man's wisdom, and the weakness of God is stronger than man's strength" (1 Co 1:23-25).

By God's grace we do believe. We through the working of his Spirit have received the hope that our Jesus is coming again. We can be sure of it. The Savior, who called us into being, who is the eternal Word of life and truth, wants to be with us in all eternity! With Peter we say, "Lord, to whom shall we go? You have the words of eternal life. We believe and know that you are the Holy One of God" (Jn 6:68,69). With the psalmist we sing, "Whom have I in heaven but you? And earth has nothing I desire besides you. My flesh and my heart may fail, but God is the strength of my heart and my portion forever" (Ps 73:25,26).

May that be our eternal song of praise in heaven!

II. Let's Be Informed about It

So far we have considered the importance of being sure of the fact that Jesus is coming again, a certainty based on Scripture, no matter how strongly man's natural wisdom argues to the contrary. A more disturbing element that has crept into eschatological teaching is the fact that not only does human reason try to lead people away from this important scriptural truth, but also the many teachings of those who claim to be of Christ but who lead people down paths where Scripture does not go. We refer here to the dispensationalists, the millennialists, the chiliasts, who have taken over most of Protestantism with their unscriptural interpretations of eschatological teaching.

The apostle Peter refers to his brother Paul's letters as containing "some things that are hard to understand, which ignorant and unstable people distort, as they do the other Scriptures, to their own destruction" (2 Pe 3:16). It's interesting to observe that Peter makes this comment in the same chapter in which he writes about "the day of the Lord" (v. 10), "the day of judgment" (v. 7), and "a thousand years" (v. 8). It is in connection with the teachings of Scripture relating to the end times that such difficulties can arise.

And they do, of course, when we fail to follow the sound hermeneutical principles that ought to guide us in our interpretation of Scripture.

Hermeneutical principles

Hermeneutics is the science of interpretation. In theology this applies to the interpretation of the Bible. Those who believe in an inerrant Scripture follow the basic hermeneutical principle that *Scripture interprets Scripture*. The more difficult passages of the Bible, interesting and revealing as they are, dare not contradict the basic truths of Scripture.

This principle must be observed especially when interpreting prophet-ical books rich in symbolism, like Daniel, Ezekiel, Zechariah, and Revelation. It also applies to poetic books full of metaphors, similes, and figurative imagery. It applies to books consisting primarily of proverbs. It applies to parables, as often used by the Lord himself. It applies to historical books written chiefly in conventional prose but also rich in prophecies, figures of speech, and symbolic pictures. This includes most of Scripture.

No less important as a hermeneutical principle is the constant *awareness of a book's purpose.* The book of Revelation, where most of the interpretive problems relating to eschatology seem to be, has the purpose of emphasizing Christ's final victory over all anti-Christian forces, a victory that reaches into all eternity. It's a message of encouragement to suffering Christians, which should lead to joy, not uncertainty. Since Revelation is written to a great extent in figurative language, we need to guard against pressing this figurative language beyond its point of comparison. Many symbols and numbers can find their interpretation through the context in which they occur and by means of comparisons with other passages of Scripture that deal with the same sub-ject in less symbolic language.

One mistake frequently made with the book of Revelation is to interpret its seven visions as occurring sequentially, as though one vision chronologi-cally follows the one that has preceded it. This is not the case. Revelation pre-sents us with a *panoramic view*, each vision relating to the *entire* New Testament period, each vision giving a different aspect of the tribulations pre-ceding Christ's final victory. The seven seals, for example, refer to various earthly calamities (4:1–7:17), the seven trumpets to false doctrines (8:1–11:19), the sixth vision more specifically to the struggle between Christ and the Antichrist (17:1–19:21). Unless we see Revelation from this panoramic perspective, we'll never appreciate what it's all about, and we'll misinterpret its message.

Sound hermeneutics interprets Scripture *literally, but not literalistically.* It is literally true that the apostle John lived on the island of Patmos and that he wrote seven letters to seven churches in Asia Minor. It is literally true that he experienced seven visions and that he actually saw the visions he wrote about. It is *literalistic,* however, to claim that the pictures, the symbols, and especially the numbers are to be understood literally instead of figuratively. Referring to a chapter in Revelation where Jesus is called both a "Lion" and a "Lamb," Professor Becker writes, "To help us understand the use of sym-bols and figurative language, it is good to point out that while in these verses Jesus is called a Lamb, just a few verses earlier he had been called a Lion. This emphatically underscores the freedom with which apocalyptic symbols are employed. It cautions the interpreter not to try to explain details for which he can find no interpretation either in the text of Revelation or in other passages in the Bible."[8]

The numbers of Revelation

The numbers of Revelation are not as mysterious as we may think at first, especially when viewed in context and in conjunction with other passages of Scripture. The number *seven* is usually associated with something holy, an outstanding feature of God's covenant with his chosen people (churches, spirits, stars, candlesticks, letters, visions, etc.). The number *three* manifests a triadic or threefold arrangement, as found in the number of persons in the Godhead (1:4; 1:8; 4:8). The number *four* is almost always connected with the earth, its four winds, its four comers, its four living creatures, its four classes of people (6:1; 7:1; 7:9). The number *three and one half* is always associated with evil forces that oppress the earth (11:9), including the 42 months found in three and one-half years (11:2) and the 1,260 days found during the same period of time (11:3; 12:6). The number *twelve,* with its multiples (24, 144, 12,000, 144,000), is the number associated with the whole church on earth, the full number of the elect of God, the church militant (4:4; 7:4; 14:1). The number *ten,* with its cube (10x10x10 or 1,000), is the number of completeness (2:10; 5:11; 20:2-7). The number *one thousand* is representative of the entire New Testament period, beginning when Christ redeemed mankind from the devil's power and commanded his church to proclaim the gospel to the ends of the earth (20:2). The *thousand years* come to an end with the day of final judgment (20:3). The number *666* (13:18), which John himself offers as a challenge to "calculate the number of the beast," is interpreted by Professor Becker as a number that perhaps "symbolizes the fact that the Antichrist will never be able to enter the same kind of covenant relationship with his followers that God has entered with his people."[9] He quickly adds that "this is one of the details about which we must speak with reserve," mentioning other possibilities of interpreting this unusual number.

Revelation 20

Bearing in mind these hermeneutical principles, we need to look more closely at the twentieth chapter of Revelation, where most of the interpretative problems relating to Christ's second coming seem to be.

vv. 1-3 *And I saw an angel coming down out of heaven, having
the key to the Abyss and holding in his hand a great*

---

[8]Siegbert W. Becker, *Revelation: The Distant Triumph Song* (Milwaukee: Northwestern Publishing House, 1985), p. 94.
[9]Ibid., p. 214.

chain. He seized the dragon, that ancient serpent, who is the devil, or Satan, and bound him for a thousand years. He threw him into the Abyss, and locked and sealed it over him, to keep him from deceiving the nations anymore until the thousand years were ended. After that, he must be set free for a short time.

The "angel" seen by John in the final vision is the Lord Jesus Christ, the eternal Son of God, revealed already in Old Testament times as "the angel of the Lord" (Ex 3:2). The "great chain" in Jesus' hand is the gospel, which proclaims the message of salvation from sin and Satan's bondage to all the world (Mt 28:19; Mk 16:15; Jude 6). Jesus "bound" Satan by his work of redemption, breaking the devil's power (Ge 3:15; Jn 16:11; Col 2:15; 1 Jn 3:8). The "thousand years" is the entire New Testament era (10x10x10, a symbolic number representing completeness). Satan's being "set free for a short time" is the period of widespread unbelief and persecution in the world before the final judgment (Mt 24; Mk 13; Lk 21; 2 Ti 3:1-9).

Summary—Jesus came into the world to carry out the work of redemption. Through this work he rescued mankind from Satan's power. This saving work marked the beginning of the New Testament era. During this era Satan's power was limited. Especially the Gentile world was evangelized. Toward the end of this era, Satan returned to power for a short time, and many people, even many in the visible church, were led astray.

vv. 4,5 *I saw thrones on which were seated those who had been given authority to judge. And I saw the souls of those who had been beheaded because of their testimony for Jesus and because of the word of God. They had not worshiped the beast or his image and had not received his mark on their foreheads or their hands. They came to life and reigned with Christ a thousand years. (The rest of the dead did not come to life* [literal translation, "did not live"] *until the thousand years were ended.) This is the first resurrection.*

The "souls" seated on "thrones" who had been "beheaded because of their testimony for Jesus" are those who suffered martyrdom. The "beast or his image" are the destructive forces of Satan (Revelation 13). The life of believers living and reigning "with Christ a thousand years" is their continued existence with Christ in heaven, even after death, during this New Testament era (Jn 5:24,25; Lk 23:43; Php 1:23; 2 Ti 4:6-8). The "rest of the dead" are those who died in unbelief. The "first resurrection" is the new spiritual life of sinners when they were brought to faith in their Savior, having received the assurance of eternal life in him (Ro 6:1-11; Eph 2:4,5; Col 3:1).

Summary—"Life" in the biblical sense is the enjoyment of the blessings of fellowship with God. "Death" is being cut off from these blessings. This new life begins with spiritual conversion to faith in Christ. Those who die in this faith continue to enjoy this spiritual life with their Lord in heaven, awaiting the "second resurrection," when soul and body will be reunited, and when Jesus comes again at the time of final judgment. (Those who die in unbelief will not enjoy these blessings, existing in a state of separation from God.)

> v. 6   *Blessed and holy are those who have part in the first res-*
> *urrection. The second death has no power over them, but*
> *they will be priests of God and of Christ and will reign*
> *with him for a thousand years.*

The "second death" is eternal death in hell (Mt 7:23; Mt 25:41,46; 2 Th 1:9). It has no power over believers, who will continue even after physical death to reign with Christ as priests of God (Jn 18:37; 1 Pe 2:9; Heb 12:1; Rev 1:6; 5:10).

Summary—Those who have come to faith in Christ during their lifetime will even after death continue to enjoy the blessings of God. Especially those who have suffered martyrdom will by their faithfulness, even unto death, serve throughout the New Testament era as an example and a source of encouragement to the sorrowing believers who remain.

> vv. 7-10 *When the thousand years are over, Satan will be*
> *released from his prison and will go out and deceive the*
> *nations in the four corners of the earth—Gog and*
> *Magog—to gather them for battle. In number they are*
> *like the sand on the seashore. They marched across the*
> *breadth of the earth and surrounded the camp of God's*
> *people, the city he loves. But fire came down from*
> *heaven and devoured them. And the devil, who deceived*
> *them, was thrown into the lake of burning sulfur, where*
> *the beast and false prophet had been thrown. They will*
> *be tormented day and night for ever and ever.*

"When the thousand years are over" are the times occurring shortly before the final judgment (Mt 24; Mk 13; Lk 21). "Gog and Magog" are anti-Christian powers, mentioned previously in Ezekiel chapters 38 and 39. John also referred to this final battle in Revelation 16 as "Armageddon" and in chapter 19 as the battle between the beast and the false prophet (anti-Christian powers in the secular and religious realms) and the rider on the white horse (Christ). The "fire . . . from heaven" and "the lake of burning sulfur" are symbols of the eternal punishment of hell (Mt 10:28; Mk 9:44; Lk 16:23; Mt 25:41,46).

Summary—Toward the close of the New Testament era, there will be an unprecedented development of anti-Christian cults, when Satan will gather together his forces from all parts of the world for a final battle. The Christian church will contend against forces of evil as never before, until God will finally step in with a final act of judgment that will destroy all his enemies. This will mark the end of the world and the final judgment of Satan and his followers, who will be condemned to suffer the eternal punishment of hell.

Yes, there is a hell. Its punishment is eternal. Our sinful flesh cringes at the thought of punishment by means of unquenchable fire, as the Scriptures picture the punishment of hell. To deny its existence, however, as the Jehovah's Witnesses do, will not cause it to disappear. Scripture does not agree with the idea of an annihilation of those who have done evil. It clearly says in the words of Revelation 20:10, "tormented day and night for ever and ever." It can't get any more explicit than that!

The concluding verses of this same chapter 20 picture Christ seated on the throne of judgment. All the dead will be judged. The second death, eternal punishment in hell, is the fate of unbelievers, together with the devil and his angels (Mt 25:41). The joys of eternal life in the "new Jerusalem" are portrayed in the following chapter.

Millennialism

We have reviewed Revelation 20 in greater detail because it is upon this chapter that the millennialists (from the Latin *mille*, 1,000) or chiliasts (from the Greek *chilioi*, 1,000) base their ideas of a thousand-year kingdom here on earth, to be ruled by Christ in connection with his return.

This literalistic interpretation is nothing new. The writings of early church leaders such as Justin Martyr and Irenaeus in the second and third centuries after Christ contain references to this false teaching. The Anabaptists of Luther's day espoused its teachings. Lutheran leaders such as the pietists Philip Spener and Johann Bengel kept it alive in the 17th and 18th centuries. Franz Delitzsch and Johann William Reu in a succeeding era had millennialistic tendencies. These men were recognized as being leaders in their church bodies, indicating how widely these teachings had spread even among Lutherans.

In more recent years, we can see the extent to which these ideas have practically taken over the preaching and teaching of the many fundamentalistic and Pentecostal sects that are springing up everywhere. In many instances it has become a focal point of their theological study and one of the chief thrusts of their evangelistic outreach.

It's very difficult to describe the details of millennialistic teachings because of their many variables. The movement has generally been divided into two chief groupings. *Premillennialists* teach that Christ will return secretly sometime during the "great tribulation," a period of time lasting seven years before Christ's second coming, to raise all those who have died

We Believe in Jesus Christ

in faith. After the seven years of tribulation, Christ will then begin his world-wide rule of righteousness and peace on earth, lasting a thousand years. The center of his rule will be in Jerusalem. There will be a general conversion of the Jews. At the end of the thousand years, Satan, who has been bound during the millennium, will be loosed. A battle will ensue between the forces of Christ and the forces of Satan at Armageddon, resulting in Satan's final defeat. Then all the dead will be raised, followed by the final judgment of all, both the good and the bad.

Postmillennialists teach that Christ's final coming will take place *after* (post) the millennium. The millennium itself will consist of a gradual reduction of evil and a gradual improvement of social, economic, and political conditions on earth—a sort of utopia on earth before judgment day. (Whether or not Christ will reign visibly during this thousand-year period is debatable among them.) This period will end with a short time of great tribulation, after which Christ will come again to judge the earth and establish his eternal kingdom, with a new heaven and new earth.

Postmillennial views are gradually dying out, especially after World War II, since it doesn't seem that the conditions in this world are getting better all the time. On the other hand, premillennialism has grown in popularity and has been accepted by many prominent TV evangelists such as Billy Graham, Jerry Falwell, and Pat Robertson. Hal Lindsey's book, *The Late Great Planet Earth*, which follows this view, has sold nearly three million copies here in the States, and has been translated and has sold many more copies worldwide.

Many millennialists may not agree with either of the millennialist summaries presented above, since each one often has his pet version and loves to proclaim his personal interpretation. The sainted Professor Walter Albrecht at Concordia Theological Seminary, Springfield, Illinois, expressed the differences between millennialists this way: "To disprove millennialism nothing more is necessary than to pit the premillennialists and the postmillennialists against each other."[10] In a thesis on millennialism for presentation to our Wisconsin Lutheran Seminary, Robert Glen Johnston has this summary of the problem: "When one reads any two millennial books written by different authors, the chances are extremely high that he will find two theological positions presented which differ considerably in the details and most likely to some extent in the basics. . . . Each time a millennial position is stated, there will be a rebuttal by a millennialist, insisting that this is not his position."[11]

The same problem arises when seeking information about the "rapture," a rather strange teaching that has arisen among millennialists in connection

---

[10]Walter Albrecht, *Notes on Eschatology*, Concordia Lutheran Seminary, Springfield, Illinois, p. 30.
[11]Robert G. Johnston, *Does Scripture Teach Millennialism?* Unpublished STM Thesis, Wisconsin Lutheran Seminary, Mequon, Wisconsin, 1983, p. 157.

with the apostle Paul's prophecy in 1 Thessalonians 4:15-17. Here Paul refers to the fact that when Christ comes at the end of the world, the believers "who are still alive, who are left till the coming of the Lord, will certainly not precede those who have fallen asleep. . . . And the dead in Christ will rise first. After that, we who are still alive and are left will be caught up together with them in the clouds to meet the Lord in the air. And so we will be with the Lord forever." Millennialists interpret this being "caught up" as a *rapture* (literally, a "snatching up") of believers as occurring in connection with the great tribulation, a period of seven years preceding the establishing the millennial reign. (The seven years of tribulation, incidentally, have been determined by them on the basis of the 70th week of Daniel's prophecy in the ninth chapter of his book.) The problem among these "tribulationists" is whether this rapture occurs before, in the midst of, or after the seven years. It may surprise us that Gleason Archer, widely known as the author of *A Survey of Old Testament Introduction*, favors a midtribulation position.

We mention this added "rapture controversy" to indicate just how ridiculous this whole millennialism business can get, even among people who ought to know better. Professor Becker makes short shrift of it all when he declares, "The whole concept of a premillennial rapture is pure fantasy."[12]

Yes, be informed about it!

While our review of Revelation 20 may have seemed rather extensive for a conference paper, there's a reason for it. With the year 2000 hard upon us, we can expect to be literally deluged with futuristic propaganda from every possible source. We've barely scratched the surface here. If there's ever a time that serious Bible study based upon proper principles of interpretation is needed, it is now.

This Bible study should preferably *not* begin with Revelation. Rather start with Genesis, and carry on through all of Scripture. Make it an ongoing course of real study, making use of prepared materials placed in the hands of Bible class members for lesson preparation *prior to the class session itself*. It should allow for dialogue between members of the class and their leader, for questions, for discussion of the many problems that arise in the lives of our people today. Let topic discussion arise out of the study of Scripture. This will lead our people to a fuller understanding and appreciation of the sermons they hear every Sunday. As our people grow in their knowledge of God's Word, they'll also want to get at books like Daniel, Ezekiel, or Revelation. We may find them less complicated and more profitable than we think. And if heaven is to be a continuation of our life with Christ reaching into all eternity, it may

---

[12]Becker, p. 82.

---

be a good idea to get better acquainted with it already now. We like to say that the Lutheran church is a Bible church. Why not make it so?

Our synod's publications department from Northwestern Publishing House offers excellent materials for such study. Recent studies on Revelation by Professor Siegbert Becker and Rev. Wayne Mueller are excellent. Let's make use of these materials!

In our own Manitowoc area we've used some Bible studies originally developed for isagogics at our seminary in Mequon, simplified for similar use at our seminary in Central Africa and adapted for ladies' Bible classes which meet at various times during the week. Several classes have met now for over four years. They have finished through 2 Kings and some of the minor prophets and are clamoring for additional studies that can take them through the entire Old Testament. They say they never realized that the Old Testament could be so interesting. There is a real hunger out there for the Word!

Some of us may recall a series of studies in the Northwestern Lutheran prepared by the sainted Professor John Meyer, beginning in August 1954 and appearing every other week until April 1957. They dealt with Eternity, Christ's Return, Chiliasm, Resurrection, Judgment, Hell, Luther on Eternity, and Heaven. Every other week for nearly three years our people had opportunity to learn more about the things to come. What a wealth of material on these subjects was to be found in these issues! What comfort in Professor Meyer's excellent use of Scripture!

III. Let's Be Ready for It

"Being ready" includes heeding Scripture's warnings, paying attention to the signs of Christ's second coming, and above all, anticipating the encouragements this second coming has to offer.

The warnings

As we read the many passages of Scripture referring to the last things, we notice phrases like "beware," "wake up," "keep watch," "be on guard," "be careful," "the time is short," "the hour has come," "watch and pray," "night is coming."

Many of these warnings are from Jesus himself as he speaks to his disciples about his second coming. Others occur in connection with his parables as he teaches the people in general, like in The Ten Virgins (Mt 25:1-13) and The Owner of the House (Mk 13:32-37). The point of these parables is the need for constant preparedness in view of the master's imminent return. Jesus also stresses this when he refers to people "in the days of Noah and Lot" as examples of those totally unprepared for God's sudden intervention into their daily affairs.

Both Paul and Peter refer to "the day of the Lord" as coming "like a thief" (1 Th 5:2; 2 Pe 3:10). Peter also refers to scoffers who ridicule the idea of a second coming, adding that God's reason for its delay is to allow more time for repentance. Do we sense a general attitude of malaise among many of our own people, including ourselves, perhaps, over against urgent warnings of this kind? Does Paul make sense to us when he writes about the Lord's second coming as "a thief in the night"? Are we being overly pessimistic when we feel that perhaps one-third of our people take these warnings seriously, one-third seem to be rather neutral about them, and the final third couldn't seem to care less?

Whether Christ comes today, tomorrow, or a hundred or a thousand years from now, isn't it true that our personal experience with a time of final judgment will occur at the moment of our death? "Man is destined to die once," the writer of Hebrews reminds us, "and after that to face judgment" (Heb 9:27). The Lord promised a dying criminal that he would be in paradise with him the very day of the criminal's death (Lk 23:43). "Blessed are the dead who die in the Lord from now on," the Spirit of God declares from heaven (Rev 14:13). "Be faithful, even to the point of death," is the Lord's message to the church at Smyrna, "and I will give you the crown of life" (Rev 2:10). Need we say more?

The signs

Yes, there is more, much more, in the many signs given us in Scripture to remind us of the need for readiness as we anticipate Christ's second coming. Think of the many signs mentioned by him that will precede his arrival. Many of them were given by him in connection with his prophecy concerning the destruction of Jerusalem, which happened only 40 years later (Mt 24; Mk 13; Lk 21).

Some of Christ's signs relate to the *world of nature*: the darkness of the sun, moon, and stars; the famines, earthquakes, floods, pestilences, and the like. In spite of the efforts of scientific experts toward improving health conditions and the billions of dollars spent in connection with natural disasters, our control over these things is not improving. A daily glance at the news media proclaims the very opposite. We are rapidly trashing our environment, from industrial pollution in America to charcoal burning in places like Africa. We are making the greenhouse effect a reality. As soon as we think we have lessened the danger of a nuclear war, the specter of an even greater disaster through biological warfare arises in the Middle East. As soon as we appear to be getting a better handle on the AIDS virus, it mutates and releases another deadly virus into so-called civilization. Disasters are not diminishing. If anything, they are on the increase.

Some of the signs have to do with *mankind's behavior*: wars and rumors of wars (Iraq), nation against nation (Bosnia; Israel vs. United Arab Republic;

We Believe in Jesus Christ

Hutu vs. Tutsi in Africa), and a general increase of wickedness. World history points to the futility of imagining that wars will serve to end War. An increasing dissolution of moral principles the world over, including in our own country (problems with greed, drugs, sex, gun control, the increase in violence, the breakdown of marriage—one could go on and on) pretty well puts an end to any thoughts of the coming of a golden age and the realization of a dreamworld. One often wonders how long the Lord will be able to put up with us!

Signs of *apostasy within the church itself*, predicted by the Lord, are being fulfilled, especially false prophets claiming "I am Christ." While some of these false prophets may not come right out and say, "I am Christ," our charismatic friends virtually claim the same with all their presumed visions from the Lord. We are also reminded of people referred to by Paul as "having a form of godliness but denying its power" (2 Ti 3:5), preachers proclaiming what "itching ears want to hear" (2 Ti 4:3).

One specific sign foretold as preceding the Lord's return is the coming of the *Antichrist* (2 Th 2:1-4). Revelation chapters 13 and 14 refer to him as the lamblike "beast, coming out of the earth," defeated in the Lord's final victory. Our Lutheran Confessions refer to the pope of Rome as "the very Antichrist."[13] A warning against him, who "will oppose and will exalt himself over everything that is called God or is worshiped, so that he sets himself up in God's temple, proclaiming himself to be God," as Paul describes him in 2 Thessalonians 2:4, is certainly timely. Especially if this "man of lawlessness," as Paul refers to him, or this lamblike beast from the earth, as John refers to him, will be revealed before Christ's second coming.

As these lines are written, Pope John Paul II is continuing his worldwide visits, this time to Cuba and Nigeria, appearing more "lamblike" every day. The Roman Catholic Church in Manitowoc County is organizing a program of spiritual revitalization known as "Renew 2000." The church of the Antichrist is alive and well. Latin American countries have been under the sway of Catholicism for centuries. Africa is rapidly catching up. Clearly, if one advocates combining Christianity with pagan beliefs, or if he asserts that Muslims and Jews all pray to the same God as Christians, he is taking his stand against Christ. This doesn't seem to worry some "Lutherans" as they continue negotiating with those who even publicly condemn anyone who believes that man is saved by faith alone without the deeds of the law. The official statement of the Roman Catholic Church—Council of Trent, Session VI, Canon 12—still declares, just as loudly and clearly as ever, "If anyone says that justifying faith is nothing else than trust in God's mercy, which remits sin for Christ's sake, or that it is this trust alone which justifies us, let him be damned."

---

[13]SA II,IV:10.

Encouragements

While these warnings caution us to be careful about complacency, they should also have a very positive effect in our lives, encouraging us to live in hopeful and joyful anticipation of Christ's second coming.

Nothing, the apostle Paul declares, can separate us from Christ's love (Ro 8:38,39). "Indeed we share in his sufferings," he says, "in order that we may also share in his glory" (Ro 8:17). In our work of the ministry, he reminds us, "we do not lose heart," for "our light and momentary troubles are achieving for us an eternal glory that far outweighs them all" (2 Co 4:16,17).

The apostle Peter reminds us that although we live here on earth as strangers, we can do so in anticipation of "an inheritance that can never perish, spoil or fade—kept in heaven" just for us (1 Pe 1:4).

John's Apocalypse, his unveiling of the future with its seven portraits, points us to a church victorious in the face of all trials and tribulations. Think of those glorious scenes portrayed for us by John in chapters 7 and 14 of Revelation, with the 144,000 (12x12x10x10x10), the full number of the elect, joining the "great multitude that no one could count, from every nation, tribe, people and language, standing before the throne and in front of the Lamb . . . wearing white robes and . . . holding palm branches in their hands" (7:9). Think of "a new heaven and a new earth" (21:1), where "the dwelling of God is with men, and he will live with them. They will be his people, and God himself will be with them and be their God. He will wipe every tear from their eyes. There will be no more death or mourning or crying or pain, for the old order of things has passed away" (Rev 21:3,4).

We sometimes have a way of saying that we don't know what heaven is like. There may be much that we don't know, but there is much revealed to us that we do know, "not in words taught us by human wisdom but in words taught by the Spirit" (1 Co 2:13). John's vision of heaven in Revelation chapter 21—describing its dimensions, its contents, its location, its precious stones, its splendor—is about as beautiful a picture as one can imagine. When children ask us to tell them about heaven, why not use some of these ideas from Revelation and simply repeat them, rather than confessing ignorance. Professor Becker writes in his commentary, "We are dealing here with realities which transcend our present experience. . . . The unquestioned beauty of that blessed place should create in us a longing to see what that world is really like."[14] "Oh, that we were there!" we sing at Christmastime (CW 34:4).

Each one of us, perhaps, may want to anticipate some favorite aspect of that heavenly home that brings special joy to our hearts. For a musician it would be playing a musical instrument or singing in a heavenly chorus. For

---

[14]Becker, p. 82.

---

an artist it would be painting the portrait of some favorite scene or enjoying the awesome beauty of some special design. For the naturalist it would be admiring the different varieties of trees, flowers, or animals or gazing at some natural setting in a perfect landscape. For a lapidary it would be admiring all the different types of precious stones mentioned by John. And then, perhaps, there are just those ordinary people like you and me who aren't too fussy but are just terribly thankful that we shall be no longer weary or sorrowful or lonely, and happy most of all to be in the presence of God himself, seeing him as he is.

For myself? Yes, I have a special preference. It's to see a heaven populated by people of "every nation, tribe, people and language" (Rev 7:9). This, to me, is John's great mission emphasis. As a former world missionary, I see this emphasis where others perhaps may not. But isn't it worthy of special emphasis that John refers to this mix of people who are saved or who need salvation no less than seven times in his book, and each time in a different chapter (5:9; 7:9; 10:11; 11:9; 13:7; 14:6; 17:15)? I'd call that quite significant!

We note also that John used four different designations—nation, tribe, people, language. Four is the number associated with the earth, here referring to the totality of the earth's people. God's number is three. Four plus three equal seven, the number of God's covenant with mankind. What a striking way of saying that God our Savior "wants all men to be saved and to come to a knowledge of the truth" (1 Ti 2:4)!

I'm sure I'm not alone in this desire to see heaven populated by people of "every nation, tribe, people and language." David sang of it: "All the ends of the earth will remember and turn to the Lord, and all the families of the nations will bow down before him" (Ps 22:27). So did Isaiah, through whom God encouraged Old Testament believers, "I will make you a light for the Gentiles, that you may bring my salvation to the ends of the earth" (Isa 49:6). Following his resurrection, Jesus not only spoke of this worldwide goal but commissioned his disciples to carry it out, as recorded in every one of the gospels (Mt 28:19; Mk 16:15; Lk 24:47; Jn 20:21). He assured them *as one of the signs of his second coming* that "this gospel of the kingdom will be preached in the whole world as a testimony to all nations, and then the end will come" (Mt 24:14).

John, we recall, was the only one of the evangelists to record the words of Jesus saying, "As long as it is day, we must do the work of him who sent me. Night is coming, when no one can work" (Jn 9:4). It was John who wrote in one of those seven references of the people in heaven, "Then I saw another angel flying in midair, and he had the eternal gospel to proclaim to those who live on the earth—to every nation, tribe, language and people" (Rev 14:6). Some exegetes have interpreted this passage to be a prophecy pointing particularly to the work of Martin Luther. Others would rather see this as referring to every historical movement in which the gospel has been emphatically proclaimed. Whatever the case, this is clearly John's mission-ary style—repetitious, circular, purposeful, effective. It may not be the same style as that of Paul, but it certainly conveys the idea that heaven will be an interesting place, one beyond all human experience in this world, as we see heaven itself with all the glorious fruits of our missionary endeavors.

Those of you who may have been in one of my homiletics classes in Mequon may be reminded of the emphasis on missions that I carried over from Africa. I recall an incident when I returned a sermon manuscript to a student with the brief notation, "You missed the mission application." Somewhat crest-fallen, he turned to me and said, "But Professor, does *every* sermon have to have a mission emphasis?" My reply? A rather overemphatic *"But of course!"*

This may have been a reaction to the general lack of urgency that one often senses in our attitude over against the rest of the world. We get so wrapped up in our projects over here, not always realizing how much we have and how comparatively little others have. Sometimes we even show a pathetic lack of awareness of the world around us, of the desperate needs confronting our mis-sionaries as they daily work among those who have never had the opportunity of hearing the unconditioned gospel of Christ. We see to it that all the bud-getary needs in our own bailiwick are taken care of first, and then wonder how much will be "left over" for the work overseas. Thank you, John, for remind-ing us again that we're not going to be the only ones up there in heaven, that many of those with whom we'll be spending eternity will be from other parts of the world, from "every nation, tribe, language and people." And thank you, John, for giving me one more chance to share this eternal truth with others.

Recently I was privileged to hear the Martin Luther College choir sing in concert their program entitled "The Believer's Walk with God." When the last part of this concert entitled "Awaits the Glory of Eternal Life" came, closing with Gretchaninof's "Nunc Dimittis," I admit to becoming emotionally over-whelmed. I thought of the many loved ones I look forward to seeing in heaven someday. I thought of my own departure from this life. When one reaches the age of 82, as I am, things like this have a way of getting to you. Call it a momentary, personal "rapture" in a good sense, experienced also by John as he describes it in chapter 4 of his Apocalypse.

What better way to close than with the final two verses of his marvelous book:

> He who testifies to these things says, "Yes, I am coming soon."
>
> Amen. Come, Lord Jesus.
>
> The grace of the Lord Jesus be with God's people. Amen.

"WE (STILL) DO NOT HAVE THE SAME SPIRIT" A CRITIQUE OF CONTEMPORARY REFORMED CHRISTOLOGY AND ITS IMPACT ON THE DOCTRINE OF THE LORD'S SUPPER

James R. Janke

Dakota-Montana District Convention
Watertown, South Dakota
June 16–18, 1998

"It is quite obvious that we do not have the same spirit." Dr. Martin Luther made that observation in October of 1529, after two days of grueling discussion with the Swiss reformer Ulrich Zwingli in a castle overlooking the German village of Marburg. The topic under discussion when Luther and Zwingli met in Marburg was the meaning of the words Jesus spoke when he instituted the Lord's Supper: "This is my body." Luther taught that the body and blood of Christ are really and truly present in the Lord's Supper. He admitted that he didn't know how this was possible; he didn't even try to explain it. He simply believed what the Savior said. Zwingli, on the other hand, taught that Christ's body and blood are not truly present in the Lord's Supper. He maintained that the word *is* cannot mean "is." The bread and wine may "stand for" Jesus' body and blood, they may "represent" or "symbolize" Christ's far-absent body and blood, but they are not and cannot be Christ's true body and true blood. The purpose of the colloquy, or discussion, at Marburg was to try to bring Zwingli and Luther to agree on the meaning of those words so that all the Protestants, the Lutheran and the Reformed Protestants, could present a united front against the errors of Rome. It was an exciting thought, but it would not happen. When at last it became apparent to Luther that his Reformed opponents were not willing to take their reason captive and make it obedient to the words of Christ by which he was "bound and held captive," he flatly rejected any union, saying, "Your spirit and our spirit cannot go together. Indeed, it is quite obvious that we do not have the same spirit."[1] To Luther it was clear that there were fundamental differences between his approach to the words of Holy Scripture and the approach of the Reformed, and yet over the years that difference has not always been so apparent to the heirs of the Lutheran Reformation.

A little more than a century ago, the Lutheran leader C. F. W. Walther wrote,

> As regards the difference between the Lutheran and the Reformed Church, my friends, the Lutheran people, at least in former times, imagined that the whole difference was this, that in reciting the Lord's Prayer in German, the Lutheran put the word "Father" first, the Reformed the word "Our" and that in the Lord's Supper, wafers, which are not broken, are used in the Lutheran Church, while the Reformed churches use ordinary bread, which they break at the distribution or before.[2]

Walther called it "horrible ignorance" when Lutherans "in former times" imagined the difference between their church and Reformed churches to be nothing more than different customs and languages, and he rejoiced that the situation had improved. He continued, "Nowadays any Lutheran child that has received at least a passable instruction in the Christian doctrine knows that there is indeed a great difference, involving the principle articles of Christian doctrine, between the Lutheran and Reformed Churches."[3]

As examples of those differences, which every Lutheran child knows, he cited the doctrine of the Lord's Supper—where Lutherans believe in a real presence of Christ's body and blood, which the Reformed reject—and the doctrine of Christ—where Lutherans believe that Christ's human nature, by virtue of its union with the divine, has received divine attributes while the Reformed contend that Christ's human nature, being incapable of divine attributes, has merely received creature gifts in the highest degree. Walther concluded, "To be brief, every Lutheran knows nowadays that the difference between the Lutheran and the Reformed Church is fundamental: it lies, not on the circumference, but in the very center of the Christian doctrine."[4] Like Luther, Walther recognized a different spirit at work in the Reformed and was sure every other Lutheran could see it too.

---

[1]Herman Sasse, *This Is My Body*, revised edition (Adelaide: Lutheran Publishing House, 1977), pp. 213,214.
[2]C. F. W. Walther, *The Proper Distinction Between Law and Gospel*, translated by W. H. T. Dau (St. Louis: Concordia Publishing House), p. 125.
[3]Ibid., p. 126.
[4]Ibid., p. 126.

However, if Dr. Walther were to look at American Lutheranism today, he would probably have to conclude that either he was overly optimistic and Lutherans really don't know that the differences between their church and the Reformed are real and fundamental, or that a majority of Lutherans in America simply don't care about those differences. For on August 18, 1997, at its Churchwide Assembly in Philadelphia, the largest Lutheran church body in America, the Evangelical Lutheran Church in America, voted 839-193 in favor of declaring "full communion" with three Reformed churches—the Presbyterian Church (USA), the Reformed Church in America, and the United Church of Christ. By voting to overlook the differences between the historic Lutheran doctrine of the Lord's Supper and the teaching of the Reformed churches, the ELCA parted company with Martin Luther, who at Marburg refused to enter into "full communion" with the Reformed because of their rejection of the real presence of Christ's body and blood in the Lord's Supper.

What about the WELS? Will our synod follow the ELCA and negotiate away the real presence? Or will it continue to stand firm on what has been called the "the Lutheran *est*?"[5] And more important, does it matter? Asked about the ELCA's willingness to overlook the historic differences between the Lutheran and Reformed doctrines of the Lord's Supper, an ELCA seminary professor commented, "Our people realize those differences exist, but they don't believe they are—in official language—church dividing, or in unofficial language, a big deal."[6] Is a little word like *is* a "big deal"? Herman Sasse answers that question this way: "It is our deep conviction that in defending the literal meaning of 'This is my body,' Martin Luther did not defend a theological view of his own or of a theological school, but a basic dogma of the Christian church. With this *est* the incarnation stands or falls. And with the reality of the incarnation stands or falls the Church of Christ."[7] The doctrine of the Lord's Supper does not stand alone. It is intimately connected with the doctrine of Christ. The difference between Lutherans and the Reformed in the doctrine of the Lord's Supper springs from a deep and fundamental difference between the Lutheran and Reformed understandings of the doctrine of Christ—who he is, what he has done, and what he is capable of doing. In this essay we will compare orthodox Lutheran Christology and the Reformed Christology of modern conservative evangelicals, and show that Luther's verdict still applies.

I. The Incarnation

Many explanations have been offered for Luther's steadfast refusal to compromise his beliefs at Marburg and offer Zwingli the right hand of fel-

---

[5]Sasse, p. 347.
[6]Quoted in *Northwestern Lutheran*, Vol. 84, No. 11 (November 1997), p. 31.
[7]Sasse, p. 347.

---

lowship. Some see nothing but the stubbornness typical of German people. Others see it merely as the cantankerousness of a sickly old man. A Reformed friend of mine attributed Luther's insistence on the real presence to the fact that Luther suffered from chronic constipation. In fact, Luther's steadfast stand on the simple meaning of the Savior's words of institution had more to do with the incarnation than with constipation. As one Luther scholar observes, "It was for [Luther] a fundamental concern which cannot be emphasized too much. We do not meet God outside of the man Jesus Christ, 'in whom the fullness of God dwells bodily' (Col. 2:9)."[8] He continues, "Luther . . . refused to consider the *logos asarkos*, i.e., the Word apart from his incarnation. It is in personal union with the humanity that the Word saved us."[9] The correctness of this judgment can be seen from an exchange between Luther and a Reformed theologian who was also present at Marburg, John Oecolampadius. At one point Oecolampadius admonished Luther, saying, "You should not cling to the humanity and the flesh of Christ, but rather lift up your mind to his divinity." To this Luther replied, "I do not know of any God except him who was made flesh, nor do I want to have another. And there is no other God who could save us, besides the God incarnate."[10] Thus Luther refused "all reflection on the Word of God apart from his incarnation, for that would be speculation, that would be to speak of God outside his incarnation, detached from the place where God wishes to be found, the humanity of Jesus Christ."[11]

So we begin our study of Christology with the incarnation, the profound mystery St. John describes when he writes, "The Word [ὁ λόγος in Greek] became flesh" (Jn 1:14). When we think of a "word," we generally think of a lifeless sound or combination of sounds. St. John, however, is not thinking in such ordinary terms when he speaks of "the Word." This becomes clear when we look at all that the apostle says about "the Word" in the prologue of his gospel. In the first verse he says, "In the beginning was the Word, and the Word was with God, and the Word was God." With the same words that introduce the creation account in Genesis 1, St. John tells us that when creation began, when time began—that is, from eternity—the Word "was" (ἦν). John doesn't say that Word "was made" in the beginning, but "was" already there when time began. As Moses in Genesis 1 started "in the beginning," so St. John starts "in the beginning." Unlike Moses, however, who started at the beginning and proceeded forward into time with the creation account, St. John starts at the beginning but then looks backward into

---

[8]Marc Lienhard, *Luther: Witness To Jesus Christ,* translated by Edwin H. Robertson (Minneapolis: Augsburg Publishing House, 1982), p. 221.
[9]Ibid., p. 233.
[10]Sasse, p. 203.
[11]Lienhard, p. 233.

We Believe in Jesus Christ

the eternity that preceded time. Already then he says, the Word was. Therefore the Word must be eternal; the Word must be God. However, John does not immediately proceed to that conclusion about the Word. Instead he tells us that "the Word was with God." In this way the Word is distinguished from God, since John is clearly speaking of two individuals, or "persons." The Augsburg Confession defines a "person" as that which exists "not a part or quality in another, but that which subsists of itself."[12] It is, as Luther says, "just as if I should say: 'He was with me; he sits at my table; he is my companion.' This would imply that I am speaking of another, that there are two of us; I alone do not constitute a companion."[13]

St. John defines the relationship between the two persons he is talking about more precisely when he later writes of the Word, "We have seen his glory, the glory of the One and Only, who came from the Father, full of grace and truth" (v. 14). The Word, then, is the eternal Son of God the Father. St. John also explains the mystery of the designation "the Word" that he uses for the Son. In verse 18 he says, "No one has ever seen God, but God the One and Only, who is at the Father's side, has made him known." In other words, the Son of God serves his heavenly Father the way our words serve us. As our words are the best way we can let others know what is in our hearts and minds, so God gave us the best insight into his loving heart by sending his Son into the world "full of grace and truth" (v. 14).

Luther says in regard to John's use of "the Word" as a name for the Son of God,

> We must realize that this Word in God is entirely different from my word or yours. For we, too, have a word, especially a "word of the heart," as the holy fathers call it. . . . A word is not merely the utterance of the mouth; rather it is the thought of the heart. Without this thought the external word is not spoken; or if it is spoken, it has substance only when the word of the mouth is in accord with the word of the heart. Only then is the external word meaningful; otherwise it is worthless. Thus God, too, from all eternity has a Word, a speech, a thought, or a conversation with Himself in His divine heart, unknown to angels and man. This is called His Word. From eternity He was within God's paternal heart, and through Him God resolved to create heaven and earth. But no man was aware of such a resolve until the Word became flesh and proclaimed this to us.[14]

---

[12]AC I:4, *Triglot*, p. 43.
[13]LW 22:15.
[14]Ibid., pp. 8,9.

Thus Luther says that the name "the Word" indicates that it is through his Son that God reveals himself to us. Professor John Meyer writes, "This Son of God in his very Essence represents, yes embodies, the deepest thoughts of God, the sum and substance of his eternal ideas and plans, and his message to man. All the heart of God is personified in the Son, and in him is revealed to us."[15]

So the Word is a person who was with God in the beginning and so is distinguished from God and yet is not to be considered subordinate to God, for John says, "the Word was God." Luther, in his German translation of this verse, stresses the fact that "the Word was God" by following the Greek word order: *"Gott war das Wort."* Yet there are not two Gods. In other words, St. John asserts a duality of persons but a unity of essence. Like *person*, the word *essence* is a technical term. When Luther and the Confessions speak of God's essence, they mean "that which makes God God, his very being, that of which all his perfections and attributes are the expression."[16] Martin Chemnitz says: "The attributes which have been ascribed to God (immutability, infinity, eternity, omnipresence, omnipotence, etc.) are the very essence of God himself."[17] The divine essence, or divine nature as it is also called, is numerically one without multiplication or division. There are not two sets of divine attributes which constitute the divine essence. John consistently refers to God in the singular. For example, in verse 6 he refers to John the Baptist as a man who came from "God" (θεός). Thus the divine essence is not multiplied as if the Father and the Son each had the same *kind* of divine essence—then there would be two gods, not one. Nor is the divine essence divided as if one part belonged to the Father and one part to the Son—then the Word would not be God, but only partly God. But St. John says, "The Word was God."

So St. John speaks of the Father and Son as two distinct persons each of whom is God, and yet he unites them so that there is only one God. Luther says John speaks of

> two, namely, God and the Word, i.e., the Father and the Son.
> But this Word was with God, yet not as a separate, distinct
> God; no, He was the true, eternal God, of one essence with
> the Father, equal in might and glory. The distinction is that
> the Father is one Person, and the Son is another Person.
> Although the latter is a different Person, He is nevertheless
> the same God as the Father. Although there are two of Them,
> yet the Son remains the one true God with the Father. The

---

[15] John Meyer, *Studies In The Augsburg Confession* (Milwaukee: Northwestern Publishing House, 1995), p. 46.
[16] Henry Eyster Jacobs, *A Summary of the Christian Faith* (Philadelphia: The United Lutheran Publication House, 1905), p. 49.
[17] Martin Chemnitz, *Loci Theologici*, translated by J. A. O. Preus (St. Louis: Concordia Publishing House, 1989), p. 72.

two Persons are distinguished thus: It is the Father who speaks; the other Person, the Son, is spoken [the Word].[18]

The writer of Hebrews speaks in very similar terms of the Son of God as a person who is truly God and yet distinct from the Father when he writes, "The Son is the radiance of God's glory and the exact representation of his being" (1:3). While St. John uses the metaphor of a speaker and the word he speaks, the writer of Hebrews uses the picture of a light source and the light rays it radiates.

In order to remove any doubt about the fact that the Son is indeed of one essence with the Father, which in the words of the Athanasian Creed means that "what the Father is, so is the Son," John explains more about the Word. He writes, "Through him [the Word] all things were made; without him nothing was made that has been made" (Jn 1:3). Thus in addition to possessing the timeless eternity of God—"In the beginning was the Word"—the apostle also predicates of him the omnipotent creative power of God. This means that when the heavens were made "by the word of the LORD" (Ps 33:6), that word was not merely a lifeless sound but was the living personal Word of God, the eternal Son. And when Moses writes "And God said . . ." in Genesis chapter 1, he is speaking of the personal Word, the eternal Son of God the Father, who is almighty in the same way the Father is almighty. The writer of Hebrews speaks of God's Son in terms very similar to St. John's when he says of God, "In these last days he has spoken to us by his Son, . . . through whom he made the universe" (1:2). The section of the Second Article of the Nicene Creed that declares the Son to be "of one being with the Father" and then goes on to say of the Son "through him all things were made" is an echo of St. John's words in the prologue of his gospel.

So with the designation "the Word," St. John teaches that the Son is a person distinct from the Father and yet of one essence with the Father. But St. John reveals still more about the Son with that unusual name. By referring to Christ as "the Word," St. John teaches how it is possible for the Son to be distinct from the Father and yet of one essence with him. For the designation "the Word" also points to the eternal origin of the Son by birth, or generation, from the Father. As our words have their origin deep within us, in our hearts, so the Son, the Word of God, has his origin deep within the Father. The Son himself describes the deep mystery of his eternal origin when he says through David in Psalm 2, "He [God] said to me, 'You are my Son; today I have become your Father'" (v. 7). This is the so-called eternal generation or birth of the Son in God's eternal "today," which we confess in our creeds. In the Nicene Creed, for example, we confess that our Lord Jesus

---

[18]LW 22:15,16.

Christ is "the only Son of God, eternally begotten of the Father, God from God, Light from Light, true God from true God, begotten, not made, of one being with the Father." The Athanasian Creed adds that Christ is "eternally begotten from the nature of the Father, . . . fully God, . . . equal to the Father as to his deity." Though the Apostles' Creed does not include as long a section on the preexistence of Christ as the Nicene and Athanasian Creeds do, rather focusing more attention on the earthly life of Christ, which began at his conception, still it identifies Jesus Christ as "his [God's] only Son, our Lord." This phrase stresses the unique relationship that exists between the Father and the Son because the Son is begotten, or born, or generated, of the Father from eternity.

The relationship between God the Father and God the Son is unique first of all because "a human son is younger than his father, but the Son of God is as old, as eternal, as the Father. As heat is as old as fire; as light is as old as the sun, so the Son of God, 'being the Brightness of the Father's glory,' is co-equal with him in eternity."[19] It is unique also because as Luther explains,

> As a human son derives his flesh, blood, and being from his father, so the Son of God, born of the Father, received His divine essence and nature from the Father from eternity. But this illustration, as well as any other, is far from adequate; it fails to portray fully the impartation of the divine majesty. The Father bestows His entire divine nature on the Son. But the human father cannot impart his entire nature to his son; he can give only a part of it. . . . In the Godhead, however, the entire divine nature and essence passes into the Son, who remains in the same Godhead with the Father, is one God together with Him.[20]

The Son of God, then, is truly God and as such has existed from all eternity according to his divine nature. He did not, however, always have a human nature. St. John says, "The Word became flesh (σάρξ)" (Jn 1:14). Luther comments on the word *flesh*: "In Scriptural parlance 'flesh' denotes a complete human being. . . . In Scriptural usage the word 'flesh' embraces both body and soul, for without the soul the body is dead."[21] This historical event is called Christ's incarnation, from the Latin word *carnis*, which means "flesh." St. Paul calls this fact that "he [God] appeared in a body" the great mystery of godliness (1 Ti 3:16). It is indeed a great mystery how the second person of the Holy Trinity could become man without the Father and the Holy Spirit at the same

---

[19]Louis Roehm, "The Person of Christ," *The Abiding Word*, Vol. 1, edited by Theodore Laetsch (St. Louis: Concordia Publishing House, 1946), p. 22.
[20]LW 22:6.
[21]LW 22:110,111.

---

time becoming man. Yet the incarnate Son refers to his Father and to the Holy Spirit as distinct from himself when he tells his disciples, "When the Counselor comes, whom I will send to you from the Father, the Spirit of truth who goes out from the Father, he will testify about me" (Jn 15:26). The manner surpasses comprehension. Yet the fact is clearly revealed in Holy Scripture. The writer of Hebrews says, "Since the children have flesh and blood, he too shared in their humanity" (2:14). The "he" in the passage is God's Son (1:2), "through whom [God] made the universe . . . [and who] is the radiance of God's glory and the exact representation of his being" (1:2,3). In keeping with the writer of Hebrews, Professor John Schaller says, "It is the basic fact of the gospel that God himself, the divine essence, united with the human nature to achieve the salvation of the world."[22]

Just as Christ received the divine nature in a unique way by his eternal generation from the Father, so he received his human nature in a unique way by being conceived and born of a virgin without the participation of a human father. The fact of the virgin birth of Christ, which St. Paul appears to assume when he writes in Galatians 4:4, "But when the time had fully come, God sent his Son, born of a woman," St. Luke clearly proclaims in his account of the announcement of the Savior's birth. In the first chapter of his gospel he tells us that God sent his angel to the town of Nazareth in Galilee to inform a virgin by the name of Mary that she would "be with child and give birth to a son" (v. 31). Mary was understandably puzzled by this news and requested more information. "How will this be?" she asked (v. 34). "The Holy Spirit will come upon you, and the power of the Most High will overshadow you," she was told by God's angel Gabriel (v. 35). Luke's account of the virginal conception of Christ is fully corroborated by St. Matthew in his gospel, where he reports that Mary "was found to be with child through the Holy Spirit" (1:18).

Thus in regard to Christ we may speak of a twofold generation, or birth. One is the eternal act of God by which, according to his divine nature, Christ is begotten of the Father from eternity. By this eternal birth of the Father, Christ is of one being with the Father and the Holy Spirit, and yet is distinguished from the Father and the Holy Spirit. The other birth is Christ's extraordinary conception by the Holy Spirit and birth of the virgin Mary in time. By his miraculous temporal birth, Christ is distinguished from other human beings and yet joins us by assuming our human nature. Luther teaches us to confess this twofold generation in his explanation of the Second Article of the Apostles' Creed: "I believe that Jesus Christ, true God, begotten of the Father from eternity, and also true man, born of the virgin Mary, is my Lord."

---

[22]John Schaller, *Biblical Christology: A Study in Lutheran Dogmatics* (Milwaukee: Northwestern Publishing House, 1981), p. 47.

Clearly, the incarnation did not "involve some sort of 'space travel' from heaven to earth."[23] For the Word "was in the world" (Jn 1:10) even before becoming flesh. As Luther writes,

> When Christ, the Son of God, was to be conceived in his mother's womb and become incarnate, he certainly had to be already present in essence and in person in the Virgin's womb, and had to assume humanity there. For the Godhead is immutable in itself and cannot pass from one place to another as creatures do. Therefore he did not climb down from heaven as on a ladder or descend as by a rope, but was already in the Virgin's womb in essence and in person, as he was also in all other places, everywhere, according to the nature and character and power of divinity.[24]

Instead of thinking of the incarnation in terms of travel from one place to another place far removed from it, Scripture leads us to think in terms of the incarnation as the manifestation of the already present Son of God. Thus to St. Paul the great mystery of godliness is the fact that "he [God] appeared in a body" (1 Ti 3:16). And St. John writes, "The reason the Son of God appeared was to destroy the devil's work" (1 Jn 3:8). Nor, as we will see, did the appearance of the Son of God in flesh on earth require his disappearance from heaven. For the moment it will suffice to remember the words of a familiar Christmas hymn: "The Word becomes incarnate and yet remains on high" (from CW 36:2).

In regard to the doctrine of Christ's incarnation, we would find little to disagree with in the writings of conservative evangelical theologians. In fact, it has been said that in many areas orthodox Lutherans have more in common with conservative evangelical theologians than they do with heterodox Lutherans. That is certainly true in regard to the doctrine of the incarnation of God's Son. For example, Carl E. Braaten, coauthor of the unofficial doctrine textbook of the Evangelical Lutheran Church in American, *Christian Dogmatics*, writes of the incarnation, "The history and phenomenology of religions have called our attention to the mythic character of the incarnation. The notion of the preexistent Son of God becoming a human being in the womb of a virgin and then returning to his heavenly home is bound up with a mythological picture of the world that clashes with our modern scientific world view."[25] After hearing that from a "Lutheran" theologian, it's refreshing to hear Wayne A. Grudem, a con-

---

[23]David Scaer, *Christology* (Fort Wayne: The International Foundation for Lutheran Confessional Research, 1989), p. 29.
[24]LW 37:62.
[25]Carl E. Braaten, *Christian Dogmatics*, Vol. 1, edited by Carl E. Braaten and Robert W. Jenson (Philadelphia: Fortress Press, 1984), p. 527.

servative evangelical who teaches at Trinity Evangelical Divinity School in Deerfield, Illinois, say in his top-selling (among evangelicals) introduction to biblical doctrine, *Systematic Theology,*

> It has been common, at least in previous generations, for those who do not accept the complete truthfulness of Scripture to deny the doctrine of the virgin birth of Christ. But if our beliefs are to be governed by the statements of Scripture, then we will certainly not deny this teaching . . . in addition to the fact that Scripture teaches the virgin birth, we can see that it is doctrinally important, and if we are to understand the biblical teaching on the person of Christ correctly, it is important that we begin with an affirmation of this doctrine.[26]

Another conservative evangelical, Millard J. Erickson, a professor of theology at Bethel Theological Seminary and the author of a major evangelical systematic theology, prefaces his book, *The Word Became Flesh,* by saying, "I have chosen to write on the doctrine of the person of Christ because it is crucial in our day. . . . I am firmly committed to the doctrine of the unique incarnation of God in the person of Jesus Christ."[27]

II. The Personal Union

The result of Christ's twofold generation is that he is one person with two natures: an eternal divine nature, and an assumed human nature. When the angel Gabriel said, "The holy one to be born will be called the Son of God" (Lk 1:35), God's own messenger proclaimed both the true deity and the true humanity of Christ. The human son born of Mary in time is the Son of God born of the Father from eternity. This truth has been expressed by using the Greek term θεάνθρωπος, "God-man," to refer to Christ. And the union of the divine and human natures, which resulted in the one person Jesus Christ, who is both God and man, is known as the personal union.

Holy Scripture abundantly testifies to the fact that there is in Christ a true, complete, and perfect human nature. St. John declares that "the Word became flesh and made his dwelling among us" (Jn 1:14), literally, "tented among us." He lived on earth with his human creatures as a human creature. John testifies to the true humanity of the Word in the first verse of his first epistle where he says that what he proclaims about the Word of life is "that . . . which we have heard, which we have seen with our eyes, which we have looked at and our hands have touched." Scripture also testifies to the true humanity of Christ in

---

[26]Wayne Grudem, *Systematic Theology* (Grand Rapids: Zondervan Publishing House, 1994), p. 532.
[27]Millard J. Erickson, *The Word Became Flesh: A Contemporary Incarnational Theology* (Grand Rapids: Baker Book House, 1991), p. 7.

---

other ways. St. Paul calls Christ a man when he writes, "There is one God and one mediator between God and men, the man Christ Jesus" (1 Ti 2:5). Scripture throughout speaks of Christ as a real human being who had the experiences and passed through all the ordinary stages that are common to mankind. His genealogy is recorded. His birth is described. He grows in wisdom and stature. He hungers and thirsts, becomes weary and weeps, and, finally, suffers and dies. Scripture declares that he has the two essential components of a human nature: a body and a soul. "The story of Christ's earthly life as told by the Evangelists, is the story of a true human being, of the same flesh and blood as ours."[28]

The importance of the biblical teaching that Christ did indeed have a true human nature is underscored by the author of Hebrews, who writes, "He [God's Son] had to be made like his brothers in every way" (2:17). The fact that Christ *had* to be like us in every way is reflected in the ancient axiom Tò ἀπρόσληπτον ἀθεράπευτον (What was not assumed was not healed [redeemed]). There is, however, a critical difference between Christ's human nature and ours. The writer of Hebrews identifies it when he says that in Christ, our high priest, "we have one who has been tempted in every way, just as we are—yet was without sin" (4:15). St. Paul confirms this when he writes in Romans that God sent his own Son "in the likeness of sinful man" (8:3) to be a sin offering. Christ assumed a human nature like that of sinful mankind, except his was without sin.

Holy Scripture also contains clear and abundant testimony to the fact that Jesus Christ is true God with the true divine nature. St. John makes this clear when he says of the Word which became flesh, "We have seen his glory, the glory of the One and Only, who came from the Father, full of grace and truth" (Jn 1:14). Thus Jesus is called God in the Bible. In Romans 9:5 St. Paul writes of the Jews, "Theirs are the patriarchs, and from them is traced the human ancestry of Christ, who is God over all, forever praised!" Jesus himself claims essential unity with the Father when he says, "I and the Father are one" (Jn 10:30). The "oneness" Jesus refers to here does not merely mean that he and the Father are of one mind and will, but refers to the fact that Christ, like the Father, has and exercises the divine attribute of omnipotence. This is clear from the previous verses where Jesus first says of his sheep, "No one can snatch them out of my hand" (v. 28), and then immediately adds, "no one can snatch them out of my Father's hand" (v. 29). Since he and the Father protect their sheep with the same omnipotence, Jesus can truly say, "I and the Father are one."

The Bible also ascribes other divine characteristics to Christ. According to Hebrews 13:8 Jesus has divine immutability: "Jesus Christ is the same yesterday and today and forever." In addition, the Bible says Jesus does works

---

[28]Schaller, p. 49.

---

that only God can do, such as the work of creation: "By him all things were created: things in heaven and on earth, visible and invisible" (Col 1:16). Scripture clearly shows that the honor and worship that God claims for himself alone (Isa 42:8) are to be accorded to Christ: "When God brings his firstborn into the world, he says, 'Let all God's angels worship him'" (Heb 1:6). Edward Koehler is correct when he says: "Whoever denies the Deity of Christ certainly cannot do so on the basis of Scriptural evidence, but does it for other reasons."[29]

Thus the eternal Word, the only begotten Son of God, who is at the Father's side, took on our human nature. In doing so, Christ received something that he did not have before, the human nature, but lost nothing of the divine nature, which he had from eternity. St. John tells us that when he says, "The Word became (ἐγένετο) flesh." On the meaning of the verb ἐγένετο, Lenski warns, "We need a caution here in regard to all the uses of γίνομαι in ordinary speech, for in all the universe no analogy occurs for the incarnation."[30] Chemnitz says that the clearest explanation of what "became" means is to be found in Genesis 2 in the account of the formation of man. There the Septuagint uses the same verb to describe what happened when God breathed the breath of life into the body he had formed of dust saying that "man became [ἐγένετο] a living being" (v. 7). In other words, just as the first man became a living being through the union of soul and body, so the Word became flesh through the union of the divine nature and the human nature. And just as there was in the first man no conversion of the body into a soul, so in Christ there is no conversion or commingling of natures.[31] God's Son became man by assuming, or taking upon himself, human flesh, but he did not give up his deity. The Word was not changed into a human being. Rather, from the moment of his conception, the Son of God was not only true God but also true man. The incarnation did not require or produce a change in God, since when the Son of God assumed a human nature, he continued to be God with the divine nature unchanged. None of his divine attributes were lost, relinquished, or impaired. The Athanasian Creed summarizes this unique miracle when it says of Christ, "He is God, eternally begotten from the nature of the Father, and he is man, born in time from the nature of his mother, fully God, fully man, with rational soul and human flesh, equal to the Father as to his deity, less than the Father as to his humanity; and though he is both God and man, Christ is not two persons but one, one, not by changing the deity into flesh, but by taking the humanity into God; one, indeed, not by mixture of the natures, but by unity in one person."

---

[29]Edward W. A. Koehler, *A Summary of Christian Doctrine* (St. Louis: Concordia Publishing House, 1971), p. 85.
[30]R. C. H. Lenski, *The Interpretation of St. John's Gospel* (Columbus: Lutheran Book Concern, 1942), p. 72.
[31]Martin Chemnitz, *The Two Natures In Christ*, translated by J. A. O. Preus (St. Louis: Concordia Publishing House, 1971), pp. 116,117.

The union of the divine nature with the human nature in Christ did not result in an essential change in either nature.

> The Christian church has always maintained that, according to the testimony of Scripture, the union effected by the incarnation of the Logos is indeed most intimate and enduring, but left both natures unaltered in their essences. As the Logos remains fully and completely true God after the incarnation, so the man Jesus remains true man in every essential aspect. Neither was the Logos transformed into a man, nor was the human nature of Christ changed into God.[32]

Each nature in the God-man retains its own properties and attributes. This is true even of the intelligence and will of each nature, which are manifestly distinct from the other. When Christ in the Garden of Gethsemane, for example, prays in regard to the cup of suffering, "Father, if you are willing, take this cup from me" (Lk 22:42), he is plainly contrasting his own human will with that of the Father with whose will his divine nature is one. When Christ then wills what he obviously dreads to will—"yet not my will, but yours be done"—he reveals a twofold will, one genuinely human, the other genuinely divine. Furthermore, it becomes clear that there is no conflict between the wills of Christ, for the human is subject to and subordinate to the divine. "The human will of Christ wills those things which the divine will wishes it to will."[33]

Again, we will find little to argue with in the works of conservative evangelicals in regard to the doctrine of the personal union. Charles (Chuck) Swindoll quotes with approval the words of G. Campbell Morgan regarding Christ: "He was the God-man. Not God indwelling a man. Of such there have been many. Not a man Deified. Of such there have been none save in the myths of pagan systems of thought; but God and man, combining in one Personality the two natures, a perpetual enigma and mystery, baffling the possibility of explanation."[34] And for himself he writes, "Who is Jesus Christ? The God-man—the most unique Person who has ever lived. The awesome Son of God!"[35] Erickson concludes his book *The Word Became Flesh* with the statement, "If our presentation has been convincing, the reader should be led to belief in the incarnation: Jesus was truly God and man in one person."[36] Grudem writes, "Jesus did not temporarily become man, but . . . his divine nature was permanently united to his human nature,

---

[32]Schaller, p. 58.
[33]Chemnitz, p. 238.
[34]Charles R. Swindoll, *Growing Deep In The Christian Life* (Grand Rapids: Zondervan Publishing House, 1995), p. 148.
[35]Ibid.
[36]Erickson, p. 627.

---

and he lives forever not just as the eternal Son of God, the second person of the Trinity, but also as Jesus, the man who was born of Mary, and as Christ, the Messiah and Savior of his people. Jesus will remain fully God and fully man, one person, forever."[37] At this point it would appear that a good foundation has been laid for agreement between Lutherans and the Reformed in a common confession of the personal union of God and man in Christ, but as we will see, that agreement breaks down in the discussion of the relationship of the two natures in Christ.

III. The Communion of Natures

The precise nature of the relationship of the two natures in Christ has been a critical christological question from the days of the Apostles to our own day. At the Fourth Ecumenical Council, which met at Chalcedon in A.D. 451, the ancient church struggled to produce a working definition of that relationship. The confession that emerged from the Council at Chalcedon has been acknowledged to express the teaching of Scripture in regard to the relationship of the two natures in Christ and says that Jesus Christ is "to be acknowledged in two natures, unconfusedly [ἀσυγχύτως], unchangeably [ἀτρέπτως], indivisibly [ἀδιαιρέτως], inseparably [ἀχωρίστως]; the distinction of natures being by no means taken away by the union, but rather the property of each nature being preserved and concurring in one person."[38]

Thus, on the one hand, the two natures in Christ are not mixed or mingled together (ἀσυγχύτως) so that a third substance comes into being "as when hydromel [honey water] is made from honey and water, which is no longer pure water or pure honey, but a mixed drink."[39] Nor did the Word become flesh in such a way that the Word is converted or changed (ἀτρέπτως) into flesh, nor the flesh into the Word, as Jesus once changed water into wine so that after the water became wine there was no longer any water in the jars but only wine. Rather, the human nature in Christ was joined to or united with the divine nature without any intervening change in either nature. "What happened when the divine, eternal Logos became flesh was a unique occurrence. It has no parallel in all of creation."[40] Pieper summarizes the danger of any kind of intermingling of the natures when he writes,

> The salvation of the world could be effected only through the theanthropic [divine-human] work of Christ, and that required a theanthropic Person. If Christ is no longer a true man, we have no claim, as Luther reminds us (St. L. VII:1557), on His

---

[37]Grudem, p. 543.
[38]Philip Schaff, *Creeds of Christendom,* Vol. 2 (New York: Harper & Brothers, 1890), pp. 62,63.
[39]FC SD VIII:19, *Triglot,* p. 1021.
[40]Wilbert Gawrisch, *Current Issues In Christology,* Wisconsin Lutheran Seminary Pastors' Institute, 1993, Part 2, p. 2.

work of redemption, since according to Scripture the true humanity of Christ was necessary for our redemption (1 Tim. 2:5: "One Mediator between God and men, the Man Christ Jesus"). And if Christ is not true God, his work of redemption has no redeeming value (Rom. 5:10: "We were reconciled to God by the death of His Son"). Any and every fusion, conversion, or curtailment of the natures does away with the theanthropic Person and His theanthropic work. We need both the unchanged deity and the unchanged humanity.[41]

Nor, on the other hand, are the two natures in Christ separated from each other. The Council of Chalcedon rejected any division (ἀδιαιρέτως) with respect to place or space, as well as any separation (ἀχωρίστως) with respect to time of the divine and human natures in Christ. In other words, Christ did not take upon himself human nature as if it were a garment, which he would again at some point lay aside, but rather made the assumed flesh his own never to abandon it. Nor can the divine nature be separated from the human nature so that in some place the divine nature can be without the human nature, nor the human nature without the divine. The Formula of Concord rejects any separation of the natures in Christ, saying that the personal union

is not to be understood, as some incorrectly explain it, as though the two natures, the divine and human, were united with one another, as two boards are glued together, so that they *realiter,* that is, in deed and truth, have no communion whatever with one another. . . . Thereby the natures are separated from one another, and thus two Christs are constituted, so that Christ is one, and God the Word, who dwells in Christ, another.[42]

The two natures in Christ are not related to each other in a way that is merely mechanical, but in a way that is personal. In this union the divine nature is active and completely pervades and energizes the human nature, while the human nature is passive and is pervaded and energized by the divine nature. This relationship has been illustrated by using the analogy of the relationship between the body and soul in a human being. We readily acknowledge the weakness of this analogy, which consists, as Schaller points out, in this: "The body does not exist in the personality of the soul, but soul and body are parts of the one personality, two incomplete natures being united to make a complete one; in Christ, however, two complete natures are united in the

---

[41]Francis Pieper, *Christian Dogmatics,* Vol. 2 (St. Louis: Concordia Publishing House, 1951), p. 92.
[42]FC SD VIII:14,15, *Triglot,* p. 1019.

We Believe in Jesus Christ

personality of one of them."[43] This weakness notwithstanding, the illustration has the approval of Holy Scripture.

St. Paul uses it to illustrate the intimate communion between the two natures in Christ when he writes in Colossians 2:9, "In Christ all the fullness of the Deity lives in bodily form." With these words St. Paul explains what St. John observed. John testified to the fact that the glory of God was visible, radiating through the human flesh of Christ Jesus (John 1:14: "We have seen his glory"). St. Paul says that happened because the Deity has made the assumed human nature of Christ its home, the place where it dwells, or resides (κατοικεῖ). When St. Paul declares that all the fullness of the Deity lives "in Christ," he is obviously speaking of the human nature of Christ. "That in which the Godhead, the divine nature dwells, cannot be Godhead, the divine nature. To say that the Godhead dwells in the Godhead, would be without sense."[44] The apostle reinforces this fact when he adds the adverb "bodily"(σωματικῶς), which confirms that the human nature, or body of Christ, is the place in which the Deity lives. Chemnitz mentions that the ancients understood Paul to say: "In Christ's assumed body dwells all the fullness of deity."[45] And he explains that as "at one time God dwelt in a disembodied state in the ark of the temple, and there he wished to be sought and thus to show his majesty; . . . now in the true temple, that is, in Christ's body (Jn 2:19), he dwells and wishes to be recognized, sought, and apprehended and to reveal in and through Christ's body the whole fullness of his deity as the glory of the Only-Begotten."[46] This is a startling truth! Remember that the Deity (τῆς θεότητος), the divine nature, is that which makes God what God is, all the divine attributes, such as omnipotence, omniscience, and omnipresence. To remove any doubt about what he is saying about Jesus, St. Paul heaps up expressions that drive home his point. "The Godhead (Deity) is in him, and not only the Godhead but the fullness of it; not only the fullness of it, however, but all the fullness of it . . . dwells in him, and dwells in him bodily, occupying him totally."[47] The Formula of Concord paraphrases Paul's words in this way: "The entire fullness of the divinity dwells in Christ, not as in other holy men and angels, but bodily, as *in its own body,* so that it shines forth with all its majesty, power, glory, and efficacy in the assumed human nature, voluntarily when and as He [Christ] wills, and in, with, and through the same manifests, exercises, and executes His exerts its divine power, glory, and efficacy, as the soul does in the body."[48]

So St. Paul himself uses the union of the body and soul in man to illustrate and clarify the nature of the union of the divine nature with the human

---

[43]Schaller, p. 50.
[44]E. Hove, *Christian Doctrine* (Minneapolis: Augsburg Publishing House, 1930), p. 182.
[45]Chemnitz, p. 118.
[46]Ibid., p. 118.
[47]Gawrisch, p. 4.
[48]FC SD VIII:64, *Triglot*, pp. 1037,1039.

---

nature in Christ. This means that the fullness of the Godhead, like the soul in a body, dwells not outside of or beside the flesh of Christ, but in his flesh. Charles Porterfield Krauth writes, "If all the fulness of the Godhead in the second person of the Trinity dwells in Christ bodily, then there is no fulness of that Godhead where it is not so dwelling in Christ."[49] The two natures in Christ are never divided by time, by place, or by space. When St. Paul uses the word κατοικεῖ ("lives"), he makes it clear that there is no "excarnation," or giving up of the human nature by the Son of God. This is indicated not only by his use of the present tense but by the fact that the verb κατοικέω denotes "permanent dwelling" as opposed to other verbs formed from οἰκέω, such as παροικέω, which means "sojourn" or "live as a stranger." Thayer says κατοικέω differs from παροικέω "as the permanent differs from the transitory."[50] So Christ never gave up the human nature which he assumed; there is no separation of the natures by time. From the first moment of Christ's conception, when "the Word was made flesh," to all eternity (St. Paul wrote that the fullness of the deity "lives" in bodily form after Christ had risen from the dead and had ascended into heaven), "the human nature of Christ is never and nowhere separated from the divine nature."[51] Nor is there any separation by place or space. "The divine nature must not be conceived as extending beyond the human, since the fulness of the Godhead dwells *in the body*. In other words, just as the soul is in the living body, but never beyond it, so the λόγος is in the flesh so as never to be beyond it or outside it."[52] The teachers of the ancient church summarized this truth with the words *Neque Logos extra carnem, neque caro extra Logon* (The Word is not outside the flesh, nor the flesh outside the Word). "It is impossible in the face of this text (Col 2:9) to believe that the divine Logos, since the incarnation, exists anywhere without the σῶμα of Christ. . . . Now the fullness of the Godhead . . . employs a human body for its entire existence, manifestation and activity."[53]

Luther writes in this connection:

> If you could show me one place where God is and not the man, then the person is already divided and I could at once say truthfully, "Here is God who is not man and has never become man." But no God like that for me! For it would follow from this that space and place had separated the two natures from one another and thus had divided the person, even though death and all the devils had been unable to sep-

[49]Charles Porterfield Krauth, *The Conservative Reformation and Its Theology* (Minneapolis: Augsburg Publishing House, 1978), p. 507.
[50]John Henry Thayer, *A Greek-English Lexicon of the New Testament* (New York, Cincinnati, Chicago: American Book Company, 1889), p. 341.
[51]Theodore Engelder, *Popular Symbolics* (St. Louis: Concordia Publishing House, 1934), p. 46.
[52]John Theodore Mueller, *Christian Dogmatics* (St. Louis: Concordia Publishing House, 1955), p. 270.
[53]W. H. T. Dau, *Doctrinal Theology*, p. 224.

arate and tear them apart. This would leave me a poor sort of Christ, if he were present only at one single place, as a divine and human person, and if at all other places he had to be nothing more than a mere isolated God and a divine person without the humanity. No, comrade, wherever you place God for me, you must also place the humanity for me. They simply will not let themselves be separated and divided from each other. He has become one person and does not separate the humanity form himself as Master Jack takes off his coat and lays it aside when he goes to bed.[54]

And yet, as the soul and body remain distinct, though they are intimately united, so the two natures in Christ are intimately united but not confused with the other or converted into the other. "As little as the body, by becoming a living body through the indwelling of the soul, becomes similar to the soul, or is thereby changed into the soul, so little does any equalizing of the natures result in Christ."[55]

It is at this point, in regard to the nature of the relationship of the natures in Christ to one another, that Lutheran and evangelical Christologies diverge. For the Christology of modern evangelicalism has its roots in the Reformed/Calvinistic Christology of the 16th Century Reformation in Europe. Whereas, as we have seen, the Bible teaches that the two natures in Christ are united as inseparably as the soul and body of man, so that the Son of God, after his incarnation, is always and everywhere incarnate, the Reformed deny this. On the basis of the philosophical principle that "the finite is not capable of the infinite" (*finitum non est capax infiniti*), the Reformed insist that the Son of God, after his incarnation, is not everywhere present according to his human nature, but that his presence is limited to a single place. The Reformed *Heidelberg Catechism* teaches this separation of natures quite plainly when it answers Question 47—"Is not then Christ with us, as he has promised, unto the end of the world?"—in this way: "Christ is true man and true God. According to his human nature, he is not now upon earth; but according to his Godhead, majesty, grace, and Spirit, he at no time departs from us." The answer to Question 48 reveals the rationalistic underpinning of that answer. Question 48 asks, "But are not, in this way, the two natures in Christ separated from one another, if the Manhood be not wherever the Godhead is?" The following answer is given: "By no means; for since the Godhead is incomprehensible and everywhere present, it must follow that it is indeed beyond the bounds of the Manhood which it has assumed, but is none the less in the same also, and remains personally united with it."[56] In contrast, our Augsburg

---

[54]LW 37:218,219.
[55]Pieper, p. 225.
[56]Philip Schaff, *Creeds of Christendom*, Vol. 3 (New York: Harper & Brother, 1890), p. 322.

Confession teaches that "there are two natures, the divine and the human, inseparably conjoined in one Person, one Christ, true God and true man."[57] The nature of the Reformed separation of natures is nicely illustrated in Grudem's *Systematic Theology*:

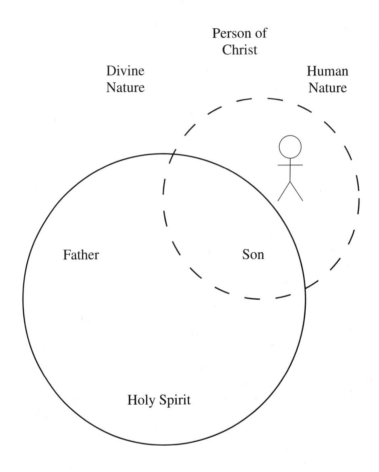

[57]AC III:2, *Triglot*, p. 45.

Though Grudem claims agreement with the Creed of Chalcedon and its four definitions of the relationship of the "two natures, unconfusedly, unchangeably, indivisibly, inseparably" united, the fact is that, in classic Reformed style, he does "separate" the natures. It is clear from his illustration that there is a separation of the divine nature from the human nature. This is what the older Lutheran theologians referred to as the *extra Calvinisticum*, or "Calvinistic outside." Because Calvin insisted that the finite human body of Christ was incapable of containing the infinite Son of God, he maintained that the divine nature of Christ must extend beyond the human nature. Charles Porterfield Krauth correctly says of the Christology illustrated by Grudem, "There is, in fact, apparently no personal union whatever, but a mere local connection—not a dwelling of the fullness of the Godhead bodily, but simply an operative manifestation; two persons separable and in every place but one separated, not one inseparable person—inseparable in space as well as in time."[58] And Sasse well says of the rationalistic axion of the Reformed which maintains that the human nature of Christ is incapable of his divine nature, "If the old question is asked how the finite human nature can comprise the infinite divine nature, the answer can only be that according to John 1:14, the Word became flesh, which cannot mean that part of the Word did not become flesh."[59]

IV. The Communication of Attributes

We have seen that Scripture uses the analogy of the body and soul in a human person to illustrate the relationship of the natures in Christ, and yet we readily acknowledge the weakness of the comparison. The Formula of Concord correctly says that the union of natures in Christ "is a far different, more sublime, and ineffable communion and union"[60] than the union of body and soul in man. That this is true is indicated by the fact that it would not be possible to say that the body of a human being is the soul nor to say that the soul is the body. Yet, on the basis of Scripture, it can be said of Christ that "God is man" and "this man is God" because in Christ, God, the divine nature, and man, a true human nature, are united in one person.

These statements, which are called personal propositions, are statements in which one of the natures of Christ occurs as the subject of a sentence and the other nature is the predicate. Apart from Christ, such mutually exclusive terms as *God* and *man* cannot be joined in one clause so that either is the subject while the other is the predicate. Apart from Christ, God is not a man, and a man is not God; indeed, anyone who would make that claim would be guilty of blasphemy. But in Christ this unusual way of speaking is possible. In

---

[58]Krauth, p. 488.
[59]Sasse, p. 122.
[60]FC SD VIII:19, *Triglot*, p. 1021.

Matthew 16:16 St. Peter speaks in precisely these terms when he gives his good confession of Christ. In response to Jesus' inquiry as to whom the disciples thought he was, Peter answers, "You are the Christ, the Son of the living God." The pronoun "You" is the subject of the statement, and it refers to Christ, who in verse 13 had called himself "the Son of Man." The predicate is "the Son of the living God." St. Peter's confession, which Jesus accepted and proclaimed to have been given to him from above, is essentially this statement: "This man is God." Romans 1:3 contains a similar proposition about the person of Christ. There St. Paul speaks of the gospel, which God promised through his prophets, "regarding his Son, who as to his human nature was a descendant of David." The subject is God's "Son," who is described in the predicate as "a descendant of David," a true man according to his human nature. Of Christ it can be said: "God is man."

In these examples, concrete terms for the natures of Christ, rather than abstract terms, are used. Concrete terms are names that refer to the person of Christ according to either nature; for example, "man," "Son of Man," and "Son of Mary" are concretes of the human nature, while "God" and "Son of God" are concretes of the divine nature. Abstracts, or terms that refer to the natures of Christ in the abstract, apart from their union in Christ, such as divinity and humanity, are not used. Therefore it would not be proper to say of Christ that deity is humanity or humanity is deity, since this would suggest a metamorphosis, or change, of one nature into another. Nor would we want to say, "Our flesh and blood is God," for the same reason. But "because, through the union, the two natures constitute one person, every concrete of the nature ultimately denotes the person itself. Since, therefore, Christ the man is the same person who is God, or this person who is God is that very person who is man, it is also said correctly: man is God, and God is man."[61]

And yet, Holy Scripture makes it clear that the union of natures in Christ is such that they have more than just names in common. It teaches that there is a true interchange or transfer between the two natures of Christ of the various attributes or qualities or characteristics of each nature, as well as the actions and works by which those characteristics manifest themselves. In other words, in a way somewhat similar to the way the soul animates the body in a human being and reveals its properties through the body, so the divine nature in Christ penetrates and permeates the human nature so that its properties reveal themselves in and through it. The ancient church used the Greek term περιχώρησις *(perichoresis)*, which means "interpenetration or permeation," to describe this relationship of the two natures in Christ. Luther also spoke of the body of Christ as "flesh and blood permeated with God."[62] Pieper

---

[61]Heinrich Schmid, *The Doctrinal Theology of the Evangelical Lutheran Church* (Minneapolis: Augsburg Publishing House, 1961), p. 320.
[62]LW 23:143.

We Believe in Jesus Christ

writes, "As the body and soul in man do not exist merely side by side, but are in each other, and this in such a way that the soul permeates the body, so also, on the basis of Scripture, the communion of natures in Christ must not be regarded as if the two natures in Christ existed merely side by side, but they rather interpenetrate each other, the divine permeating the human."[63]

This means it is impossible to ascribe an attribute to either nature which does not belong to the person of Christ, designated by either nature, nor can there be an act performed by either nature in which the other does not participate. There is a communication of attributes of both natures to the person of Christ, and of the natures to each other. This mutual participation of each nature in Christ in the attributes of the other is known as the communication of attributes. The doctrine of the communication of attributes simply applies what the personal propositions declare about Christ and shows how the truths expressed by the personal propositions in Scripture actually operate in Christ.

An example of this communication of attributes may be seen in those Scripture passages in which attributes of either nature are ascribed to the person of Christ without regard to the nature according to which Christ is named. This class of passages may be illustrated this way: "A person consists of body and soul; each of these has its own peculiar attributes and properties. But as both, body and soul, belong to the same person, the attributes of either body or soul are ascribed to the entire person. Example: 'N.N. weighs 150 pounds,' which can properly be said only of his physical body. 'N.N. is happy and joyful,' which can properly be predicated only of his soul."[64] Scripture speaks the same way of the attributes of the two natures and the person of Christ. For example, the name "Christ" refers to the person of Christ according to both natures, and Scripture assigns characteristics of both natures to him. For example, St. Peter writes, "Christ suffered for you" (1 Pe 2:21). On the other hand, the writer of Hebrews says, "Jesus Christ is the same yesterday and today and forever" (Heb 13:8). In these passages, attributes of both natures— the divine nature (immutability) and the human nature (suffering)—are ascribed to the person of Christ. So Scripture ascribes to the person of Christ both human and divine attributes. It ascribes to him eternity: "Before Abraham was born, I am!" (Jn 8:58)—and time, for it says that Jesus went to the temple when "he was twelve years old" (Lk 2:42). Both properties are really and truly Christ's, the first according to his divine nature, the second according to the assumed human nature. The Bible says Jesus is omniscient: "He knew what was in a man" (Jn 2:25)—and that he has limited knowledge: "Jesus grew in wisdom" (Lk 2:52). We are told that Jesus is omnipotent: "The Father had put all things under his power" (Jn 13:3)—and that he had limited strength, for as a boy Jesus "grew and became strong" (Lk 2:40). Holy

---

[63]Pieper, p. 123.
[64]Koehler, p. 90.

Scripture thus ascribes to the person of Christ two sets of attributes, one divine and the other human. "Both kinds of attributes, the divine and the human, belong to Christ, equally, really, and truly because both natures, the divine and human, really and truly belong to him."[65]

Even more striking is the fact that the Scriptures do not hesitate to ascribe attributes of either nature to the person of Christ without regard to the nature according to which Christ is named. The inspired writers ascribe human characteristics—such as being born, suffering crucifixion, and dying—to Christ even when he is designated by a name that refers specifically to his divine nature, that is, a concrete of the divine nature. For example, St. Paul says, "God sent his Son, born of a woman" (Gal 4:4). Paul also accuses the rulers of this age of having "crucified the Lord of glory" (1 Co 2:8). St. Peter says that the Jews killed "the author of life" (Ac 3:15). Being born, being crucified, and dying are properly attributes of the human nature, but Scripture ascribes these human attributes to Christ when referring to him by a name that designates him according to his divine nature— "Son," "Lord of glory," and "author of life." These passages confront us with the mysterious truth that the deity, which cannot be born or suffer and die, was truly born and did indeed suffer and die on account of the personal union of the divine and human natures in Christ. On the basis of Scripture we may then truly call Mary "the mother of God" and say that "the Son of God suffered and died."

In other passages the Savior is designated according to his human nature, but things are predicated of him that properly apply to his divine nature. For example, when some of his disciples began to grumble about the "hard teaching" Jesus had proclaimed in his "bread of life" discourse (Jn 6:35-58), he said, "What if you see the Son of Man ascend to where he was before" (v. 62). Here Jesus uses a name (the Son of Man) that designates himself according to his human nature and, yet he asserts that he is in heaven, according to his divine nature, before he came to earth in his incarnation. It can truly be said with regard to Jesus, "This man is God," since not only the divine nature but divine attributes such as eternity are ascribed to him. So we see that in Scripture characteristics that are peculiar to either the divine or the human nature are ascribed to the entire person of Christ, and this is true whether he is designated by either nature or by both.

The fact that the Scriptures assign both human and divine attributes to the person of Christ does not mean that divine attributes become essential characteristics of the human nature or that human attributes become essential characteristics of the divine nature. Christ possesses the divine attributes essentially according to his divine nature and the human characteristics essentially

---

[65]Mueller, p. 274.

---

according to his human nature. The Formula of Concord explains that "in this mode of speaking, it does not follow that what is ascribed to the person is at the same time a property of both natures, but it is distinctively explained what nature it is according to which anything is ascribed to the person."[66] Thus St. Paul speaks of God's Son "who as to his human nature was a descendant of David" (Ro 1:3). St. Peter also adds what are called diacritical, or distinguishing, particles when he speaks of Christ's suffering. In his first letter he writes that "Christ suffered in his body" (4:1) and "bore our sins in his body" (2:24). Yet because of the union of the human nature with the divine nature in Christ, the Son of God was born, suffered, and died, since it was not only the human nature that was born, suffered, and died but the person of Christ. God's Son, who assumed a true human nature, thus assumes to himself all that happens to his human nature, that is, being born, suffering, and dying.

This confronts us with the great mystery that the Son of God, who cannot be born, suffer, or die according to his divine nature, according to Holy Scripture really and truly did share in the suffering of his human nature. Although it is true that God cannot die, yet because God and man are united in the person of Christ, it is scriptural to sing as German Lutherans once did: *"O große Not, Gott selbst ist tot!"* (Oh, sorrow dread, God himself is dead!). To be more specific, we would add that "God" here is a concrete term that refers to the person of Christ, who died according to his human nature. We are here confronted with a mystery that exceeds human understanding—even human expression. One teacher of the church expressed the mystery of Christ's suffering with words that appear paradoxical: "Without suffering the Son of God suffered."[67] Yet the truth taught by these passages—which are classified as the *genus idiomaticum*, namely, that the Son of God was born, suffered, and died—is critically important since "it is this very fact that *God* suffered and died for us which gives to the blood of Christ the power to cleanse from sin."[68] As Luther says,

> If God is not in the scale to give it weight, we, on our side, sink to the ground. I mean it this way: if it cannot be said that God died for us, but only a man, we are lost; but if God's death and a dead God lie in the balance, his side goes down and ours goes up like a light and empty scale. Yet he can also readily go up again, or leap out of the scale! But he could not sit on the scale unless he had become a man like us, so that it could be called God's dying, God's martyrdom, God's blood, and God's death. For God in his own nature cannot die; but

---

[66]FC SD VIII:37, *Triglot*, p. 1027.
[67]Pieper, p. 140.
[68]Mueller, p. 274.

---

now that God and man are united in one person, it is called God's death when the man dies who is one substance or one person with God.[69]

It is at this place that the christological differences between Zwingli and Luther become very apparent. While Luther can write, "He who kills Christ has killed God's Son, indeed, God and the Lord of glory himself,"[70] Zwingli insisted that the suffering and death of Christ must be referred only to his human nature. In order to "explain" why Scripture ascribes suffering and death to the whole person of Christ, the Son of Man and the Son of God, Zwingli resorted to a figure of speech, which he called the αλλοίωσις (*alloeosis*), which means "exchange" or "interchange." In assuming this figure of speech, wherever suffering or death was predicated of Christ, the Son of Man or the Son of God, the subject was changed to read as only the human nature. For example, when Jesus asks the Emmaus disciples, "Did not the Christ have to suffer these things and then enter his glory?" (Lk 24:26), Zwingli here explains that "the term 'Christ' stands for the human nature only, which could suffer and die, while the divine nature could not die."[71] In response, Luther wrote, "If I believe that only the human nature suffered for me, then Christ would be a poor Savior for me, in fact, he himself would need a Savior."[72]

The *alloeosis*—the substitution of the appropriate nature in the subject to fit the description given in the predicate—is still found among conservative evangelicals. Grudem resorts to it, for example, in a paragraph entitled "One Nature Does Some Things That the Other Nature Does Not Do." There he says, "When we are talking about Jesus' human nature, we can say that he ascended to heaven and is no longer in the world (John 16:28; 17:11; Acts 1:9-11). But with respect to his divine nature, we can say that Jesus is everywhere present: 'Where two or three are gathered in my name, there am I in the midst of them' (Matt. 18:20); 'I am with you always, to the close of the age' (Matt. 28:20)."[73] Notice how "with respect to his divine nature" is substituted for the person of Christ, "I," in the two passages from Matthew's gospel. Again, Grudem writes, "In his human nature, Jesus was weak and tired (Matt. 4:2; 8:24; Mark 15:21; John 4:6), but in his divine nature he was omnipotent (Matt. 8:26,27; Col. 1:17; Heb. 1:3)."[74] Notice again how "in his divine nature" is substituted in the Matthew passage, although the disciples, amazed that the Jesus who slept could awake and still a storm with his word, actually ask, "What kind of *man* is this?" (8:27).

---

[69]LW 41:103,104.
[70]LW 37:62.
[71]Pieper, p. 137.
[72]LW 37:210.
[73]Grudem, p. 559.
[74]Ibid.

We Believe in Jesus Christ

Chuck Swindoll has the same tendency to divide the natures and indicate that one nature does this and another does that. In writing about the account in Matthew 14, of Jesus walking out to his disciples on the storm-tossed Sea of Galilee after having gone away by himself to pray, Swindoll concludes, "Only man prays. Only God walks on water. According to Matthew, Jesus Christ did both."[75] Again, in reference to the healing of a leper in Mark 1, he writes of the Savior who was moved with compassion: "That's an example of Jesus' humanity." And then he says of the miracle of healing, "Only God can do that." When he adds "and God in man had done his work," you think he may be ready to actually unite the two natures in Christ. But then he goes on to the miracle of stilling the storm on the Sea of Galilee and writes, "Here, as a man, weary from the day. . . . He falls sound asleep in the boat. . . . And suddenly with a word, everything is calm. Only God could do such a thing!"[76] While that observation is true, the startling truth was that the *man* Christ Jesus had done this thing that only God could do.

Chemnitz writes,

> These two natures in Christ do not subsist individually, by themselves, or separately, so that there is one Christ the God and another person who is Christ the man; but they are united into one hypostasis or person, so that there is one Christ who is at the same time God and man . . . as Luther rightly says, the hypostatic union does not permit the kind of division whereby I can properly say that the divine nature of Christ does this or the human nature does that. For such a division of works would be followed by a division of the person, for the actions, as Damascenus says, are not of the natures but of the person.[77]

In other words, one does not say of Christ that he did human things as a man and divine things as God. Instead, we say that Christ did both human and divine things. The divine things he did according to his divine nature, and the human things he did according to the human nature, but "the one nature does not lie otiose, or perform its functions entirely alone, while the other does something else . . . but each nature in Christ performs in communion with the other that which is the proper activity of each."[78]

When Reformed theology envisions the two natures in Christ as united in a merely mechanical way—"like two boards glued together"—and separates the natures, it commits a serious error. Pieper says that "it inevitably denies

---

[75]Swindoll, p. 145.
[76]Ibid., p. 147.
[77]Chemnitz, pp. 162,163.
[78]Ibid., p. 157.

---

the incarnation of the Son of God and Christ's vicarious atonement, and so destroys the foundation of the Christian faith."[79] For Scripture bases the redemptive value of Christ's suffering on the fact that not a mere man but the Son of God suffered; for it says, "we were reconciled to him [God] through the death of his Son" (Ro 5:10). However, insofar as Reformed Christology is inconsistent and ignores its basic error, it returns to the Christian faith. Grudem illustrates this happy inconsistency when he writes,

> By virtue of its union with Jesus' human nature, his divine nature somehow tasted something of what it was like to go through death. The *person* of Christ experienced death. Moreover, it seems difficult to understand how Jesus' human nature alone could have borne the wrath of God against the sins of millions of people. It seems that Jesus' divine nature had somehow to participate in the bearing of wrath against sin that was due us.[80]

Even Grudem senses the inconsistency of this correct assessment of Christ's death with the rest of his Christology when he adds the remarkable (in view of Romans 5:10) comment: "(though Scripture nowhere explicitly affirms this)."[81]

V. The Communication of Majesty

Scripture not only teaches a communication of qualities and works of either nature to the person of Christ, but also teaches a communication of attributes from the divine nature to the human nature. The passages that teach the communication of attributes from the divine to the human nature are called the *genus majestaticum.* This genus may be illustrated in this way: "The human body in itself is dead; but when joined to the living soul, this soul imparts and communicates life to the body. Thereby the life of the soul is not diminished or divided, but it remains fully intact. However, at times this life manifests itself in the body less than at other times, less, for example, when a person sleeps than when he is awake; but the body does not impart anything to the soul."[82] The second genus deals with those passages that teach that the Son of God communicates properties of his divine nature to his human nature for its possession and use.

Since the divine nature is complete and perfect and cannot be increased or diminished, it is clear at once that the human nature cannot communicate anything to the divine; instead, the communication is completely from the

---

[79]Pieper, p. 271.
[80]Grudem, p. 560.
[81]Ibid., p. 560.
[82]Koehler, p. 91.

divine nature to the human. According to his divine nature, the Son of God always had all divine glory and majesty. Jesus testified to that when he prayed on the night he was betrayed: "And now, Father, glorify me in your presence with the glory I had with you before the world began" (Jn 17:5). Jesus is speaking of the glory of the divine majesty, which he had according to his eternal divine nature with the Father prior to the creation of the world. Thus, according to the divine nature, Christ could not be given or receive glory. It is according to his human nature that Christ asks to be glorified, and to the human nature that Scripture says divine glory and majesty were given. It is in regard to his human nature that Jesus says, "All authority in heaven and on earth has been given to me" (Mt 28:18), and again, "All things have been committed to me by my Father" (Mt 11:27). The Formula of Concord says, "There is a unanimously received rule of the entire ancient orthodox Church that what the Holy Scripture testifies that Christ received in time He received not according to the divine nature (according to which He has everything from eternity), but the person has received it in time . . . , that is, as referring and with respect to, according to the assumed human nature."[83] This ancient rule of the church is based squarely on the words of our Lord, who claims for himself the power to raise the dead and judge the world on the Last Day, saying, "[The Father] has given him authority to judge because he is the Son of Man" (Jn 5:27). "This authority [to execute judgment] the Father has given Him because He is a son of man, that is, because He is man and hence cannot of Himself have the authority to execute judgment; nor would He have it had it not been given to Him by the Father."[84]

Scripture makes it even more clear that divine glory and majesty have been communicated to the human nature of Christ by virtue of the personal union when it ascribes divine characteristics to the human nature which is referred to by so-called abstract terms. Abstract terms are expressions that refer to the human nature by itself apart from the divine nature, for example, "flesh" and "blood." Yet even when using these abstract expressions, characteristics that are truly divine are predicated of Christ. In John 6, for example, Jesus says, "I am the living bread that came down from heaven. If anyone eats of this bread, he will live forever. This bread is my flesh, which I will give for the life of the world" (v. 51). Here the "flesh" of Christ, his human nature by itself, so to speak, is called the living, life-giving bread, which when eaten by faith gives eternal life. When the Jews took exception to this teaching and asked, "How can this man give us his flesh to eat?"(v. 52), Jesus did not take back his claim but intensified it, saying, "I tell you the truth, unless you eat the flesh of the Son of Man and drink his blood, you have no life in you"

---

[83]FC SD VIII:57, *Triglot*, p. 1035.
[84]Meyer quoted in Pieper, p. 160.

(v. 53). He adds "blood" to "flesh" to make it even clearer that he is speaking of his human nature and yet again ascribes to it life-giving, soul-saving power. St. John does the same in the first chapter of his first letter when he says that "the blood of Jesus, his Son, purifies us from all sin" (v. 7). Here the divine characteristic of taking away sin is ascribed to Christ's blood, his human nature as such. Now clearly it would be wrong to make such bold statements about the human nature apart from its union with the divine in the person of Christ, but in the context of the personal union these passages emphatically affirm the doctrine that in Christ the attributes of the divine nature are communicated to the human nature.

There is, however, no essential or natural infusion of the properties of the divine nature into the human nature. The Formula of Concord says,

> We believe, teach, and confess that to be almighty, eternal, infinite, to be of itself everywhere present at once naturally, that is, according to the property of its nature and its natural essence, and to know all things, are essential attributes of the divine nature, which never to eternity become the essential properties of the human nature.

> On the other hand, to be a corporeal creature, to be flesh and blood, to be finite and circumscribed, to suffer, to die, to ascend and descend, to move from one place to another, to suffer hunger, thirst, cold, heat, and the like, are properties of the human nature, which never become properties of the divine nature.[85]

Thus the human nature comes into possession of all the divine attributes of the Logos not essentially, but mediately; by communication they are received into the personality of the Logos. "In no way is conversion, confusion, or equalization of the natures in Christ or of their essential properties to be maintained or admitted."[86] The divine nature imparts its properties to the human nature, not essentially, or as if the human nature would possess them even if separated from the divine nature, but in a way somewhat similar to the way the soul acts in and through the body in a human being. Though the soul imparts its life to the members of the body and enables the body to do what it could not do without the soul, the soul does not cease to be soul, and the body does not cease to be body. The union of a body with a soul does not transform the body into a spirit. A piece of iron may be thrown into a fire, may be affected by and permeated by the fire, so that the properties of the fire (such

---

[85]FC SD VIII:9,10, *Triglot*, pp. 1017,1019.
[86]FC SD VIII:62, *Triglot*, p. 1037.

as heat and light) become active through the iron. Yet the properties of fire are not properties of iron.

Therefore while the human nature of Christ did not possess divine attributes essentially, by communication it came into possession of all the divine attributes of the eternal Word. And it cannot be denied that Scripture ascribes divine power, majesty, and glory to the human nature of Christ. Scripture makes it clear that Jesus Christ is an omniscient, omnipotent, and omnipresent man. St. John says of Jesus, "He did not need man's testimony about man, for he knew what was in a man" (Jn 2:25). To know the thoughts of the heart is the prerogative of God, who alone "looks at the heart," while mere men are limited to looking "at the outward appearance" (1 Sa 16:7). Even the Samaritan woman at Sychar recognized the omniscience of God in Christ's human nature, for she urged the people of her town, "Come, see a man who told me everything I ever did" (Jn 4:29). Christ, according to his human nature, possessed and exercised divine omniscience—and divine omnipotence.

Every miracle our Lord performed during his earthly ministry is evidence of the fact that he possessed divine omnipotence. For while others such as the apostles Peter and Paul were also able to do miracles, they did not do them, as Jesus did, by their own power. St. Peter made that clear when after healing the lame man at the temple, he asked the amazed crowd, "Why do you stare at us as if by our own power or godliness we had made this man walk?" (Ac 3:12). Jesus, on the other hand, was able to perform miracles by the divine omnipotence which he possessed as the eternal Son of God and which was communicated to his human nature. St. John therefore says that Jesus, through the miracle of changing water into wine at the wedding at Cana, "revealed his glory" (Jn 2:11). It was the very fact that the man Jesus Christ performed miracles that amazed those who witnessed them. For example, the disciples on the Sea of Galilee, which had been turned from stormy to still in an instant, asked: "What kind of man is this? Even the winds and the waves obey him!" (Mt 8:27). When some doubted that a man like Jesus had the authority to do the works of God, namely, to forgive sins (Mt 9:2,3), Jesus performed a miracle to confirm that very fact for them, saying as he healed the paralytic, "But so that you may know that the Son of Man has authority on earth to forgive sins. . . . Get up, take up your mat and go home" (Mt 9:6).

Because his work on earth required Jesus to be seen and touched and handled, he had fewer opportunities to demonstrate that in addition to possessing divine omniscience and omnipotence, his human nature was also omnipresent, and yet the Scriptures do contain evidence of that fact. When St. John wants to contrast the preaching ministry of Christ with that of the prophets and apostles, he says the latter speak as "from the earth" (Jn 3:31), which means by revelation or inspiration, which takes place on earth, while Christ speaks as "the one who comes from above" (v. 31) and "testifies to what he has seen and heard" (v. 32). In other words, while on earth Christ declared "what He had seen and heard 'in the council of the Holy Trinity.' "[87] And yet St. John makes it clear that although Jesus "came from the Father" (Jn 1:14), he is still with the Father in heaven, for even while the Father "made him known" during his earthly ministry, St. John declares him to be "God the One and Only, who is at the Father's side" (Jn 1:18). In other words, while Jesus was making the Father known on earth, an activity in which Jesus was engaged only after his incarnation, he was at still at the Father's side in heaven.

That Christ's presence in heaven was not interrupted by his incarnation is made clear by the Savior himself in his conversation with Nicodemus in which he claims to be "the one who came from heaven—the Son of Man, *who is in heaven*" (Jn 3:13). While it is true that the NIV places the italicized words in a footnote, it is also true that the textual support for their inclusion is both ancient and widespread. In addition, the truth contained in those words, that even while he was on earth Jesus continued to be in heaven, is completely consistent with the theology of the apostle who proclaims Christ to be the Word who became flesh.[88] It is on the basis of the omnipresence of his human nature that the man Jesus can promise not only, "Where two or three come together in my name, there am I with them" (Mt 18:20), but also, "Surely I am with you always, to the very end of the age" (28:20). Note that while the latter promise was made after Jesus' resurrection, the former was made prior to the resurrection. Friedrick Philippi correctly observes: "As He (the Son of Man) after His resurrection entered through closed doors, so also, before His resurrection, He vanished out of the sight of His enemies (John 8:59; Luke 4:30); and so we see that even then His body was not subject to the conditions and limitations of space and matter as are ours."[89]

In fact, far from being subject to the same limitations of space and matter as our bodies are, the Bible reveals that the human nature of Christ has at least four different modes or ways of being present. First, there is the local presence according to which Christ's body lay in the manger of Bethlehem (Lk 2:7), was anointed at Bethany (Jn 12:3), hung on the cross (Jn 19:18), and was placed in the tomb (Jn 19:42). Luther calls this "the comprehensible, bodily mode, as He went about bodily upon earth, when, according to His size, He vacated and occupied space [was circumscribed by a fixed place]."[90]

By virtue of the personal union, Christ's human nature possesses also "the incomprehensible, spiritual mode, according to which He neither occupies nor vacates space, but penetrates all creatures wherever He pleases."[91] Christ

---

[87]Pieper, p. 162.
[88]John Brug, *Wisconsin Lutheran Quarterly*, Vol. 93, No. 2 (Spring 1996), pp. 140,141.
[89]Philippi quoted in Pieper, p. 177.
[90]FC SD VII:99, *Triglot*, p. 1005.
[91]FC SD VII:100, *Triglot*, pp. 1005,1007.

employed this manner of presence "when he suddenly appeared to his disciples as they were crossing the Sea of Galilee by night (Mt 14:25) and when he escaped from his enemies by miraculously disappearing from their midst (Lk 4:30; Jn 8:59)."[92] Luther elaborates, "As, to make an imperfect comparison, my sight penetrates and is in air, light, or water, and does not occupy or vacate space; as a sound or tone penetrates and is in air or water or board and wall, and also does not occupy or vacate space; likewise, as light and heat penetrate and are in air, water, glass, crystals, and the like, and also do not vacate or occupy space."[93]

In addition, Scripture reveals that the human nature of Christ is present in still a third way since the human body of Christ is the home of the person of the Son of God (Col 2:9). Regarding this so-called supernatural or divine mode of presence, Luther says, "Here we come with a Christ beyond all creatures, both according to his humanity and his divinity; with his humanity we enter a different land from that in which it moved here on earth, viz. beyond and above all creatures and purely in the Godhead."[94] Here we must not think of Christ's human nature filling the universe in a physical way, by a diffusion or expansion of his body, but rather we must think in terms of an illocal, supernatural presence. Luther explains that something is present in this way when it "is simultaneously present in all places whole and entire, and fills all places, yet without being measured or circumscribed by any place, in terms of the space which it occupies. . . . Since he [Christ] is a man who is supernaturally one person with God, and apart from this man there is no God, it must follow that according to the third supernatural mode, he is and can be wherever God is and that everything is full of Christ through and through, even according to his humanity."[95] Anticipating our curious questions in regard to this mode of presence, Luther adds, "Here you will say with Nicodemus, 'How can this be?' [John 3:9]. . . . I answer: Here you must with Moses take off your old shoes, and with Nicodemus be born anew."[96]

In addition to this so-called *omnipraesentia generalis*, or general omnipresence, the Bible also teaches a special presence of Christ according to his human nature, also known as the *voli*-presence, that is, the volitional presence, because he effects it "when, how, and wherever he wishes"[97] or wills. The Savior speaks of this special presence when he promises, "Where two or three come together in my name, there am I with them" (Mt 18:20). That is clearly a special kind of presence with believers distinct from his general omnipresence with all creatures. So also, according to his promise, Christ's body and

---

[92]Wilbert Gawrisch, *No Other Gospel* (Milwaukee: Northwestern Publishing House, 1980), p. 242.
[93]FC SD VII:100, *Triglot*, p. 1007.
[94]LW 37:229.
[95]LW 37:216,218.
[96]LW 37:219.
[97]Chemnitz, p. 448.

---

blood are present in the Lord's Supper in, with, and under the bread and wine. This again is a special presence of Christ's human nature, which is above and beyond the presence according to which "all things are through and through full of Christ, also according to the humanity."[98] Luther distinguishes this special presence from the general omnipresence when he writes,

> It is one thing if God is present, and another if he is present for you. He is there for you when he adds his Word and binds himself, saying, "Here you are to find me." . . . He also now exceeds any grasp, and you will not catch him by groping about, even though he is in your bread, unless he binds himself to you and summons you to a particular table by his Word, and he himself gives meaning to the bread for you, by his Word, bidding you to eat him. This he does in the Supper, saying, "This is my body."[99]

Bente summarizes the difference between Christ's general omnipresence and his special presence this way: "In virtue of the personal union Christ is present everywhere also according to His human nature; while the peculiarly gracious manner of His presence in the Gospel, in the Church, and in the Lord's Supper depends upon His will and is based upon His definite promises."[100]

If we have trouble understanding how the human nature of Christ can be omnipotent, omniscient, or omnipresent without being annihilated or destroyed, or if we worry that a human nature endowed with those qualities must be something less than a true human nature, then let us remember that "the highest possible authority relieves us of this worry. In the Scriptures we have God's Word for it that the human nature of Christ did not lose anything by its assumption into the Person of the Son of God; Scripture describes Christ not only as true God, but throughout also as a true, complete man."[101] The Formula reminds us that

> the best, most certain, and surest way in this controversy is this, namely, that what Christ has received according to His assumed human nature through the personal union, glorification, or exaltation, and of what His assumed human nature is capable beyond the natural properties, without becoming annihilated, no one can know better or more thoroughly than the Lord Christ Himself; and He has revealed it in His Word, as much as is needful for us to know of it in this life."[102]

---

[98]FC SD VIII:81, *Triglot,* p. 1045.
[99]LW 37:68,69.
[100]F. Bente, "Historical Introductions to the Symbolical Books," *Triglot,* p. 184.
[101]Pieper, pp. 81,82.
[102]FC SD VIII:53, *Triglot,* p. 1033.

We Believe in Jesus Christ

It is in regard to the communication of majesty from the divine nature in Christ to his assumed human nature that the Reformed tendency to separate the two natures in Christ from each other becomes most apparent. The Reformed stress the individuality of the two natures in Christ to such an extent that they practically create two persons in Christ—one human and one divine. Grudem provides excellent examples of this tendency in his theology. He writes, "Particularly striking is the scene on the Sea of Galilee where Jesus was asleep in the stern of the boat, presumably because he was weary (Matt. 8:24). But he was able to arise from his sleep and calm the wind and sea with a word (Matt. 8:26,27)! Tired yet omnipotent! Here Jesus' weak human nature completely hid his omnipotence until that omnipotence broke forth in a sovereign word from the Lord of heaven and earth."[103] Grudem says in effect: "Jesus slept as man and stilled the storm as God." In fact, though, what amazed Jesus' disciples was that Jesus stilled the storm in his "weak human nature" (to use Grudem's phrase) for they asked, "What kind of man is this? Even the winds and the waves obey him!" (Mt 8:27).

The same is true in regard to the divine attribute of omniscience. Grudem writes, "On the one hand, with respect to his human nature, he had limited knowledge (Mark 13:32; Luke 2:52). On the other hand, Jesus clearly knew all things (John 2:25; 16:30; 21:17). Now this is only understandable if Jesus learned things and had limited knowledge with respect to his human nature but was always omniscient with respect to his divine nature."[104] Again the explanation is that Jesus had limited knowledge as man and all knowledge as God. Interestingly, Grudem attempts to buttress his Nestorianizing tendencies with a reference to R. C. H. Lenski, a Lutheran commentator. He says that Lenski and others, "attribute this ignorance of Jesus to his human nature only, not to his divine nature." That is true as far as it goes, but it doesn't tell the whole story. For while Grudem ascribes only limited knowledge to the human nature of Christ, Lenski affirms that Christ's human nature did possess divine omniscience but that he did not fully use it during the state of humiliation. Lenski writes,

Whereas Jesus thus names himself according to his divine person ('the Son') and nature, what he predicates of himself is something that pertains to his human nature (namely, limited knowledge). . . . In their essential oneness the three persons know all things, but in his humiliation [which Lenski correctly applies only to Christ's human nature; See his *Interpretation of Philippians*, p. 781] the second person did not use his divine attributes save as he needed them in his mediatorial work. So the divine omniscience was used by Jesus only in this restricted way.[105]

---

[103]Grudem, p. 559.
[104]Ibid., p. 561.
[105]R. C. H. Lenski, *The Interpretation of St. Mark's Gospel* (Columbus, The Wartburg Press, 1951), p. 590.

In other words, Lenski actually affirms the very thing Grudem rejects: the communication of divine attributes to Christ's human nature.

Very clearly Grudem rejects the communication of divine omnipresence to the human nature of Christ: "The divine attribute of *omnipresence* is not directly affirmed to be true of Jesus during his earthly ministry. However, while looking forward to the time that the church would be established, Jesus could say, 'Where two or three are gathered in my name, *there am I* in the midst of them' (Matt. 18:20). Moreover, before he left the earth, he told his disciples, 'I am with you always, to the close of the age' (Matt. 11:25-27)." Grudem then clarifies in a footnote: "I do not mean to imply that these verses show that Jesus' human nature was omnipresent. Jesus' human nature, including his physical body, was never more than one place at one time. It is probably best to understand these verses to refer to Jesus' divine nature."[106] Certainly it is true that Jesus is both God and man, and has both human and divine characteristics, but what makes Christ truly remarkable is that "he presents these two aspects not successively, not alternatingly, not in two individuals, but one."[107]

A contemporary Reformed theologian, Richard Muller, puts his finger on the difference between evangelical and Lutheran Christology when he writes,

> Whereas the greatest difference between the Lutherans and the Reformed appears in the *genus maiestaticum*, which the Reformed utterly reject, we note that the Reformed view of the *communicatio*, which tends to be restricted to the *genus idiomaticum*, approaches the communication more as a *praedicatio verbalis*, or verbal communication, of *idiomata* from both natures of the person, whereas the Lutheran view insists that the person actually bears the *idomata* of both natures. . . . the Lutheran teaching is a real *communicatio* while the Reformed . . . is . . . a mutual interchange or reciprocation of names, rather than a transfer or communication of properties.[108]

John Theodore Mueller says in response, "If we must regard as nominal or topical in Scripture everything to which man's blind reason opposes itself, then, in the last analysis, every article of faith must be denied."[109]

The result of the Reformed refusal to admit the communication of majesty to the human nature in Christ can be clearly seen in the doctrine of the Lord's Supper. Erickson writes,

---

[106]Grudem, p. 548.
[107]Dau, p. 219.
[108]Richard Muller, *Dictionary of Latin and Greek Theological Terms* (Grand Rapids: Baker Book House,1985), p. 74.
[109]Mueller, p. 271.

If we take 'This is my body' and 'This is my blood' literally, an absurdity results. If Jesus meant that the bread and wine were at that moment in the upper room actually his body and his blood, he was asserting that his flesh and blood were in two place simultaneously, since his corporeal form was right there beside the elements. To believe that Jesus was in two places at once is something of a denial of the incarnation, which limited his physical human nature to one location.[110]

In fact, the charge of denying the incarnation is more accurately directed at the Reformed, who profess to believe that the Word became flesh but deny the necessary result of that union of natures—namely that since the incarnation, the Word is never and nowhere outside of his assumed flesh. Krauth correctly summarizes the inconsistency of this position on the part of someone like Erickson who confesses the doctrine of the incarnation when he writes,

> Accepting the doctrine of a real incarnation, the omnipresence of the human nature of Christ, not in itself, in which respect its presence is determinate, but through the divine, is a necessary result and involves no new mystery. If that whole Godhead which dwells in Christ's body can, without motion, without leaving heaven, or extending itself, be present with us on earth, then can it render present with us, without motion or extension, that other nature which is one person with it.[111]

VI. The State Of Humiliation

While Scripture makes it clear that when the Son of God assumed a human nature and imparted to it divine majesty, glory, and attributes, it is also clear from the biblical record of his life that Christ "did not always, nor in the same manner make use of the divine attributes communicated to his human nature."[112] There is a distinct period in the life of Christ when his majesty is seen only occasionally, and for the most part he appears bearing all the weaknesses and infirmities of all other men since the fall into sin.

At this point it is important to distinguish between the incarnation and the state of humiliation, that is, the taking of human flesh and blood by the Son of God (the incarnation), and the fact that Christ did not make full and constant use of the divine prerogatives that were communicated to his human nature at the incarnation (the humiliation). The two events, the incarnation and humiliation, are not always distinguished as clearly as they might be.

---

[110]Millard J. Erickson, *Christian Theology*, Vol. 3 (Grand Rapids: Baker Book House, 1985), p. 1121.
[111]Krauth, p. 350.
[112]Schaller, p. 82.

"We (Still) Do Not Have the Same Spirit"

Even the words of the *Te Deum,* "When you became man to set us free, you humbled yourself to be born of a virgin," are apt to be misunderstood if we don't distinguish between the incarnation in the first phrase and the humiliation in the second. "In point of time the humiliation starts with the incarnation, but it is not the same thing. By his incarnation Christ did not abdicate his divine glory, but brought it with him and filled his body with the fullness of the Godhead."[113] Schaller points out that the incarnation of the eternal Word "being an act of the Logos, was not a humiliation, but a demonstration of supreme power. Though the human nature of Christ entered upon the state of exinanition (humiliation) at the first moment of its existence, logically the beginning of its existence preceded its humiliation."[114] It was not a sign of weakness but a "demonstration of supreme power" for the Word to become flesh. Imagine pouring the water of all the oceans of the world into the pail a child plays with at the beach! Something similar but far more amazing happened when the Son of God became flesh.

St. Paul reminds us of that when he writes in Philippians 2:5,6, "Your attitude should be the same as that of Christ Jesus: Who, being in very nature God, did not consider equality with God something to be grasped." A correct understanding of this passage begins with a correct understanding of the Greek word μορφή, which is translated "nature" in the NIV but would better be translated "form," as it was in the KJV. According to Thayer's Greek-English Lexicon of the New Testament, the word μορφή means "the form by which a person or thing strikes the vision" or "the external appearance." Yet Paul is not saying that Christ was merely a man who "appeared" as God to others. Thayer contrasts μορφή with σχῆμα, a synonym, saying, "μορφή *form* differs from σχῆμα *figure, shape, fashion,* as that which is intrinsic and essential, from that which is outward and accidental."[115] "The nature or essence of God is presupposed in one who manifests the form of God, since only one who possesses the essence of God can exist in the form of God."[116] Thus the μορφῇ θεοῦ is the external manifestation or form of God, whereby one who is God is known and seen to be God. But how does God who is spirit (Jn 4:24), that is, a real being without a body of flesh and blood, manifest his essence so that it can be seen and known? St. John says it happened when the Word became flesh in the man Christ Jesus, for those who have seen him have seen "the glory of the One and Only, who came from the Father" (Jn 1:14). "The μορφή θεοῦ is equivalent to the δόξα θεοῦ . . . the aggregate of all divine attributes, especially his omnipotence, his omniscience and his omnipresence."[117]

---

[113]Dau, p. 233.
[114]Schaller, p. 84.
[115]Thayer, p. 418.
[116]Louis Wessel, *Proof Texts of the Catechism* (St. Louis: Concordia Publishing House, 1927), p. 179.
[117]Ibid., p. 178.

We Believe in Jesus Christ

Like St. John, then, St. Paul is speaking of the incarnate Christ, not the pre-incarnate Christ. Unless we are prepared to believe that St. Paul wants us to imitate the way the eternal Word became flesh, we must insist that it is the *man* Christ Jesus, the Word in the flesh, who is set before us as an example to be imitated. For, as Schaller points out, the pre-incarnate Christ *is* true God, not in the *form* of God, and the preincarnate Christ is not *equal* with God, but *is* God.[118] And to say that the pre-incarnate Christ, who *is* God from all eternity, has the form of God is self-evident. It would make little sense for the apostle to say that Christ is God in the form of God. "However, if this phrase ("being in the form of God") is understood of the incarnate Christ, of the Word made flesh, it is a very fitting expression of a most unusual fact, namely, that . . . when he became man, he did not lay aside his divine nature or leave it in heaven apart from the human nature, but that when the eternal Logos became flesh, the divine nature was intimately united with the human nature it assumed."[119] Thus it is in the human nature of Christ that "the aggregate of all divine attributes, especially his omnipotence, his omniscience and his omnipresence" are revealed.

However, St. Paul goes on to say that the man Christ Jesus, who being in the form of God, possessing all divine glory in his human nature, "did not consider equality with God something to be grasped, but made himself nothing, taking the very nature of a servant, being made in human likeness. And being found in appearance as a man, he humbled himself and became obedient to death—even death on a cross!" (Php 2:6-8). Though he possessed the aggregate of divine prerogatives, Jesus did not consider his divine majesty "something to be grasped," ἁρπαγμὸν, that is, he didn't treat it like "the loot of a victorious warrior who uses it according to his desires and for his own selfish purposes."[120] Instead, he "made himself nothing," or emptied himself, ἑαυτὸν ἐκένωσεν, according to the human nature which had been filled with all the majesty of God by "taking," λαβών (an instrumental participle), upon himself the "form of a servant," μορφὴν δούλου. This then is the essence of the humiliation: Christ freely exchanged the form of God, the full and open use of the divine attributes by which God is seen to be God, for the form of a servant, the form and appearance of a lowly person. The term "form of a servant" does not mean the human nature as such, but the way Christ conducted himself, the appearance or condition in which the incarnate Christ was found. The incarnate Son of God might have shown himself at all times to be the wonderful human being that he was by the exercise of his divine powers. He might have come into the world by creating a fully grown human nature and uniting it with his divine nature; he might have appeared at all times as the

---

[118]Schaller, pp. 71,87.
[119]F. W. Wenzel, *The Wenzel Commentary Book II* (Bemidji: Arrow Printing, 1988), p. 65.
[120]Schaller, p. 86.

glorious man who was seen by the disciples on the Mount of Transfiguration; he might have conducted himself as a heavenly and earthly king and demanded to be treated accordingly. But instead of doing that, he was "made in human likeness . . . being found in appearance as a man." This means that he became a man like all other men—in the "likeness" of human nature as it was weakened by the fall—and that in his appearance among men he was "found" not in the form of God but in the form of a common man, yes, among the serving class of men. All this was done deliberately and for a specific purpose. As the apostle says, "He humbled himself [ἐταπείνωσεν ἑαυτόν] and became obedient to death—even death on a cross!"

St. Paul declares the same truths about the humiliation of Christ in another place when he says, "You know the grace of our Lord Jesus Christ, that though he was rich, yet for your sakes he became poor, so that you through his poverty might become rich" (2 Co 8:9). On the words "Christ . . . became poor," Professor J. P. Meyer comments, "This does not refer to the incarnation as such; that was merely a preparatory step enabling him to become poor. Even after the incarnation he was in the form of God; but because he did not consider it as ἁρπαγμὸν, something to be displayed jealously at all times, namely to live on an equal footing with God, he emptied himself and took on the form of a servant (Php 2:6,7)."[121] In this simple way Scripture describes Christ's humiliation, or exinanition as it is also known. The term *exinanition* comes from the Latin translation of the Greek ἑαυτὸν ἐκένωσεν in Philippians 2:7, which reads *semet ipsum exinanivit* in the Vulgate and means "made himself empty" or "made himself of none effect." These words are a reminder that the humiliation of Christ was not merely a concealment of his divine majesty, as if Christ did not really give up anything and as if his poverty, lowliness, temptation, sufferings, and death were only apparent. Scripture makes it clear that the humiliation of Christ was a real "emptying" of himself, a true renunciation of the divine glory that was really his according to his divine nature. Thus Jesus can ask his heavenly Father to restore that which he had freely given up: "And now, Father, glorify me in your presence with the glory I had with you before the world began" (Jn 17:5).

Since God "does not change like shifting shadows" (Jas 1:17), it goes without saying that the exinanition or self-renunciation of the full use of the divine prerogatives applies only to the human nature of Christ and not in any way to his divine nature. However, even according to the human nature, the fact that Christ "emptied himself" does not mean that he relinquished or gave up possession of any of his divine attributes. The continued possession of the divine attributes by Christ also in the state of humiliation is confirmed by

---

[121]John P. Meyer, *Ministers of Christ* (Milwaukee: Northwestern Publishing House, 1963), p. 175.

We Believe in Jesus Christ

every miracle he performed. Jesus clearly testified to the fact that his human nature, also in the state of exinanition, shares in the divine work of preserving and governing the world together with his heavenly Father. When he was criticized for doing a miracle of healing on the Sabbath, Christ responded by saying, "My Father is always at his work to this very day, and I, too, am working" (Jn 5:17). That these words do not refer only to the single act of healing the sick man at the pool of Bethesda but to the perpetual preservation and government of the universe by Christ is made clear by the words which follow: "Whatever the Father does the Son also does" (v. 19). The exinanition then is not an emptying or self-renunciation of the possession of the divine attributes by Christ, but of the full use of the divine attributes by Christ according to his human nature. Chemnitz says,

> The humiliation was not the absence, deprivation, loss, lack, despoliation, setting aside, or laying down of the divine attributes in the divine nature of the Logos, as if it did not then possess them or did not in itself use them, so that they had to be given back or returned to the deity; for Christ says at the time when his Passion was imminent, at the depth of his humiliation, 'All things which the Father has are mine' (Jn 16:15); and in John 5:17 he says, 'My Father works hitherto, and I work.' But he is said to have emptied himself because he did not always exercise his divine majesty through the assumed flesh in the time of his humiliation.[122]

John William Baier, a Lutheran theologian of the 17th century, defines the exinanition this way: "The exinanition of Christ pertains to his human nature and consists in this, that Christ for a time abdicated the full use of the divine majesty which the human nature received in the personal union by communication."[123]

The doctrine of Christ's humiliation must be maintained if we are to begin to understand and safeguard the biblical doctrine of the true human development of Christ. Remember that Scripture contains seemingly contradictory statements about Christ. On the one hand it says Jesus is omniscient: "In [Christ] are hidden all the treasures of wisdom and knowledge" (Col 2:3). On the other hand, we are told that he had limited knowledge and in fact that "Jesus grew in wisdom" (Lk 2:52). We are told that Jesus is omnipotent, "By him all things were created" (Col 1:16), and that he had limited strength, for the boy Jesus "became strong" (Lk 2:40). While Jesus can claim, according to his human nature, to be "the Son of Man, who is in heaven" (Jn 3:13), it can

---

[122]Chemnitz, p. 281.
[123]Schmid, p. 377.

also be said that the human body of Jesus "grew in . . . stature" (Lk 2:52). On the basis of these seemingly contradictory assertions, theologians distinguish between natural and personal acts on the part of Christ. Natural acts are those that Christ has in common with all other human beings, such as to learn and to grow taller and stronger. Personal acts are those that belong to the human nature of Christ only by virtue of the personal union, such as to be omniscient, omnipotent, and omnipresent. So Christ possessed the knowledge, strength, and size that belong to the human nature as its own essential attribute and the omniscience, omnipotence, and omnipresence that belong to his human nature by virtue of the personal union. The divine wisdom, power, and presence that are communicated to his human nature are infinite and incapable of growth, while the wisdom, strength, and size that he had as essential attributes of his human nature are finite and capable of growth. When we are told that Jesus increased in wisdom, strength, and stature, this is to be understood as an actual increase in the natural wisdom, strength, and stature that are essential to his human nature. The Formula of Concord says, "This majesty [the divine attributes] He [Christ] always had according to the personal union, and yet He abstained from it in the state of His humiliation, and on this account [of the exinanition] truly increased in all wisdom and favor with God and men; therefore He exercised his majesty, not always, but when it pleased Him."[124]

The fact that Christ did not always exercise his majesty in the state of exinanition also "explains" how Scripture can make another series of assertions regarding Christ that appear contradictory. For example, we are told that the same Christ in whose body all the fullness of the deity lives, thus being "rich," was also "poor" (2 Co 8:9). The same Jesus whose amazed disciples gasped, "Even the winds and the waves obey him!" (Mt 8:27), also sat down at Jacob's well "tired as he was from the journey" (Jn 4:6). This Jesus who knows "all things" (Jn 21:17) is able to honestly tell his disciples, "No one knows about that day [the Last Day] or hour, not even the angels in heaven, nor the Son, but only the Father" (Mk 13:32). The same Jesus who can promise according to his human nature, "Where two or three come together in my name, there am I with them" (Mt 18:20), can also tell his disciples when Lazarus died in Bethany, "I am glad I was not there" (Jn 11:15). The same Jesus who has "life in himself" (Jn 5:26) also suffers and dies. Francis Pieper observes, "Such utterly opposite statements have never been predicated of any other person. History indeed tells of many mighty men who became utterly powerless, and of rich men who became exceedingly poor. But no man ever was powerful and weak, rich and poor, at the same time. . . . But in the case of Christ, possession of all things and extreme poverty, omnipotence and limited power, are ascribed to the same Person simultaneously."[125]

---

[124]FC Ep VIII:16, *Triglot*, p. 821.
[125]Pieper, p. 285.

We Believe in Jesus Christ

"These apparently contradictory statements Scripture explains by the fact that the Son of Man did not always and fully use the divine prerogatives that were communicated to him as man."[126] The Savior himself declares that he did not always make use of the power that was his to use. In John 10:18 Jesus says of his own life, "No one takes it from me, but I lay it down of my own accord. I have authority to lay it down and authority to take it up again." In John 18 we have an example of Christ's use and non-use of the divine glory according to his human nature. In verse 6 we are told that when Jesus told those who had come to arrest him that he was the one they were looking for, saying, " 'I am he,' they drew back and fell to the ground." Had Jesus made full and constant use of that divine power, he could not have been bound and led away to the cross. But having given evidence that he possessed almighty power, Jesus refrained from using it with the result as St. John records: "Then the detachment of soldiers with its commander and the Jewish officials arrested Jesus" (18:12). Chemnitz writes that Christ "did not exercise his power at that time [the state of humiliation] but kept it withdrawn as it were, and in quiet, as Irenaeus so nicely put it, yielding to the wrath of the Father against the sin of the human race"[127] so that he could suffer, be crucified, and die. In Mark 13 we have another example of the same phenomenon. There Jesus, who has demonstrated divine omniscience as he spoke in great detail of all that will take place as the end of the world approaches, at the same time tells his disciples, "No one knows about that day or hour, not even the angels in heaven, nor the Son, but only the Father" (v. 32).

How could both limited strength and knowledge and divine omniscience and omnipotence exist in the same person? The answer Scripture gives is simply that in the state of exinanition the divine attributes did not always become operative in the human nature. Why weren't the divine attributes always fully operative in the human nature of Christ? Jesus answered that question when he said, "The Son of Man did not come to be served, but to serve, and to give his life as a ransom for many" (Mk 10:45). Pieper adds, "He came into the world not to parade His deity before men, but to suffer and die in the place of men and by His death to destroy him who had the power of death over men."[128]

How did Christ decide when to use the divine attributes, which for the most part "rested" or remained "quiescent" during the state of exinanition? Christ's words again give the answer. He came into the world for a very definite reason, namely, "to give his life as a ransom for many." When the execution of his redemptive work required it, Christ refrained from the use of his divine attributes, and when the work he had come to do required their use, he

---

[126]Mueller, p. 288.
[127]Chemnitz, p. 83.
[128]Pieper, p. 161.

---

used his divine attributes. Divine omniscience, for example, did not become functional with regard to the day and hour of the world's end since according to God's plan that information is to remain hidden from man. It did, however, become functional when Jesus told his disciples on Palm Sunday that they would find a donkey and colt waiting for them in the next village so that the Scriptures could be fulfilled. Divine omnipotence did not become functional when Jesus was arrested, bound, and led away to Annas (Jn 18:12), but it did become functional when Jesus "walked right through" the angry mob at Nazareth that was bent on throwing him down a cliff (Lk 4:28-30). The reason for the difference was that in the one case "his time had not yet come" (Jn 7:30), while in the other case "Jesus knew that the time had come for him to leave this world" (Jn 13:1).

A number of analogies have been suggested to illustrate the quiescence of the divine attributes during Christ's state of exinanition. Koehler, for example, says Christ in his use of his divine omnipotence during the state of humiliation was "like a king, who hides his royal garments beneath a beggar's cloak. He was like a strong giant who does not use the strength he has, but allows little children to capture and crucify him."[129] Others, to illustrate the way divine knowledge could "rest" in the human nature of Christ, point to a person who while sleeping has certainly not lost his knowledge, but that knowledge has become inactive or lies dormant. "This, then, is the case: As by 'the resting of the λόγος,' that is, by the inactivity of the divine omnipotence in the human nature, there could be in Christ both limited power—with poverty, weariness, suffering, and death—and divine omnipotence, so by the 'resting of the λόγος,' that is, by the inactivity of the divine knowledge in the human nature, there could be in Christ both limited knowledge and divine omniscience."[130] This, of course, does not mean that divine knowledge and divine omnipotence in and of themselves can actually ever be "dormant"— they function without ceasing (Jn 5:17)—but they are either active or inactive in and through Christ's human nature as the exercise of his office required.

While it is impossible for us to truly comprehend the distinction between the possession and the use of divine omniscience and omnipotence by Christ according to his human nature in the state of humiliation, the matter becomes even more difficult for our reason in regard to the possession and the use of divine omnipresence in the state of humiliation. And yet Scripture clearly testifies to the fact that while Christ possessed the divine attribute of illocal omnipresence according to his human nature also in the state of humiliation, he refrained from the full and constant use of that divine attribute. Thus, on

---

[129]Koehler, p. 96.
[130]Pieper, p. 164.

the one hand, Jesus can profess to be "the Son of Man, who is in heaven" (Jn 3:13) and promise already in the state of humiliation, "Where two or three come together in my name, there am I with them" (Mt 18:20). And, on the other hand, he can say in regard to the death of Lazarus in Bethany, "I am glad I was not there" (Jn 11:15). Clearly it would be incorrect on the basis of the Lord's words to his disciples to deny that Christ was present with Lazarus in Bethany according to the illocal omnipresence his human nature possessed also in the state of humiliation. For if St. John is right and "the Word became flesh," then "no man, least of all a theologian who professes to believe Holy Scripture, can rightly think of the incarnate Son of God as being outside His human nature."[131] And if St. Paul is correct when he claims that "in Christ all the fullness of the deity lives in bodily form," and the divine nature in its entirety has made its home in the human nature of Christ, that means his human nature must also share in the divine characteristic of illocal omnipresence. As the Formula of Concord says of Christ, "Wherever you place God, there you must also place with Him humanity."[132]

The "solution" to what again seems to be a hopeless contradiction begins with an understanding of the divine attribute of omnipresence. Abraham Calov defines the omnipresence of God as "an attribute which is related to creation, an attribute whereby God is present to all creatures, present not only by the nearness of his substance but also effectively and operatively."[133] In other words, God's omnipresence is not "mere presence," or simply a "being there," but a dynamic presence whereby God actually upholds and affects his creation. As St. Paul said in his sermon on Mars Hill: "He is not far from each one of us. 'For in him we live and move and have our being'" (Ac 17:27,28). Where God is at work, there he is. And where God is, there he is at work. In other words, the divine attributes of omnipotence and omnipresence go hand in hand. Thus when Jesus says, "All authority in heaven and on earth has been given to me" (Mt 28:18), he claims not only omnipotence according to his human nature but also omnipresence. For as Charles Porterfield Krauth writes, "To have all power, implies that the power shall be everywhere. . . . The power of omnipresence is a part of all power."[134] When Jesus says, "My Father is always at his work to this very day, and I, too, am working" (Jn 5:17), he assures us that with the Father and the Holy Spirit, according to his human nature, he is administering "all things everywhere powerfully and efficaciously."[135] He is claiming the all-ruling illocal omnipresence of God according to his human nature.

---

[131]Ibid., p. 206.
[132]FC SD VIII:84, *Triglot*, p. 1045.
[133]Robert Preus, *The Theology of Post-Reformation Lutheranism*, Vol. 2 (St. Louis: Concordia Publishing House, 1972), p. 85.
[134]Krauth, p. 505.
[135]Chemnitz, p. 490.

But it is precisely the full, constant, and open exercise of that all-ruling illocal omnipresence through his human nature from which Christ refrained during his state of humiliation. As Chemnitz writes, "The whole fullness of the Godhead, which dwells personally in Christ's assumed nature, exercises his power, authority, and activity in and through the assumed nature even at the time of the humiliation, *although not without means, and not always fully and openly.*"[136] This is what John Schaller means when he speaks of the difficulty the question of the *presence* of Christ's human nature presents for our reason: "Since we cannot conceive of presence except in terms of space and time, it is impossible for us really to conceive that the human nature of Christ, because it is received into the person of the Son of God, is thereby actually lifted out of the relations of time and space, and that it was part of Christ's exinanition to submit for a period to the confinements of those relations, in order to accomplish the work of our redemption."[137] And so while Jesus was certainly present in Bethany according to his omnipresent human nature, and according to that nature he certainly possessed the omnipresent dominion of God, he refrained from the use of that all-ruling dominion through the illocal omnipresence of his human nature. In that sense Jesus can say, "I was not there"—in the sense of not exercising his universal dominion through the illocal omnipresence of his human nature. For while Jesus clearly intended to awaken Lazarus from death, and was fully capable of doing so without actually going to Bethany, he refrained from exercising his divine all-ruling omnipresence immediately, or without means, and in the interest of his saving mission physically journeyed to Bethany in order that his disciples might believe in him (Jn 11:15). Again Chemnitz writes, "In the incarnation the personal union took place between the divine Logos and the assumed humanity, in which dwelt the fullness of the Godhead personally from the moment of conception. But because of the humiliation the use and manifestation of this fullness was deferred and in a sense suspended for a time, so that it did not exercise itself immediately, but always did so through the assumed humanity."[138]

Since, as we have seen, the Reformed deny the communication of divine majesty to the human nature of Christ in the incarnation, it follows that they will not understand Christ's humiliation. Indeed, Grudem says that Philippians 2:7 "talks about Jesus giving up the status and privilege that was his in heaven: He 'did not count equality with God a thing to be grasped' (or 'clung to for his advantage'), but 'emptied himself' or 'humbled himself' for our sake, and came to live as a man."[139] If there is any doubt that he confuses the incarnation and the humiliation, he removes it when he writes, "Thus, the

---

[136]Ibid.
[137]Schaller, p. 60.
[138]Chemnitz, p. 491.
[139]Grudem, p. 551.

We Believe in Jesus Christ

doctrine of the 'twofold state of Christ' is the teaching that Christ experienced first the state of humiliation. . . . Within the humiliation of Christ are included his incarnation, suffering, death and burial."[140] However, as Pieper points out, "if, as it is wrongly affirmed, the exinanition consisted in the assumption of the human nature, the succeeding exaltation would by the very force of contrast mean the dehumanization of Christ or His putting aside of the human nature."[141] This would contradict Paul's teaching that "all the fullness of the Deity" κατοικεῖ, has taken up permanent residence in the body of Christ.

Erickson too, in his three-volume *Christian Theology*, lists the incarnation, along with Christ's death and descent into hades, as "steps" in his humiliation.[142] And in *The Word Became Flesh* he asks, "May not the incarnation be a matter of divine self-limitation, freely chosen and appropriate to deity?" Now while this question sounds as if Erickson is swerving into the biblical doctrine of the incarnation and humiliation, he soon reveals his true Reformed colors. For he continues,

> For example, the divine ability to be everywhere (or omnipresence, as theologians prefer) was not lost by the Second Person of the Trinity. In that sense, what he was did not diminish. He did, however, limit himself to exercising that power only in connection with the restrictions imposed by a human body, which meant that he could be in only one physical location at a time. . . . In like manner, when Jesus asked how long a child had suffered from a disease, or when he professed that he did not know that time of his second coming, he was not pretending. He had chosen to subject his omniscience to the veiling or cloaking effect of humanity.[143]

Thus Erickson's idea of self-limitation is not the same as non-use according to the human nature, but actually is the old Calvinistic principle "the finite is not capable of the infinite" dressed in "Lutheran" language. The Bible, however, knows nothing of Christ's human body restricting his divine omniscience, omnipotence, or omnipresence. Instead, it says, "The Word became flesh and made his dwelling among us. We have seen his glory, the glory of the One and Only" (Jn 1:14). John and the other disciples saw the aggregate of divine attributes radiating through the human flesh of Christ. Far from limiting the divine, the church father Cyril says of Christ's human nature in his work *On the Incarnation*, "The Word introduced Himself into that which He was not, in order that the *nature of man* also might become what it was not,

---

[140]Ibid., p. 620.
[141]Pieper, p. 288.
[142]Millard J. Erickson, *Christian Theology*, Vol. 2 (Grand Rapids: Baker Book House, 1984), p. 769.
[143]Erickson, *Word Became*, p. 549.

resplendent, by its union, with the grandeur of divine majesty, which has been raised beyond nature rather than that it has cast the unchangeable God beneath [its] nature."[144] The only restriction on the divine attributes came not from Christ's human nature itself but from the fact that during the state of humiliation he refrained from the full and constant use of those divine attributes according to his human nature.

A correct understanding of the Savior's state of humiliation is critical for understanding the doctrine of the Lord's Supper. For if the state of humiliation consists in the loss of divine prerogatives in regard to Christ's human nature, then Erickson was right when he called it an "absurdity" to take Christ's words at the first Lord's Supper, "This is my body," at face value. For the possibility of the true presence of Christ's body and blood in the Lord's Supper is not correctly explained by saying that he is now in a glorified state and now possesses a glorified body. The fact that the body of Christ was not glorified did not prevent its presence at the first celebration of the Lord's Supper, nor does its subsequent glorification contribute to its presence at future celebrations. The possibility of his body and blood being present is established by the personal union, more specifically, by the communication of divine majesty to the human nature of Christ. Since the humiliation did not deprive Christ's human nature of the possession of divine majesty, Krauth's comments apply also to the state of humiliation:

> Jesus Christ our adorable Lord is not only essentially omnipotent and omnipresent as God, but is personally omnipotent and personally omnipresent in that human nature also which has been taken into absolute and inseparable unity with the divine. All objections vanish in the light of his glorious and all-sufficient person. That the true and supernatural communion with his Lord in his 'Supper'—which is the Christian's hope—can be, rests upon the fulness of the Godhead dwelling in Christ's body; that it will be, rests upon the absolute truth of him who cannot deceive us. He who is incarnate God can do all things: He who is the Truth will fulfill all his assurances.[145]

VII. The State Of Exaltation

A biblical understanding of our Savior's state of exinanition as that period of Christ's life from his conception in the virgin's womb to his burial in Joseph's tomb, during which he did not make full and constant use of the divine majesty which belonged to his human nature by virtue of the personal

---

144"Catalogue of Testimonies," *Triglot*, p. 1127.
145Krauth, p. 819.

union, enables us to properly define the ensuing state of exaltation. St. Paul speaks of the exaltation of Christ when after describing the amazing depths of Christ's humiliation, "became obedient unto death—even death on a cross!" (Php 2:8), he continues, "Therefore God exalted him to the highest place and gave him the name that is above every name, that at the name of Jesus every knee should bow, in heaven and on earth and under the earth, and every tongue confess that Jesus Christ is Lord, to the glory of God the Father" (vv. 9-11). Whereas in the state of exinanition Christ did not fully and constantly use the divine majesty imparted to his human nature, having been "highly exalted" in the state of exaltation, he now does so. The NIV's translation of the verb ὑπερύψωσεν, "exalted . . . to the highest place," may be a bit misleading since its mention of an exaltation to "the highest place" seems to speak of the exaltation of Christ in terms of his ascension into heaven and session at the right hand of God.

In fact, though, the Greek verb simply speaks of a "super- (ὑπερ) exaltation," which did not begin with Christ's ascension and session but with his coming to life again in the grave. As St. Paul says in Romans 6:4, "Christ was raised from the dead through [διά, that is, "in" or "with" (attendant circumstance)] the glory of the Father." St. Peter also links the exaltation with the resurrection when he writes of Christ, "He was put to death in flesh but was made alive in spirit" (1 Pe 3:18; GWN). It is evident that the contrast between flesh and spirit in this passage cannot be a way of contrasting Christ's body and his soul, since that would suggest that while Christ died "bodily," he did not rise bodily but only "spiritually" from the dead. It was that very notion that the risen Savior took pains to dispel by urging his disciples, "Touch me and see; a ghost does not have flesh and bones, as you see I have" (Lk 24:39). It is much better to understand the contrast St. Peter draws between Christ's flesh and spirit as standing for his human nature in its earthly mode of existence ("flesh") and its exalted, superterrestrial, supermundane, glorified mode of existence ("spirit"), which we call the state of exaltation and which St. Peter says began when Christ was made alive.

St. Paul explains the exaltation of Christ when he says that the same Jesus who humbled himself to serve and save mankind was given by God "the name that is above every name," in other words, God bestowed on him the highest glory, "that at the name of Jesus every knee should bow, in heaven and on earth and under the earth, and every tongue confess that Jesus Christ is Lord, to the glory of God the Father" (Php 2:9-11). St. Peter says much the same thing when he tells the Jews in Jerusalem that by raising Jesus from the dead and exalting him to God's right hand, "God has made this Jesus, whom you crucified, both Lord and Christ" (Ac 2:36). Nor is the title "Lord" merely honorary. It expresses the reality that Christ actually, actively rules over everything. Looking ahead to Christ's exaltation, in Psalm 8 King David says of God, "You made him ruler over the works of your hands; you put everything under his feet: all flocks and herds, and the beasts of the field, the birds of the air, and the fish of the sea, all that swim the paths of the seas" (vv. 6-8). Summarizing these verses, the writer of Hebrews simply says, "God left nothing that is not subject to him" (2:8). On the basis of these passages, David Hollaz defines the exaltation as "the solemn enthronization and inauguration of the revived Christ to the full and perfect employment of the heavenly government and the rule of heaven and earth, especially of the church."[146] And the Formula of Concord says, "Hence also the human nature, after the resurrection from the dead, has its exaltation above all creatures in heaven and on earth; which is nothing else than that He entirely laid aside the form of a servant, and yet did not lay aside His human nature, but retains it to eternity, and is put in the full possession and use of divine majesty according to His assumed human nature."[147]

One cannot help but notice the striking contrast between Christ's mode of existence in his state of exinanition, during which time he adopted the form of a servant, and the state of exaltation, when he resumed the form of God. Whereas in the state of exinanition Christ answered the question about the day and hour of the world's end by saying, "No one knows . . . not even . . . the Son" (Mk 13:32), in the state of exaltation he tells his disciples when they come with a similar inquiry, "It is not for you to know the times or dates the Father has set by his own authority" (Ac 1:7). Whereas in the state of exinanition Christ's enemies seized him and led him away captive (Lk 22:54), in the state of exaltation St. Paul writes of Christ, "When he ascended on high, he led captives in his train" (Eph 4:8). And whereas during the days of his humiliation Jesus can say, "I am glad I was not there" (Jn 11:15), the Scriptures say that when "the disciples went out and preached everywhere," the Lord who was taken up into heaven and sat down at the right hand of God "worked with them" wherever they went (Mk 16:20). In other words, the power, knowledge, and all-ruling omnipresence of God that had been present in Christ's human nature but which had "rested" for the most part of his earthly ministry now became fully and perpetually operative in and through his assumed human nature. The Formula of Concord defines the state of exaltation when it says,

> This majesty He [Christ] always had according to the personal union, and yet He abstained from it in the state of his Humiliation . . . until after His resurrection He entirely laid aside the form of a servant, but not the [human] nature, and was established in the full use, manifestation, and declaration of the divine majesty, and thus [Christ] entered into His glory, Phil. 2,6ff., so that now not only as God, but also as man He

---

[146]Schmid, pp. 385,386.
[147]FC SD VIII:26, *Triglot*, p. 1023.

knows all things, can do all things, is present with all creatures, and has under His feet and in His hands everything that is in heaven and on earth and under the earth, as He Himself testifies Matt. 28,18; John 13,3: *All power is given unto me in heaven and in earth.* And St. Paul says Eph. 4,10: *He ascended up far above all heavens, that he might fill all things.* And this His power, He, being present, can exercise everywhere, and to Him everything is possible and everything is known.[148]

Note that the exaltation, like the exinanition, applies only to the human nature of Christ. The writer of Hebrews reminds us of that when in describing the exalted Christ he says, "We see Jesus, who was made a little lower than the angels, now crowned with glory and honor" (2:9). The glory and honor of the exaltation that were given to Jesus could not be given to his divine nature. The "unanimously received rule of the entire ancient orthodox church that what Holy Scripture testifies that Christ received in time he received not according to the divine nature . . . but . . . according to the assumed human nature" prevents us from ascribing the exaltation to Christ's human nature. For "to refer these statements [which say divine majesty was given to Christ in time] to Christ's divine nature would be tantamount to denying His eternal, essential deity and to reducing Christ to a person who was made or came to be God in time."[149]

Since the full majesty of God belonged to Christ's human nature already at the moment of his incarnation, it is clear that at the time of his exaltation Christ did not receive new power and glory which he had not possessed before, but rather in his exaltation began to exercise all the divine power that already belonged to his human nature constantly and completely. The Formula of Concord says, "Now as regards this majesty, to which Christ has been exalted according to His humanity, He did not first receive it when He arose from the dead and ascended into heaven, but when He was conceived in his mother's womb and became man, and the divine and human natures were personally united with one another."[150] John Brenz writes, "One must not think that the humanity of Christ was then first exalted to the highest majesty and received all power in heaven and on earth when he ascended visibly into heaven, but when the Word was made flesh and when in the womb of the Virgin God assumed man, that is, the human nature, into the same person."[151]

---

[148]Ibid., VIII:16, p. 821.
[149]Pieper, p. 157.
[150]FC SD VIII:13, *Triglot,* p. 1019.
[151]John Brenz quoted in Gawrisch, *No Other,* p. 251.

That Christ did not receive new majesty when God exalted him but began to make full and constant use of the majesty he had possessed according to his human nature at his conception, when the Word became flesh, becomes clear when we consider the question of Christ's presence in the state of exaltation. We have already seen from Scripture that Christ's human nature, even in the state of humiliation, was capable of multiple modes of presence. As a true man Christ's body was present in a visible, local manner in the manger at Bethlehem and on the cross at Calvary. Since the nature of Christ's work on earth required him to be touched and handled and seen, Christ was ordinarily present according to his human nature in this local, circumscribed manner during the state of humiliation. And it was this manner of presence—in which he was subject to the limitations of space and time—that he laid aside in the state of exaltation. He had foretold as much when he said to his disciples before his death and burial, "The poor you will always have with you, but you will not always have me" (Mt 26:11). The Lord himself made it clear in what sense he meant that the disciples would not always have him, when he appeared to them on Easter evening. Luke tells us that after Jesus had permitted the disciples to touch his body and after he had eaten in their presence, he said, "This is what I told you while I was still with you" (Lk 24:44). Jesus was no longer "with" his disciples even when he was obviously among them. It was in terms of a local, tangible presence, which would make it possible for them to perform acts of personal bodily service, that Jesus in Mt 26:11 means he will no longer be with his disciples. The reason for this was that the limitations of time and space to which he had made his human nature subject in order to carry out the work of the world's salvation were laid aside after he rose from the dead.

Thus when "Christ was raised from the dead through the glory of the Father" (Ro 6:4), though he rose with the same body that had suffered death on the cross, that body was endowed with new qualities. In Philippians 3:21 St. Paul calls it a "glorious [glorified] body." It was no longer subject to the weaknesses common to man—such as the need for food, drink, rest, and sleep—which Christ had taken upon himself during his humiliation. "That he ate and drank before his disciples, does not show his continued need of food; his body no longer required nourishment, yea, it could not any longer be nourished by earthly food."[152] In the same way, during the so-called "forty days sojourn of the glorified Christ on earth," rather than moving about from place to place with the normal movements of a human body as he had prior to rising from the dead, Jesus would suddenly appear and then disappear as he willed. The disciples in the locked room in Jerusalem on Easter evening "were startled and frightened, thinking they saw a ghost" (Lk 24:37) because Jesus

---

[152]Schaller, p. 106.

We Believe in Jesus Christ

did not knock at the door and walk through the open door in the usual way but rather suddenly stood among them. When the eyes of the Emmaus disciples were opened so that they recognized the risen Savior, "he disappeared from their sight" (Lk 24:31). "He was now risen from the dead, and had put on that glorious body which evades our grosser sense, and needs an act of will to make it visible. In his ubiquitous Godhead everywhere present, at any moment, or in any place, he could emerge to view and reappear in corporeal guise . . . and as soon as the purpose was fulfilled, without necessarily quitting the spot, the glorified body ceased to be seen."[153]

And yet the capabilities of the glorified body in which Christ rose from the dead were not something that he had not possessed before. For even in the state of humiliation, when it was necessary for him to do so, by virtue of the personal union with the divine nature, Christ's body was capable also of that same invisible, illocal yet definitive presence, similar to that of angels, according to which he was able to appear and disappear at will. It was in this manner that he was able to suddenly appear to his disciples on the Sea of Galilee (Mt 14:25) and to miraculously escape from his enemies by passing through their midst (Lk 4:30; Jn 8:59). The difference between the states of exinanition and exaltation then is not between possession and non-possession of divine majesty on the part of Christ, but between use and non-use. One writer summarizes the difference this way: "When the body was 'earthly,' the thing supernatural was for his 'face to shine as the sun,' so now that it was 'heavenly,' the thing supernatural was for that body to come out appreciable by untransfigured organs—perceptible to eyes and ears which were not yet immortal like itself."[154]

The same is true of Christ's presence after his ascension into heaven, which took place forty days after Jesus had risen and had appeared to his disciples on a number of occasions to give them proof of his resurrection. While this disappearance was not essentially different from previous disappearances during the forty days after Easter, and while it was not necessary for Christ according to his visible human nature to actually ascend in a real, gradual upward motion in order to enter heaven, Jesus did so to show his disciples that they should no longer expect him to be with them any longer in the same visible, tangible way that he had been with them before his resurrection. The manner in which Christ ascended proclaimed that he would no longer live among them here on earth in visible and physical form and in the ordinary and familiar way as he did before his resurrection. So in its visible, tangible, physical form the glorified body of Christ has been taken into heaven, and "in that form he now appears to his saints who are in heaven, as Augustine says, for they follow the Lamb wher-

---

[153]Krauth, p. 485.
[154]Ibid., p. 485.

---

ever he goes (Rev 14:4)."[155] "Christ is also in heaven, yet not according to local circumscription, but definitively and according to the manner of a glorified body."[156] But from this it does not follow that he "neither knows nor has another mode of presence."[157] For even after his ascension, his presence according to his human nature was not absolutely and completely removed from the earth. For it was the Savior who had risen in his true body who promised his disciples to the end of time, "Surely I am with you always" (Mt 28:20). Pieper well says of this promise, "It has always appeared doubtful to us whether even a Christian theologian is capable of conceiving of Christ as present outside His flesh, that is, only according to His divine nature, when he reads: 'I am with you alway, even unto the end of the world'."[158] Therefore, even as Christ according to the illocal omnipresence in which his human nature shared by virtue of the personal union with the divine nature was "in heaven" (Jn 3:13) as he sat in Jerusalem and spoke with Nicodemus, so Christ whose glorified body appears visibly to the saints and angels in heaven is also present with us on earth according to that same illocal omnipresence.

St. Paul speaks of that mode of presence when he writes that Christ who "descended to the lower, earthly regions" as a humble man in his state of exinanition "is the very one who ascended higher than all the heavens, in order to fill the whole universe" (Eph 4:9,10). St. Paul is obviously speaking of Christ according to his human nature when he says Christ ascended "in order to fill the whole universe," because if those words were applied to the divine nature, it would imply that prior to his ascension Christ's divine nature was not omnipresent, and thereby deny the deity of Christ. Therefore the only understanding of Paul's words that is permissible is the one which predicates omnipresence—or the repletive (all-filling) presence of the Son of God—also to Christ's human nature. Abraham Calov speaks of Christ's ascension in this way when he defines the ascension as "the visible and glorious triumph of Christ as victor, raising his body above the clouds, and then, in an invisible way, extending it above all heavens, so as to occupy his kingdom unto the end of the world, and everywhere, in a heavenly manner, afford us aid."[159] Therefore we may say that just as Christ appeared on earth in one manner of presence without ever leaving heaven according to another manner of presence, so he went to heaven in his ascension in one mode of presence without ever leaving the earth according to another.

The same is true of the infinite power of God, which Christ, according to his human nature began to exercise fully, openly, and constantly when "he sat

---

[155]Martin Chemnitz, *The Lord's Supper*, translated by J. A. O. Preus (St. Louis: Concordia Publishing House, 1979), p. 211.
[156]Schmid, p. 402.
[157]Chemnitz, *Lord's Supper*, p. 211.
[158]Pieper, p. 257.
[159]Calov quoted in Jacobs, p. 156.

We Believe in Jesus Christ

down at the right hand of God" (Mk 16:19). The term *sit* is not a sitting of idleness or ease, but an official sitting that expresses the activity of a judge or ruler. For example, Psalm 9:4 says with reference to God, "You have sat on your throne, judging righteously." Thus, as Schaller says, "This phase of the exaltation is not merely a state of existence, but of omnipotent and paramount activity."[160] This understanding of "the right hand of God" is confirmed by Moses, who sang in Exodus chapter 15, "Your right hand, O LORD, was majestic in power. Your right hand, O LORD, shattered the enemy" (v. 6). "As man commonly uses his right hand for most of the things he does, so the attribute by which God does His work, namely, His unlimited power, or His omnipotence, is figuratively called His right hand."[161] That same right hand of God, according to King David, was at work guiding and upholding him wherever he was, for he writes in Psalm 139:9,10, "If I rise on the wings of the dawn, if I settle on the far side of the sea, even there your hand will guide me, your right hand will hold me fast." John Gerhard thus agrees with Scripture when he says, "The sitting at the right hand of God must be understood to be of like nature with the right hand of God. Now the right hand of God is not a bodily, circumscribed, limited definite place, but it is the infinite power of God and his most efficacious dominion by which God preserves and governs all things."[162] In regard to the concept of God's right hand, the Formula of Concord says it "is no fixed place in heaven, as the Sacramentarians assert without any ground in the Holy Scriptures, but nothing else than the almighty power of God, which fills heaven and earth," and says again, "God's right hand is everywhere."[163]

Therefore when Scripture says of Christ that "[God] seated him at his right hand in the heavenly realms"(Eph 1:20), it means that "sitting at the right hand of God is the highest degree of glory, in which Christ, the God-Man, having been exalted according to His human nature to the throne of divine majesty, most powerfully and by His immediate presence governs all things."[164] And yet Christ possessed the omnipresent dominion of God according to his human nature also in the state of humiliation. As Chemnitz writes, "Christ says at the time when his Passion was imminent, at the depth of his humiliation, 'All things which the Father has are mine' (Jn 16:15)."[165] Also, the work of preserving and governing the world that Jesus claims for himself when he says, "My Father is always at his work to this very day, and I, too, am working" (Jn 5:17), was performed in and through his human nature also in the state of humiliation. Isaiah said of the Child to be born for us, "The gov-

---

[160]Schaller, p. 110.
[161]Pieper, p. 329.
[162]Schmid, p. 403.
[163]FC SD VIII:28, *Triglot*, p. 1025; FC Ep VII:12, *Triglot*, p. 811.
[164]Hollaz quoted in Pieper, pp. 329,330.
[165]Chemnitz, *Two Natures*, p. 281.

---

ernment will be on his shoulders" (Isa 9:6). The Formula says of the majesty bestowed on Christ in his exaltation, "This majesty He had immediately at His conception, even in His mother's womb, but . . . did not employ it always, but only when He wished."[166] When St. Paul then explains the significance of the session of Christ at the right hand of God by saying, "God placed all things under his feet and appointed him to be head over everything for the church, which is his body, the fullness of him who fills everything in every way" (Eph 1:22,23), this means that "he entered into a fuller and more open use and manifestation of the power, authority, and glory of the Deity which in complete fullness had dwelt personally in the assumed nature from the beginning of the union."[167] This agrees with Scripture, which says on the one hand that Jesus "thus revealed his glory" (Jn 2:11), and on the other that he prayed for his Father to glorify him (Jn 17:5). "Scripture thus teaches that the possession [of divine majesty] in the state of humiliation becomes possession in the full sense of the word only with the exaltation."[168]

In summary, then, the difference between the states of humiliation and exaltation is not possession of divine attributes in the latter and non-possession of those attributes in the former, but the use and non-use of the divine attributes that Christ possessed from the moment of his conception when his human nature was personally united with the Son of God. Chemnitz writes in this regard,

> Neither was it only after his resurrection that the entire fulness of the divine nature began to dwell bodily in Christ as though, after the concurrence of the hypostatic union in conception and before the ascension, and sitting at the right hand, either any empty vacancy or partialness of divine nature dwelt bodily in Christ; or as though the hypostatic union or personal indwelling of the entire fulness of the Godhead, in the assumed nature of Christ, became in the process of years constantly greater, more intimate, fuller, and more complete: for, from the first moment of the hypostatic union, the entire fulness of the Godhead dwelt bodily, or, in other words, in the flesh, or assumed nature, of Christ.[169]

Since the Reformed, refusing to take Colossians 2:9 at face value, deny that Christ's human nature possessed divine attributes even in the state of humiliation, it is clear that their definition of the exaltation will differ from

[166]FC SD VIII:26, *Triglot*, p. 1023.
[167]Chemnitz, *Two Natures*, p. 492.
[168]Pieper, p. 303.
[169]Chemnitz, *Two Natures*, p. 488.

We Believe in Jesus Christ

the biblical definition. Grudem makes this difference clear in a paragraph dealing with the Ascension entitled "Christ Received Glory and Honor That Had Not Been His Before As The God-Man." Under that heading he writes, "When Jesus ascended into heaven he received glory, honor and authority that had never been his before as one who was both God and man. Before Jesus died, he prayed, 'Father, glorify me in your own presence with the glory which I had with you before the world was made' (John 17:5)." And in a footnote dealing with the Savior's prayer, he writes, "This verse shows that the glory Jesus received had been his before as eternal Son of God, but it had not been his before in his incarnate form as God-man."[170] In making that statement, however, Grudem forgets what St. John says of the same Savior who prayed to be glorified: "We have seen his glory, the glory of the One and Only, who came from the Father" (Jn 1:14). Just exactly what kind of honor, glory, and authority Christ received when he ascended is not really clear from Grudem's explanation. He consistently uses the term *authority* and carefully avoids ascribing *all power* or *omnipotence* to Christ. In regard to the presence of Christ's risen and ascended body, he says, "Jesus had a resurrection body that was subject to spatial limitations (it could be at only one place at one time)."[171] Luther's analysis of the Reformed is still accurate: "But what Christ's ascension into heaven and his sitting are, they do not know. It is not like climbing into a house by means of a ladder; but it means that he is above all creatures and in and outside all creatures."[172] Krauth is also correct in his analysis of the effect of Grudem's position, which "has taken our Lord out of the world he redeemed, and has made heaven, not his throne, but a great sepulchre, with a stone rolled against its portal."[173]

The effect that this kind of Christology will have on the doctrine of the Lord's Supper is obvious. In dismissing Luther's doctrine of the real presence, Grudem says, "In order to affirm this doctrine, Luther had to answer an important question: 'How can Christ's physical body, or more generally Christ's human nature, be everywhere present? Is it not true that Jesus in his human nature ascended into heaven and remains there until his return? Did he not say that he was leaving the earth and would no longer be in the world but was going to the Father?' (John 16:28; 17:11)."[174] So where Erickson rejected the real presence at the first Supper as an "absurdity" because Christ was sitting at the table with the disciples, Grudem now rejects that presence because of Christ's ascension. Krauth observes,

---

[170]Grudem, p. 618.
[171]Ibid., p. 610.
[172]Luther quoted in Werner Elert, *The Structure of Lutheranism*, translated by Walter A. Hansen, (St. Louis: Concordia Publishing House, 1962), p. 252.
[173]Krauth, p. 351.
[174]Grudem, p. 994.

It is interesting here to see the lack of consistency between two sorts of representations made by the objectors to the sacramental presence of Christ. The first is, We cannot believe that he was sacramentally present then at the first Supper because he was bodily so near. The second is, He cannot be sacramentally present now, because his body is so far off. But alike to the argument from mere natural proximity, or from mere natural remoteness, the answer is: The whole human nature of our Lord belongs on two sides, in two sets of relations, to two diverse spheres. That his body was before their eyes in the manner of the one sphere, is no reason why it should not be imparted to them, after the supernatural and heavenly manner of the other, in the sacramental mystery.[175]

And, we may add, the fact that his body is removed from our eyes in the manner of the one sphere is no reason why it cannot be imparted to us after the supernatural and heavenly manner of the other sphere.

Erickson's understanding of Christ's exaltation appears at first to be more promising than Grudem's. Speaking of the differences between Christ's mode of existence in the state of humiliation and in the state of exaltation, Erickson writes,

Now [!] Jesus is the God-man. There is a continuing incarnation. In I Timothy 2:5 Paul says, "There is one God, and there is one mediator between God and men, the man Christ Jesus." This gives every indication that Jesus currently is a man who mediates between God and us. His, however, is not the type of humanity that we have, or even the humanity that he had while he was here. It is a perfected humanity of the type which we will have after our resurrection. Thus, his continuing incarnation imposes no limitation upon his deity. Just as our bodies will have many of their limitations removed, so it has been with the perfect, glorified humanity of Jesus, which continues to be united with the deity, and thus will forever exceed what we will ultimately be.[176]

In another place he speaks more guardedly: "The incarnation continues and maintains a permanent modification in the second person of the Trinity, but the limitations involved are greatly reduced. Now it is a glorified humanity that is in union with the deity, and such a humanity imposes even less restriction

---

[175]Krauth, p. 783f.
[176]Erickson, *Christian Theology*, Vol. 2, p. 778.

upon the functioning of the divine nature."[177] While he does not specifically indicate what possibilities the glorified human nature may have since it now "imposes even less restriction upon the functioning of the divine," it is doubtful whether he would be willing to allow the possibility of the true presence of Christ's body and blood in the Lord's Supper. We say "the possibility" because he clearly rejects the real presence, saying, "We should think of the sacrament not so much in terms of Christ's presence as in terms of his promise and the potential for a closer relationship with him. We also need to be careful to avoid the neoorthodox conception that for the true communicant the Lord's Supper is a subjective encounter with Christ. He is objectively present. The Spirit is capable of making him real in our experience and has promised to do so."[178]

It's interesting that Erickson expresses a fear that the Lord's Supper, without any real presence of Christ's body and blood, could turn into the kind of subjective encounter with Christ that is found in neoorthodoxy. Swindoll seems to describe that very thing Erickson fears when he writes of one of his most memorable communion services:

> We were sitting on a windswept, chilly beach. We had sung a few songs around sunset. All we had to serve were chips and cola. Yet it was marvelous! I have never before or since served chips and cola at the Lord's Supper, but the elements were insignificant. Our Lord's presence was there in the sunset over the Pacific, in the pounding of the surf, in the faces of those young believers, in the tears that fell, in the testimonies that were spoken. And we worshiped our God as we met at that open place, sand between our toes, swimming suits on, towels wrapped around us as we shivered around the fire and passed the chips and cola among us. We did it all 'in remembrance of Me.'[179]

Amazing how the Lord's presence could be discerned everywhere except where the Lord promised to be present—in his Word and Sacrament. Krauth was right when he said that if you lock Christ up in heaven, separating his human nature from his church and his true body and blood from the Sacrament, then all the light, peace, and joy that an incarnate Christ sheds upon the soul "vanish in a haze of hyperboles, a miserable twilight of figures of speech, and the vigorous and soul-sustaining objectivity of faith faints into a mere sentimentalism."[180]

---

[177]Erickson, *Word Became*, p. 576.
[178]Erickson, *Christian Theology*, Vol. 3, p. 1123.
[179]Swindoll, p. 361.
[180]Krauth, p. 351.

VIII. The Communication of Official Acts

Since Christ truly was the God-man in the state of humiliation just as he is in the state of exaltation, it is clear that the official acts of the Savior were, and are, never performed by one nature alone, but always by both natures participating jointly, each one contributing its proper share to the act in intimate communion with the other. The Creed of Chalcedon summarizes this truth when it states, "The distinction of natures being by no means taken away by the union, but rather the property of each being preserved and concurring in One Person and One Subsistence."[181] The Formula of Concord has this in mind when it says,

> As to the execution of the office of Christ, the person does not act and work in, with, through, or according to only one nature, but in, according to, with, and through both natures, or, as the Council of Chalcedon expresses it, one nature operates in communion with the other what is the property of each. Therefore Christ is our Mediator, Redeemer, King, High Priest, Head, Shepherd, etc., not according to one nature only, whether it be the divine or the human, but according to both natures.[182]

This is known as the *genus apotelesmaticum*, from the Greek word ἀποτέλεσμα, "an official act."

This genus may be illustrated in the following way: "Whenever a person performs a voluntary act, not only his body, nor only his soul acts, but both act conjointly, each contributing its part. Without the soul the body does not move nor do anything, and we know of no soul action which does not somehow employ the organs of the body."[183] This genus has its solid foundation in the Holy Scriptures, which refer the divine works by which the Son of God became, and still is, the Savior of mankind sometimes to Christ when he is named according to his divine nature and at other times to the same person named according to his human nature. For example, St. John writes in his first letter, "The reason the Son of God appeared was to destroy the devil's work" (3:8). Here Christ is named according to his divine nature, "the Son of God," and the divine work of destroying the devil's work is ascribed to him. And yet that work was accomplished through the organ, or instrument, of the human nature in which the Son of God "appeared." On the other hand, Scripture also names the Savior according to his human nature and still ascribes divine works to him. For example, Jesus tells Zacchaeus, "The Son of Man came to

---

[181]Schaff, *Creeds*, Vol. 2, p. 62.
[182]FC SD VIII:46,47, *Triglot*, p. 1031.
[183]Koehler, p. 92.

We Believe in Jesus Christ

seek and to save what was lost" (Lk 19:10). These passages simply remind us that our redemption was not the work of the human nature alone, nor of the divine nature alone, but of the entire person of the God-man—each nature doing what naturally belongs to it, with the participation of the other. Chemnitz gives an example of how the two natures in Christ "concur" in Christ's death when he writes,

> When Christ in his human nature suffers and dies, even this takes place in communion with the divine nature, but not with the result that the divine nature in itself also suffers and dies. For this is a property only of the human nature. But the divine nature is present personally in the suffering human nature and wills this suffering for the human nature. The divine nature does not turn away from the suffering, but permits the human nature to suffer and die, yet strengthens and sustains it so that it can endure the immeasurable burden of the sins of the world and the total wrath of God, thus making those sufferings precious before God and saving for the world.[184]

That the death of Christ was an act of the God-man is clear from the infinite value St. Paul places on the blood of Christ when he urges the Ephesian elders, "Be shepherds of the church of God, which he bought with his own blood" (Ac 20:28). Schaller adds, "The *necessity* of this joint activity of the two natures becomes apparent if we consider that, whereas sinners could be saved only by the vicarious suffering and death of the Savior, the Godhead could not in itself suffer and die, nor could a mere man offer a sacrifice sufficing for the redemption of a whole world of men."[185]

The *genus apotelesmaticum* is the logical result of the *genus majestaticum*, since the operative attributes of God (omnipotence, omniscience, omnipresence) were communicated to the human nature of Christ so that they might operate, as their name suggests, in union with the human nature. Since the Savior is a divine-human person, it follows that all his acts will be divine-human.

> The testimony of this truth runs through the entire Bible and is properly its scope. As the Seed of the woman, that is, through His human nature as His organ, the Son of God crushes the head of the serpent (Gen. 3:15). As the Seed of Abraham, that is, in and through His human nature, He brings the blessings of salvation to all nations of the earth (Gen. 22:18). As He that is made of a woman, and that

---

[184]Chemnitz, *Two Natures*, p. 216.
[185]Schaller, p. 80.

---

means, in and through the human nature, the Son of God was made under the Law, that He might redeem those that were under the Law, so that we might received the adoption of sons (Gal. 4:4-5).[186]

In regard to this fact that the human nature of Christ participates in all his activities not alone with its human attributes but also with its endowment of divine prerogatives, Schaller observes that this is true not only during the state of exinanition but "especially since his exaltation to glory."[187]

Again, the Scripture testimony to this point is abundant. The Savior himself proclaimed that his human nature would participate in the all-ruling omnipresence of God when he told the high priest, "From now on, the Son of Man will be seated at the right hand of the mighty God" (Lk 22:69). St. Paul says that "Christ Jesus, who died . . . is at the right hand of God and is also interceding for us" (Ro 8:34). Again, he speaks of Christ according to the human nature when he says that God "raised him from the dead and seated him at his right hand in the heavenly realms" (Eph 1:20), which means that God "placed all things under his feet and appointed him to be head over everything for the church" (v. 22). Chemnitz comments,

> Christ's human nature, therefore, cannot and ought not be removed or excluded from the general dominion which he possesses and exercises over all things, or from the administration of the world, since Scripture expressly affirms that all things, even those which are outside the church have been put under Christ's feet. . . . But the humanity in and with the Logos rules all things, not in the sense of being absent, far away, or removed by an immense interval of space, or through some kind of vicarious work and administration, such as kings are accustomed to exercise when their power is extended widely through many distant provinces. But just as the human nature subsists in the Logos and insofar as it personally adheres to the Logos, it also has all things before it in the Logos and in being present it rules over all things in the Logos.[188]

Finally, Jesus speaks of himself according to his human nature and in that nature promises to perform the divine act of judging the world when he says, "The Son of Man is going to come in his Father's glory with his angels, and then he will reward each person according to what he has done" (Mt 16:27).

---

[186]Pieper, pp. 249,250.
[187]Schaller, p. 80.
[188]Chemnitz, *Two Natures*, pp. 432,433.

We Believe in Jesus Christ

While it is surely true that it is not out of necessity that the human nature of Christ participates in all his activities in the state of exaltation, the reality that the human nature does participate serves for our comfort in this world of sin. Chemnitz reminds us of that when he writes,

> I do not say that the divine nature of the λόγος could not perform its divine operations without the support of the assumed nature; for it could do this before the Incarnation, and to this day it can do the same. But in his great good will he wished to assume our human nature into the communion of his divine operations as an organ primarily in his office as Messiah in order to exhibit to us a sure pledge in himself of the beatification of our nature, and in order that we might know that we have access to, and communion with, the offices and benefits of the Son of God, our King, High Priest, and head, because he assumed our human nature for the performance and communion of these offices, according to which [nature] he is consubstantial to us, our blood relative, nay, rather, our Brother, Flesh of our flesh, no man hating his own flesh, but nourishing and cherishing it, even as the Lord of the Church (Ephesians 5:29).[189]

Again the Reformed reject the possibility of Christ's human nature participating in all the divine works which the exalted Savior carries out for the good of his church. For example, in regard to Christ's priestly work of interceding for the saints at the throne of God, Grudem writes,

> Yet in his human nature alone Jesus could not of course be such a great high priest for all his people all over the world. He could not hear the prayers of persons far away, nor could he hear prayers that were only spoken in a person's mind. He could not hear all requests simultaneously (for in the world at any one moment there are millions of people praying to him). Therefore, in order to be the perfect high priest who intercedes for us, he must be God as well as man. He must be one who in his divine nature can both know all things and bring them into the presence of the Father.[190]

As to the exercise of Christ's kingly office in the state of exaltation, Grudem writes,

> The fact that Jesus now sits at the right hand of God in heaven does not mean that he is perpetually "fixed" there or that he

---

[189]Ibid., p. 303.
[190]Grudem, p. 628.

---

is inactive. He is also seen as standing at God's right hand (Acts 7:56) and as walking among the seven golden lampstands in heaven (Rev. 2:1). Just as a human king sits on his royal throne at his accession to kingship, but then engages in many other activities throughout each day, so Christ sat at the right hand of God as a dramatic evidence of the completion of his redemptive work and his reception of authority over the universe, but he is certainly engaged in other activities in heaven as well.[191]

The Formula of Concord speaks of the comfort that is taken away from Christians by those who deny that the human nature participates in the activities of the exalted Savior when it says,

> We regard it as a pernicious error when such majesty is denied to Christ according to His humanity. For thereby the very great consolation is taken from Christians which they have . . . concerning the presence and dwelling with them of their Head, King, and High Priest, who has promised them that not only His mere divinity would be with them, which to us poor sinners is as a consuming fire to dry stubble, but that He, He, the man who has spoken with them, who has tried all tribulations in His assumed human nature, and who can therefore have sympathy with us, as with men and His brethren,—He will be with us in all our troubles also according to the nature according to which He is our brother and we are flesh of His flesh.[192]

IX. Conclusion

There is no question that the doctrine of Christ is of supreme importance to the Christian faith and must be kept absolutely pure. For as Pieper says, while "we generally call the doctrine of justification the central article of the Christian doctrine, the *articulus stantis et cadentis ecclesiae*. But this article is directly based on the doctrine of Christ, on the doctrine of Christ's theanthropic Person and theanthropic work. . . . Whoever denies that Christ in His theanthropic Person and His theanthropic work of redemption is the object of saving faith cancels the Christian doctrine of justification and does away with all of Christianity."[193] Unfortunately, as we have seen, the rationalistic errors of 16th century Reformed theologians such as Zwingli and Calvin continue to

---

[191]Ibid., p. 619.
[192]FC SD VIII:87, *Triglot*, p. 1047.
[193]Pieper, p. 55.

We Believe in Jesus Christ

taint the Christology of today's conservative evangelicals, and those same errors are at the heart of their persistent rejection of the biblical doctrine of the real presence of Christ's body and blood in the Lord's Supper.

What Luther observed at Marburg in 1529 regarding the Reformed theologians and their approach to the doctrines of Christ and Holy Communion continues to be true today of those who truly teach what Luther taught, and of conservative evangelicals: "It is quite obvious that we do not have the same spirit." What Walther said a century ago likewise remains true: "There is indeed a great difference, involving the principle articles of Christian doctrine, between the Lutheran and the Reformed Churches." Therefore, we must conclude with Luther, "Your spirit and our spirit cannot go together." Taking that position, however, will continue to call down on us the scorn of a religious world which for the most part considers that conclusion to be evidence of small-minded sectarianism. Is it worth the cost to remain confessional? Herman Sasse answers that question this way:

> The rejection, by Luther and the Lutheran Church, of Zwingli's and Calvin's teachings concerning the Sacrament can be understood only in the light of their consequences: these teachings must inevitably, although certainly against the will of those who represent them, eventuate in undermining belief in the Incarnation and particularly belief in the presence of Christ. A spiritualism which will have nothing to do with Christ's humanity, and concerns itself, instead, solely with His divine nature, will soon lose even this. The separation of the divine and human natures of the Lord in such a way that one is thought of apart from the other, will easily result in a rejection of the doctrine of the two natures as an absurdity and in a complete abandonment of belief in the Incarnation. To what extent this opinion has been confirmed by the doctrinal development in Reformed Protestantism we shall refrain from judging. But within Lutheranism, at least, it is true that every defection from belief in the real presence of the whole Christ in the Sacrament of the Altar has resulted in an abandonment of belief in the Incarnation of the eternal Son of God.[194]

May God graciously preserve us from such a tragic defection from the truth. And may he instead grant us grace to believe and teach as our fathers believed and taught on the basis of God's Word: "Thus when we begin with the Word and promise concerning the presence of Christ's body and blood and against all objection add his divine power, the personal union, and his session

---

[194]Herman Sasse, *Here We Stand,* translated by Theodore Tappert (St. Louis: Concordia Publishing House, 1938), pp. 147,148.

at the right hand to his will as it is revealed in the Word, it is surely manifest that the Son of God can accomplish what he teaches and promises in his Word concerning his body, while still leaving its true reality intact, so that with his body he can be present when, how and wherever he wishes."[195]

> God's Word is our great heritage
> And shall be ours forever;
> To spread its light from age to age
> Shall be our chief endeavor.
> Through life it guides our way;
> In death it is our stay.
> Lord, grant, while worlds endure,
> We keep its teachings pure
> Throughout all generations. Amen. (CW 293)

---

[195]Chemnitz, *Two Natures*, pp. 432,433.

We Believe in Jesus Christ